PRISONERS *of* SHANGRI-LA

PRISONERS
of ... of
SHANGRI-LA

TIBETAN
BUDDHISM
and the
WEST

Donald S. Lopez, Jr.

THE
UNIVERSITY
of CHICAGO PRESS
CHICAGO *and*
LONDON

The University of Chicago Press, Chicago 60637
The University of Chicago Press, Ltd., London
© 1998 by The University of Chicago
Paperback edition 1999
All rights reserved. Published 1998
Printed in the United States of America

07 06 05 04 03 02 01 00 99   2 3 4 5

ISBN: 0-226-49310-5 (cloth)
ISBN: 0-226-49311-3 (paperback)

Library of Congress Cataloging-in-Publication Data

Lopez, Donald S., 1952–
    Prisoners of Shangri-La : Tibetan Buddhism and the West / Donald S. Lopez, Jr.
        p.   cm.
    Includes index.
    ISBN 0-226-49310-5 (alk. paper)
    1. Buddhism—China—Tibet.   I. Title.
BQ7604.L66   1998
294.3'923—dc21   97-41202
                                                                        CIP

for TOMOKO

Contents

Acknowledgments

The greater part of this book was written at the scholars' Shangri-La otherwise known as the National Humanities Center, where I held the Benjamin N. Duke Fellowship, which is endowed by the Research Triangle Foundation of North Carolina. I received additional support from the Office of the Vice President for Research at the University of Michigan.

The writing of this book would have been much more difficult without the support of excellent staff at the National Humanities Center, under the direction of Robert Connor and Kent Mullikin. I would especially like to thank two of the librarians, Eliza Robertson and Jean Houston, whose indomitable efforts gave me access to scores of obscure books, long unread. That the resulting book may sometimes appear to be little more than a string of potent quotations is due to the riches they provided me with such skill and dedication. Susan Meinheit of the Library of Congress kindly provided photocopies of a number of Tibetan texts that would have otherwise been unavailable to me.

The days of writing were punctuated by stimulating conversations with my fellow fellows, among whom I would like especially to thank David Armitage, Paul Berliner, George Chauncey, Constantin Fasolt, Jane Gaines, Jacquelyn Hall, Joy Kasson, William Ray, Charles Stewart, and Paul Strohm.

For reading the manuscript in whole or part, I am grateful to Janet Gyatso, Clare E. Harris, Elizabeth Horton Sharf, Robert Sharf, and especially to Catherine Bell. Alan Thomas of the University of Chicago Press provided patient and wise counsel throughout the project.

One of the pleasant coincidences of my fellowship at the National Humanities Center was that the Center is located near Chapel Hill and the University of North Carolina, where my wife, Tomoko Masuzawa, serves on the faculty. Thus, my fellowship provided the rare opportunity, understood only by other commuting couples, to live with my spouse. This book is dedicated to her, with my heartfelt gratitude for the many ways she has sustained me over the ten years of our partnership.

Introduction

At the Opening Ceremonies of the 1996 Olympic Games in Atlanta, a work entitled "Call to Nature," by Mickey Hart, percussionist of the Grateful Dead, was performed. It began with the chant of a Tibetan monk from Gyuto monastery. In 1993 chants of Tibetan monks from the same monastery were broadcast at deafening volume by agents of the Federal Bureau of Investigation in Waco, Texas, as part of their psychological assault on the Branch Davidians. The 1995 film *Ace Ventura: When Nature Calls* finds the protagonist living in a Tibetan monastery, doing penance for having failed to rescue a raccoon. He is dressed in the red robes and yellow hat of a Geluk monk, seeking to attain a state of "omnipresent supergalactic oneness."[1] On June 16, 1996, fifty thousand people gathered at Golden Gate Park for a "Free Tibet" benefit concert, which featured performances by Smashing Pumpkins, the Red Hot Chili Peppers, the Beastie Boys, Yoko Ono, and John Lee Hooker (among others). Prior to performing, the bands were blessed by Tibetan monks. The 1992 Christmas issue of Paris *Vogue* had as its guest editor the Dalai Lama. In the 1990 series *Twin Peaks*, Special Agent Dale Cooper tells the local police force, "Following a dream I had three years ago, I have become deeply moved by the plight of the Tibetan people and filled with a desire to help them. I also awoke from the same dream realizing that I had subconsciously gained knowledge of a deductive technique involving mind-body coordination operating hand in hand with the deepest level of intuition."[2] In the better grocery stores one can purchase Tibetan Root Beer: "gently invigorating cardamom and coriander in a Tibetan adaptation of Ayurvedic herbs." In a 1991 episode of *The Simpsons,* Mayor "Diamond" Joe Quimby tells the assembled citizens awaiting the arrival of Michael Jackson, "This is the most exciting thing to happen to our fair town since the Dalai Lama visited in 1952. And so, I hereby declare that Route 401, currently known as the Dalai Lama Expressway, will henceforth be known as the Michael Jackson Expressway." Thus when we see advertised, under the heading "Booty, Spoils & Plunder," a "Tibetan Shaman's Jacket" (for women, $175) in a 1995 J. Peterman catalog we are not surprised to read the accompanying copy that says, "It's official. Crystals are out, Tibetan Buddhism is in."

But Tibetan Buddhism has been in for some time. In the 1983 film *The Return of the Jedi,* the teddy-bear like creatures called Ewoks spoke high-speed Tibetan. In 1966, when the Beatles recorded "Tomorrow Never Knows," which begins "Turn off your mind, relax, and float downstream," John Lennon asked the recording engineer to make his voice sound like "the Dalai Lama on a mountain top." In 1925 the French poet Artaud wrote "Address to the Dalai Lama," which begins "We are your most faithful servants, O Grand Lama, give us, grace us with your illuminations in a language our contaminated European minds can understand, and if need be, transform our Mind, create for us a mind turned entirely toward those perfect summits where the Human Mind no longer suffers. . . . Teach us, O Lama, the physical levitation of matter and how we may no longer be earthbound."[3] In 1948 the presidential campaign of Progressive Party candidate Henry Wallace (vice president under Franklin Roosevelt, 1940–44) foundered when it was revealed that he had written letters to a Russian Tibetophile that began "Dear Guru." And in "The Adventure of the Empty House," Sherlock Holmes accounts for his whereabouts during the years he was assumed dead—after plunging with Professor Moriarty over Reichenbach Fall—by telling Watson, "I travelled for two years in Tibet, therefore, and amused myself by visiting Lhassa, and spending some days with the head lama. You may have read of the remarkable explorations of a Norwegian named Sigerson, but I am sure that it never occurred to you that you were receiving news of your friend."

On September 6, 1995, the Raleigh, North Carolina, *News & Observer* carried on the front page a color photograph of the Dalai Lama being embraced by Senator Jesse Helms, under the headline "Buddhist Captivates Hero of Religious Right." The next day the photograph appeared on T-shirts in Chapel Hill. But by then, the words below the picture seemed redundant. They read "Anything Is Possible." This book is an attempt to understand how it is possible.

Tibet and Tibetan Buddhism have long been objects of Western fantasy. Since the earliest encounters of Venetian travelers and Catholic missionaries with Tibetan monks at the Mongol court, tales of the mysteries of their mountain homeland and the magic of their strange—yet strangely familiar—religion have had a peculiar hold on the Western imagination. During the last two centuries, the valuation of Tibetan society and, particularly, its religion, has fluctuated wildly. Tibetan Buddhism has been portrayed sometimes as the most corrupt deviation from the Buddha's true dharma, sometimes as its most direct descendant. These fluctuations have occurred over the course of this century, at its beginning as Tibet resisted the colonial ambitions of a European power and at its end as it succumbed to the colonial ambitions of an Asian power.

Typical of those who have held the negative view is Susie Carson Rijnhart, a medical missionary who traveled in Tibet from 1895 to 1899. In her account of her journey, *With the Tibetans in Tent and Temple,* she writes:

> But nothing could be further from the truth than the belief entertained by many occidentals that the lamas are superior beings endowed with transcendent physical and intellectual gifts. On the contrary, they are mere children in knowledge, swayed by the emotions that play on the very surface of being. During all our four years' sojourn among the Tibetans of various tribes and districts, we did not meet a single lama who was conversant with even the simple facts of nature . . . , for the great mass of them we found to be ignorant, superstitious and intellectually atrophied like all other priesthoods that have never come into contact with the enlightening and uplifting influence of Christian education. They are living in the dark ages, and are themselves so blind that they are not aware of the darkness. Ten centuries of Buddhism have brought them to their present state of moral and mental stagnation, and it is difficult to believe that any force less than the Gospel of Christ can give them life and progress in the true sense.[4]

At the same time, many, notably Theosophists, held quite a different view:

> A prophecy of Tsong-ka-pa is current in Tibet to the effect that the true doctrine will be maintained in its purity only so long as Tibet is kept free from the incursions of western nations, whose crude ideas of fundamental truth would inevitably confuse and obscure the followers of the Good Law. But, when the western world is more ripe in the direction of philosophy, the incarnation of the Pban-chhen-rin-po-chhe—the Great Jewel of Wisdom—one of the Teshu Lamas, will take place, and the splendour of truth will then illuminate the whole world. We have here the true key to Tibetan exclusiveness.[5]

We see here a play of opposites: the pristine and the polluted, the authentic and the derivative, the holy and the demonic, the good and the bad. This opposition has functioned throughout the history of Europe's relation to Asia: "West" and "East," "Occident" and "Orient"—each a historical rather than a geographic construct. As will be evident in the chapters that follow, the play of opposites has been both extreme and volatile in the case of Tibet, and it remains at work in contemporary attitudes toward Tibet and Tibetan Buddhism.

The opposition of the authentic and the derivative was also imagined to operate inside Tibet. In his popular 1951 survey *Buddhism* (which invokes, like so many others, the landscape of Tibet), Christmas Humphreys writes, "The great spaces . . . and the silence where men are scarce and wildlife is rarer still, all lend themselves to introverted thought, to the development of abnormal ways of thought, to the practice of the best and worst of the manifold powers of the mind."[6] For many decades, what interested scholars about Tibet was not Tibetan literature or practice, but the translations of Sanskrit texts lost in India but preserved in Tibet, held as if in deep freeze, safe from the dangers of Muslim fire and monsoon water. These texts, even in translation, were valued as the authentic documents of Mahayana Buddhism, which had been condemned by an earlier generation of scholars as a deviation from the Buddha's original teachings. Yet Tibetan commentaries on these works and their articulations in various ritual forms were generally dismissed as arid repetition devoid of the animation of authenticity. "Indigenous" Tibetan religion was portrayed as a debased practice. The French explorer André Guibaut wrote of Tibet, "Nowhere but here, in this atmosphere, could the lofty conception of Buddha unite with the dark, primitive rites of ancient Shamanism, to culminate in the monstrosity of Lamaism."[7]

Even those Europeans with a more fanciful interest in Tibet distinguished between the Tibetans' own religious practice and the secret knowledge of occult masters. The Theosophists believed Tibet to be the abode of the Mahatmas (Great Souls), keepers of the wisdom of Atlantis who congregated in a secret region of Tibet to escape the increasing levels of magnetism produced by civilization; they believed as well that the Tibetans were unaware of the Mahatmas' presence in their land. In James Hilton's 1933 novel *Lost Horizon*, what makes Shangri-La invaluable is not the indigenous knowledge of the indigenous people, but that over the centuries of his long life, a Belgian Catholic missionary had gathered all that was good in European culture—first editions of great books, priceless works of art, musical scores—and that a brotherhood of foreigners (mostly Europeans but some Americans and Chinese) protected them from the impending world conflagration. They lived in the lamasery of Shangri-La, which towered physically and symbolically above the Valley of the Blue Moon, where the happy Tibetans lived their simple lives. For centuries many of Tibet's devotees have most valued not the people who live there but the treasures it preserves.

These nineteenth- and early-twentieth-century constructions of Tibetan Buddhism are part of the legacy of colonialism. Yet unlike most of Asia's Buddhist societies, Tibet neither came under direct European control nor did it make any real attempt to "modernize" (despite certain failed attempts by the thirteenth Dalai Lama) by establishing European-style universities, importing European technologies, or sending elites to Europe for education. Among the many reasons the European powers were deterred is that in 1792 the Manchu Emperor Qianlong declared imperial control over all Tibetan communications with foreign countries. This did not sever Tibet's longstanding relations with Inner Asia and China. Instead, until the twentieth century, further relations of Europeans with Tibet were conducted from the borderlands. During the nineteenth century, Tibet became a cherished prize in the Great Game played by Britain and Russia, the two great European powers of the region. Both repeatedly attempted to establish relations with the government in Lhasa, and often sent spies, sometimes disguised as Buddhist pilgrims, into Tibet on map-making missions. It was during this period that Tibet came to be consistently portrayed as "isolated" or "closed," characterizations that meant little except in contrast with China, which had been forcibly "opened" to British trade after the Opium War of 1839. Tibet was thus an object of imperial desire, and the failure of the European powers to dominate it politically only increased European longing and fed the fantasy about the land beyond the Snowy Range. Highly romanticized portrayals of traditional Tibet emerged, some of which continue to hold sway.

Many of these hyperrealities, ruled by the law of opposites, have come into play in the depiction of the Chinese invasion and occupation of Tibet that began in 1950. There were times prior to the nineteenth century when India and China were exalted by the poets and philosophers of Europe. China had been a particular favorite of the French Enlightenment, which saw the rule of a huge population by a class of scholar-gentlemen, the mandarins, as an ideal. India was a favorite of the German Romantics, who saw it as an abode of Spirit. This was an early manifestation of the continuing European romance in which the West perceives some lack within itself and fantasizes that the answer, through a process of projection, is to be found somewhere in the East. But by 1800, as European colonial interests in Asia were accelerating, the valuation of both societies had plummeted; they now seemed corrupt and backward, so incapable of governing themselves that their colonization seemed fully justified. During this period of European exploration and colonization, Tibet was closed to Europeans. Bounded on the south by the highest mountains in the world, at a time when mountains signified a cold and pristine purity, Tibet could be imagined as a domain of lost wisdom. Because Tibet did not become a European colony, many of Europe's fantasies about India and China, dispelled by colonialism, made their way across the mountains to an idealized Tibet. But many myths were of Tibetan making. Long before the Theosophists wrote of the secret region where the Mahatmas reigned, before James Hilton described the Edenic Valley of the Blue Moon in *Lost Horizon*, Tibetans wrote guidebooks to idyllic hidden valleys (*sbas yul*).

During the nineteenth century Tibet and China were regarded by many European scholars and colonial officers as "Oriental despotisms," one ruled by a Dalai Lama, an ethereal "god-king," the other by an effete emperor.[8] As early as 1822, Hegel, discussing Lamaism in his *Lectures on the Philosophy of History*, found it both paradoxical and revolting that the Dalai Lama, a living human being, was worshipped as God. During the Second World War, the Chinese, and Chinese Communists, were briefly portrayed as freedom-loving, in contrast to the despotic Japanese. After the success of the Communists in 1949, the image of the Oriental despot resurfaced and was superimposed onto Chairman Mao, not as emperor but as the totalitarian leader of faceless Communists. The Chinese invasion and occupation of Tibet was perceived not as a conquest of one despotic state by another, but as yet another case of opposites, the powers of darkness against the powers of light. The invasion of Tibet by the People's Liberation Army in 1950 was (and often is still) represented as an undifferentiated mass of godless Communists overrunning a peaceful land devoted only to ethereal pursuits, victimizing not only millions of Tibetans but the sometimes more lamented Buddhist dharma as well. Tibet embodies the spiritual and the ancient, China the material and the modern. Tibetans are superhuman, Chinese are subhuman. According to this logic of opposites China must be debased for Tibet to be exalted; for there to be an enlightened Orient there must be a benighted Orient; the angelic requires the demonic. The German Tibetophile who called himself Lama Govinda wrote in 1966:

> [W]hat is happening in Tibet is symbolic for the fate of humanity. As on a gigantically raised stage we witness the struggle between two worlds, which may be interpreted, according to the standpoint of the spectator, either as the struggle between the past and future, between backwardness and progress, belief and science, superstition and knowledge—or as the struggle between spiritual freedom and material power, between the wisdom of the heart and the knowledge of the brain, between the dignity of the human individual and the herd-instinct of the mass, between the faith in the higher destiny of man through inner development and the belief in material prosperity through an ever-increasing production of goods.[9]

Since the Tibetan diaspora that began in 1959 (a true diaspora in that it was a forced dispersal by an oppressor of a morally superior dispersed), Tibetan Buddhist culture has been portrayed as if it were itself another artifact of Shangri-La from an eternal classical age, set high in a Himalayan keep outside time and history. According to a 1968 documentary, "Tibet seemed not to belong to our earth, a society left on the shelf, set in amber, preserved in deep freeze, a land so close to the sky that the natural occupation of her people was to pray."[10] The history of Tibet was portrayed as pre- and post-pivot, having turned, with the introduction of Buddhism in the seventh century, from a society that had been directed outward, to conquer the world, into one that directed all its energies inward, to conquer the mind. As one scholar explains, "[Buddhism] turned their society from a fierce grim world of war and intrigue into a peaceful, colorful, cheerful realm of pleasant and meaningful living."[11]

The Chinese takeover exposed Tibet's timeless culture to time, time that would cause the contents of the culture to wither and turn to dust like the bodies of those who dare leave Shangri-La. In a closing scene of Frank Capra's *Lost Horizon,* Maria, the young and beautiful Russian, ages and dies when she leaves the Valley of the Blue Moon. In this apocalyptic vision the Tibetans are portrayed as ancient conservators of a timeless wisdom in a timeless realm, now thrust from their snowy sanctuary into history, where time is coming to an end and, with it, their wisdom. (A 1995 television documentary in Time-Life's *Lost Civilizations* series was entitled "Tibet: The End of Time.") In this particular version of the fantasy, those left in Tibet seem lost, while those in exile have to cope with the body blows of modernity, moving, as is often noted, from a country that even in the twentieth century had prayer wheels but no wheels on wagons, multiple metaphoric vehicles to liberation but no carts.

The ravages wrought by China's policies resulted not only in the destruction of monasteries, temples, texts, and works of art, but also in the deaths of hundreds of thousands of Tibetans. This would seem to be enough to sustain the contrast with life in Tibet before the invasion. But here again the logic of opposites is at work. To the growing number of Western adherents of Tibetan Buddhism "traditional Tibet" has come to mean something from which strength and identity are to be derived. It represents an ideal that once existed on the planet in high Tibet, a land free from strife, ruled by a benevolent Dalai Lama, his people devoted to the dharma and (we have recently learned) the preservation of the environment and the rights of women.[12] The mountaineer Marco Pallis wrote, "Sheltered behind the rampart of the Himalaya, Tibet has looked on, almost unscathed, while some of the greatest traditions of the world have reeled under the attacks of the all-devouring monster of modernism."[13] It is here that we see the volatility of the mythologizing and mystification of Tibetan culture. We often hear, for example, that Tibetan society was hermetic, sealed off from outside influence. Yet the reports of travelers from the early eighteenth century note that Tartars, Chinese, Muscovites, Armenians, Kashmiris, and Nepalese were established in Lhasa as merchants. The monasteries in Lhasa drew monks from as far west as the Kalmyk region of western Russia, between the Caspian Sea and the Black Sea; from as far east as Sichuan Province in China; from as far north as the Buryiat region near Lake Baikal in Siberia; and from as far south as the Sherpa regions of Nepal.

Nor was Tibet, in Georges Bataille's phrase, "an unarmed society."[14] Tibet did not renounce armed conflict when it converted to Buddhism in the eighth century, or in the eleventh century, or under the fifth Dalai Lama. The fifth Dalai Lama assumed temporal power over Tibet through the intervention of his Qoshot Mongol patron, the Gushri Khan, whose troops defeated the king of Tsang, patron of the Karma Kagyu. Tibetan armies fought against Ladakh in 1681, against the Dzungar Mongols in 1720, in numerous incursions into Bhutan during the eighteenth century, against invading Nepali forces from 1788 to 1792 and again in 1854, against Dogra forces invading Ladakh from Kashmir in 1842, and against the British in 1904.

Tibet prior to Chinese invasion and colonization has been portrayed in the West as an idyllic society devoted to the practice of Buddhism, a nation that required no police force because its people voluntarily observed the laws of karma, a society in which, through the workings of an "inner democracy," a peasant boy might become a great lama. But traditional Tibet, like any complex society, had great inequalities, with power monopolized by an elite composed of a small aristocracy, the hierarchs of various sects (including incarnate lamas), and the great Geluk monasteries. The subordinate members of the society included nonaristocratic laymen, non-Buddhists, and women.

The turn-of-the-century colonialist saw incarnate lamas as "an incarnation of all vices and corruptions, instead of the souls of departed Lamas."[15] In contrast, an extreme form of the view held by many in the West today argues that the Tibetan "gross national product of enlightened persons must have been proportionally higher than any other country ever."[16] Although the sons of peasants were chosen as Dalai Lamas and the sons of nomads mastered the monastic curriculum to become respected scholars and abbots, the system of incarnation was not a cosmic meritocracy above the mundane world of power and politics.

But the point is not to debunk with a catalog of facts our most cherished notions about Tibet (as useful as such a project might be) to more accurately depict what Tibet was or is "really like." The search for the real Tibet, beyond representation, lies at the heart of the fantasy of Tibet and contains its own ideology of control, which was put to devastating use during the colonial period. Nor is the point to suggest that Tibetan Buddhism is merely an instrument of oppression exercised in bad faith by power-hungry clerics. The important questions are why these myths persist and how they continue to circulate unchallenged.

In his 1991 *Sacred Tibet*, Philip Rawson explained that "Its real interest for us is that Tibetan culture offers powerful, untarnished and coherent alternatives to Western egotistical lifestyles, our short attention span, our gradually more pointless pursuit of material satisfactions, and our despair when these, finally, inevitably, disappoint us." [17] Tibet is seen as the cure for an ever-ailing Western civilization, a tonic to restore its spirit. And since the Tibetan diaspora that began in 1959 there seems an especial urgency about taking this cure, before it is lost forever. Today, however, it is no longer necessary to go to Tibet when Tibet can come to us. Tibetan monks now tour Europe and the United States, chanting and dancing to raise funds to support their monasteries in India. Of the first such show in 1924, an English journalist writing for the *Sunday Express* expressed a sentiment that would not be shared by today's audiences: "I cannot imagine anything more likely to kill the romance and mystery of Tibet than this ill-conceived idea of bringing some of the holy men of Buddhism to play in a masquerade of the religion on a London stage." [18]

Indeed, amid the many meanings ascribed to Tibet, it is often tempting to see Tibet as a vacuum, its emptiness attracting assorted influences and associations from the outside, whether Nepalese or Chinese artistic forms or fascist fantasies, which have styled Tibet both as the headquarters of an anti-Aryan conspiracy (in concert with Jews, Catholics, and Freemasons) and as the preserve, in its caves, of the esoteric wisdom of an ancient Aryan civilization, where all that was imagined to be good and true about the premodern had been preserved.

In the process, Tibet's complexities and competing histories have been flattened into a stereotype. Stereotypes operate through adjectives, which establish chosen characteristics as if they were eternal truths. Tibet is "isolated," Tibetans are "content," monks are "spiritual." With sufficient repetition, these adjectives become innate qualities, immune from history. And once these qualities harden into an essence, that essence may split into two opposing elements. [19] Thus, Lamaism may be portrayed in the West as the most authentic and the most degenerate form of Buddhism, Tibetan monks may be portrayed as saintly and rapacious, Tibetan artists may be portrayed as inspired mystics and mindless automatons, Tibetan peasants may be portrayed as pristine and filthy. This language about Tibet not only creates knowledge about Tibet, in many ways it creates Tibet, a Tibet that Tibetans in exile have come to appropriate and deploy in an effort to gain both standing in exile and independence for their country.

In the continual play of opposites, the view of old Tibet as good is put forward by the Tibetan government-in-exile. The representation of old Tibet as bad, so familiar from European accounts of the nineteenth century, is appropriated by the Chinese colonial government (as evidenced in their recent virulent attacks on the Dalai Lama) in their campaign to incorporate the nation of Tibet into China. To recognize this play of opposites strengthens the case against the Chinese occupation and underscores the dangers of romanticizing Tibet and Tibetan Buddhism.

We may be disillusioned to learn that Tibet is not the place we have dreamed of. Yet to allow Tibet to circulate in a system of fantastic opposites (even when Tibetans are the "good" Orientals) is to deny Tibet its history, to exclude it from a real world of which it has always been a part, and to deny Tibetans their agency in the creation of a contested quotidian reality.[20] During the past three decades fantasies of Tibet garnered much support for the cause of Tibetan independence. But those fantasies are ultimately a threat to the realization of that goal. To the extent that we continue to believe that Tibet prior to 1950 was a utopia, the Tibet of 1998 will be no place.

THE CREATION MYTH of this book began when I attended a conference on Tibet some years ago. The keynote speaker gave a public lecture that romanticized Tibetan history and demonized the Chinese. At the conclusion of the speech, the audience rose as one in a standing ovation. It seemed clear that several hundred people had been converted to the cause of Tibetan independence. The question that the lecture raised for me was whether it was possible to make the case for Tibetan independence, which, one assumes, all people of good will (when presented with the facts) would support, without invoking the romantic view of Tibet as Shangri-La. Invoking the myth seems at times almost irresistible; without it the Chinese occupation and colonization of Tibet seems just one of many human rights violations that demand our attention. What sets the plight of Tibet apart from that of Palestine, Rwanda, Burma, Northern Ireland, East Timor, or Bosnia is the picture of Tibetans as a happy, peaceful people devoted to the practice of Buddhism, whose remote and ecologically enlightened land, ruled by a god-king, was invaded by the forces of evil. This is a compelling story, an enticing blend of the exotic, the spiritual, and the political. But I have become convinced that the continued idealization of Tibet—its history and its religion—may ultimately harm the cause of Tibetan independence.[21] I set out to investigate some of the factors that have contributed to the formation and persistence of the romance of Tibet. This book is the result of those investigations.

It is not a history of Western relations with and attitudes toward Tibet; the materials that I have examined derive largely from the last century. It is not a detailed social history, within which the romance of Tibet would play a highly allusive role. I have not attempted to catalog every case of Western intercourse with Tibet, even during this century. Nor have I considered in any detail, for example, the substantial body of popular literature about Tibet, both travel accounts and fiction (including *Tintin in Tibet*),[22] written both by those who have crossed the Tibetan frontier and those who have never approached it.[23] I have not considered the role of British, Russian, and Japanese espionage in the formation of knowledge about Tibet and Tibetan Buddhism: just as, during the ninth century, Indian *paṇḍitas* walked into Tibet carrying rosaries and perhaps prayer wheels, Indians and Tibetans of the nineteenth century, working as British agents (known as "the pundits"), walked into Tibet disguised as pilgrims, their rosaries used to measure distance, their prayer wheels emptied of mantras to conceal a compass.[24] The two groups of pilgrims, separated by a millennium, each played a role in the formation of an archive and in the delineation of the Tibetan state, the first by acting as translators, making a sacred canon for Tibet, the second by acting as surveyors, making maps for the British.

In 1942 the United States Office of Strategic Services (the forerunner of the CIA) sent two army officers, Captain Ilya Tolstoy (grandson of Count Leo) and Lieutenant Brooke Dolan, to survey Tibet for routes for roads and sites for airfields, both of which would be used to transport materials from India to China.[25] Tibet's neutral government refused permission to the Allies to convey any war materials across Tibetan territory. On November 30, 1943, an American C-87, a cargo plane flying the "hump" from China to India, ran out of fuel and its crew bailed out, landing near the monastery of Samye. They were rescued by Tibetans and escorted safely back to the Indian border.[26] Although a landing strip was not constructed until after the Chinese invasion, flights of fancy and imagination had been launched from "Tibet" for centuries. Some returned to earth, sometimes in Tibet, sometimes elsewhere, only to refuel and fly off again. But most have remained in orbit. Some, launched at the same time, took off in opposite directions, their paths crossing only high above the earth where it is neither day or night. Without constant propulsion, however, a satellite, drawn by gravity, will eventually fall into the earth's atmosphere.

This book attempts to plot the trajectories of a few of these flights, noting their points of origin and their routes, decoding the signals the satellites send to earth, tracing the intersections of their orbits, investigating what keeps them aloft and why they occasionally fall flaming to earth. They include a name (Lamaism), a book (*The Tibetan Book of the Dead*), an impostor

(T. Lobsang Rampa), a mantra (*oṃ maṇi padme hūṃ*), an aesthetic (Tibetan Buddhist art), an academic discipline (Tibetan Buddhist Studies), and a prison, in which Tibetan lamas in exile and their students are at once the inmates and the guards. Each ship is launched from Tibet through a complex network of discourse, and one often finds simulacra in Tibet: the hidden valley, the memory of a past life, the secret meaning of a mantra. In each case, however, it becomes clear that, once free of the specificity of Tibet, anything Tibetan begins to attract associations, whether Roman Catholic, sexual (the meaning of a mantra), or psychedelic (the reading of a Buddhist text); things Tibetan become not particular to a time and place, but universal, and in the process Tibet is everywhere and hence nowhere, functioning as an element of difference in which anything is possible.

This book does not set out to apportion praise and blame. Neither is its purpose to distinguish good Tibetology from bad, to separate fact from fiction, or the scholarly from the popular, but to show their confluence. The question considered is not how knowledge is tainted but how knowledge takes form. The book then is an exploration of some of the mirror-lined cultural labyrinths that have been created by Tibetans, Tibetophiles, and Tibetologists, labyrinths that the scholar may map but in which the scholar also must wander. We are captives of confines of our own making, we are all prisoners of Shangri-La. This book, then, is not written outside the walls of the prison, nor does it hold a key that would permit escape. Hidden in its pages, however, some may find a file with which to begin the slow work of sawing through the bars.

CHAPTER ONE

The Name

❀

It hardly seems necessary to remark that the term Lamaism *is a purely European invention and not known in Asia.*   ISAAC JACOB SCHMIDT, 1835

Altogether, therefore, "Lāmaism" is an undesirable designation for the Buddhism of Tibet, and is rightly dropping out of use.   L. A. WADDELL, 1915

Lamaism was a combination of the esoteric Buddhism of India, China, and Japan with native cults of the Himalayas.   NATIONAL GALLERY BROCHURE, 1991

A 1992 exhibition at the National Gallery of Art, in Washington, D.C., entitled "Circa 1492: Art in the Age of Exploration" contained four rooms devoted to Ming China. Commenting on one of the Ming paintings, a well-known Asian art historian wrote, "The individual [Tang and Song] motifs, however, were woven into a thicket of obsessive design produced for a non-Chinese audience. Here the aesthetic wealth of China was placed at the service of the complicated theology of Tibet." [1] The painting was of an Indian Buddhist monk, a disciple of the Buddha. The non-Chinese audience for whom the work was produced perhaps included Mongol or Tibetan Buddhists. However, the complicated theology that China's aesthetic wealth was made to serve was not identified as Buddhism, or even Tibetan Buddhism. The art historian used the term "Lamaism," an abstract noun that does not appear in the Tibetan language but has a long history in the West, a history inextricable from the ideology of exploration and discovery that the National Gallery cautiously sought to celebrate.

"Lamaism" is often regarded as a synonym for "Tibetan Buddhism." The terms, however, have different connotations. "Tibetan Buddhism" suggests a regional version of a world religion, as distinguished from Japanese Buddhism or Thai Buddhism, for example. "Lamaism" carries other associations. The art historian's comment echoes the nineteenth-century portrait of Lamaism as something monstrous, a composite of unnatural lineage devoid of the spirit of original Buddhism. Lamaism was seen as a deformity unique to Tibet, its parentage denied by India (in the voice of British Indologists) and by China (in the voice of the Qing empire), an aberration so unique in fact that it would eventually float free of its Tibetan abode, and that abode would vanish.

In the discourse of the Christian West, we find, among its many associations, a rather consistent pairing of "Lamaism" with "Roman Catholicism." For example, a 1992 book review in the *New York Times* said of Tibetan Buddhism, "It has justly been called the Roman Catholicism of the East: ancient and complex, hierarchical and mystical, with an elaborate liturgy, a lineage of saints, even a leader addressed as His Holiness." [2] The reviewer seemed unaware, however, of the long history of this particular comparison, one that began centuries before Ogden Nash reminded us that "A one -*l* lama, he's a priest. A two -*l* lama, he's a beast." [3] It is as if a certain amnesia has set in, under which the association of Tibetan Buddhism, called "Lamaism," with Roman Catholicism seems somehow free, somehow self-evident, even to be construed as somehow also objective by recourse to theories of causation, influence, borrowing, and diffusion. But the association of Lamaism with Catholicism, like all associations, is not free.

Europe refused to identify any legitimate ancestors of Lamaism in Asia; it seemed unlike anything else. And it is in this state of genealogical absence that Lamaism was most susceptible to comparison, that it could begin to look like Catholicism. The use of the term "Lamaism" in European discourse as a code word for popish ritualism, and as a substitute for "Tibet," is, in its own way, not unrelated to the recent disappearance of Tibet as a nation. During the nineteenth century Tibet's existence was both threatened and contested by Britain and China. And during the twentieth century Tibet's absence became manifest in art-exhibition catalogs and maps of Asia as it was forcibly incorporated into China. The history of these effects begins with the particular vicissitudes that led to the invention of the term "Lamaism" through a process that the nineteenth-century philologist Max Müller might have termed "the decay of language."

This chapter will trace this process of decay. It will begin with the term "lama," which today conjures the image of a smiling, bespectacled Buddhist monk, but in fact is derived from Tibet's pre-Buddhist past. Only during the ninth century did it become the official Tibetan translation of the Sanskrit term "guru." From Tibet, the term traveled to Mongolia and to China, where it eventually came to signify not simply a Tibetan Buddhist teacher but also his teaching. It was perhaps from Mongolia, perhaps from China, that Europeans derived the abstract noun "Lamaism," which would name the religion of Tibet, and by the late eighteenth century the term was being used to serve a wide range of agendas. One of the constants during this period was the comparison of Lamaism with Roman Catholicism. The comparison was first drawn by Catholics, who felt constrained to account for the many similarities they observed between this form of heathenism and their own true faith. The comparison would later be drawn by Protestants seeking to demonstrate that the corrupt priestcraft observed in Tibet had its counterpart in Europe. With the rise in Europe of the academic study of Buddhism, Lamaism was the term used to describe the state to which the original teachings of the Buddha had sunk in the centuries since his death. As with much European discourse about Tibet, Tibetans have been largely absent from the scene: the term Lamaism has no correlate in the Tibetan language. It was only after the Dalai Lama and thousands of Tibetans fled to India in 1959 that they confronted the term, which they have generally regarded as pejorative, suggesting as it does that their religion does not deserve the designation "Buddhism." Yet the term, so deeply engrained, persists (especially among those who fear that the very use of the term "Tibet" would occasion the wrath of the People's Republic of China, into which Tibet has now been subsumed), "Lamaism" sometimes serving as a substitute for "Tibet," and "Lamaist" for "Tibetan." This chapter will trace some of the trajectories of the term.

THE TIBETAN TERM "lama" (*bla ma*) is derived from two words, *la* and *ma*. The notion of *la*, generally translated as "soul," "spirit," or "life," predates the introduction of Buddhism into Tibet. The *la* is said to be an individual's life force, the essential support of the physical and mental constitution of the person. It is mobile; it can depart from the body and wander or be carried off by gods and demons, to the detriment of the person it leaves, who will become either ill or mentally unbalanced as a result. There are therefore rites designed to call the *la* back into the body.[4] Even when the *la* is properly restored to its place in the body, it may simultaneously reside in certain external abodes, such as a lake, tree, mountain, or animal. The person in whom the *la* resides is in what Sir James Frazer would call a sympathetic relationship with these phenomena: if the *la* mountain is dug into, the person will fall ill. In an attempt to conquer a certain demoness, the Tibetan epic hero Gesar of Ling cuts down her *la* tree and empties her *la* lake; he fails because he does not kill her *la* sheep. The identity of these external *la* is thus commonly kept secret, and portable abodes of the *la*, usually a precious object of some kind (often a turquoise), are placed in special receptacles and hidden by the person who shares the *la*.[5] Perhaps in relation to the concept of this soul, the term *la* also has the common meaning of "above" or "high."

With the introduction of Buddhism in the seventh, eighth, and ninth centuries, Tibetan monks and visiting Indian *paṇḍitas* undertook the task of translating Buddhist texts from Sanskrit into Tibetan, in the process inventing hundreds of neologisms. When these exegetes came to decide upon a Tibetan equivalent for *guru*, the Sanskrit term for teacher, they departed from their storied penchant for approximating the meaning of the Sanskrit and opted instead for the word "lama" (*bla ma*). Here they combined the term *la* with *ma*, the latter having at least three meanings: as a negative particle meaning "no" or "not," as a substantive indicator (as in *nyi ma*, "sun," or *srung ma*, "protector"), and as the word for "mother." Subsequent Buddhist etymologies, drawing on the meaning of *la* as "high" rather than its pre-Buddhist usage as "soul," were then construed, which explained *la ma* as meaning either "highest" (literally "above-not," that is, "none above") or "exalted mother."[6] Lama came to be the standard term for one's religious teacher, a person so significant as to be appended to the threefold Buddhist refuge formula: Tibetans say, "I go for refuge to the lama, I go for refuge to the Buddha, I go for refuge to the dharma [his teaching], I go for refuge to the sangha [the community of monks and nuns]."[7]

The other common use of the term lama is as a designation of incarnations. The institution of incarnation (*sprul sku*) has existed in Tibet since at least the fourteenth century, when the then recently deceased Karma pa monk

Rangjung Dorje (Rang byung rdo rje, 1284–1338) was identified in his biography as having been the incarnation of Karma Pakshi (1206–1283).[8] Since then, every sect of Tibetan Buddhism has adopted the practice of identifying the successive rebirths of a great teacher, the most famous instance of which being, of course, the Dalai Lamas. But there are several thousand other lines of incarnation in Tibetan Buddhism. In ordinary Tibetan parlance, such persons are called lamas whether or not they have distinguished themselves as scholars, adepts, or teachers in their present lives. To ask whether a particular monk is a lama is to ask whether he is an incarnation, and the terms *bla chung* and *bla chen* refer to minor and major incarnate lamas. The ambiguity in usage between "lama" as a religious preceptor and "lama" as an incarnation has led the current Dalai Lama in his sermons to admonish his followers that a lama (as one's religious teacher) need not be an incarnation and that an incarnation is not necessarily a lama.[9]

One Western scholar has argued that "guru" was translated as *bla ma* to mean "mother to the soul" in order to "facilitate assimilation of the 'role' of the *guru* in Buddhism into the existing shamanic beliefs of the Tibetan people."[10] Whether Tibetan beliefs were "shamanic" or not, the more likely possibility is that lama meant "one endowed with the soul."[11] What is noteworthy, however, is that this meaning is lost in the Buddhist etymologies, that as Buddhism was introduced into Tibet the archaic meaning of *la* as "life" or "soul" disappeared.

As the *la* would sometimes leave the body, Tibetan lamas would leave Tibet, traveling to the courts of Mongol khans and Manchu emperors. And it was in these realms, beyond Tibet, that "lama" would become "Lamaism." But this process took time, for when Tibetan Buddhist teachers made their way from Tibet to the Mongolian and Chinese centers of power it seems that they were referred to not as lamas but by terms derived from the languages of their hosts. Marco Polo, for example, refers to the Tibetans at the court of Kublai Khan as *Bacsi* (*bakshi*, the Mongolian word for "teacher"): "The sorcerers who do this [prevent storms] are TEBET and KESIMUR [Kashmir], which are the names of two nations of idolaters. . . . There is another marvel performed by those BACSI of whom I have been speaking as knowing so many enchantments. . . . These monks dress more decently than the rest of the people, and have the head and the beard shaven."[12] At the Chinese court of the early Ming dynasty, Tibetan monks were simply called *seng*, as were Chinese monks, and the religion of Tibet was called Buddhism (*fo jiao*).[13]

In 1775 during the reign of the Manchu Emperor Qianlong we find perhaps the first official usage of the Chinese term *lama jiao,* one of the sources from which "Lamaism" seems to derive. *Jiao* is the standard Chinese term for "teaching," being employed in terms such as *dao jiao* (the teaching of the dao, "Daoism"), *ru jiao* (the teaching of the literati, "Confucianism"), and *fo jiao* (the teaching of the Buddha, "Buddhism"). By the reign of Qianlong, "lama" had come to be used as an adjective to describe Tibetan religion in contexts that in the past would have simply used the term "Buddhist."[14] In 1792 Qianlong composed his *Lama Shuo* (Pronouncements on Lamas), pre-served in a tetraglot inscription (in Chinese, Manchu, Mongol, and Tibetan) at the Yonghe-gong (today known to tourists as the "Lama Temple") in Bei-jing. Here Qianlong defends his patronage of a Tibetan sect the Chinese called the "Yellow Hats" (the Geluk) from his Chinese critics by claiming that his support has been merely expedient: "By patronizing the Yellow Church we maintain peace among the Mongols. This being an important task we cannot but protect this (religion). (In doing so) we do not show any bias, nor do we wish to adulate the Tibetan priests as (was done during the) Yuan dynasty."[15] Here are some of Qianlong's comments on the term "lama":

> [Buddhism's] foreign priests are traditionally known as Lamas. The word Lama does not occur in Chinese books. . . . I have carefully pondered over its meaning and found that *la* in Tibet means "superior" and *ma* means "none." So *la-ma* means "without superior," just as in Chinese a priest is called a "superior" (*shang-jên*). Lama also stands for Yellow Religion.[16]

Qianlong had clearly learned the standard Tibetan Buddhist gloss of the term as "highest." He seems determined to place the term "lama" at some distance from his reign, to declare to the subjects who speak the four languages of his realm that lamas are foreigners and that his patronage of them has been motivated by political expediency. We also see in Qianlong's discussion an example of the implication of the term "lama" and, later, "Lamaism" in Manchu imperial projects directed toward Tibet. In this case, Qianlong, who had been a generous patron and dedicated student of Tibetan lamas, sought to assure his Chinese subjects that foreign priests exercised no influence over him. As the term "Lamaism" gained currency in Europe, it would gain fur-ther implications and associations from other imperial projects, as during the nineteenth century Tibet would become an object of European colonial in-terests. European ideologues, however, would be far less explicit than the Manchu emperor about the political connotations of their use of the term.

BEFORE MOVING to Europe and the nineteenth century, it would be useful to have some sense of what Europeans knew about Tibet. By the middle of the eighteenth century, knowledge of the world, gathered from the accounts of explorers, traders, and missionaries, was compiled in works like Bernard Picart's *The Ceremonies and Religious Customs of the Various Nations of the Known World*, published in London in 1741. His description of Tibetan Buddhism follows, although nowhere do the words "Tibet" or "Buddhism" appear. Instead he describes the religion of the Mongols (called Tartars) and the Kalmyks ("Calmoucks"—Mongols living in the region of Russia between the Black Sea and the Caspian Sea), suggesting that this knowledge was gained from travelers to those regions rather than from travelers to Tibet. Picart describes Tibet's religion as Marco Polo described it almost five centuries earlier: as idolatry. During the seventeenth century, only four religions were identified: Christianity, Judaism, Islam, and Idolatry. And here we see the seeds of the association of this form of idolatry with Catholicism, in terms like "convent" and "pontiff," and in the glossing of "lama" as "priest."

> The *Mongolian Tartars, Calmoucks,* and others, according to them, have, properly speaking, no other God but their *Dalai-Lama,* which signifies, as we are informed, *Universal Priest.* This Sovereign Pontiff of all the *Tartarian* Idolaters, and whom they acknowledge as their God, resides toward the Frontiers of *China,* near the City of *Potola,* in a Convent, situate on the Summit of an high Mountain, the Foot whereof is inhabited by above twenty thousand *Lamas,* . . . who have their separate Apartments round about the Mountain, and, according to their respective Quality and Function, are planted nearer, or at a greater Distance from their Sovereign Pontiff. . . . The Term *Lama,* in the *Mongolian* Language, signifies *Priest;* and that of *Dalai,* which in the same Language implies *vast Extent,* has been translated in the Language of the Northern *Indians,* by *Gehan,* a Term of the same Signification. Thus *Dalai-Lama,* and *Prete-Gehan* are synonymous Terms, and the Meaning of them is *Universal Priest.*
>
> There are two Monarchs, one Temporal, and the other Spiritual, at *Lassa,* which, some say, is the Kingdom of *Tanchuth,* or *Boratai,* or *Barantola.* The Spiritual Monarch is the *Grand Lama,* whom these Idolaters worship as a God. He very seldom goes abroad. The Populace think themselves happy, if they can by any Means procure the least Grain of his Excrements, or Drop of his Urine; imagining either of them as infallible Preservative from all Maladies and Disasters. These Excrements are kept as sacred Relicks, in little Boxes, and hung around their Necks. Father *Le*

Comte imagines *Fo* [the Chinese term for "Buddha"] and the *Grand Lama* to be one and the same Deity; who, according to the Idea of these *Tartars*, must for ever appear under a Form that may be felt or perceiv'd by the Senses, and is supposed to be immortal. He is close confined, adds he, to a Temple, where an infinite Number of *Lama's* attend him, with the most profound Veneration, and take all imaginable Care to imprint the same awful Ideas of him on the Minds of the People. He is very seldom expos'd to View, and whenever he is, 'tis at such a Distance, that it would be morally impossible for the most quick-sighted Person to recollect his Features. Whenever he dies, another *Lama*, who resembles him as near as possible, is immediately substituted in his Stead; for which Purpose, as soon as they perceive his Dissolution drawing nigh, the most zealous Devotees, and chief Ministers of the imaginary God, travel the whole Kingdom over, to find out a proper Person to succeed him. This pious Intrigue is carried on, says he, with all the Dexterity and Address imaginable. The Deification of the *Lama*, if we may depend on the Veracity of Father *Kircher*, was first owing to the extraordinary Trust and Confidence which those People re-pos'd in their *Prester-John.*[17]

There are hints of blasphemy here, as a mere mortal is regarded as God, and of pollution, as the populace worships human waste. There is also a hint of the sinister, as Picart, unaware that the new Dalai Lama is found only after the death of the present one, explains that the priests search the realm for a credible substitute when the death of the Dalai Lama draws near. Finally, there is the familiar suggestion, which we will encounter again, that anything authentic in this religion is due to the influence of a Christian. Here Picart explains that the people once placed their faith in Prester John, the fabled Catholic priest whose utopian kingdom was located sometimes in Asia, sometimes in Africa. Only later was their trust transferred to a false god, the Dalai Lama.

Tibetan religion was not only described but also explained. Thus, in a fascinating entry on Tibet in his 1784 *Outlines of a Philosophy of the History of Man*, Johann Herder speculated that the religion of the lamas (still not identified as Buddhism) could not have originated in the robust northern zones of Tibet, but must have come from a warmer clime because it was "the creature of some enervate minds, that love above all things to indulge in bodily rest, and freedom from thought." He concludes: "If there be a religion upon Earth, that deserves the epithets of monstrous and inconsistent, it is the religion of Tibet."[18] Such condemnation of Tibetan religion was widespread.

In *The Social Contract* (1762), Rousseau makes a reference to "the religion of the Lamas," which, along with that of the Japanese and Roman Catholicism, may be classified as "the religion of the priest," a type of religion that "is so clearly bad, that it is a waste of time to stop to prove it as such." [19]

Perhaps the first occurrence of the term "Lamaism" in a European language appears in the reports of the German naturalist Peter Simon Pallas, who traveled through the realm of Catherine the Great for the Royal Academy of Sciences in Petersburg. His reports of 1769, translated into English by the Reverend John Trusler and published in 1788 in his *The Habitable World Described*, contain a long description of the religion of the Kalmyks, based largely on conversations with Kalmyk converts to Christianity. There Pallas refers to the "religion of Lama" and the "tenets of Lamaism." [20] In 1825 Jean Pierre Abel Rémusat, in his "Discours sur l'origine de la hiérarchie lamaïque," uses the term *des lamistes*. [21] In the account of his travels in western Ladakh from 1819 to 1825, William Moorcroft refers to "those places where Lamaism still predominates." [22] Hegel discusses Lamaism in his *Lectures on the Philosophy of Religion* of 1824 and 1827 and in his *Lectures on the Philosophy of History*, delivered between 1822 and 1831, in which he finds the notion of a living human being worshipped as God, as he describes the Dalai Lama, paradoxical and revolting, just as Picart had almost a century earlier. Hegel writes, "The Abstract Understanding generally objects to this idea of a God-man; alleging as a defect that the form here assigned to the Spirit is an immediate [unrefined, unreflected] one—that in fact it is none other than Man in the concrete. Here the character of a whole people is bound up with the theological view just indicated." [23]

Hegel seems to have based his discussion on some version of the reports of Catholic missionaries rather than on any Tibetan text. When the first translations from Tibetan into English became available the impression they created was of a religion not nearly as coherent as Hegel had postulated. The French explorer Victor Jacquemont, in a letter from Ellora on May 22, 1832, described the translations done by the Hungarian scholar Alexander Csoma de Kőrös: "They are unspeakably boring. There are some twenty chapters on what sort of shoes it is fitting for lamas to wear. Among other pieces of preposterous nonsense of which these books are full, priests are forbidden to take hold of a cow's tail to ford a swift river. There is no lack of profound dissertations on properties of griffins', dragons', and unicorns' flesh or the admirable virtues of hoofs of winged horses. To judge by what I have seen of that people and what M. Csoma's translations tell us about them, one would take them for a race of madmen or idiots." [24] It would seem then that neither access to translations of Tibetan texts nor eyewitness description could consistently dispel European fantasies about Tibet. There were, however, occasional voices of dissent.

In his 1835 essay "Ueber Lamaismus und die Bedeutungslosigkeit dieses Nahmens" (On Lamaism and the Meaninglessness of This Term), Isaac Jacob Schmidt (1779–1847), who had studied Buddhism among the Kalmyks in Russia from 1804 to 1806, explains that *la* means "soul" and *ma* means "mother," and challenges an assumption that would persist far into the next century:

> It is well-known that the Tibetan and Mongolian peoples, as far as their religious faith is concerned, were until not long ago almost universally called *Lamaites* (*Lamaiten*) and their religion, Lamaism. Indeed, even now there are many people, otherwise quite well-informed, who imagine that there is an essential difference between Buddhism and Lamaism. The purpose of this essay is to demonstrate the non-existence of this imagined difference and to show at the same time the extent to which the religion of Tibetans and Mongols represents a particular manifestation in the history of Buddhism. It seems hardly necessary to remark that the term *Lamaism* is a purely European invention and not known in Asia. The peoples of that faith call themselves followers of the teachings of the Buddha and are consequently, according to the European expression, Buddhists; the meaning of this term agrees completely with the Sanskrit *Bauddha*. [25]

Schmidt (a Mongolist) seems unaware of the Chinese term *lama jiao*, from which "Lamaism" may derive. Nonetheless, his assertion that Lamaism is essentially a European category remains remarkable, both for its insight as well as for the fact that it has gone unnoticed in the long history of Western discourse about Lamaism.

To trace the movements of this discourse we must go back before the late Qing dynasty in China and the early nineteenth century in Europe to the time of Marco Polo and other early European visitors to the Chinese court during the Yuan dynasty. It is there that we hear the first recitations of the similarities between Tibetan Buddhism and Roman Catholicism. The trope is employed differently by two distinct groups of European exegetes of the Orient, first the Catholic, then the Protestant. One of the earliest Catholic observers was the Dominican Jourdain Catalani de Séverac, who visited the empire of the "Grand Tartar":

In that empire, there are temples of idols and monasteries of men and women, as there are at home, with choirs and the saying of prayers, exactly like us, the great pontiffs of the idols wearing red robes and red hats, like our cardinals. Such luxury, such pomp, such dance, such solemn ceremony is incredible in the sacrifices to idols.[26]

The Portuguese Jesuit Antonio de Andrade, writing in 1626 after a Tibetan lama had watched him perform the Mass, learned from the lama that the "Grand Lama in Utsang [Central Tibet] offers small quantities of bread and wine, that he drinks of them himself and distributes the remainder to the other lamas and that he blows and breathes with his mouth over the wine he presents to God, which he alone and no one else may do. And he added that this Grand Lama wears on his head a tiara like mine but much larger."[27] The German Jesuit John Grueber, who reached Lhasa in 1661, observed of the Tibetans:

Thus they celebrate the Sacrifice of the Mass with Bread and Wine, give extreme Unction, bless married Folks, say Prayers over the Sick, make Nunneries, sing in the Service of the Choir, observe divers Fasts during the year, undergo most severe Penances, and, among the rest, Whippings; consecrate Bishops, and send-out Missionaries who live in extream Poverty, and travel bare-foot through the Desarts as far as *China*.[28]

Once such a similarity was observed it had to be accounted for, and Catholic missionaries to China and Tibet turned to history and theology to explain why Tibetan lamas looked like priests of the Holy Mother Church. The Vincentian missionaries Huc and Gabet, who traveled in China and Tibet from 1844 to 1846, noted the affinities between what they called "Lamanesque worship" and Catholicism:

The cross, the mitre, the dalmatica, the cope which the Grand Lamas wear on their journeys, or when they are performing some ceremony out of the temple; the service with double choirs, the psalmody, the exorcisms, the censer, suspended from five chains, and which they can open or close at pleasure, the benedictions given by the Lamas over the heads of the faithful; the chaplet, ecclesiastical celibacy, spiritual retirement, the worship of the saints, the feasts, the processions, the litanies, the holy water, all these are analogies between the Buddhists and ourselves. Now, can it be said that these analogies are of Christian origin? We think so.[29]

They then recount a story about Tsong kha pa (1357–1419), the deified "founder" of the Geluk sect, which by the time of the Vincentians' visit had wielded political control over Tibet for two centuries. They tell of the young Tsong kha pa's encounter with a lama "from the most remote regions of the West," who took him as his disciple and "initiated [him] into all the doctrines of the West" in the few years before his peaceful death. What was remarkable about this lama, besides his unfathomable learning, were his gleaming eyes and his large nose. Huc and Gabet predictably speculate that this stranger with the prominent nose was a Catholic missionary. "It may be further supposed that a premature death did not permit the Catholic missionary to complete the religious education of his disciple, who himself, when afterwards he became an apostle, merely applied himself, whether from having incomplete knowledge of Christian doctrine, or from having apostatized from it, to the introduction of a new Buddhist liturgy." [30] The implication and regret, of course, is that if the Catholic missionary had lived longer, Tsong kha pa would have received full instruction in the dogmas of the Church and so could have converted Tibet to Christianity.

Here is perhaps the most common strategy for explaining similarity, called borrowing or, more properly, "genealogy" (also known as "diffusionism" in anthropology)—that is, accounting for coincidental phenomena or traits by appealing to historical influence. The recourse to genealogy attempts to establish not only a direct historical relation, but also a hierarchy based on the chronological proximity of the influencing agent to the originary ancestor. Hence Huc and Gabet could lay claim to all that they found "authentic" in Tsong kha pa's Buddhism by ascribing its origin to one of their own, and at the same time dismiss Tibetan Buddhism as deficient because Tsong kha pa's instruction in the Gospel remained incomplete, their own mission thereby legitimated as the fulfillment of the mysterious Westerner's work. The Europeans thus claimed a position of power, indeed the power of origin, over Tsong kha pa, whom they perceived as the most important figure in the history of Tibetan Buddhism. [31]

The first European encounters with Tibetan Buddhism occurred long before the rise of the science of philology, long before any notion of an ancestral heritage of "mankind" that could attempt to explain the manifestation of parallel developments in different parts of the globe. Thus, there were only two possible (but not necessarily mutually exclusive) explanations for the apparent similarities between Tibetan lamas and Catholic priests: they were either the result of the work of one of their own or they were the result of the work of another. Those who believed the former included the Jesuit mission-aries to Cathay and Tibet, who were motivated by the belief (which persisted into the eighteenth century, as evidenced in the passage from Picart) that they would find remnants of the church of Prester John, who some thought may have been the first Dalai Lama.[32] If this was not the case, then the similari-ties must be the work of an other, a cause not for the delight expressed by Huc and Gabet, but for a deep anxiety, reflected in the words of the Jesuit Athanasius Kircher (apparently Picart's chief source), who in 1667 described the adulation afforded the Dalai Lama:

> Strangers at their approach fall prostrate with their heads to the ground, and kiss him with incredible Veneration, which is no other than that which is performed upon the Pope of *Rome*; so that hence the fraud and deceit of the Devil may easily and plainly appear, who by his innate malignity and hatred, in way of abuse hath transferred, as he hath done all the other Mysteries of the Christian Religion, the Veneration which is due unto the Pope of Rome, the only Vicar of Christ on Earth, unto the superstitious Worship of barbarous people.
>
> Whence as the Christians call the *Roman* High-Priest Father of Fa-thers, so these *Barbarians* term their false Deity the Great *Lama*, that is, the Great High-Priest, and the *Lama* of *Lamas*, that is, the High-Priest of High-Priests, because that from him, as from a certain Fountain, floweth the whole form and mode of their Religion, or rather mad and brain-sick idolatry, whence also they call him the Eternal Father.[33]

This is an extreme form of the theory of demonic plagiarism articulated by Justin Martyr and other church fathers during the second and third centuries, in which any similarity between ritual elements of the Church and those of rival cults is attributed to the work of the devil. In many cases, components of the Christian rituals were derived from these very same rival cults, such that the doctrine of demonic plagiarism served as a means of appropriating the purity of the origin, consigning the other to the corrupt state of the derivative.[34]

Why must this appearance be demonic? The answer derives in part from the Christian Church's claim to historical and ontological particularity. It is the task of the missionary to transmit the word of that particularity to those realms where it has not yet spread, to diffuse it from its unique point of origin. To carry its accoutrements from Rome in a time and to a place they could not possibly have been taken before, and to find them already there, suggests the workings of a power beyond history, which could only be seen as demonic. But what is described in this passage is a visual image: the dress and the liturgy were derived from their authentic source; they are a copy. It is as if the priest arrived in distant China only to see himself reflected in a mirror, with the inversion of the image so typically ascribed to the demonic. He sees the very aim of his long journey, what he hopes will have been when the last domain of the globe has been brought to the true faith—namely, that as a result of his ministry the bodies of the once idolatrous Orientals will have worn the vestments of the Christian father and will have performed the liturgy of the holy church. But to the priest, the image of the Buddhist monk at the first encounter appears to already be what it can only become later. This distant goal, a mirage of the maturation of his power, has already been achieved. The monk stands before the priest, as if he were looking in a mirror.

Unlike the infant in the "mirror stage" who regards the integrated vision of his body in the mirror with jubilation, for the priest it is a moment of dread; he recognizes the reflected image, as the child does not, as a trap and a decoy. What is monstrous is not the presence of the Buddhist monk, but the priest's identification with the monk's image, "with the automaton in which, in an ambiguous relation, the world of his own making tends to find completion." [35] The priest sees identity where it is absent: the dress and liturgies of Buddhism, whether Chinese or Tibetan, are not the same as those of a Roman Catholic priest. But for such a perception to occur, the fragmented body of the church must imagine itself complete, already present before its arrival, in the regalia of the Lamaist priest. The original has arrived too late, after its image, and this late arrival has as its consequence both self-constitution and alienation. The Catholic priest simultaneously identifies with the image of his foreign counterpart and armors himself against it by condemning it as demonic. It is as if the image of the Buddhist, the counterpart, throws the priest forward in time, out of the "natural" dissemination of the word, projecting him out of the process of conversion. The missionary's confrontation with his Tibetan counterpart is then, like the mirror stage, "high tragedy: a brief moment of doomed glory, a paradise lost." [36]

Even at the Qing court, a Portuguese missionary to China was quoted as saying of Tibetan rituals, "There is not a piece of dress, not a sacerdotal function, not a ceremony of the court of Rome, which the Devil has not copied in this country." [37] Thus this Roman Catholic genealogy of Tibetan

Buddhism was not merely a case of pre-Enlightenment demonology, it persisted into the eighteenth and nineteenth centuries.[38]

As early as the mid-eighteenth century Protestants were comparing Tibetan Buddhism with Roman Catholicism, but for a different reason. Their intent was not to account for the *possibility* of similarity between idolaters and Roman Catholics, as Catholic authors had sought to do, but to claim the *necessity* of such similarities, because Roman Catholics were, in effect, idolaters as well. Thus the English Protestant Thomas Astley's *A New Collection of Voyages and Travels Consisting of The most Esteemed Relations which have been hitherto published in any Language Comprehending Everything Remarkable in its Kind in Europe, Asia, Africa, and America*, published between 1745 and 1747, is in many ways similar to the French Catholic Picart's *The Ceremonies and Religious Customs of the Various Nations of the Known World*, which was published during the same decade. Yet Astley draws conclusions different from Picart's in his discussion of the Tartar court in China:

> From the above Accounts of the Religion of *Fo* [Buddha], however imperfect, or disguised, the Reader may perceive a most surprizing Conformity between it, and that of *Rome*: We shall not say of Christians in general, although it is circumstanced with an incarnate God, a Saviour, a Holy Spirit, a Ternary, which some of the Missioners consider as an Emblem of the Trinity, and others a Trinity in Effect. However that may be, we find, in this Religion, every individual article, great and small, of which the *Romish* system is composed: Such as the Worship of Images, praying to Saints, and for the Dead; Purgatory, Pardons, Indulgences, Confession, Absolution, Penance; Exorcism, the Treasure of the Church, Merits and Works of Supererogation; the Pretence to work Miracles; a Hierarchy, or different Order of Priests, with a Pope at their Head; Monks and begging Friars, Nuns; in short, every Thing in Speculation and Practice down to Holy-Water and the Beads. They have not, indeed, a Wafer-God, which they first adore, and then devour; but they have a living Divinity in human Form [the Dalai Lama] transubstantiated, or transformed, as they believe, from Time to Time; who dwells among them personally, and is therefore, we think, a much more rational Object of Worship.
>
> The Missioners, confounded at this exact Conformity of the Romish Faith, with a Religion which is confessedly idolatrous, and one continued Scene of Priestcraft, use several Arts to conceal the Resemblance; some mentioning one Part of its Doctrines, others different Parts, none the Whole; and those who are most copious on the Occasion, recite them in a

loose, scattered Way, without any Method, or Order. After all these Disguisements, the Resemblance appears so glaring, that many, to account-for it, have made a hardy Step, and pretend, that it is a Corruption of Christianity, meaning the *Romanish* Religion. Some affirm, that the *Nestorians* converted the People of *Tibet* and *Tartary* about the seventh and eighth Centuries: Others will have it, that the Faith was preached there in the Time of the Apostles. We call this a hardy Step, because they know, that according to the *Chinese* History, *Fo*'s Religion sprung-up above a thousand years before Christ.[39]

Astley thus catalogs the similarities, which he claims the Catholics try to hide, finding the religion of the Buddha and the Romish faith identical in every way, except for that most preposterous article of faith, the Eucharist, which is unique to Catholics. He dismisses the possibility of historical influence, noting that Buddhism antedates Christianity (although Buddhism was introduced in Tibet only in the seventh century). For Astley, it is the very resemblance of the two that accounts for the failure of the Roman Catholic missions in China and Tibet: the Buddhists would gain nothing by converting:

> But the greatest Security the *Bonʒas* [Buddhist monks] can have against the Progress of Popery among them, is the great Conformity between the two Religions: For, by the Change, their Followers see they will be just in the same Condition they were before; there being nothing of Novelty to induce them, excepting what arises from the Difference of a few Forms. Besides, they must naturally have a greater Respect for the Saints, Images, and Ceremonies of their own, than those of a foreign Manufacture.[40]

The apparent similarities between Lamaism and Roman Catholicism continued to fascinate Protestants into the twentieth century. In 1901 Dr. Susie C. Rijnhart, a Dutch missionary who had traveled in Tibet from 1895 to 1899, wrote, "No more interesting question offers itself to Christian scholarship than that concerning the resemblances between the ritual of the Gelupa [*sic*] sect and that still in vogue in the Roman Catholic and Anglican branches of Christendom."[41] But the question had already been considered in depth, especially in Britain during the last decades of the nineteenth century. Buddhism enjoyed great popularity then, as evidenced by the success of Edwin Arnold's life of the Buddha, *The Light of Asia*. The Buddha was seen in such works as the greatest philosopher of India's Aryan past, and his teachings were regarded as a complete philosophical and psychological system, one based on reason and restraint, and opposed to ritual, superstition, and sacerdotalism, demonstrating how the individual could live a moral life without the trappings of institutional religion. Standing in sharp contrast to the spiritual and sensuous exoticism of modern India, this Buddhism was also a fitting candidate for classical status because, like the civilizations of Greece, Rome, and Egypt, and unlike Hinduism, the Buddhism of India was long dead.[42]

The leading British Orientalists of the late Victorian period saw in Buddhism a rationalist and humanist reaction against the priestcraft of sixth-century B.C.E. India, subsumed under yet another of the "isms" of the Western study of Asia, Brahmanism. "Being opposed to all sacerdotalism and ceremonial observances, it abolished, as far as possible, the sacrificial system of the Brāhmans, and rejected the terrible methods of self-torture, maintaining that a life of purity and morality was better than all the forms and ceremonies of the Vedic ritual."[43] Early Buddhism was thus consistently, and mistakenly, portrayed as lacking any element of ritual; ignored, for example, were the ordination ceremonies for monks and nuns; the communal confession of infractions of the monastic code, and the ceremonial conclusion of the retreat at the end of the rainy season, all said to have been sanctioned by the Buddha. As Monier-Williams, Boden Professor of Sanskrit at Oxford, described it in his 1888 Duff Lectures, "It had no hierarchy in the proper sense of that term—no church, no priests, no true form of prayer, no religious rites, no ceremonial observances."[44]

Among the factors contributing to such a portrayal was the Victorian interpreters' almost exclusive reliance on the texts selected and edited by the Pali Text Society (and then translated in Max Müller's Sacred Books of the East series and the Pali Text Society's Sacred Books of the Buddhists series), which were thought to constitute the canon of primitive Buddhism. This portrayal, moreover, supported the interpreters' comparative model, in which the Buddha's rejection of sacerdotalism could be interpreted as foreshadowing a similar rejection in the West during the Reformation. As Müller wrote, "The ancient history of Brahmanism leads on to Buddhism, with the same necessity with which mediaeval Romanism led to Protestantism."[45] The point was made more emphatically and extensively by James Freeman Clarke in his *Ten Great Religions* in the chapter "Buddhism, or the Protestantism of the East":

Why call Buddhism the Protestantism of the East, when all its external features so much resemble those of the Roman Catholic Church?

We answer: Because deeper and more essential relations connect Brahmanism and the Romish Church, and the Buddhist system with Protestantism. The human mind in Asia went through the same course of experience, afterward repeated in Europe. It protested, in the interest of humanity, against the oppression of the priestly caste. . . .

Buddhism in Asia, like Protestantism in Europe, is a revolt of nature against spirit, of humanity against caste, of individual freedom against the despotism of an order, of salvation by faith against salvation by sacraments. . . . Finally, Brahmanism and the Roman Catholic Church are more religious; Buddhism and Protestant Christianity, more moral.[46]

The rise of interest in Buddhism in England during the last half of the nineteenth century coincided with the "No Popery" movement, which was marked by the Murphy riots of 1866 to 1871 and the wide popularity of works such as Richard Whately's *Essays on the Errors of Romanism* (1856) and *The Confessional Unmasked,* distributed to each member of Parliament in 1865 by the Protestant Evangelical Mission and Electoral Union.[47]

It is against the background of original Buddhism and anti-Papism that the Protestant discourse on Lamaism must be placed: Lamaism, with its devious and corrupt priests and vapid sacerdotalism, would be condemned as the most degenerate form of Buddhism (if it was a form of Buddhism at all) in the decades just after Roman Catholicism was being scourged in England, in the decades before the turn of the century and the 1903 invasion of Tibet, when British troops under the command of Colonel Younghusband marched on Lhasa to demand trade privileges.

In 1877 Thomas W. Rhys Davids, the nineteenth century's leading British scholar of Buddhism and the founder of the Pali Text Society, produced a popular manual on Buddhism. It was published by the Society for Promoting Christian Knowledge as part of its Non-Christian Religious Systems series. (Rhys Davids was the son of a Welsh Congregationalist minister.) Near the end of the book Rhys Davids considers "developments in doctrine" beyond those in the Pali canon, the locus of which was interchangeably termed "primitive Buddhism," "true Buddhism," or "original Buddhism." He writes:

The development of Buddhist doctrine which has taken place in the Panjab, Nepal, and Tibet is exceedingly interesting, and very valuable from the similarity it bears to the development which has taken place in Christianity in the Roman Catholic countries. It has resulted at last in the complete establishment of Lāmāism, a religion not only in many points different from, but actually antagonistic to, the primitive system of Buddhism; and this is not only in its doctrine, but also in its church organization.[48]

Two comparisons are drawn here, one of similarity and one of contrast. The value of developments in Buddhist doctrine lies in their similarity to the changes undergone by Christianity in those countries that remain Roman Catholic. At the same time, Lamaism is contrasted with primitive Buddhism, such that Lamaism is seen as not merely different from but inimical to the doctrine and organization of primitive Buddhism, now long past. As Monier-Williams said, "In truth, Tibetan Buddhism is so different from every other Buddhistic system that it ought to be treated of separately in a separate volume."[49]

Rhys Davids's most sustained comparison of Roman Catholicism and Lamaism appears in his 1881 Hibbert Lectures, "Lectures on the Origin and Growth of Religion as Illustrated by Some Points in the History of Indian Buddhism." There he provides a full page of parallels, all of which constitute "one of the most curious facts in the whole history of the world." "[E]ach with its services in dead languages, with choirs and processions and creeds and incense, in which the laity are spectators only; each with its mystic rites and ceremonies performed by shaven priests in gorgeous robes; . . . each, even ruled over by a Pope, with a triple tiara on his head and the sceptre of temporal power in his hand, the representative on earth of an eternal Spirit in the heavens!"[50]

The litany of parallels is now familiar. Like Thomas Astley a century before, the late Victorian interpreters of Buddhism to the West, especially the British and the Americans, no longer held to the view that the apparent similarities between Lamaism and Romanism were due to direct historical contact between the two.[51] Instead, Rhys Davids explains, in a vocabulary of violation, mixing begets mixing:

Each had its origin at a time when the new faith was adopted by the invading hordes of barbarian men bursting in upon an older, a more advanced civilization—when men in body, but children in intellect, quick to feel emotion, and impregnated with Animistic fallacies, became at once the conquerors and the pupils of men who passed through a long training in religious feeling and in philosophical reasoning. Then do we find that strange mixture of speculative acuteness and emotional ignorance; of earnest devotion to edification, and the blindest confidence in erroneous methods;

of real philanthropy, and a priestly love of power; of unhesitating self-sacrifice, and the most selfish struggles for personal pre-eminence, which characterize the early centuries of Roman Catholicism and Tibetan Lāmaism alike.[52]

Whether or not the genealogical view put forward by the Roman Catholic missionaries anticipated the anthropological theory of diffusionism, the Protestant interpreters held firmly to a variation of the theory that diffusionism briefly replaced: the "comparative method," made famous by Sir James Frazer, in which it was postulated that all societies develop according to a similar pattern, and that each is distinguished by the stage it occupies in the continuum of development and the rate at which it progresses along it. The comparative method was so named because of its claim that societies at the same stage of development, regardless of their location in time and place, share the same characteristics, allowing knowledge of one to inform analysis of another. Such a theory cast primitive societies as contemporary reminders of the archaic stages through which Western civilization had passed, and from which the savages themselves, with the encouragement and support of the West, would eventually emerge. That Frazer's comparative method made its mark on Buddhist Studies is evident from this 1896 statement by Rhys Davids:

> For it is precisely in India that for us Westerns the evolution of religious beliefs is most instructive. It can be traced there with so much completeness and so much clearness; we can follow it there with so much independence of judgement and so great an impartiality; and it runs, in spite of the many differences, on general lines so similar to the history of religion in the West, that the lessons to be learnt there are of the highest value. . . . Yet nowhere else do we find a system at once so similar to our own in the stages and manner of its growth, and so interestingly and absolutely antagonistic to our own in the ultimate conclusions it has reached.[53]

The same observation had been made a year earlier, this time about Tibet, by L. Austine Waddell in his *The Buddhism of Tibet, or Lamaism*: "For Lāmaism is, indeed, a microcosm of the growth of religion and myth among primitive people; and in large degree an object-lesson in their advance from barbarism toward civilization. And it preserves for us much of the old-world lore and petrified beliefs of our Aryan ancestors."[54] More interesting, however, although not noted by Rhys Davids or Waddell, is the fact that this same (and equally anti-Papist) view had been advanced more forcefully in German by Isaac Jacob Schmidt a half century earlier, although unlike the British scholars he did not distinguish Buddhism from Lamaism. Writing in 1835, he concluded his essay on the term "Lamaism":

This brief review of a not unimportant subject in the cultural history of humankind . . . should suffice to demonstrate the lack of foundation for the European idea of Lamaism, above all else, however, to refute this bizarre notion that Lamaism somehow owed its existence to Christianity and its organization to the papal hierarchy, an idea that was brought to Europe about 150 years ago by some Capuchins who had visited Tibet as missionaries and that found unquestioning agreement in Europe. . . . This monkish prejudice had absolutely no awareness of the fact that equal circumstances must produce similar results, that just as the earlier semi-barbarism of Europe in its time produced the papacy out of Christianity, so, under equal conditions, the semi-barbarism of Asia, which continues until today, could not find it very difficult to produce a similar dominating priesthood out of the considerably older and no less dogmatically constructed Buddhism, and that it was not at all necessary for one [of those priesthoods] to assist the other. Every spiritual corporation, just as soon as its power is able to reach a certain height and to govern and dominate the benightedness of the ignorant masses arbitrarily through the mental predominance of an elevated culture, will not fail to demonstrate similar manifestations at any time in any country, but these manifestations must gradually grow more obscure and disappear eventually just as soon as the inheritance of all humankind, namely the spirit of examination, discrimination, and knowledge, gradually achieves maturity.[55]

Schmidt's hopeful conclusion is perhaps a reflection of Enlightenment social philosophy. Nonetheless, he anticipates the evolutionary model to which Rhys Davids and Waddell subscribed. Here the Buddhism of Tibet, or Lamaism, figured prominently as the end point in the Victorian version of the history of Buddhism, according to which, after the early centuries of the brotherhood, Buddhism in India followed a course of uninterrupted deterioration from its origins as a rational, agnostic faith to a degenerate religion rife with ritual and superstition. The specific course charted by the British Buddhologists was as follows: With the rise of the Mahayana, the agnostic idealism and simple morality of primitive Buddhism was replaced by "a speculative theistic system with a mysticism of sophistic nihilism."[56] Further deterioration occurred with the rise of the Yogācāra school, which, for reasons that remain unclear, was regarded with particular antipathy: "And this Yoga parasite, containing within itself the germs of Tantrism, seized strong hold of its host and soon developed its monster outgrowths, which crushed and cankered most of the little life of purely Buddhist stock yet left in the Mahāyāna." [57] (The author of these two statements, L. Austine Waddell, the son of a Scottish Presbyterian minister, conducted his research while serving as the assistant sanitary commissioner for the Darjeeling district; in 1889 his "Are Venomous Snakes Autotoxic?" was published in *Scientific Memoirs by Medical Officers of the Army of India*.) Were this not enough, the progress of the contamination continued as the pure essence of primitive Buddhism was once more polluted in India with the rise of tantrism.

It was this mere shadow of original Buddhism that was belatedly transmitted to Tibet. Prior to the introduction of Buddhism, Waddell recounts, the Tibetans were "rapacious savages and reputed cannibals, without a written language, and followers of an animistic and devil-dancing or Shamanistic religion, the Bön, resembling in many ways the Taoism of China." [58] The introduction of a corrupt form of Indian Buddhism into this atmosphere resulted in something that Waddell calls "primitive Lāmaism," which he defines as "a priestly mixture of Ṣivaite [*sic*] mysticism, magic, and Indo-Tibetan demonolatry, overlaid by a thin varnish of Mahāyāna Buddhism. And to the present day Lāmaism still retains this character." [59] Thus the corrupt form of Buddhism that arrived in Tibet was further adulterated with the demon worship of the Tibetans: "The Lamaist cults comprise much deep-rooted devil-worship. . . . For Lamaism is only thinly and imperfectly varnished over with Buddhist symbolism, beneath which the sinister growth of poly-demonish superstition darkly appears." [60] Once again, the discourse of the demonic comes into play, as the superstitions of the non-Buddhist religions, both Indian and Tibetan, portrayed as parasites, eventually overwhelm the Buddhist host. Lamaism thus stands at the nadir of a long process of contamination and degeneration from the origin. In *Kim*, Rudyard Kipling has the Teshu Lama (as the British referred to the Panchen Lama) express this view: "[I]t was in my mind that the Old Law was not being followed; being overlaid, as thou knowest, with devildom, charms, and idolatry." [61] Colonel Younghusband, who had led Waddell to Lhasa, was not impressed by one of the great scholars of his age, the Holder of the Throne of Ganden (dGa' ldan khri pa Blo bzang rgyal mtshan): "And his spiritual attainments, I gathered from a long conversation I had with him after the Treaty was signed, consisted mainly of a knowledge by rote of vast quantities of his holy books. The capacity of these

Tibetan monks for learning their sacred books by rote is, indeed, something prodigious; though about the actual meaning they trouble themselves but little." [62] Even Madame Blavatsky, whose Mahatmas lived in Tibet, decried the degradation of their wisdom in the hands of Tibetans: "How the pristine purity of these grand revelations was dealt with may be seen by studying some of the so-called 'esoteric' Buddhist schools of antiquity in their modern garb, not only in China and other Buddhist countries in general, but even in not a few schools in Thibet, left to the care of uninitiated Lamas and Mongolian innovators." [63] She accepts the view of Lamaism as a degenerate form of pure Buddhism, writing in *Isis Unveiled*, "From pure Buddhism, the religion of these districts has degenerated into Lamaism; but the latter, with all its blemishes—purely formalistic and impairing but little the doctrine itself—is yet far above Catholicism." [64]

Once identified as an endpoint in the process of degeneration, Lamaism also seemed to creep backward in time. In a discussion of the Mahayana sutras in his 1877 *Buddhism*, Rhys Davids writes:

> The later books were afterwards translated into Tibetan, and a new doctrine attained in Tibet to so great a development that Tibetan Buddhism, or rather Lamaism, has come to be the exact contrary of the earlier Buddhism. It has been worked up there into a regular system which has shut out all of the earlier Buddhism, although a few of the earlier books are also to be found in Tibetan translations. [65]

It is perhaps noteworthy that in this work Rhys Davids subsumes all of Mahayana Buddhism, the Buddhisms of China, Japan, and Tibet, under the heading Tibetan Buddhism. All "subsequent" Buddhisms are thereby absorbed under the category of Lamaism, as if the parasite identified by Waddell had spread retroactively to infect all Buddhisms that existed in a form other than the texts preserved in European libraries, all Buddhisms that were not under European control.

Tibetan Buddhism was thus regarded as doubly other in a complex play of Orientalist ideologies: with the discovery and translation of Sanskrit and Pali texts, Romantic Orientalism invented and controlled Buddhism, casting it in the role of the mimetic other—the other that is like oneself—and called it "original Buddhism." In Victorian Britain this Buddhism was represented as a "religion of reason," within which morality and free intellectual inquiry were possible without the institution of a church and its rituals. European and

American philologists thus became the true and legitimate conservators of this "classical tradition." Tibetan Buddhism was then constructed as the other of this other ("original Buddhism"). It was a product not of the religion of reason but of the degeneration of the Indian textual tradition, namely, the Mahayana and tantra, the latter of which had been excoriated for centuries. "Tantra," a notoriously vague term used generally to designate an Indian movement that made use of activities traditionally proscribed in the religious path (most notably sexual intercourse), was regarded by nineteenth-century Orientalists as the most depraved of abominations. Such regard went back at least to 1730, when the Capuchin missionary Orazio della Penna described the tantric literature of Tibet: "I have not read this infamous and filthy law of Khiute [tantra], so as not to stain my mind, and because it is unnecessary. For to confute it one must know in the abstract of what it treats, and there is little good or indifferent that is not mixed up with much more witchcraft, magic incantations, and obscenity." [66]

A nexus of forces were therefore brought to bear to create this degenerate form of Buddhism found in Tibet, "Lamaism." This history, from its pristine origins in the distant past to the present state of decay and corruption, was derived from two different modes of representation, both controlled by the European Orientalist: what is known of early Buddhism, of primitive Buddhism, of true Buddhism, is based on texts, while the knowledge of "modern Buddhism," which deviated wildly from the texts, is derived from direct observation. Again, Monier-Williams from the Duff Lectures: "For it is certain that without any practical experience of what Buddhism has become in modern times—I mean such an experience as can only be gained by residing or traveling in countries where Buddhism now prevails—the mere study of ancient scriptures is likely to be misleading." [67] That is, texts can elucidate only true Buddhism; to understand the current state of what Buddhism "has become," "practical experience" of the missionary and the colonial officer is essential.

Victorian scholars were not unanimous in their portrayal of Lamaism as an extreme deviation from the Buddha's original teachings. For those connected with the missionaries, such as Monier-Williams, the root cause of the corruption lay in the Buddha himself, who denied the existence of human aspirations to the transcendent, who rejected the possibility of a supernatural force that could aid in the struggle for salvation, who could find no place in his system for a Ruler of the Universe. Thus, despite the high order of his moral precepts, the system of the Buddha was destined to turn into its opposite:

> In point of fact it was not a development that took place, but a recoil—like the recoil of a spring held down for a time by a powerful hand and then released. And this resulted from the simple working of the eternal instincts of humanity, which insisted on making themselves felt notwithstanding the unnatural restraint to which the Buddha had subjected them; so that every doctrine he taught developed by a kind of irony of fate into a complete contradiction of itself.[68]

Lamaism was the collective embodiment of those contradictions. For others who were more sympathetic to their creation of true Buddhism, Lamaism was not a natural outcome of the founder's original faith but a deviation from it. In either case, however, comparisons with Roman Catholicism served as a further form of condemnation, where "Lamaism" becomes a substitute for "Papism." The Tibetans, having lost the spirit of primitive Buddhism, now suffered under the oppression of sacerdotalism and from the exploitation of its priests, something that England had long since thrown off. But it is not simply analogy that Pali Buddhism (which by the end of the nineteenth century was largely under British control) is to Tibetan Buddhism (which at the end of the nineteenth century Britain was actively seeking to control) as Protestantism is to Roman Catholicism. It is rather a strategy of debasing the distant and unsubjugated by comparing it with the near and long subjugated, subjugated both by its relegation to England's pre-Reformation past and to its present European rivals and Irish subjects. For example, Waddell begins his chapter "The Hierarchy and Re-Incarnate Lāmas" with two epigraphs— "Le roi est morte, vive le roi!" and a passage from the Talmud—and then heads a subsequent page with "The First Dalai Lāma-Pope," associating Lamaists with the French, Jews, and Catholics in only two pages.[69] "Lamaism" thus served as a code word for "Papism" in a master narrative that used its representation of the other without to attack the other within. This was not the first time Protestant polemics had figured in scholarship on other religions; such polemics had shaped the study of the religions of Late Antiquity, sometimes referred to as "Pagano-Papism."[70] And just as Papism was implicated in theories of world domination, so also was Lamaism. In Sax Rohmer's 1917 *The Hand of Fu Manchu*, the headquarters of the sinister doctor's conspiracy to dominate the globe is in Tibet, "a mystery concealed from the world behind the veil of Lamaism." [71] In 1937 the Nazi J. Strunk published *Zu Juda und Rom-Tibet: ihr Ringen um die Weltherrschaft* (On Juda and Rome-Tibet: Their Struggle for World Domination).[72]

At the end of both his tomes on Tibet, Waddell offers his vision of Tibet's future, when "its sturdy overcredulous people are freed from the intolerable tyranny of the Lāmas, and delivered from the devils whose ferocity and exacting worship weigh like a nightmare upon all." [73] There is reason for hope, he argues, when one considers that during the twelfth century the Catholic Church seemed in hopeless decay, but then Dante and then the Renaissance appeared. Indeed, Waddell claims, a knowledge of Buddhism might have saved the Catholic Church from the degeneration it suffered soon after "the disappearance of its immortal founder." Waddell, with apparent magnanimity, next demonstrates his possession of true Buddhism (which the Tibetans lack) by claiming that Christians are finally coming to understand that the teachings of Jesus are more akin to those of the Buddha than they are to Paul, Augustine, or Luther. Completing the gesture of control, he ends by proclaiming that rather than burying Tibetan Buddhism as a decadent cult, it is the mission of England "to herald the rise of a new star in the East, which may for long, perhaps for centuries, diffuse its mild radiance over this charming land and interesting people. In the University, which must ere long be established under British direction at Lhasa, a chief place will surely be assigned to studies in the origin of the religion of the country." [74] Waddell wrote these words not from a position of imperial longing at the border, but at the conclusion of *Lhasa and Its Mysteries,* his account of the British invasion of Tibet in 1903 and 1904, during which he served as chief medical officer.

Lamaism thus serves as a fundamental trope in the history that late Victorian colonialism wrote for itself. Like all historicisms, it has its fantasy of pristine origin, here embodied in true Buddhism, and its fantasy of the end, here embodied in Tibetan Buddhism, called Lamaism, which is seen as an inevitable end whether it is a perversion of the Buddha's intention or its fulfillment. As the end point in the process of degeneration, Tibetan Buddhism after a certain stage has no history, only stasis. Change must be introduced from the outside. Whether Tibet was to be cured by the restoration of true Buddhism or by conversion to Christianity, the cure seemed to be in the possession of the West, and the colonization of Tibet was considered by some to be the best means of its administration. By defining Tibetan Buddhism as something apart, as disconnected from the other Buddhisms of Asia, all of which were under the sway of the West by the end of the nineteenth century, it was easier to portray Tibet as entirely other and hence incapable of its own representation.

These nineteenth-century denotations of Lamaism are succinctly captured, under the more archaic "Lamanism," in the current *Oxford English Dictionary*:

> + lamanism. *Obs.* [After F. *lamanisme* (Huc).] = LAMAISM. So la'manical
> a. = LAMAIC
>   1852 *Blackw. Mag.* LXXI. 339 The Tibetan portion . . . is inhabited by a rough race, . . . retaining many primitive superstitions beneath the engrafted Lamanism. 1867 M. JONES *Huc's Tartary* 243 The foundation of the lamanical hierarchy, framed in imitation of the pontifical court. *Ibid.* 252 It is with this view [of enfeebling the strength of the Mongol princes] that the Emperors patronise lamanism.

In the 1852 reference Lamaism is not native to Tibet but had at some point been "engrafted" to the primitive superstitions of the people living in the Tibetan region of another country. In the first 1867 reference the Lamaist church is a copy of the original Roman Catholic hierarchy. And in the third reference, which is reminiscent of Qianlong's declaration, there is a disavowal of allegiance; the Chinese emperor's support has been a pretense. In all three references, none of which mentions "Buddhism," Lamaism is portrayed as somehow inauthentic, with that inauthenticity determined in relation to what is more original and more real: in the first reference, Lamaism is an appendage of Tibetan superstition; in the second it is a late copy of an original; in the third it is the object of the pretense of realpolitik.

As is the case with so many of the "isms" in the study of religion, those designated by the term come to use it only when they enter into the fray of defining their "lost culture" and are confronted by the definitions of the West, definitions created by competing ideologies of authenticity. As stated at the outset, there is no term in the Tibetan language for "Lamaism"; Tibetans refer to their religion as the "Buddhist religion" (*sangs rgyas pa'i chos*) or, more commonly, "the religion of the insiders" (*nang pa'i chos*). The use of the term "Lamaism" has been condemned by the spokesman for Tibetan culture, whose own name recalls the circumstances of its coinage, the current Dalai Lama. His first book on Tibetan Buddhism, published in 1963 and composed in part for foreign consumption, concludes:

Some people say that the religion of Tibet is "Lamaism" (literally, "religion of lamas," *bla ma'i chos*), as if it were a religion not taught by the Buddha, but this is not so. The original author of the sūtras and tantras that are the root source of all schools of Tibetan Buddhism is the teacher Śākyamuni Buddha. . . . Tibetan lamas took these as the basis and root and then listened to them, contemplated them, and meditated upon them; among the main points they did not fabricate a single doctrine that does not accord with [the teachings of the Buddha].[75]

Here we see the rhetoric of authenticity again at work, upholding (in opposition to the claims of Victorian scholars) the fidelity of Tibetan Buddhism to the teachings of the Buddha and the Indian masters and therefore minimizing Tibetan contributions to the development of Tibetan Buddhism. The response to "Lamaism" by Tibetans has not been unambiguous, however. The first Tibetan Buddhist monastery in the United States, founded in 1955 by the Mongolian monk Geshe Wangyal in Freewood Acres, New Jersey, took as its name the Lamaist Buddhist Monastery of America.[76]

During the 1960s and 1970s, in the years following Tibet's invasion and annexation by China, the earlier Buddhological valuation of Tibetan Buddhism (sometimes still called Lamaism) as degenerate reached its antipodes, as young scholars came to exalt Tibet as a pristine preserve of authentic Buddhist doctrine and practice. Unlike the Buddhisms of China, Japan, and Southeast Asia, Tibetan Buddhism had not been tainted by Western domination. Tibet was no longer valuable to scholars of Buddhism only as an archive of the scriptures of Indian Buddhism, long lost in the original Sanskrit but preserved in a highly accurate Tibetan translation.[77] The Tibetan diaspora that followed the Dalai Lama's flight to India in 1959 brought with it a great flood of autochthonous Tibetan Buddhist literature, heretofore unstudied, that, largely through the efforts of the Library of Congress office in New Delhi, was made available to the universities of Europe and North America. Scorned by Waddell at the end of the last century as "contemptible mummery," this literature was now hailed by Orientalists of a new age, both professional and amateur, as a repository of ancient wisdom whose lineage, as the Dalai Lama himself claimed, could be traced back to the Buddha himself.[78] The comparisons with Catholicism continued, but with Tibetan Buddhism now being valued as the truer faith, the Dalai Lama was the better pope. Typically avant garde, Artaud wrote in his 1925 "Address to the Dalai Lama," "We are surrounded by bellowing popes, poetasters, critics, dogs, our Mind is gone to the dogs who think directly in terms of the earth, who think incorrigibly in the present. . . . For you well know what transparent liberation of souls, what freedom of Mind in the Mind we mean, O acceptable Pope, O true Pope of the Mind." [79]

What is the site of Lamaism in the late twentieth century, decades after the Orientalists used Lamaism for the rhetorical subjugation of Tibet in anticipation of its colonial subjugation? "Lamaism" is still used as a subject heading by the Library of Congress. It also retains currency among art historians. Pratapaditya Pal, regarded as the leading Western authority on Tibetan art, wrote in 1969, "The word lama is generally used in Tibet to designate a Buddhist monk [in fact, only a tiny percentage of the monks in Tibet were referred to as lamas]; and since in Tibet the monks ultimately controlled both the temporal and spiritual life of the people, *Lamaism* is particularly apposite to define that form of Buddhism that developed in Tibet." [80] The Victorian view of Lamaism as a mixture of Buddhist elements from India and primitive Tibetan animism persists. In 1991 the Asian art historian Sherman Lee defined the Sanskrit term *vajrayāna*, used in India long before Buddhism was introduced into Tibet, as "Tantric Buddhism with an admixture of pre-Buddhist Tibetan 'Bön' worship of nature deities and demons." [81]

The following definition appeared in the free brochure dispensed to the public at the "Circa 1492" exhibition: "Lamaism was a combination of the esoteric Buddhism of India, China, and Japan with native cults of the Himalayas." [82] Among the many observations that might be made about this sentence, it is initially noteworthy that the verb is in the past tense, that Lamaism and hence its substitute Tibetan Buddhism no longer exist but inhabit a static past. Beyond the tense of the verb, there is little to suggest that this sentence was not composed a century ago. There are the same subtle differentiations from true Buddhism: Lamaism is not Buddhism or even esoteric Buddhism (a "late development"), but a combination of various forms of esoteric Buddhism with native cults. (The Victorian scholars would have corrected the erroneous attribution of any Japanese influence on Tibetan Buddhism.) Lamaism is thus a hybrid, a mixture, a concoction of outside influences and native primitivism. It therefore follows that the signifier "Tibet" should occur nowhere in the definition.

Although the power of representation did not lead to Western political domination of Tibet, that power has been appropriated by China, which was finally able to bring Tibet under colonial dominion in a process that began with the invasion by its People's Liberation Army in 1950. The rhetorical trajectory that began when *lama jiao* became Lamaism has thus come full circle, as Lamaism, invested with two centuries of Orientalist discourse, has once again become *lama jiao* and been returned to the Orientals. This is not to suggest that the Chinese do not have their own long history of denigrating Tibetan culture. Yet the term that had been coined during the Qing, and used to isolate Tibet from Chinese culture, is now used to dissolve it into the motherland. In post-1959 Chinese publications on Tibet, Tibetan Buddhism is easily subsumed under the critique of Buddhism and religion in general and condemned for its suppression of the masses. Nonetheless, the Western representation of Tibetan Buddhism as Lamaism, a corruption of original Buddhism, has been appropriated by the Chinese to justify to the West the invasion and colonization of Tibet. In 1964 the only Westerners allowed to visit Tibet were apologists for the Chinese Communist Party. In a 1964 travelogue, *The Timely Rain: Travels in New Tibet*, Stuart and Roma Gelder resuscitated the Victorian rhetoric of Lamaism to defend the Chinese destruction of Buddhist institutions in Tibet: "The rich spiritual inheritance which, according to some who fear Communism more than they understand Tibetan Buddhism, is being destroyed by the Chinese, was in fact not there to be destroyed. It existed only in the imaginations of those who mistook the mechanical observance of ritual and religious custom for spiritual experience." [83]

The abstract noun, coined in the West, has become naturalized as if it were an empirical object, the manipulation of which has effects beyond the realm of rhetoric. Eventually, Lamaism becomes so particular, so different, so often described as not this and not that, that it becomes unbound and starts to float freely, like "Zen" or "mysticism." In the process the "original" site of Lamaism, Tibet, loses its boundaries and is declared missing, dissolving into the People's Republic of China. As an Australian missionary to Tibet observed earlier in the century in *The Land of Mystery, Tibet*, "Tibetan national existence and Lamaism are one and the same thing." [84] Tibet, unexplored and uncolonized by the European, is absorbed into China. The very use of the term Lamaism is a gesture of control over the unincorporated and the unassimilated, used first by the Qing over Tibet, then as a code word for "Papism" by the British over Catholic Ireland and Europe, and finally by European Buddhology over the uncolonized and unread Tibet. Long the blank spot on the map marked only by the word "Thibet," the contours have now been drawn, the rivers traced to their sources, the mountains measured, only to have the borderlines, and the name "Tibet," effaced. Even among the partisans of the Tibetan cause, the focus remains largely on the unsited, on the ethereal and transhistorical, on Tibetan religion as the sole legacy, even the irreducible essence, of Tibetan culture. There is not now and never was Tibet, there was only Lamaism. The term used to mark off Tibet remains; Tibet is nowhere to be found.

Tibetans are said to believe that if the *la*, the soul, leaves the body, the person becomes unbalanced or insane. With the formation of lama from *la*, the original meaning of *la* left lama, causing a loss of equilibrium that resulted finally in "Lamaism." My purpose here has been to attempt a belated ritual of "calling the *la*" back to its lost abode.

CHAPTER TWO

The Book

Instead of being something said once and for all—and lost in the past like the result of a battle, a geological catastrophe, or the death of a king—the statement, as it emerges in its materiality, appears with a status, enters various networks and various fields of use, is subjected to transferences or modifications, is integrated into operations and strategies in which its identity is maintained or effaced. MICHEL FOUCAULT, THE ARCHAEOLOGY OF KNOWLEDGE

In "The Enigma of Edward FitzGerald," Jorge Luis Borges ponders the miracle that occurred when a nineteenth-century English eccentric came upon a manuscript of five hundred quatrains by a thirteenth-century Persian astronomer. In his translation of a selection of the poems, the Englishman "interpolated, refined and invented" to produce one of the nineteenth century's most popular works of European literature, assuring, as Swinburne observed, "Omar Khayyám a permanent place among the major English poets." The case calls for "conjecture of a metaphysical nature," and Borges wonders whether Umar was reincarnated in England or whether, around 1857, the spirit of Umar lodged in FitzGerald.[1]

Like the Rubaiyat, the work known in the West as *The Tibetan Book of the Dead* is the product of a chance meeting between a fourteenth-century Tibetan author and a latter-day eccentric, Walter Wentz of San Diego, California. Since its publication in 1927, it has been reincarnated several times. The Tibetan work known by this title, one of many Buddhist texts known by the name *Bar do thos grol* (literally, liberation in the intermediate state [through] hearing), is a *terma* (*gter ma*), a "treasure text," one of the thousands of works said to have been secreted by Padmasambhava during his visit to Tibet in the late eighth century, works that he hid in stones, lakes, pillars, and in the minds of future generations because Tibetans of the eighth century were somehow unprepared for them. Thus were they hidden to be discovered at the appropriate moment.

The *Bar do thos grol* is one such work. In its incarnation as *The Tibetan Book of the Dead*, it has been discovered and rediscovered in the West over the course of almost a century; five major (and several minor)[2] discoveries of this text, each somehow suitable for its own time, have occurred since 1919. Together they illuminate much about the various purposes that the *Bar do thos grol* has been meant to serve. Each of the five, in the order of their appearance in the West, will be considered here: *The Tibetan Book of the Dead*, by Walter Y. Evans-Wentz (1927); *The Psychedelic Experience*, by Timothy Leary, Ralph Metzner, and Richard Alpert (1964); *The Tibetan Book of the Dead*, translated by Francesca Fremantle and Chögyam Trungpa (1975); *The Tibetan Book of Living and Dying*, by Sogyal Rinpoche (1992); and *The Tibetan Book of the Dead*, translated by Robert Thurman (1994). From its first incarnation in English in 1927, the work has taken on a life of its own as something of a timeless world spiritual classic. It has been made to serve wide-ranging agendas in various fields of use, agendas that have far more to do with the twentieth-century cultural fashions of Europe and America than with how the text has been used over the centuries of its history in Tibet.

The first and most famous of these is, of course, Evans-Wentz's work, which has served as the progenitor of the later versions to a greater extent even than the "original" Tibetan text. It alone has had a number of reincarnations, in the form of editions, each successive with more prefaces and forewords added to the text. Since publication in 1927 its various editions have sold more than 525,000 copies in English; it has also been translated into numerous European languages. Its full title is *The Tibetan Book of the Dead or the After-Death Experiences on the* Bardo *Plane, according to Lāma Kaẓi*

Dawa-Samdup's English Rendering. It was "compiled and edited by W. Y. Evans-Wentz." This was the first of four books on Tibetan Buddhism that Evans-Wentz would produce from lamas' translations; the others are *Tibet's Great Yogī Milarepa* (1928) and *Tibetan Yoga and Secret Doctrines* (1935), both based on translations by Kazi Dawa-Samdup, and *The Tibetan Book of the Great Liberation* (1954), based on translations done for Evans-Wentz by three Sikkimese.[3] The first edition of *The Tibetan Book of the Dead* contains a preface by Evans-Wentz and a foreword, "Science of Death," by Sir John Woodroffe, an official of the British Raj who, during his tenure as judge of the High Court of Calcutta, became a scholar and devotee of Hindu tantra, publishing works such as *The Serpent Power* under the pseudonym Arthur Avalon. There is also Evans-Wentz's own extensive introduction and his copious annotations on Lama Kazi Dawa-Samdup's translation. The second edition (1949) contains an additional preface by Evans-Wentz. The third edition (1957) brought the book close to the form in which it is best known today, adding a "Psychological Commentary" by C. G. Jung, translated by R. F. C. Hull from the original German version that appeared in *Das Tibetanische Totenbuch*, which was published in Zurich in 1935. The third edition also contains an introductory foreword by Lama Anagarika Govinda. Finally, Evans-Wentz contributed a preface to the first paperback edition (1960).

Although the first sentence of Evans-Wentz's preface to the first edition reads, "In this book I am seeking—so far as possible—to suppress my own views and to act simply as the mouthpiece of a Tibetan sage, of whom I am a recognized disciple," the version of the book that we have today is filled with other voices (the various prefaces, introductions, forewords, commentaries, notes, and addenda comprise more than half of the book).[4] Together they overwhelm the translation, the increasing popularity of the work having compelled this unusual assortment of authorities to provide their own explanations of the text.

This amalgam of commentaries appended to a translation of a Tibetan text has become the most widely read "Tibetan text" in the West. Its initial appeal may have been due in part to the resurgence of spiritualism after the First World War and a renewed interest in knowing the fate of the dead. It was then that Sir Arthur Conan Doyle, for example, turned to spiritualism and tried to contact his son, who had been killed in the war.[5] But the text has proved remarkably resilient in subsequent generations, gaining far more readers in its English version (with subsequent translations into other European languages) than the Tibetan text upon which it is based ever had in

Tibet. Prior to 1959 "The Tibetan Book of the Dead" (or a Tibetan translation of this title) was unheard of among traditional Tibetan scholars. The Tibetan text upon which it is based, the *Bar do thos grol,* would have been familiar to scholars who knew the literature of the Nyingma sect; they would have recognized it as the name of a large genre of mortuary texts used by Nyingma lamas. The translation in Evans-Wentz's work is a portion of a well-known work in that genre.[6]

Before turning to Evans-Wentz's text, let me briefly summarize the *Bar do thos grol* for those of a younger generation who may not have committed it to memory. It is traditionally used as a mortuary text, read aloud in the presence of a dying or dead person. The text describes the process of death and rebirth in terms of three intermediate states or *bardos* (*bar do,* a Tibetan term that literally means "between two"). The first, and briefest, is the bardo at the moment of death (*'chi kha'i bar do*), when a profound state of consciousness called the clear light dawns. If one is able to recognize the clear light as reality, one is immediately liberated from rebirth. If not, the second bardo, called the bardo of reality (*chos nyid bar do*), begins. The disintegration of the personality brought on by death reveals reality, but in this case not as the clear light but in the form of a mandala of fifty-eight wrathful deities and a mandala of forty-two peaceful deities. These deities appear in sequence to the consciousness of the deceased in the days immediately following death. If reality is not recognized in this second bardo, then the third bardo, the bardo of mundane existence (*srid pa'i bar do*), dawns, during which one must again take rebirth in one of the six realms: in that of gods, demigods, humans, animals, hungry spirits, or in hell.

Prior to his encounter with the Tibetan text, Evans-Wentz studied another system of reincarnation. Born in Trenton, New Jersey, in 1878, he took an early interest in the books on spiritualism in his father's library and read both Madame Blavatsky's *Isis Unveiled* and *The Secret Doctrine* during his teen years.

The Theosophical Society was founded in New York in 1875 by Madame Helena Petrovna Blavatsky and Colonel Henry Steele Olcott. Its goals included the formation of a universal brotherhood regardless of race, creed, sex, caste, or color; the encouragement of studies in comparative religion, philosophy, and science; and the investigation of unexplained laws of nature and the powers latent in man. It was in many ways a response to Darwin, yet rather than seeking in religion a refuge from science, it attempted to found a scientific religion, one that accepted the new discoveries in geology and embraced an ancient and esoteric system of spiritual evolution more so-phisticated than Darwin's. The society was founded at the height of late-nineteenth-century America's interest in spiritualism, the belief that one could contact and communicate with the spirits of the dead through seances, mate-rialization, automatic writing, and other techniques.[7] Madame Blavatsky was herself adept at these and other occult arts.

During the eighteenth century Europeans saw India as a land of origin; some claimed that Christianity had begun there.[8] During the nineteenth and the twentieth centuries India was increasingly displaced by Tibet, especially by occult movements, as the source and preserve of secret knowledge and as the abode of lost races. Some offered evidence that Jesus had spent his lost years there.[9] Madame Blavatsky herself claimed to have spent seven years in Tibet as an initiate of a secret order of enlightened masters called the Great White Brotherhood. These masters, whom she called Great Teachers of the White Lodge or Mahatmas (great souls), lived in Tibet but were not them-selves Tibetans. Madame Blavatsky's disciple A. P. Sinnett explained in *Eso-teric Buddhism*:

> From time immemorial there had been a certain secret region in Tibet, which to this day is quite unknown to and unapproachable by any but initiated persons, and inaccessible to the ordinary people of the country as to any others, in which adepts have always congregated. But the country generally was not in the Buddha's time, as it has since become, the chosen habitation of the great brotherhood. Much more than they are at present were the Mahatmas in former times distributed about the world. The prog-ress of civilization, engendering the magnetism they find so trying, had, however, by the date with which we are now dealing—the fourteenth cen-tury—already given rise to a general movement towards Tibet on the part of the previously dissociated occultist. Far more widely than was held to be consistent with the safety of mankind was occult knowledge and power then found to be disseminated. To the task of putting it under the control of a rigid system of rule and law did Tsong-ka-pa address himself.[10]

Under the tutelage of the Mahatmas, Madame Blavatsky studied the *Stanzas of Dzyan*, which were to form the basis of her magnum opus, *The Secret Doctrine*. In volume five she writes:

> The BOOK OF DZYAN—from the Sanskrit word "Dhyâna" (mystic medi-tation)—is the first volume of the Commentaries upon the seven secret

folios of *Kiu-te,* and a Glossary of the public works of the same name. Thirty-five volumes of *Kiu-te* for exoteric purposes and the use of laymen may be found in the possession of the Tibetan Gelugpa Lamas, in the library of any monastery; and also fourteen books of Commentaries and Annotations on the same by the initiated Teachers.

Strictly speaking, those thirty-five books ought to be termed "The Popularised Version" of THE SECRET DOCTRINE, full of myths, blinds and errors; the fourteen volumes of *Commentaries,* on the other hand—with their translations, annotations, and an ample glossary of Occult terms, worked out from one small archaic folio, the BOOK OF SECRET WISDOM OF THE WORLD—contain a digest of all the Occult Sciences. These, it appears, are kept secret and apart, in the charge of the Teshu Lama of Tji-gad-je. The Books of *Kiu-te* are comparatively modern, having been edited within the last millennium, whereas, the earliest volumes of the Commentaries are of untold antiquity, some fragments of the original cylinders having been preserved.[11]

Throughout her career she (and, later, other members of the society) claimed to be in esoteric communication with the Mahatmas, sometimes through dreams and visions but most often through letters that either materialized in a cabinet in Madame Blavatsky's room or that she transcribed through automatic writing. The Mahatmas' literary output was prodigious, conveying instructions on the most mundane matters of the society's functions as well as providing the content of its canonical texts, which included A. P. Sinnett's *Esoteric Buddhism,* Madame Blavatsky's *The Secret Doctrine,* and, more recently, the works of Alice Bailey, dictated to her by the master Djwaul Khul, whom she referred to simply as "the Tibetan."[12]

The Theosophical Society enjoyed great popularity in America, Europe, and India (despite repeated scandals and a report by the Society for Psychical Research that denounced Madame Blavatsky as a fraud), playing an important but ambiguous role in the Hindu renaissance in India and the Buddhist renaissance in Sri Lanka. Its popularity continued after the death of its founders and into the present century, when in 1909 Blavatsky's heir, Annie Besant, chose a young Hindu boy as the messiah, the World Teacher Krishnamurti. He renounced his divine status and broke with the society in 1930. The death of Besant and other leaders followed soon after and the society fell into decline. Nonetheless, the Theosophical Society has had a profound effect on the reception of Buddhism in Europe and America during the twentieth century. Of *The Voice of the Silence,* a work Madame Blavatsky claimed to have translated from the secret Senzar language, D. T. Suzuki wrote, "Here is the real Mahayana Buddhism."[13] Christmas Humphrey's 1960 anthology *The Wisdom of Buddhism* included only five works from Tibet. One was actually of Indian origin, but the last and longest was an extended extract from *The Voice of the Silence*. The scholar of Perfection of Wisdom literature, Edward Conze, remained a Theosophist throughout his life, telling Mircea Eliade that he considered Madame Blavatsky the reincarnation of Tsong kha pa.[14] The Dalai Lama's first book, *The Opening of the Wisdom Eye*, was published by the Theosophical Society.

At the turn of the century Walter Wentz moved to California, where in 1901 he joined the American Section of the Theosophical Society. Headquartered in Point Loma, it was headed by Katherine Tingley, known as the "Purple Mother."[15] At Tingley's urging, he enrolled at Stanford, where he studied with William James and William Butler Yeats. (Yeats had joined the Esoteric Section of the Theosophical Society in 1888 only to be expelled by Madame Blavatsky two years later.) After graduating from Stanford, Wentz went to Jesus College Oxford to study Celtic folklore. It was there that he added a family name from his mother's side to his surname and became Walter Evans-Wentz. After completing his thesis, later published as *The Fairy Faith in Celtic Countries* (1911), he began a world tour financed by income he received from rental properties in Florida. He was in Greece when the First World War broke out, and spent most of the war in Egypt.

From Egypt, he traveled to Sri Lanka and then on to India, where he visited the Theosophical Society headquarters in Adyar and met with Annie Besant. In north India he studied with various Hindu gurus, especially Swami Satyananda. In 1919 he arrived in Darjeeling, on the southern slope of the Himalayas in Sikkim. A great collector of texts in languages he never learned to read (he amassed a collection of Pali palm leaf manuscripts in Sri Lanka), he acquired some Tibetan texts from a British army officer who had recently returned from Tibet. These were portions of the *Profound Doctrine of Self-Liberation of the Mind [through Encountering] the Peaceful and Wrathful Deities* (*Zab chos zhi khro dgongs pa rang grol*), by Karma gling pa, also known as the *Peaceful and Wrathful Deities according to Karmalingpa* (*Kar gling zhi khro*). (One wonders how the course of Western history might have changed had Major Campbell, the British officer, given Evans-Wentz a monastic textbook on Buddhist logic, for example.) With a letter of introduction from the local superintendent of police, Evans-Wentz took these texts to the English teacher at the Maharaja's Boy's School in Gangtok, one Kazi Dawa-Samdup.

He was already acquainted with Western enthusiasts of Buddhism, having served as a translator for Alexandra David-Neel (who had received her Theosophical Society diploma in 1892).[16] She described him in *Magic and Mystery in Tibet*:

> Dawasandup was an occultist and even, in a certain way, a mystic. He sought for secret intercourse with the Dâkinîs and the dreadful gods hoping to gain supernormal powers. Everything that concerned the mysterious world of beings generally invisible strongly attracted him, but the necessity of earning his living made it impossible for him to devote much time to his favourite study. . . .
>
> Drink, a failing frequent among his countrymen, had been the curse of his life. This increased his natural tendency to anger and led him, one day, within an ace of murder. I had some influence over him while I lived in Gangtok. I persuaded him to promise the total abstinence from fermented beverages that is enjoined on all Buddhists. But it needed more energy than he possessed to persevere. . . .
>
> I could tell many other amusing stories about my good interpreter, some quite amusing, in the style of Boccaccio. He played other parts than those of occultist, schoolmaster, writer. But, peace to his memory. I do not wish to belittle him. Having acquired real erudition by persevering efforts, he was sympathetic and interesting. I congratulate myself on having met him and gratefully acknowledge my debt to him.[17]

Evans-Wentz took his texts to Kazi Dawa-Samdup and during the next two months met with him each morning before the school day began. The translation that Kazi Dawa-Samdup did for Evans-Wentz was the germ of what would become *The Tibetan Book of the Dead*. Their time together was brief. Evans-Wentz soon returned to the ashram of Swami Satyananda to practice yoga, where he learned to sit motionless for four hours and forty minutes each day. Though a student of several prominent neo-Vedantin teachers of the day, including Sri Yuketswar and Ramana Maharshi, Evans-Wentz seems never to have been a devotee of Tibetan Buddhism. Of his relationship with Kazi Dawa-Samdup, Evans-Wentz's biographer writes: "The few letters that have survived that they exchanged show a surprisingly distant and formal tone. Even in Dawa-Samdup's diaries there is no word to suggest otherwise. There is nothing at all foreshadowing the later declarations that the Lama was the guru of Walter Evans-Wentz, nothing about the 'teachings' the American was supposed to have received."[18]

Evans-Wentz returned to Darjeeling in 1935, after Kazi Dawa-Samdup's death, and employed three Sikkimese of Tibetan descent to translate another text for him, later published in *The Tibetan Book of the Great Liberation*. He remained a Theosophist and wrote for various Theosophical publications for the rest of his life, the last twenty-three years of which were spent in the Keystone Hotel in San Diego. He spent his final months at the Self-Realization Fellowship of Swami Yogananda in Encinitas, California.

Evans-Wentz subscribed to a version of reincarnation that was first put forth in 1885 in A. P. Sinnett's *Esoteric Buddhism* and elaborated (and "corrected") in Madame Blavatsky's *The Secret Doctrine* (1888). Having claimed to have studied the ancient *Book of Dzyan*, written in the secret language of Senzar, Blavatsky describes a system of seven rounds, seven root races, and seven subraces. The Earth has passed through three rounds during which it has evolved from a spiritual to a material form. We are now in the fourth round. During the final three rounds it will slowly return to its spiritual form. The universe is populated by individual souls, or monads, themselves ultimately identical to the universal oversoul. Monads are reincarnated according to the law of karma. During the fourth round, the monads inhabit the Earth in the form of seven successive races. The first was a race of spiritual essences called the "Self-born," who had no physical form; they inhabited the Imperishable Sacred Land until it sank into the ocean. The second race, the Hyperboreans, lived at the North Pole. They, too, had no physical form. The Lemurians, the third root race, were the first humans, although they had no sense of taste or smell. Their homeland, the vast continent of Lemuria, stretched across the Pacific to include Africa before being destroyed by fire, although remnants of it, Australia and Easter Island, still exist. The fourth root race inhabited the continent of Atlantis. An advanced race, they used electricity and flew in airplanes. Their civilization ended in the great flood.[19] The last subrace of Atlanteans was absorbed into the early subraces of the fifth root race, the Aryans. These early subraces included the Greeks, Egyptians, and Phoenicians. The Aryans later defeated the remaining Atlanteans, the "yellow and red, brown and black," and drove them into Africa and Asia.[20] As the Mahatma explained in *Esoteric Buddhism*:

> I told you before that the highest people now on earth (spiritually) belong to the first subrace of the fifth root race, and those are the Aryan Asiatics, the highest race (physical intellectuality) is the last sub-race of the fifth —
> yourselves, the white conquerors. The majority of mankind belongs to the

seventh sub-race of the fourth root race—the above-mentioned Chinamen and their offshoots and branchlets (Malayans, Mongolians, Tibetans, Javanese, &c., &c.)— with remnants of other sub-races of the fourth and the seventh sub-race of the third race.[21]

In 1888 Madame Blavatsky found the seeds of the sixth subrace of the fifth root race already evident in the Americans, "the pioneers of that race which must succeed to the present Europeans."[22] Other Theosophists identified California as the center of this civilization. After twenty-five thousand years, the seventh subrace will appear. Eventually Europe and the Americas will be destroyed in a cataclysm, heralding the dawn of the sixth root-race of the Earth's fourth round.[23]

Since the midpoint of the Atlantean race a finite number of monads have reincarnated again and again, and will continue to do so throughout the entire cycle of evolution.[24] Only rebirth as a human is possible; animals may reincarnate as higher species, but never vice versa.[25] Those who evolve from the animal stage first take human form as what the *Stanzas of Dzyan* call the "narrow-brained," which includes South Sea islanders, Africans, and Australians. "Those tribes of savages, whose reasoning powers are very little above the level of animals, are not the unjustly disinherited, or the *unfavoured,* as some may think—nothing of the kind. They were simply those *latest arrivals* among the human Monads, which *were not ready*: which have to evolve during the present Round . . . so as to arrive at the level of the average class when they reach the Fifth Round."[26]

The 1927 preface to the first edition of *The Tibetan Book of the Dead* must be read with Evans-Wentz's commitment to Theosophy in mind. He begins, "In this book I am seeking—so far as possible— to suppress my own views and to act simply as the mouthpiece of a Tibetan sage, of whom I am a recognized disciple." This is precisely the kind of claim that Madame Blavatsky made so often. He goes on to report that he spent more than five years "wandering from the palm-wreathed shores of Ceylon, and thence through the wonder-lands of the Hindus, to the glacier-clad heights of the Himalayan Ranges, seeking out the Wise Men of the East" (p. xix). In his travels he encountered philosophers and holy men who believed that there were parallels between their own beliefs and practices ("some preserved by oral tradition alone") and those of the Occident and that these parallels were the result of some historical connection (p. xix).

In the 1948 preface to the second edition Evans-Wentz emphasizes what is a consistent theme in his annotations to the translation, that the West has largely lost its own tradition on the art of dying, an art well-known to the Egyptians, to the initiates of the "Mysteries of Antiquity," and to Christians of the Middle Ages and the Renaissance. It was a pre-Christian tradition (as, Evans-Wentz claims in his addendum to the translation, the Tibetan art of dying was a pre-Buddhist tradition) that had been wisely incorporated into the rituals of "various primitive Churches of Christendom, notably the Roman, Greek, Anglican, Syrian, Armenian, and Coptic" (p. xiv), whose traditions have been ignored by modern medical science. The late lama and other learned lamas shared the hope, he says, that their rendering of *The Tibetan Book of the Dead* would inspire the West to rediscover and to once again practice an art of dying, in which they would find the inner light of wisdom taught by the Buddha "and all the Supreme Guides of Humanity" (pp. xvi–xvii).

In the 1955 preface to the third edition there is no further mention of the rediscovery of an Occidental tradition. Instead, "To each member of the One Human Family, now incarnate on the planet Earth, this book bears the greatest of all great messages. It reveals to the peoples of the Occident a science of death and rebirth such as only the peoples of the Orient have heretofore known" (p. vii). This was the edition in which the commentaries of Jung and Govinda were first incorporated, and Evans-Wentz's preface takes due notice of their insights. Beyond that, the references to Hindu works, especially the Upanishads and *Bhagavad Gita*, already evident in the notes and epigraphs, seem to outweigh the references to Buddhism and Tibet. Jung's commentary, he says, demonstrates that Western psychologists have moved beyond Freud; they will "advance much further when they no longer allow the Freudian fear of metaphysics to bar their entrance into the realm of the occult" (p. ix). He repeats the view found in much of the spiritualist and Theosophical literature of the nineteenth century (which is held as well by the present Dalai Lama): that Western science will eventually evolve to the point at which it can confirm the insights of the East, most importantly, the existence of rebirth:

> Thus it is of far-reaching historical importance that the profound doctrine of pre-existence and rebirth, which many of the most enlightened men in all epochs have taught as being realizable, is now under investigation by our own scientists of the West. And some of these scientists seem to be approaching that place, on the path of scientific progress, where, as with respect also to other findings by the Sages of Asia long before the rise of

Western Science, East and West appear to be destined to meet in mutual understanding. (P. ix)

It is when the current "heretical" psychologists adopt the methods of meditation and self-analysis taught by master yogins that "Western Science and Eastern Science will, at last, attain at-one-ment" (p. x). This leads him to a pronouncement worthy of Madame Blavatsky:

> Then, too, not only will Pythagoras and Plato and Plotinus, and the Gnostic Christians, and Krishna and the Buddha be vindicated in their advocacy of the doctrine, but, equally, the Hierophants of the Ancient Mysteries of Egypt and Greece and Rome, and the Druids of the Celtic World. And Western man will awaken from that slumber of Ignorance which has been hypnotically induced by a mistaken Orthodoxy. He will greet wide-opened his long unheeded brethren, the Wise Men of the East. (P. x)

In his 1935 "Psychological Commentary," C. G. Jung (who had read widely in the work of Madame Blavatsky's former secretary, G. R. S. Mead) says that *The Tibetan Book of the Dead* (which he consistently refers to as the *Bardo Thödol*) has been his constant companion ever since its publication in 1927 and "to it I owe not only many stimulating ideas and discoveries, but also many fundamental insights" (p. xxxvi). He thus sets for himself the modest task of making "the magnificent world of ideas and the problems contained in this treatise a little more intelligible to the Western mind" (p. xxxvi). He declares the Tibetan work to be psychological in its outlook, and begins to compare its insights to the more limited views of Freud. He makes extensive use of the three Tibetan terms used to describe the stages of death and rebirth. The first is *Chikhai Bardo* (*'chi kha'i bar do*), literally, the intermediate state of the moment of death, in which the various dissolutions that end in the dawning of the clear light occur. The second is the *Chönyid Bardo* (*chos nyid bar do*), literally, the intermediate state of reality, the actual period between death and the next rebirth during which the visions so vividly described in the text appear. The third is the *Sidpa Bardo* (*srid pa'i bar do*), literally, the intermediate state of existence, which occurs with the entry of the wandering consciousness into the womb, which is itself preceded by the witnessing of the primal scene of parental intercourse.

Jung argues that Freudian psychoanalysis, working backwards, has been able to discover only the last of the three bardos, the *Sidpa Bardo,* which is marked by infantile sexual fantasies. Some analysts claim even to have uncovered intrauterine memories. It is at this point that "Western reason reaches its limit, unfortunately" (p. xli). He expresses the wish that Freudian psychoanalysis could have continued even further, to the pre-uterine: "[H]ad it succeeded in this bold undertaking, it would surely have come out beyond the *Sidpa Bardo* and penetrated from behind into the lower reaches of the *Chönyid Bardo*" (p. xlii), that is, Freud could have proven the existence of rebirth. Here Jung is reminiscent of classical Buddhist proofs on the existence of rebirth, in which it is claimed that one moment of consciousness is produced by a previous moment of consciousness, and that once it is conceded that consciousness at the moment of conception is the product of a previous moment of consciousness, rebirth has been proven. But more important for Jung is this opportunity to dismiss Freud before moving on to his own project. Some might judge this particular condemnation to be disingenuous, since Jung did not himself pursue the question of existence of rebirth (beyond the symbolic level) in the decades that followed.

But Jung offers his criticism of Freud only in passing as he moves on to his larger task, evident also in his other commentaries on Asian texts, that is, the incorporation of Asian wisdom into his own psychological theory. He begins with the suggestion that the Westerner read the *Bardo Thödol* backwards, that is, first the *Sidpa Bardo*, then the *Chönyid Bardo*, and then the *Chikhai Bardo*. The neurosis of the *Sidpa Bardo* has already been identified. The next step is to move on to the *Chönyid Bardo*, which is a state of "karmic illusion" (p. xliii). He takes this as an opportunity to interpret karma as psychic heredity, which leads quickly to the archetypes of the collective unconscious. Of the archetypes to be mined from comparative religion and mythology, he writes, "The astonishing parallelism between these images and the ideas they serve to express has frequently given rise to the wildest migration theories, although it would have been far more natural to think of the remarkable similarity of the human psyche at all times and in all places" (p. xliv). Thus, apparently in contrast to Evans-Wentz, Jung sees Asian yogins and the initiates of Greek mystery cults as having had no influence on one another. Instead their ideas are primordial and universal, originating from an omnipresent psychic structure. How else could one account for the fact that the very same idea, that the dead do not know that they are dead, is to be found in the *Bardo Thödol*, American spiritualism, and Swedenborg? (pp. xliv–xlv).[27]

The horrific visions of the *Chönyid Bardo*, then, represent the effect of surrendering to fantasy and imagination, uninhibited by the conscious mind:

"the *Chönyid* state is equivalent to a deliberately induced psychosis" (p. xlvi). Here Jung reiterates a warning that appears in almost all of his writings about Asia: that the Westerner who practices yoga is in great danger. The dismemberments that occur in the Buddhist hells described in the Tibetan text are symbolic of the psychic dissociation that leads to schizophrenia (p. xlvii).

Thus, a fundamental distinction between East and West is that in Christianity initiation is a preparation for death, while in the *Bardo Thödol* initiation is a preparation for rebirth, preparing "the soul for a descent into physical being" (p. xlix). This is why the European should reverse the sequence of the *Bardo Thödol* such that one begins with the experience of the individual unconscious, then moves to the experience of the collective unconscious, and then moves finally to the state in which illusions cease and "consciousness, weaned away from all form and from all attachment to objects, returns to the timeless, inchoate state" (pp. xlviii–xlix). This sequence, Jung says, "offers a close parallel to the phenomenology of the European unconscious when it is undergoing an 'initiation process,' that is to say, when it is being analyzed" (p. xlix). He closes with the statement that "The world of gods and spirits is truly 'nothing but' the collective unconscious inside me" (p. liii).

Jung thus uses the *Bardo Thödol* (as he did the other Asian texts about which he wrote)[28] as raw material for his own theories. Like the colonial industrialist, he mined Asian texts (in translation) for raw materials, without acknowledging the violence (both epistemic and otherwise) that he did to the texts in the process; reversing the order of the three bardos is but one example. He then processed these raw materials in the factory of his analytic psychology, yielding yet further products of the collective unconscious. These products were then marketed to European and American consumers as components of a therapy and exported back to Asian colonials as the best explanation of their own cultures.

The next preface to the 1948 edition was by Lama Govinda, one of the most influential figures in the representation of Tibetan Buddhism to the West. Lama Anagarika Govinda was born Ernst Lothar Hoffmann in Kassel, Germany, in 1895.[29] He served at the Italian front during World War I, after which he continued his studies at Freiburg University in Switzerland. He became interested in Buddhism while living with expatriate European and American artists in Capri, publishing his first book, *The Basic Ideas of Buddhism and Its Relationship to Ideas of God*, in 1920. (The work is apparently no longer extant.) In 1928 he sailed for Ceylon, where he briefly studied meditation and Buddhist philosophy with the German-born Theravada monk

Nyānatiloka Mahāthera (who gave him the name Govinda) before leaving to travel in Burma and India. While visiting Darjeeling in the Himalayas in 1931 he was driven by a spring snowstorm to a Tibetan monastery at Ghoom, where he met Tomo Geshe Rinpoche (Gro mo dge bshes rin po che), a Gelukpa lama. In his autobiographical *The Way of the White Clouds*, published over thirty years later, Govinda would depict their meeting and his subsequent initiation as the pivotal moment in his life. It is difficult to imagine what transpired between the Tibetan monk and the German traveler (dressed in the robes of a Theravada monk, although he seems not to have been ordained), who spoke no Tibetan, or what this "initiation" may have been (it was perhaps the most preliminary of Buddhist rituals, the refuge ceremony). Govinda's description of any instruction he may have received is vague. He seems, however, to have understood the term differently from its Tibetan meaning of an empowerment by a lama to engage in specific tantric rituals and meditations. In *Foundations of Tibetan Mysticism according to the Esoteric Teachings of the Great Mantra Oṁ Maṇi Padme Hūṁ* he writes, "By 'initiates' I do not mean any organized group of men, but those individuals who, in virtue of their own sensitiveness, respond to the subtle vibrations of symbols which are presented to them either by tradition or intuition." [30]

After making a pilgrimage to Mount Kailash in southwestern Tibet in 1932, he held brief teaching positions at the University of Patna and at Shantiniketan (founded by Rabindranath Tagore), publishing essays in *Mahabodhi*, the journal of a Buddhist society in Calcutta, as well as in various Theosophical journals. His lectures at Patna resulted in *The Psychological Attitude of Early Buddhist Philosophy*, and his lectures at Shantiniketan resulted in *Psycho-Cosmic Symbolism of the Buddhist Stūpa*. While at Shantiniketan he met a Parsi woman, Rati Petit, whom he would marry in 1947. (She also assumed a new name, Li Gotami, and like her husband dressed in the Tibetan-style robes of his design.) During the 1930s he founded a number of organizations, including the International Buddhist University Association, the International Buddhist Academy Association, and the Arya Maitreya Mandala. In 1942 he was interned by the British at Dehra Dun with other German nationals, including Heinrich Harrer (who would escape to spend seven years in Tibet) and Nyānaponika Mahāthera, another German Theravada monk best known as the author of *The Heart of Buddhist Meditation*.

In 1947 and 1948 Lama Govinda and Li Gotami led an expedition sponsored by the *Illustrated Weekly of India* to photograph some of the temples of western Tibet, notably those in Tsaparang and Tholing. (Li Gotami's photographs, important as archives since the Chinese invasion, appear in Govinda's *The Way of the White Clouds, Foundations of Tibetan Mysticism*, and her own *Tibet in Pictures*.) During their travels they met a lama named Ajorepa Rinpoche at Tsecholing monastery, who, according to Govinda, initiated them into the Kagyu order. No sect of Tibetan Buddhism has such an initiation ceremony, such that the nature of this ceremony also remains nebulous. As with Tomo Geshe Rinpoche, Lama Govinda is mute on the teachings they received. Nonetheless, from this point on he described himself as an initiate of the Kagyu order or, as he often styled himself, "an Indian National of European descent and Buddhist faith belonging to a Tibetan Order and believing in the Brotherhood of Man."

Returning from Tibet, Lama Govinda and Li Gotami set up permanent residence in Sikkim, living as tenants of a house and property rented to them by Walter Evans-Wentz. During the 1960s their home at Kasar Devi became an increasingly obligatory stop for spiritual seekers (including the Beat poets Gary Snyder and Allen Ginsberg in 1961) until they were forced to put up signs around the property warning visitors away. With the publication of *The Way of the White Clouds* in 1966, Govinda's fame only grew, and he spent the last two decades before his death in 1985 lecturing in Europe and the United States. His last years were spent in a home in Mill Valley provided by the San Francisco Zen Center. In 1981 Govinda published what he regarded as his most important work, *The Inner Structure of the I Ching*, a work that he undertook because "We have heard what various Chinese and European philosophers and scholars thought about this book, instead of asking what the *I Ching* itself has to say." [31] His study seeks to remedy the situation, unimpeded and perhaps enhanced, it seems, by Lama Govinda's apparent inability to read Chinese. The book was published with support from the Alan Watts Society for Comparative Research.

Indeed, throughout his career Govinda seems to have drawn on a wide variety of Western-language sources but never on untranslated Buddhist texts. The translations of the Pali in his *The Psychological Attitude of Early Buddhist Philosophy* (first delivered as lectures at the University of Patna in 1935) are drawn from the British scholars Thomas and Caroline Rhys Davids and from his fellow German, Nyānatiloka Mahāthera. His *Psycho-Cosmic Symbolism of the Buddhist Stūpa* draws entirely on Western sources. In his book of essays, painting, and poetry published by the Theosophical Society, *Creative Meditation and Multi-Dimensional Consciousness* (which includes the essays "Concept and Actuality," "The Well of Life," and "Contemplative

Zen Meditation and the Intellectual Attitude of Our Time"), he cites Martin Buber, D. T. Suzuki, Alan Watts, Heinrich Zimmer, and Evans-Wentz. Nonetheless, he represents himself as a spokesman for Tibetan Buddhism in ways that are above all reminiscent of the Theosophy of Evans-Wentz:

> The importance of Tibetan tradition for our time and for the spiritual development of humanity lies in the fact that Tibet is the last living link that connects us with the civilizations of a distant past. The mystery-cults of Egypt, Mesopotamia and Greece, of Incas and Mayas, have perished with the destruction of their civilizations and are for ever lost to our knowledge, except for some scanty fragments.
>
> The old civilizations of India and China, though well preserved in their ancient art and literature, and still glowing here and there under the ashes of modern thought, are buried and penetrated by so many strata of different cultural influences, that it is difficult, if not impossible, to separate the various elements and to recognize their original nature.[32]

Like Evans-Wentz, who portrayed himself as a mere mouthpiece for Kazi Dawa-Samdup, Lama Govinda suggests that his musings derive from teachings he received from Tomo Geshe Rinpoche, to whom his *Foundations of Tibetan Mysticism according to the Esoteric Teachings of the Great Mantra Oṁ Maṇi Padme Hūṃ* is dedicated: "The living example of this great teacher, from whose hands the author received his first initiation twenty-five years ago, was the deepest spiritual stimulus of his life and opened to him the gates to the mysteries of Tibet. It encouraged him, moreover, to pass on to others and to the world at large, whatever knowledge and experience he has thus gained—as far as this can be conveyed in words."[33] The fact that this work contains an interpretation that appears in no Tibetan text may explain (as we shall see in the case of Evans-Wentz) why he describes them as "esoteric teachings."

In his introductory foreword to *The Tibetan Book of the Dead*, Lama Govinda, like Jung, draws on a psychological vocabulary when he says that "There are those who, in virtue of concentration and other *yogic* practices, are able to bring the subconscious into the realm of discriminative consciousness and, thereby, to draw upon the unrestricted treasury of subconscious memory, wherein are stored the records not only of our past lives but the records of the past of our race, the past of humanity, and of all pre-human forms of life, if not of the very consciousness that makes life possible in this universe" (p. liii). Govinda thus seems to combine Jung's notion of a collective and archaic repository of memory with Evans-Wentz's belief that *The Tibetan Book of the Dead* is drawn from the actual memories of Eastern yogins who could remember their past lives. Such knowledge, however, would crush those not trained to receive it; therefore, the *Bardo Thödol* has remained secret, "sealed with the seven seals of silence." Echoing Evans-Wentz's call, Govinda declared, "But the time has come to break the seals of silence; for the human race has come to the juncture where it must decide whether to be content with the subjugation of the material world, or to strive after the conquest of the spiritual world, by subjugating selfish desires and transcending self-imposed limitations" (p. liv). The remainder of his foreword is taken up largely with a defense of the authenticity of the Tibetan *terma,* the texts hidden by Padmasambhava during the eighth century, and an argument for the purely Buddhist nature of the *Bardo Thödol,* untainted by Bönpo influence. On this point, as we shall see, he appears to part company with Evans-Wentz.

Sir John Woodroffe's foreword is noteworthy for its persistent attempts at finding in the Hindu literature, particularly the Hindu tantric literature to which Woodroffe was so devoted, parallels and even precedents for the doctrines set forth in *The Tibetan Book of the Dead.* He pauses, however, to include an obligatory swipe at Tibetans for the way in which they mispronounce Sanskrit mantras (p. lxxix).

Evans-Wentz's own lengthy introduction begins with a note explaining its function, which is worth quoting in full:

> This Introduction is—for the most part—based upon and suggested by explanatory notes which the late Lāma Kazi Dawa-Samdup, the translator of the *Bardo Thödol,* dictated to the editor while the translation was taking shape, in Gangtok, Sikkim. The Lāma was of the opinion that his English rendering of the *Bardo Thödol,* dictated to the editor while the translation was taking shape, in Gangtok, Sikkim. The Lāma was of the opinion that his English rendering of the *Bardo Thödol* ought not to be published without his exegetical comments on the more abstruse and figurative parts of the text. This, he thought, would not only help to justify his translation, but, moreover, would accord with the wishes of his late *guru* (see p. 80) with respect to all translations into a European tongue of works expository of the esoteric lore of the great Perfectionist School into which that guru had initiated him. To this end, the translator's exegesis, based upon that of the translator's *guru,* was transmitted to the editor and recorded by the editor herein.

The editor's task is to correlate and systematize and sometimes to expand the notes thus dictated, by incorporating such congenial matter, from widely separated sources, as in his judgement tends to make the exegesis more intelligible to the Occidental, for whom this part of the book is chiefly intended.

The translator felt, too, that without such safeguarding as this Introduction is intended to afford, the *Bardo Thödol* translation would be peculiarly liable to misinterpretation and consequent misuse, more especially by those who are inclined to be, for one reason or another, inimical to Buddhistic doctrines, or to the doctrines of his particular Sect of Northern Buddhism. He also realized how such an Introduction as is here presented might itself be subject to adverse criticism, perhaps on the ground that it appears to be the outcome of a philosophical eclecticism. However this may be, the editor can do no more than state here, as he has stated in other words in the Preface, that his aim, both herein and in the closely related annotations to the text itself, has been to present the psychology and teachings peculiar to and related to the *Bardo Thödol* as he has been taught them by qualified exponents of them, who alone have the unquestioned right to explain them.

If it should be said by critics that the editor has expounded the *Bardo Thödol* doctrines from the standpoint of the Northern Buddhist who believes in them rather than from the standpoint of the Christian who perhaps would disbelieve at least some of them, the editor has no apology to offer; for he holds that there is no sound reason adducible why he should expound them in any other manner. Anthropology is concerned with things as they are; and the hope of all sincere researchers in comparative religion devoid of any religious bias ought always to be to accumulate such scientific data as will some day enable future generations of mankind to discover Truth itself— that Universal Truth in which all religions and all sects of all religions may ultimately recognize the Essence of Religion and the Catholicity of Faith. (Pp. 1–2 n. 1)

This remarkable note accomplishes many tasks. First, it locates the authority for the contents of the introduction that is to follow not in Evans-Wentz but in the translator, the Tibetan lama. It is the lama's oral teachings that provide the basis of Evans-Wentz's words. Indeed, it raises the level of authority one step higher by invoking the power of lineage, stating that the exegesis derives from the lama's own guru, and that it was transmitted first to Kazi Dawa-Samdup and then from him to Evans-Wentz, in the tradition of guru to disciple. Evans-Wentz, then, has for the most part, as he states in his own preface to the first edition, acted only as the mouthpiece for his lama, only occasionally "incorporating such congenial matter, from widely separated sources, as in his judgement tends to make the exegesis more intelligible to the Occidental." He reports that the late lama called him his "living English dictionary" (p. 78). As we shall see, there will be much such congenial matter, especially concerning the theories of karma and rebirth, and concerning "symbolism," matter that deviates significantly from the contents of the *Bardo Thödol* but that is represented by this note as having the sanction of the lama and the lama's lama. For Evans-Wentz is claiming for himself the status of the initiate; he is setting forth the teachings "as he has been taught them by qualified initiated exponents of them, who alone have the unquestioned right to explain them." He thus vouchsafes that right for himself as the student of these masters, although whether his reference here is to Tibetan lamas or Mahatmas is unclear.[34] At the same time, in the final paragraph, he professes as well the authority of the scholar, the anthropologist who is concerned with "things as they are," unconcerned with the articles of any particular faith. Thus he claims for himself both the authority of Eastern religion (through his Tibetan lama) and Western science (through his Oxford degree). His task is the accumulation of scientific data, data that will one day lead all sects of all religions to see the Essence of Religion. One assumes that by this he means Theosophy.

Evans-Wentz begins the body of the introduction by claiming an "ultimate cultural relationship" between the *Bardo Thödol* and the *Egyptian Book of the Dead*: the germ of this teaching has been "preserved for us by a long succession of saints and seers in the God-protected Land of the Snowy Ranges, Tibet" (p. 2). He launches immediately into a discussion of symbolism, claiming that "some of the more learned lāmas" have believed that "since very early times there has been a secret international symbol-code in common use among the initiates, which affords a key to the meaning of such occult doctrines as are all still jealously guarded by religious fraternities in India, as in Tibet, and in China, Mongolia, and Japan" (p. 3). It is this supposed code that will allow him to make his most dubious deviations from the Tibetan text. Symbol codes, he notes, are not unique to Buddhists but have been used throughout the world, in Egyptian and Mexican hieroglyphics, by Plato and the Druids, by Jesus and the Buddha. In the case of the Buddha, his disciples have over the centuries preserved teachings of his that were never written down, teachings that form "an extra-canonical, or esoteric Buddhism" (p. 5).

Throughout the introduction, he refers to occult teachings known only to initiates of the esoteric tradition. Again, all of this takes on new meaning when read through the lens of Theosophy, in which symbolism is of central importance. One quarter of the fifteen hundred pages of the 1888 edition of *The Secret Doctrine* is concerned with symbolism, of which Madame Blavatsky writes, "The study of the hidden meaning in every religious and profane legend, of whatsoever nation, large or small—pre-eminently the traditions of the East—has occupied the greater portion of the present writer's life."[35] It is therefore easy to see why Evans-Wentz would have sought the esoteric meaning in all that he read. In this pursuit he would even be encouraged by Tibetan lamas, at least the lamas whom Madame Blavatsky claimed to know. In 1894 she published in *Lucifer* a letter she had received from one of the Mahatmas, "Chohan-Lama of Rinch-cha-tze (Tibet) the Chief of the Archives-registrars of the secret Libraries of the Dalai and Ta-shü-hlumpo Lamas-Rimboche." In discussing the Tibetan canon, the Chohan-Lama explains (in a passage no Tibetan scholar of the nineteenth century could have written):

> Could they even by chance had seen them, I can assure the Theosophists that the contents of these volumes could never be understood by anyone who had not been given the key to their peculiar character, and to their hidden meaning.
>
> Every description of localities is figurative in our system; every name and word is purposely veiled; and a student, before he is given any further instruction, has to study the mode of deciphering, and then of comprehending and learning the equivalent secret term or synonym for nearly every word of our religious language. The Egyptian enchorial or hieratic system is child's play to the deciphering of our sacred puzzles. Even in those volumes to which the masses have access, every sentence has a dual meaning, one intended for the unlearned, and the other for those who have received the key to the records.[36]

Evans-Wentz then launches into a discussion of the symbolism of the number seven, for the bardo lasts for a maximum of forty-nine days, seven times seven. The number also has symbolic meaning in Hinduism, in Hermetic writings, and in the Gospel of John. In nature, seven is important in the periodic table and in the "physics of color and sound." This proves that the *Bardo Thödol* is "scientifically based" (p. 7).[37] In his discussion of the esoteric meaning of the forty-nine days of the bardo, Evans-Wentz refers the reader to several passages from Madame Blavatsky's *The Secret Doctrine*, to which he adds, "The late Lāma Kazi Dawa-Samdup was of the opinion that, despite the adverse criticisms directed against H. P. Blavatsky's works, there is adequate internal evidence in them of their author's intimate acquaintance with the higher *lāmaistic* teachings, into which she claimed to have been initiated" (p. 7 n. 1). Later in the introduction he writes, "In other words, the *Bardo Thödol* seems to be based upon verifiable data of human physiological and psychological experiences; and it views the problem of the after-death state as being purely a psycho-physical problem; and it is therefore, in the main scientific" (p. 31). His view, then, seems to be that the *Bardo Thödol*, or at least its esoteric teachings, is most ancient, confirmed by the saints and seers of all the great civilizations of the past. The judgment scene, for example, has parallels in ancient Egypt, in Plato's *Republic*, and in "the originally pagan St. Patrick's Purgatory in Ireland" (p. 37). At the same time the esoteric teachings are also most modern, waiting to be confirmed by visionary scientists of the future. This is a conviction that later exponents of *The Tibetan Book of the Dead*, especially Leary and Thurman, would reprise in subsequent decades.

As mentioned above, Evans-Wentz's most creative contribution to the introduction to *The Tibetan Book of the Dead*, and the point least likely to have been endorsed by "the late Lāma Kazi Dawa-Samdup," and, most especially, by Dawa-Samdup's teacher, is the interpretation of the doctrine of rebirth.

In standard Buddhist doctrine one finds descriptions of a cycle of birth and death, called *saṃsāra* (wandering), which consists of six realms of rebirth: gods, demigods, humans, animals, ghosts, and hell beings (although sometimes the realm of demigods is omitted). The entire cycle of rebirth in which the creations and destructions of universes are encompassed has no ultimate beginning. The realms of animals, ghosts, and hell beings are regarded as places of great suffering, whereas the godly realms are abodes of great bliss. Human rebirth falls in between, bringing as it does both pleasure and pain. The engine of samsara is driven by karma, the cause and effect of actions. Like other Indian religions, Buddhist doctrine holds that every intentional act, whether physical, verbal, or mental, leaves a residue in its agent. That residue, like a seed, will eventually produce an effect at some point in the future, an effect in the form of pleasure or pain for the person who performed the act. Thus Buddhists conceive of a moral universe in which virtuous deeds create experiences of pleasure and nonvirtuous deeds create experiences of pain. These latter are often delineated in a list of ten nonvirtuous deeds: killing, stealing, sexual misconduct, lying, divisive speech, harsh speech, senseless speech, covetousness, harmful intent, and wrong view. Buddhist texts include extensive discussions of the specific deeds that constitute these ten nonvirtues and their respective karmic weights.

These deeds not only determine the quality of a given life but also determine the place of rebirth after death. Depending on the gravity of a negative deed (killing being more serious than senseless speech and killing a human more serious than killing an insect, for example), one may be reborn as an animal, a ghost, or in one of the hot or cold hells, where the life span is particularly lengthy. Among the hells, some are more horrific than others. The most torturous is reserved for those who have committed one of five heinous deeds: killing one's father, killing one's mother, killing an arhat, wounding a buddha, and causing dissent in the community of monks and nuns.

Rebirth as a god or human in the realm of desire is the result of a virtuous deed, and is considered very rare; the vast majority of beings in the universe are said to inhabit the three unfortunate realms of animals, ghosts, and the hells. Rarer still is rebirth as a human who has access to the teachings of the Buddha. In a famous analogy, a single blind tortoise is said to swim in a vast ocean, surfacing for air only once every century. On the surface of the ocean floats a single golden yoke. It is rarer, said the Buddha, to be reborn as a human with the opportunity to practice the dharma than it is for the tortoise to surface for its centennial breath with its head through the hole in the golden yoke. One is said to be reborn as a god in the realm of desire as a result of an act of charity: giving gifts results in future wealth. Rebirth as a human is said to result from consciously refraining from a nonvirtuous deed, as when one takes a vow not to kill humans. The greater part of Buddhist practice throughout Asia and throughout history has been directed toward securing rebirth as a human or (preferably) a god in the next lifetime, generally through acts of charity directed toward monks and monastic institutions.

For Evans-Wentz, however, this is only the exoteric teaching; the esoteric doctrine is quite different.[38] "In examining the Rebirth Doctrine, more particularly as it presents itself in our text, two interpretations must be taken into account: the literal or exoteric interpretation, which is the popular interpretation; and the symbolical or esoteric interpretation, which is held to be correct by the initiated few, who claim not scriptural authority or belief, but knowledge" (pp. 39–40). He concedes that the exoteric view, "accepted universally by Buddhists, both of the Northern and Southern Schools—as by Hindus," is that consciousness can be embodied in a subhuman form in a lifetime after, even immediately after, embodiment as a human. This view is based on "the untested authority of *gurus* and priests who consider the literally interpreted written records to be infallible and who are not adept in *yoga*" (p. 42). That "the brute principle of consciousness in its entirety and the human principle of consciousness in its entirety are capable of exchanging places with each other" is, for Evans-Wentz, an "obviously irrational belief." Yet this, he concedes, is the view that the *Bardo Thödol* conveys, when it is read literally.

The esoteric view, "on the authority of various philosophers, both Hindu and Buddhist, from whom the editor has received instruction," is quite different. The human form is the result of evolution, as is human consciousness. Thus, just as it is impossible for an animal or plant to devolve into one of its previous forms, so it is impossible for "a human life-flux to flow into the physical form of a dog, or fowl, or insect, or worm" (p. 43). Thus, "man, the highest of the animal-beings, cannot become the lowest of the animal beings, no matter how heinous his sins" (pp. 43–44). Such a view was believed by the esotericists to be quite unscientific (p. 48). (Note here Colonel Olcott's rendering of Buddhist doctrine in his 1881 *The Buddhist Catechism*: "143. Q. *Does Buddhism teach that man is reborn only upon our earth?* A. As a general rule that would be the case, until he had evolved beyond its level.") There can be gradual progression and retrogression only within a species. Only after ages of continual retrogression would it be possible for a human form to revert to the subhuman. Evans-Wentz claims that this was the view of the late lama, and he quotes him speaking of "a mere faded and incoherent reflex of the human mentality," an utterance difficult to imagine from a Tibetan lama, whether in English or Tibetan. What Evans-Wentz found particularly remarkable, however, was that the lama "expressed it while quite unaware of its similarity to the theory held esoterically by the Egyptian priests and exoterically by Herodotus, who apparently became their pupil in the monastic college of Heliopolis" (p. 45).

It appears that Evans-Wentz held to the conviction throughout his life that in Buddhism rebirth as an animal is impossible, referring readers of his 1954 *Tibetan Book of the Great Liberation* and his 1958 *Tibetan Yoga and Secret Doctrines* to this exposition in *The Tibetan Book of the Dead*. Commenting on an incident in the life of Padmasambhava in *The Tibetan Book of the Great*

Liberation in which Padma Tsalag is reborn as a fly, Evans-Wentz explains, "While the many, the exotericists, may accept this strange folk-tale literally, the more spiritually advanced of the Great *Guru's* devotees interpret it symbolically, as they do very much else in the Biography as a whole, the fly being to them significant of the undesirable characteristics of the unbridled sensuality associated with Padma Tsalag." [39]

But if this is the true teaching, why does the *Bardo Thödol* appear to teach otherwise? "The *Bardo Thödol*, as a Doctrine of Death and Rebirth, seems to have existed at first unrecorded, like almost all sacred books now recorded in Pali, Sanskrit, or Tibetan, and was a growth of unknown centuries. Then by the time it had fully developed and been set down in writing no doubt it had lost something of its primitive purity. By its very nature and religious usage, the *Bardo Thödol* would have been very susceptible to the influence of the popular or exoteric view; and in our opinion it did fall under it, in such manner as to attempt the impossible, namely, the harmonizing of the two interpretations. Nevertheless, its original esotericism is still discernible and predominant" (pp. 54–55). [40] Thus, it seems that even the sacred teachings of the lamas, preserved for centuries in Tibet (Evans-Wentz argues, in contrast to Govinda, that the essentials of the text are pre-Buddhist in origin [pp. 73, 75], perhaps deriving from the Atlantean age), were subject to degeneration when the esoteric knowledge was committed to writing; the higher teaching of the *Bardo Thödol* is confused, perhaps, "because of corruptions of text" (p. 58). But the true meaning is still accessible: if the "Buddhist and Hindu exotericists re-read their own Scriptures in light of the Science of Symbols their opposition to Esotericism would probably be given up" (p. 57). [41]

Thus, the *Bardo Thödol* is a reshaping of ancient teachings handed down orally over the centuries, recording the belief of countless generations concerning the postmortem state. Once written down, corruptions inevitably crept into the text, such that it cannot be accurate in all details. Yet it remains scientific in its essentials. "In its broad outlines, however, it seems to convey a sublime truth, heretofore veiled to many students of religion, a philosophy as subtle as that of Plato, and a psychical science far in advance of that, still in its infancy, which forms the study of the Society for Psychical Research [which had condemned Madame Blavatsky as a fraud]. And, as such, it deserves the serious attention of the Western World, now awakening to a New Age, freed, in large measure, from the incrustations of medievalism, and eager to garner wisdom from all the Sacred Books of mankind, be they of one Faith or of another" (pp. 77–78).

The book ends with his opinion that "the greater part of the symbolism nowadays regarded as being peculiarly Christian or Jewish seems to be due to the adaptations from Egyptian and Eastern religions. They suggest, too, that the thought-forms and thought-processes of Orient and Occident are, fundamentally, much alike—that, despite differences of race and creed and of physical and social environment, the nations of mankind are, and have been since time immemorial, mentally and spiritually one" (p. 241).

This sentiment engendered a reincarnation of *The Tibetan Book of the Dead* not forty-nine days but thirty-seven years later (in 1964) in the form of *The Psychedelic Experience: A Manual Based on the Tibetan Book of the Dead*, by Timothy Leary, Ralph Metzner, and Richard Alpert (later to become Baba Ram Dass). It was their claim that the oneness, both mental and spiritual, that Evans-Wentz had proclaimed could now be confirmed through the use of psychotropic drugs. Thus their book is a guide to the use of hallucinogens in which the various stages of death, the intermediate state, and rebirth described in the *Bardo Thödol* are transposed onto the stages of what at the time was called an "acid trip." "If the manual is read several times before a session is attempted, and if a trusted person is there to remind and refresh the memory of the voyager during the experience, the consciousness will be freed from the games which comprise 'personality' and from positive-negative hallucinations which often accompany states of expanded awareness."[42] Their book has generally been forgotten, invoked perhaps only by collectors of Beatles esoterica who might remember that the opening lines of "Tomorrow Never Knows" on the 1966 album *Revolver* come from this book: "Whenever in doubt, turn off your mind, relax, float downstream" (p. 14).

The book's premise, now well-worn and easily dismissed but perhaps exciting in 1964, is stated at the outset:

> A psychedelic experience is a journey to new realms of consciousness. The scope and content of the experience is limitless, but its characteristic features are the transcendence of verbal concepts, of space-time dimensions, and of the ego or identity. Such experiences of enlarged consciousness can occur in a variety of ways: sensory deprivation, yoga exercises, disciplined meditation, religious or aesthetic ecstasies, or spontaneously. Most recently they have become available to anyone through the ingestion of psychedelic drugs such as LSD, psilocybin, mescaline, DMT, etc. . . .

Here then is the key to a mystery which has been passed down for over 2,500 years—the consciousness-expansion experience—the premortem death and rebirth rite. The Vedic sages knew the secret; the Eleusinian initiates knew it; the Tantrics knew it. In all their esoteric writings they whisper the message: it is possible to cut beyond ego-consciousness, to tune in on neurological processes which flash by at the speed of light, and to become aware of the enormous treasury of ancient racial knowledge welded into the nucleus of every cell in your body. . . .

The present moment in human history (as Lama Govinda points out) is critical. Now, for the first time, we possess the means of providing the enlightenment to any prepared volunteer. (The enlightenment always comes, we remember, in the form of a new energy process, a physical, neurological event.) For these reasons we have prepared this psychedelic version of *The Tibetan Book of the Dead*. The secret is released once again, in a new dialect, and we sit back quietly to observe whether man is ready to move ahead and to make use of the new tools provided by modern science.[43]

Leary and Alpert believed, at least in the early years of their work with LSD, that the experiences of the mystics and the yogins of the world's religions were essentially the same, that they were insights into the fundamental and eternal truths of the universe, truths that are now being or will soon be confirmed by modern science, but were already known to the sages of the past. "Indeed, eastern philosophic theories dating back four thousand years adapt readily to the most recent discoveries of nuclear physics, biochemistry, genetics, and astronomy" (p. 20). Furthermore, those same experiences could be induced through the use of psychedelic drugs. In order to put the Tibetan text (or, more precisely, Evans-Wentz's book) to such use, it was necessary for the authors to decontextualize it from its traditional use as a mortuary text. To effect this change, they, like Evans-Wentz before them when he found Theosophical doctrines there, resort to the trope of the esoteric meaning: "The concept of actual physical death was an exoteric facade adopted to fit the prejudices of the Bonist tradition in Tibet. Far from being an embalmers' guide, the manual is a detailed account of how to lose the ego; how to break out of personality into new realms of consciousness; and how to avoid the involuntary limiting processes of the ego; how to make the consciousness-expansion experience endure in subsequent daily life" (p. 22).

The book is dedicated to Aldous Huxley and begins with tributes to Evans-Wentz, Jung, and Lama Govinda. It then moves through the three bardos set forth in *The Tibetan Book of the Dead,* providing its own gloss. Thus here the first bardo, the bardo of the time of death (*'chi kha'i bar do*), during which the mind of clear light dawns, is called the Period of Ego Loss or Non-Game Ecstasy. At this first stage of the psychedelic experience the voyager has the opportunity to see reality directly and thereby achieve liberation, with liberation defined as "the nervous system devoid of mental-conceptual activity," and thus able to see the "silent unity of the Unformed" (p. 36). The authors then translate the Tibetan imagery into their own:

> The Tibetan Buddhists suggest that the uncluttered intellect can experience what astrophysics confirms. The Buddha Vairochana, the Dhyani Buddha of the Center, Manifester of Phenomena, is the highest path to enlightenment. As the source of all organic life, in him all things visible and invisible have their consummation and absorption. He is associated with the Central Realm of the Densely-Packed, i.e., the seed of all universal forces and things are densely packed together. This remarkable convergence of modern astrophysics and ancient *lamaism* demands no complicated explanation. The cosmological awareness—and awareness of every other natural process—is there in the cortex. You can confirm this preconceptual mystical knowledge by empirical observation and measurement, but it's all there inside your skull. Your neurons "know" because they are linked directly to the process, are part of it. (P. 36)

The second bardo, in which visions of peaceful and wrathful deities occur (*chos nyid bar do*), is called the Period of Hallucinations. The authors again translate the Tibetan deities that appear during this stage into their own vocabulary, renaming the visions of the sixth day, for example, the Retinal Circus. During this stage the voyager is told not to become attracted or repulsed by the visions that occur, that he or she should sit quietly, "controlling his expanded awareness like a phantasmagoric multi-dimensional television set" (p. 47). Indeed, television (and to a lesser extent robots) provides the dominant metaphor for the author's gloss of the experience of the bardo.

> The fact of the matter is that all apparent forms of matter and body are momentary clusters of energy. We are little more than flickers on a multi-dimensional television screen. This realization directly experienced can be delightful. You suddenly wake up from the delusion of separate form and hook up to the cosmic dance. Consciousness slides along the wave matrices, silently at the speed of light.

The terror comes with the discovery of transience. Nothing is fixed, no form solid. Everything you can experience is "nothing but" electrical waves. You feel ultimately tricked. A victim of the great television producer. Distrust. The people around you are lifeless television robots. The world around you is a facade, a stage set. You are a helpless marionette, a plastic doll in a plastic world. (P. 66)

Consistent with their reading of *The Tibetan Book of the Dead* as an esoteric guide to the use of psychedelic drugs, Leary, Metzner, and Alpert see the third and final of the three bardos not as an explanation of the process by which the spirit of a dead person is reborn in one of the six realms of samsara (as a god, demigod, human, animal, ghost, or denizen of hell), but rather as an instruction on how to "come down" when the effects of the drug begin to fade. The third bardo is thus called the Period of Re-Entry. "In the original Bardo Thodol the aim of the teachings is 'liberation,' i.e., release from the cycle of birth and death. Interpreted esoterically, this means that the aim is to remain at the stage of perfect illumination and not to return to social game reality" (p. 77). All but the most advanced, however, must return to one of six "game worlds." Thus, like Evans-Wentz, the authors of *The Psychedelic Experience* offer their own version of the Buddhist doctrine of rebirth:

The Tibetan manual conceives of the voyager as returning eventually to one of six worlds of game existence (*sangsara*). That is, the re-entry to the ego can take place on one of six levels, or as one of six personality types. Two of these are higher than the normal human, three are lower. The highest, most illuminated, level is that of the *devas*, who are what Westerners would call saints, sages or divine teachers. They are the most enlightened people walking the earth. Gautama Buddha, Lao Tse, Christ. The second level is that of the *asuras*, who may be called titans or heroes, people with a more than human degree of power and vision. The third level is that of most normal human beings, struggling through game-networks, occasionally breaking free. The fourth level is that of primitive and animalistic incarnations. In this category we have the dog and the cock, symbolic of hyper-sexuality concomitant with jealousy; the pig, symbolizing lustful stupidity and uncleanliness; the industrious, hoarding ant; the insect or worm signifying an earthy or grovelling disposition; the snake, flashing in anger; the ape, full of rampaging primitive power; the snarling "wolf of the steppes;" the bird, soaring freely. Many more could be enumerated. In all cultures of the world people have adopted identities in the image of animals. In childhood and in dreams it is a process familiar to all. The fifth

level is that of neurotics, frustrated lifeless spirits forever pursuing unsatis-
fied desires; the sixth and lowest level is hell or psychosis. Less than one
percent of ego-transcendent experiences end in sainthood or psychosis.
Most persons return to the normal human level. (P. 83)

This reading is at wild variance with the way in which the doctrine of rebirth
is understood in Tibet, or any other Buddhist culture. The Buddha appeared
in the form of a human, not as a god, and was superior to a god because,
unlike them, he was free from future rebirth. Like Evans-Wentz, Leary,
Metzner, and Alpert are also committed to the view that the human level is
the most common abode, whereas in Tibet there is a well-known saying that
the number of beings born in the unfortunate realms of animals, ghosts, and
the hells is like the number of stars visible on a clear night, while the number
of beings born as gods, demigods, and humans is like the number of stars
seen a clear day. This insistence on rejecting a literal interpretation of
rebirth in favor of psychologizing the six realms would persist in future incarnations of *The Tibetan Book of the Dead*.

The next section of the book, "Some Technical Comments about Psychedelic Sessions," includes detailed instructions on the amount of time to be
cleared on one's calendar; the setting, including the choice of lighting, music,
furnishings, art work, and food (preferably "ancient foods like bread, cheese,
wine, and fresh fruit"); the number of people who should make the voyage
together, including their personality traits; the qualifications for the guide,
the person (or ideally two people, one high, the other straight) who will serve
as air traffic controller; and, of course, the dosage. "The dosage to be taken
depends, of course, on the goal of the session. Two figures are therefore
given. The first quantity indicates a dosage which should be sufficient for an
inexperienced person to enter the transcendental worlds described in this
manual. The second quantity gives a smaller dosage figure, which may be
used by more experienced persons or by participants in a group session"
(p. 101). Voyagers are instructed to study the book closely before embarking,
even tape-recording portions to be played back at appropriate points during
the voyage.

Yet the authors close with an instruction regarding "religious expecta-
tions": "Again, the subject in early sessions is best advised to float with the
stream, stay 'up' as long as possible, and postpone theological interpretations
until the end of the session, or to later sessions" (p. 104). What the authors
fail to acknowledge, however, is that their apparently clinical reading of the

psychedelic experience is itself a richly theological interpretation, a theology founded, like that of Evans-Wentz, on the conviction that there is an ancient brotherhood of mystics who, throughout history and across cultures, have shared in an experience of gnosis. What Leary, Metzner, and Alpert add to Evans-Wentz is the conviction that the harmony between science and religion that Evans-Wentz could only prophesy had now become true, and was accessible to all through the use of LSD. They assume that there is a deep structure in human consciousness that has remained the same across time and space. This remains a topic of debate among anthropologists, who would ask us to consider to what extent even the idea of "consciousness" is translatable cross-culturally. Leary, Metzner, and Alpert assume further that the states of consciousness described in Buddhist texts are records of meditative experience. Here scholars of Buddhism would ask to what extent one might regard the baroque pure lands described in the Mahayana sutras as the records of a vision experienced in meditation. Should they be taken instead as literary descriptions, not unlike the paradise described by Dante?

But the fundamental assumption that supports the view that there is a structural similarity between the results of Buddhist meditation and those of drug use is that Buddhism is compatible with science, that the Buddha knew long ago what scientists are only now beginning to discover, that Buddhist meditators gained access to the deepest levels of consciousness long before scientists invented chemical agents that demonstrated the existence of such states. What is it about Buddhism that would make us draw such conclusions? When we read the claims of Hindu fundamentalists that locomotives and rocket travel are described in the Vedas or that the beam of light emitted from Śiva's brow is really a laser, we smile indulgently. But when we read Buddhist descriptions (products of the same time and the same culture that produced the Vedas and Śiva), descriptions, for example, of a universe that moves through periods of cosmic evolution and devolution, we assume that this is simply something that physicists have not yet discovered. This assumption would reappear in future incarnations of *The Tibetan Book of the Dead*.

The second English translation of *The Tibetan Book of the Dead* was published in 1975 by Shambhala Publications as part of its Clear Light Series, dedicated to Evans-Wentz. The translators were Francesca Fremantle and Chögyam Trungpa, a prominent incarnate lama of the Kagyu sect who gained a large following in the United States beginning in the early 1970s.[44] Unlike previous and subsequent translations, the translators' and editors' commentaries did not equal or surpass in length the actual translation of the

Tibetan text. Trungpa provides a relatively brief, twenty-nine-page commentary devoted largely to how to recognize while living the visions (which he calls "projections") described in *The Tibetan Book of the Dead,* with much emphasis on overcoming duality. It is a highly psychologized reading, with much talk of neurosis, paranoia, and unconscious tendencies. Fremantle explains, in terms reminiscent of Leary, Metzner, and Alpert, that "It is noticeable that several of the words which best express the teachings of Buddhism are part of the language of contemporary psychology, for the attitudes of certain schools of Western psychology often come closer to Buddhism than do those of Western philosophy or religion. . . . Concepts such as conditioning, neurotic patterns of thought, and unconscious influences, seem more appropriate in this book than conventional religious terms."[45]

Their decision to psychologize the text is evident throughout. For example, in Tibetan texts on the dying process, one of the early stages described is that in which the physical elements of earth, water, fire, and wind dissolve in succession, one into the other. An eighteenth-century Tibetan text states, "when the power of the wind that serves as the basis of the physical earth constituent declines, and it dissolves into the water constituent, the external sign is that the strength of the body is lost, that is, one says, 'I am being pulled down,' thinking that one is sinking into the earth. Similarly, when the water constituent dissolves into the fire constituent, the external sign is that the moisture of the mouth and nose dry up and the lips become puckered. When the fire constituent dissolves into the wind constituent, the external sign is that warmth of the body gathers from the extremities at the heart and one's luster deteriorates. The external sign of the wind constituent dissolving into consciousness is a gasping for breath and one makes a wheezing sound from [the breath] collecting unevenly within."[46] Leary, Metzner, and Alpert took the instructions on the bardo out of their traditional context of death and made them into a description of hallucinations. In discussing these stages of the dissolution of the elements, Trungpa also moves the discussion away from the experience of death, explaining that these dissolutions happen every day:

> Such experiences happen constantly. . . . First the tangible quality of physical, living logic becomes vague; in other words, you lose physical contact. Then you automatically take refuge in a more functional situation, which is the water element; you reassure yourself that your mind is still functioning. In the next stage, the mind is not quite sure whether it is functioning

properly or not, something begins to cease operating in its circulation. The only way to relate is through emotions, you try to think of someone you love or hate, something very vivid, because the watery quality of the circulation does not work any more, so the fiery temperature of love and hate becomes more important. Even that gradually dissolves into air, and there is a faint experience of openness, so that there is a tendency to lose your grip on concentrating on love or trying to remember the person you love. The whole thing seems to be hollow inside.[47]

It is not surprising, then, to see that Trungpa reads the six realms of rebirth as "different types of instinct," and that each of the traditional descriptions of the abodes of rebirth are "a psychological portrait of oneself." The cold hells are thus "the aggression which refuses to communicate at all."[48] We learn that (contrary to the experience of many pet owners) "the animal realm is characterised by the absence of sense of humour."[49]

In 1992 a second best-selling book of the dead was published, this time by Sogyal Rinpoche, a Tibetan lama living in England. *The Tibetan Book of Living and Dying* is described on the dust jacket as "a spiritual masterpiece" that "brings together the ancient wisdom of Tibet with modern research on death and dying and the nature of the universe." Sogyal intends the book as "the quintessence of the heart advice of all my masters, to be a new *Tibetan Book of the Dead* and a *Tibetan Book of Life*."[50] To date, the book has sold over three hundred thousand copies. Part of its appeal is certainly its approachable style, so different from translations of Tibetan texts or transcriptions of teachings by contemporary lamas.[51] The work is filled with Sogyal Rinpoche's reminiscences about great masters he knew in Tibet and how they died, but there are many such stories available in the current popular literature on Tibetan Buddhism. The book contains classic Buddhist teachings illustrated by classic stories, also available elsewhere. But there is much here from genres of literature not included in the standard lineage of teaching. There are approving citations from the works of Elisabeth Kübler-Ross on "death and dying," Ian Stevenson on "cases suggestive of reincarnation," and Raymond Moody on the "near-death" experience. The Brazilian Minister on the Environment is quoted on the threat to the environment posed by modern industrial society. Accounts of the deaths of ordinary people are interwoven with scenes of the passing of great masters, illustrated by quotations from Milarepa, Padmasambhava, and the current Dalai Lama. But Sogyal's points are also supported by citations from other masters. There are quotations from Montaigne, Blake, Rilke, Henry Ford, Voltaire, Origen, Shelley, Mozart, Balzac, Einstein, Rumi, Wordsworth, and the Venerable Bede, which together create a cosmopolitan eclecticism around Sogyal's message, as if what the book conveys is not a Tibetan Buddhist tradition but a universal message, a perennial philosophy, that has always been known to those who know, a secret brotherhood not unlike Madame Blavatsky's Mahatmas. Indeed, the vast popularity of Evans-Wentz's and Sogyal's versions may derive from the way they homogenize the Tibetan text into an ahistorical and universal wisdom. (The Tibetan text is so thoroughly appropriated in Sogyal's work that its translation need not be included.)

Sogyal Rinpoche has said that Tibet is lost, that all that remains is its wisdom.[52] He places that wisdom in a global and ahistorical spiritual lineage of thinkers that no other Tibetan author has ever cited. Referring to a revered contemporary Tibetan lama, Sogyal writes, "Whenever I think of him, I always say to myself, 'This is what St. Francis of Assisi must have been like'" (p. 109).[53] This is the kind of statement that makes the reader suspect the presence of a ghost writer, and Sogyal acknowledges the assistance of Patrick Gaffney and Andrew Harvey, who perhaps collaborated with him as Evans-Wentz did with Lama Kazi Dawa-Samdup. In this case, however, the author named on the spine of the book is the Tibetan, not the Westerner. Harvey is a best-selling author on the spiritual, a term that by the beginning of this decade meant something different than it had in Madame Blavatsky's day. "Spiritual" no longer refers to contact and communication with the spirits of the dead. Instead it evokes an ethos beyond the confines of the merely religious, pointing back to that which was the original life blood of religious traditions but was ultimately free from them, confined as they were by institution and by history. The spiritual was instead at once both universal and personal, accessible not only through the experiences of the mystics of the great "world religions" but also, perhaps in a more pristine form, through Asian traditions or through shamanism, nature worship, or the cult of the goddess, what was once regarded as primitive.

It is to the spiritual seeker that Sogyal's book, like Evans-Wentz's before it, is directed. And, indeed, the parallels between the two books are striking. Both speak of a universal message known to mystics of all traditions but preserved most perfectly in Tibet; both speak of the urgency of transmitting this teaching to a modern world in crisis, rich in knowledge of the external but bereft of the ancient science of the internal; both are collaborations between a Tibetan and a Westerner, with the determinative role of the latter largely effaced. And like Evans-Wentz (and Leary and Trungpa), Sogyal provides his own reading of the Buddhist doctrine of reincarnation. Although he concedes that the realms of rebirth "may, in fact, exist beyond the range of perception of our karmic vision" (p. 112), he is more interested in the way in which the six realms of rebirth "are projected and crystallized in the world around us":

> The main feature of the realm of the gods, for example, is that it is devoid
> of suffering, a realm of changeless beauty and sensual ecstasy. Imagine the
> gods, tall, blond surfers, lounging on beaches and in gardens flooded by
> brilliant sunshine, listening to any kind of music they choose, intoxicated
> by every kind of stimulant, high on meditation, yoga, bodywork, and ways
> of improving themselves, but never taxing their brains, never confronting
> any complex or painful situation, never conscious of their true nature, and
> so anesthetized that they are never aware of what their condition really is.
>
> If some parts of California and Australia spring to mind as the realm
> of the gods, you can see the demigod realm being acted out every day
> perhaps in the intrigue and rivalry of Wall Street, or in the seething corri-
> dors of Washington and Whitehall. And the hungry ghost realms? They
> exist wherever people, though immensely rich, are never satisfied, craving
> to take over this company or that one, or endlessly playing out their greed
> in court cases. Switch on any television channel and you have entered im-
> mediately the world of demigods and hungry ghosts. (P. 113)

Perhaps Sogyal believes that his audience would recoil at a literal rendering of the doctrine of the six realms of rebirth—as physical realms where beings are reborn after death. That may be why he locates them instead in North America, with gods in California and demigods on the East Coast.

The most recent translation of *The Tibetan Book of the Dead* is, according to the title page, "*Composed by* Padma Sambhava, *Discovered by* Karma Lingpa, *Translated by* Robert A. F. Thurman." It was published in 1994 as part of the Bantam Wisdom Edition series, which also includes translations of the *Tao Te Ching*, the *Bhagavad Gita*, the *I Ching*, *The Book of Five Rings* (a book on swordsmanship by the seventeenth-century samurai Musashi Miyamoto), a book of "mystical poetry" by Rumi, and a book on unlocking the Zen koan. The placement of the *Book of the Dead* among these world spiritual classics is in itself indicative of the radical decontextualization that the Tibetan text has achieved.

In the preface, Thurman describes his initial reluctance at doing yet another translation of the so-called *Tibetan Book of the Dead*. His own research had centered on another genre of Tibetan literature that deals with death, "an ancient tradition of spiritual techniques every bit as sophisticated as modern material technologies," which he found in the works of Tsong kha pa, "founder" of the Geluk sect.[54] In comparison, *The Tibetan Book of the Dead*, which derives from the Nyingma sect, was not as clear and systematic; it seemed "less relevant." He eventually decided, however, to undertake the project when he realized that "people who are dying need something more clear, usable, and accessible than those translations" of Evans-Wentz and Fremantle and Trungpa (p. xx). Like the Evans-Wentz version, about half of Thurman's work is taken up with his own commentary and glossary. The former includes sections such as "Tibet: A Spiritual Civilization," "Buddhism in Summary," "The Body-Mind Complex," and "The Reality of Liberation." In the latter, karma is glossed as "evolution," *gotra* (lineage) as "spiritual gene," *abhidharma* as "Clear Science," and *ḍākinī* as "angel."

Thurman's choice of translation terms supports his larger project of representing *The Tibetan Book of the Dead*, and Buddhism in general, as scientific rather than religious (he renders *vidyadhara*—literally, "knowledge holder," a class of advanced Indian tantric masters—as "Hero Scientist": "they have been the quintessential scientists of that nonmaterialist civilization" [p. 110]). For Thurman Tibet's civilization was unique. While the West has devoted itself to the investigation and conquest of the material world and outer space, the direction of Tibetan society has been inward and its product has been generations of spiritual adepts who have studied spiritual technologies (tantras) and have become "inner world adventurers of the highest daring" (he calls them "psychonauts") who have "personally voyaged to the furthest frontiers of that universe which their society deemed vital to explore: the inner frontiers of consciousness itself, in all its transformations of life and beyond death" (p. 10). As a product of this society, *The Tibetan Book of the Dead* (or, as he renders the Tibetan title, the *Great Book of Natural Liberation through Understanding in the Between*) is not a Buddhist approach to death and dying, but a scientific description of the death process, derived from the research of psychonauts. Tibetan views on death are no more or less religious than modern Western views on the structure of the solar system (p. 18). In fact, Buddhism is not a religion; the Buddha did not found a religion. Instead, he founded an educational movement in which reality is "freely open to unprejudiced experience" (p. 16). He founded educational and research institutions (these institutions are referred to by others as monasteries and convents) in which "the study of death, between, and rebirth processes in particular, was conducted by researchers within these Mind Science institutions, the results being contained in a huge, cumulative scientific literature on the subject" (p. 17).

Thurman then argues in favor of the existence of rebirth and against those "emotional annihilationists," "closet cosmic escapists," and "materialist scientists" who dogmatically dismiss evidence of the postmortem continuity of consciousness in order to preserve their belief in nothingness. He still finds Pascal's wager compelling. Pascal argued that if God exists, then his existence is incomprehensible. Thus, it is impossible to know with certainty whether or not God exists. If God does exist, the consequences of belief and disbelief are profound, both for the present and for eternity. To believe that God exists, therefore, is the prudent and reasonable course, in which nothing is lost and everything may be gained (*Pensées* 343).[55] Thurman simply substitutes belief (or faith) in "rebirth" for "God." From here, it is a short step to accepting the Tibetan view:

A nourishing, useful, healthful faith should be no obstacle to developing a science of death. In developing such a science, it behooves the investigator to consider all previous attempts to do so, especially those traditions with a long development and a copious literature. Of all these, the science of death preserved in the Indo-Tibetan tradition is perhaps the most copious of all. (P. 27)

Having argued for the scientific value of the Tibetan system of rebirth, Thurman must, like previous translators of *The Tibetan Book of the Dead*, deal with the specific question of the existence of the realms of gods, ghosts, and hell beings. Thurman is the only translator of *The Tibetan Book of the Dead* who did not collaborate directly with a Tibetan lama in the rendering of the text into English. And he is the only translator who rejects the "metaphorical" view of the realms of rebirth, arguing that the Buddhist heavens and hells are just as real as the realm of humans. "Those who have remembered their own previous lives have reported this to be the case. And it makes logical sense that the life forms in the ocean of evolution would be much more numerous than just the number of species on this one tiny little material planet we can see around us nowadays" (p. 33).

How are we to account for Thurman's unique position in the history of the text? According to Evans-Wentz, Lama Kazi Dawa-Samdup supported the "esoteric" view of rebirth as an evolutionary system in which regression to the brutish realms was impossible. Leary and his collaborators, following the Evans-Wentz translation, extended the metaphor further, arguing that *The Tibetan Book of the Dead* was really about life. From this they concluded that it could profitably be read as an account of an eight-hour acid trip. Trungpa Rinpoche portrays the realms of rebirth as psychological states. Sogyal Rinpoche uses his discussion of the six realms as an opportunity to lampoon California surfers and New York bankers. Only Thurman appears to believe what real Tibetans believe.

Evans-Wentz, Leary, Trungpa, and Sogyal can all interpret the six realms of rebirth as a matter of popular belief rather than fact because they have no contract with the practices of ordinary Tibetans.[56] Their investments have been made elsewhere: in Theosophy for Evans-Wentz, in LSD for Leary, in transpersonal psychology for Trungpa, in the New Age for Sogyal. Only Thurman seems invested in a more literal (perhaps "orthodox") presentation of Tibetan doctrine. Precisely because he is not Tibetan, he was not born into the lineage that naturally bestows authenticity but must derive his authenticity from other sources. These include his scholarly credentials, his ordination in 1964 (since lapsed) as the first American to become a Tibetan Buddhist monk, his description of himself as a "lay Buddhist," his characterization by journalists as America's leading Buddhist, his occasional role as unofficial spokesperson for the Dalai Lama (who does not speak of rebirth symbolically), and his position as the Jey Tsong Khapa Professor of Buddhist Studies at Columbia University. Taken together his credentials accord him an official status, a certain orthodoxy, that would not constrain a Tibetan lama living in America, such as Sogyal, for example. His active role in the Tibetan independence movement is a further impetus for his identification with a central tenet of Tibet's endangered civilization. Thus for Thurman rebirth is not a symbol; it is, or will be, a scientific fact.

But his identification with Tsong kha pa provides its own problems. Here and in other works Thurman represents the life and works of Tsong kha pa as the pinnacle of Tibetan civilization, ushering in a renaissance. He writes elsewhere, "After the renaissance led by Tsong Khapa, the spiritual synthesis of Tibetan Buddhism was complete."[57] Although many Tibetans associated with the Geluk sect of Tibetan Buddhism (of which Tsong kha pa is regarded retrospectively as the "founder") would probably not object to this characterization, those of other sects would. The problem is that the *Bar do thos grol* is a Nyingma text. This does not deter Thurman, however, from interpreting the work as if it were a Geluk text. His discussion of the "Ordinary Prepa-rations for Death" is drawn not from the extensive Nyingma literature on the topic (some of which is available in English)[58] but from Tsong kha pa's "three primary aspects of the path" (*lam tso rnam gsum*). His discussion of the "Ex-traordinary Preliminaries" is drawn, again, not from Nyingma literature but from the standard presentation of the Geluk. Thurman is aware of the prob-lem, explaining it away in a spirit of ecumenism:

> There are numerous Tantras used in the different Tibetan Buddhist orders, all inherited from the creative pioneer work of the great adepts of India. . . . All these Tantras emerge from the same path of transcendent renuncia-tion, the enlightenment spirit of universal love, and the wisdom of selfless voidness [i.e., Tsong kha pa's categories]. . . . That they present the process of achieving this one goal of supreme integration of Buddhahood variously as Great Perfection, Great Seal, bliss-void indivisible, and so on is a differ-ence of conceptual scheme and terminology, not a difference of path or its fruition. (Pp. 73–74)

Thus, it is all the same, except that Tsong kha pa's version is the best, one that can be fruitfully applied in any situation. In outlining simple mindfulness meditation, Thurman explains that the meditation object should be chosen according to one's beliefs. "If you are a Christian, an icon of Christ. If you are a Moslem, a sacred letter. If you are a secularist, a Mona Lisa, a flower, or a satellite picture of the planet" (p. 55). When it comes to more advanced stages of tantric practice, however, other traditions are somewhat bereft:

> The genuine shaman knows of the dissolution process, knows of divine allies and demonic interferences, and usually finds a ground of benevolence and trust, some sort of Lord of Compassion. The monastics of all ages have experimented with journeys of the soul, and some have lived to recount their experience in useful works. Sufi and Taoist adepts have given instruc-tions and maintain living traditions. The Tibetan tradition can be used by any seeker in any of these traditions for its systematic technologies and its penetrating insight. (Pp. 80–81)

The technology is thus available to all presumably because it is, simply, the truth. It is no longer necessary, as it was for the other translators, to read the Tibetan text as symbol in an effort to find an accommodation between Bud-dhism and science, part of the endless attempt that goes back to Blavatsky and beyond to neutralize Darwin. For Thurman, Buddhism is science.

In each of the previous incarnations of *The Tibetan Book of the Dead,* the text is always read away from itself; it is always pointing at something else, at a meaning that requires so much elaboration that the translation of the Tibetan text (except in the case of Fremantle and Trungpa) is dwarfed by introductions and commentaries; in Leary and Sogyal's renditions the Tibetan text is so superfluous that it need not be included at all. Despite the claims of the translators, their readings are not symbolic (in either the Romantic or the Peircean senses of the term): missing is the requisite arbitrariness between the symbol and the symbolized. Instead the book is read as a code (a system of constraints) to be deciphered against another text that is somehow more authentic, or perhaps as an allegory for another, anterior text with which it can never coincide; *The Tibetan Book of the Dead* is construed as referring "to one specific meaning and thus exhausts its suggestive potentialities once it has been deciphered."[59] For Evans-Wentz, the urtext is Madame Blavatsky's *The Secret Doctrine,* itself her decoding of the *Stanzas of Dzyan* from Senzar, the secret language. For Leary, Metzner, and Alpert the text was the script for the paradigmatic acid trip; for Trungpa it contained the tenets of transpersonal psychology; for Sogyal it embodied the language of self-help in the New Age; and for Thurman the Nyingma text was forced into a Geluk template. For each, *The Tibetan Book of the Dead* must be read against something else in order for its true meaning to be revealed.

But, ironically, perhaps each of these modern interpreters was in his own way traditional. For the Tibetan work called the *Bar do thos grol* is a treasure text (*gter ma*) said to have been written long ago, in the eighth century, during a time when the people of Tibet were unprepared to appreciate its profundity. So it was hidden away, only to be discovered six centuries later. Even then it was revealed to its discoverer in the secret *ḍākinī* language, a kind of code that only he was able to decipher and translate into a public language. It was necessary, then, for the discoverer, finding the text at the prophesied moment, to become a kind of embodied ghost writer, translating it in such a way as to make it meaningful for its time, creating a text that is original because it is already a copy.

The Eye

❀

The word *mystify*, the dictionary tells us, is derived from the Greek *mystos*, meaning to close the eyes and lips during an initiation or religious rite. T. Lobsang Rampa, whose books about "Tibet" have sold more copies than any other author on the subject, claimed to be an initiate into the secret cults of Lamaism. Rampa's eyes were closed, however, to the authorized knowledge of Tibetan history and culture because he was not an initiate of another cult, the cult of Tibetology. He might then be called a *mystifier,* in two senses of the modern meaning of the word. First, he mystified Tibet, embellishing its various realities with his own mystical fancies, and, second, he mystified his readers, playing on the credulity of the reading public. This latter sense of mystify has a strong connotation of intentional deceit, a charge vehemently denied by Rampa, who is regarded as the greatest hoaxer in the history of Tibetan Studies. Although Alexandra David-Neel dressed as a Tibetan to hide her true identity and Lama Govinda dressed as a Tibetan to signal his new identity, the Englishman who wrote under the name of T. Lobsang

Rampa claimed to have been possessed by a Tibetan lama, and over the course of seven years to have become a Tibetan, not just in his dress but in his molecules. He accomplished this through his ability to float free, first from the forces of gravity in a man-bearing kite, and later from the constraints of time and space, floating free in the astral plane.

This chapter considers notions of embodiment and possession in an effort to raise the question of what authorizes the author of a book about Tibet. The occasion for these reflections is provided by three books published under the name of T. Lobsang Rampa, who claimed not to have had his eyes closed but to have had a new eye opened, an eye that allowed him in his words "to see people as they are and not as they pretend to be."

The Third Eye, first published in Britain in 1956, tells the autobiographical story of Tuesday Lobsang Rampa, the son of a Lhasa aristocrat, who was one of the leading members of the Dalai Lama's government. The author begins with his childhood. He had an elder brother, Paljör, and an elder sister, Yasodhara. Paljör died before his seventh birthday "and returned to the Land of Many Temples." Tibetan children, however, are generally hardy, having survived a test during infancy to determine their ability to endure the harsh climate. Newborn infants are immersed in icy streams by their grandmothers, the child turning first red then blue until its cries cease. "If the baby survives, then it is as the gods decree. If it dies, then it has been spared much suffering on earth."[1] He grew up in a fashionable home in Lhasa, under the strict tutelage of one of the "men of Kham," a seven-foot former member of the monk police named Old Tzu, who was wounded while fighting the troops of Colonel Younghusband during the British invasion of Tibet in 1904. Rampa attended school, where he studied Tibetan, Chinese, arithmetic, and wood carving (for printing blocks). Every day, the students recited the laws: "(1) Return good for good. (2) Do not fight with gentle people. (3) Read the Scriptures and understand them. (4) Help your neighbors. (5) The Law is hard on the rich to teach them understanding and equity. (6) The Law is gentle with the poor to show them compassion. (7) Pay your debts promptly."[2] Among sports, he enjoyed archery, pole vaulting, stilt walking, and especially kite flying, the national sport of Tibet. The kite season began on the first day of autumn, signaled when a single kite rose from the Potala.

A great celebration was planned for Rampa's seventh birthday. All of the noble families of Lhasa attended. They were served shark's-fin soup and candied rhododendron blossoms in a festive setting where butter lamps hung from the branches of trees and floated in an ornamental lake. It was at this celebration that astrologers predicted the boy's future: "A boy of seven to enter a lamasery, after a hard feat of endurance, and there to be trained as a priest-surgeon. To suffer great hardships, to leave the homeland, and go among strange people. To lose all and have to start again, and eventually to succeed" (p. 44).

He thus sought to join the Chakpori lamasery, the Temple of Tibetan Medicine. But those who aspire to the higher ranks of that order must pass a test, and the young boy was made to sit motionless in the posture of contemplation in front of the temple gate before he was finally allowed to enter. He began a rigorous course of study, with a strong emphasis on mathematics and on the memorization of the Buddhist scriptures. The teachers shot questions at the students such as "You, boy, I want to know the fifth line of the eighteenth page of the seventh volume of the Kan-gyur" (p. 82). Rampa soon showed himself to be an excellent student and was chosen to receive the esoteric teachings so that the knowledge would be preserved after Tibet had fallen under an alien cloud. He thus began a period of intensive training designed to impart in a few years what a lama normally would learn over the course of a lifetime. The abbot warned him, "The Way will be hard, and often it will be painful. To force clairvoyance is painful, and to travel in the astral planes requires nerves that nothing can shatter, and a determination as hard as the rocks" (p. 61). He was given the ordination name of Yza-mig-dmar Lah-lu and placed under the tutelage of the great lama Mingyar Dondup, who oversaw the performance of a surgical procedure designed to force clairvoyance, after which Rampa could be instructed hypnotically. The operation, performed on Rampa's eighth birthday, involved drilling a hole in his skull at the point between his eyes to create the third eye, an eye that allowed him to see auras, "to see people as they are and not as they pretend to be" (p. 88). When he recovered from the surgery he was summoned to the Potala, where he met privately with the Dalai Lama, the "Inmost One," who, having scrutinized both the records of Rampa's last incarnation (he had been the abbot of Sera monastery) and the predictions for his future, reminded him of the great work that lay before him in preserving the wisdom of Tibet for the world.

Shortly after his twelfth birthday, Rampa took the examinations that one must pass in order to become a *trappa*, or medical priest. Each student was sealed inside a stone cubicle that was six feet wide, ten feet long, and eight feet high. Once inside, he was passed written questions to which he composed written answers. The students wrote for fourteen hours a day on a single subject; the battery of tests lasted six days. During that time they were locked inside the cubicle; tea and tsampa were passed through a small trap in the wall. After successfully passing his examinations, Rampa accompanied Lama Mingyar Dondup on an expedition to collect medicinal herbs. During their travels, they stopped at the monastery of Tra Yerpa, where the monks built box kites large enough to bear the weight of an adult. Rampa made several flights in such kites, and later suggested design modifications to the monastery's kite master to improve their airworthiness.

Upon his return to Lhasa, he was called upon by the Dalai Lama to sit in hiding in the audience room of the summer palace, the Norbulinga, and use his third eye to observe the auras, and thus learn the intentions, of the Chinese emissaries to the Dalai Lama. The Chinese were filled with hate, their auras showing "the contaminated hues of those whose life forces are devoted to materialism and evil-doing" (p. 175). Later he was called upon to read the aura of an English visitor. Rampa was astonished by his dress; the man wore trousers and shoes, neither of which he had ever seen before. Occasionally the man would hold a white cloth to his nose and make the sound of a small trumpet, which Rampa took to be a form of salute to the Dalai Lama. He assumed that the man was crippled because he had to sit on a wooden frame supported by four sticks. His aura showed him to be in poor health. However, he had a genuine desire to help Tibet but was constrained by the fear that if he were to do so he would lose his government pension. Rampa was to learn that the man's name was C. A. Bell (Sir Charles Bell, 1870–1945, British political officer for Sikkim, Bhutan, and Tibet).[3]

Rampa later accompanied Lama Mingyar Dondup on an expedition to the northern plain, the Chang thang, where after a perilous journey through frozen wastelands they came upon an Edenic valley, warm and luxuriant, where they encountered the yeti. Upon his return to Lhasa, around the time of his sixteenth birthday, he again entered the examination boxes, this time for ten days, taking written tests on topics such as anatomy, divinity, metaphysics, and yoga, followed by two more days of oral examinations. When the results came in, Rampa was at the top of his class, and was promoted from the rank of *trappa* to the rank of lama. He went on to study anatomy by working side by side with the Body Breakers, the disposers of the dead.

Finally, the Dalai Lama declared that Rampa must undergo the initiation rites to become an abbot, the Ceremony of the Little Death. After three months of preparation and a rigorous regime of fasting and meditation, he was led by three aged abbots through the labyrinthine caves beneath the Potala until they reached a shining black house. Inside were three black coffins in which lay the huge golden bodies of gods from Tibet's prehistoric age. Rampa was locked inside the house with the bodies of the gods, and traveling astrally returned through time to the great civilization of the giants, who inhabited Tibet before the earth was struck by another planet, moving Tibet from the warm seaside into the snowy mountains. When he returned from his astral travels after three days in the tomb, he had returned from death.

Shortly thereafter he was again summoned by the Dalai Lama, who instructed him to leave immediately for China, yet warned, "The ways of foreigners are strange and not to be accounted for. As I told you once before, they believe only that which they can do, only that which can be tested in their Rooms of Science. Yet the greatest Science of all, the Science of the Overself, they leave untouched. That is your Path, the Path you chose before you came to this Life" (p. 217). *The Third Eye* ends with Tuesday Lobsang Rampa departing for China on horseback, looking back for the last time at the Potala, where a solitary kite is flying.[4]

Rampa published a sequel in 1959 called *Doctor from Lhasa*. It begins where *The Third Eye* ends, as Tuesday Lobsang Rampa departs Lhasa for China. The year is 1927. He travels on horseback from Lhasa to Chungking, encountering many things unknown in Tibet such as heavy, moist air; fishing (in Tibet fish had no fear of humans and were often pets); motor vehicles; bicycles; indoor plumbing; spring beds; and Russians preaching the glories of Communism from the backs of oxcarts. In Chungking he enrolls in a Chinese medical college, where he registers as "Tuesday Lobsang Rampa, Lama of Tibet. Priest-Surgeon Chakpori Lamasery. Recognised Incarnation. Abbot Designate. Pupil of Lama Mingyar Dondup."[5] His curriculum includes both Chinese medicine and American methods of medicine and surgery, with special attention given to electricity and magnetism. (In his electricity class he amazes the professor by painlessly enduring a 250-volt shock and by sketching a magnetic field, which he sees through his third eye.) By combining what he learns of Chinese and Western medicine with his knowledge of esoteric Tibetan healing techniques, he hopes to be able to reproduce a device he once saw in the ruins of a prehistoric city in a hidden valley in the Chang thang. It was an apparatus for reading auras that could be used to predict the onset of diseases, both physical and mental.

Rampa's most extraordinary confrontation with the modern world was his first encounter with an airplane. After being taken for a brief flight by a

Chinese pilot interested in Tibet, he "borrowed" the plane and took off alone, teaching himself various maneuvers as he went, finally executing a smooth landing. He was soon recruited to join a special corps of medical airmen in Chiang Kai-shek's army.

Some years later he received a telepathic message from Lhasa that "the Inmost One, the thirteenth Dalai Lama, the last of his line, [was] shortly to pass from this world" (p. 103). He was summoned to Lhasa, and returned by car and then horseback to participate in the funeral ceremonies. Shortly after the ceremonies he returned to China with the knowledge that "Tibet was without a Dalai Lama, the last one had left, and the one yet to come [the fourteenth and current Dalai Lama], according to prophecy, would be one who would serve alien masters, one who would be in the thrall of the Communists" (p. 112).

By the time he arrived back in China, war with Japan was imminent. He was given a commission as a medical officer in the Chinese army and, at the request of a Chinese general, went to Shanghai, where he set up a private medical and psychological practice while continuing to study navigation and the theory of flight. War with Japan broke out in 1937 and Rampa went into service flying an air ambulance; he was eventually shot down and taken prisoner. He was tortured brutally by the Japanese for information but said only that he was a noncombatant officer in the Chinese army. His training as a lama enabled him to withstand the torture and privation, which he describes in detail. He eventually escaped by feigning death and made his way back to the Chinese lines and to Chungking, where he recuperated from the many injuries inflicted by the Japanese.

He returned to service as the director of a hospital, only to be captured by the Japanese again. Again he was beaten and interrogated; the Japanese wanted to know why a Tibetan lama was serving on the Chinese side. He was sent to a prison camp and escaped. But he was betrayed and recaptured; the Japanese broke both of his legs to prevent further attempts. He remained in the camp providing medical assistance to the other prisoners, using his Tibetan knowledge of herbs to cure many tropical maladies. Toward the end of the war the most incorrigible prisoners, including Rampa, were transferred to a special prison camp in Japan. The camp was located in a village near Hiroshima and on the day the bomb was dropped he escaped from the camp, made his way to the seashore, stole a fishing boat, and drifted into the Sea of Japan and into the unknown. *Doctor from Lhasa* ends there.

The final work in the trilogy, *The Rampa Story* (1960), opens fifteen years later, in 1960. In Tibet, the lamas, through astral exploration, have located a network of caves and tunnels in the most remote region of the country and are busy physically transporting the most sacred and secret artifacts of the faith from Lhasa to this new site, where they can be hidden from the Communists. These include the golden figures of past incarnations, sacred objects, ancient writings, as well as the most learned priests. The abbots, having known clairvoyantly of the Chinese invasion, had been preparing for this for years, secretly selecting the most spiritually advanced monks for the new home where the ancient knowledge would be preserved by a new order called the School of the Preservation of Knowledge. At that time Tuesday Lobsang Rampa was living in Windsor, Canada. He was in telepathic communication with the lamas in Tibet. They informed him that his next task was to write a book "stressing one theme, that one person can take over the body of another, with the latter person's full consent."[6] The author summarizes much of the first two books, adding incidents that were not included there, such as an account of an astral journey he made with Lama Mingyar Dondup to another planet in which he received instructions from extraterrestrials.

Rampa recounts that the Japanese fishing boat eventually ran aground, and that he was left for dead, only to wake up in a cottage where an old Buddhist priest was watching over him. The boat had crossed the Sea of Japan and landed near the Russian lines. Because of his telepathic ability to calm the fiercest Russian mastiff patrol dogs ("not so fierce as Tibetan mastiffs" [p. 44]), he was drafted into the Russian army in Vladivostok to be a dog trainer. There he became known as "Comrade Priest."

Some weeks later he hid on a freight train bound for Moscow and was there arrested by security police. After being tortured in Lubianka prison, he was released and deported to Poland. On the way there the Russian truck he was riding in was involved in an accident and he was seriously injured. While in the hospital he was transported to a world beyond the astral, "The Land of Golden Light," to recuperate, and there was met by Lama Mingyar Dondup (who had been murdered by the Communists in Tibet) and Sha-lu, a talking cat. He also met the thirteenth Dalai Lama, who urged him to return to earth and continue his work. The problem was that his body was in deplorable condition. But the Dalai Lama had a plan: "We have located a body in the land of England, the owner of which is most anxious to leave. His aura has a fundamental harmonic of yours. Later, if conditions necessitate it, you can take over his body" (p. 71). After the transfer was made, it would take seven years for a complete molecular transformation to take place, after which the new body would be the same as the old one, even bearing the same scars.[7] He was warned, however, that should he decide to return to earth, he would "return to hardship, misunderstanding, disbelief, and actual hatred, for there is a force of evil which tries to prevent all that is good in connection with human evolution" (p. 71).

Back on earth he recovered sufficiently to be deported to Poland, where he was assigned to a road crew. He and another prisoner commandeered a car and escaped to Czechoslovakia, where he was hired by a Viennese smuggler and later an American automobile dealer. He was eventually hired to drive a piece of heavy construction equipment to France. In Cherbourg he signed on as third engineer on a merchant vessel bound for New York. "So, probably for the first time in history, a Tibetan Lama, posing as an American, took his place aboard ship as a watch-keeping engineer" (p. 101).

In America he was hit by a car in the Bronx and while unconscious found himself once more with Lama Mingyar Dondup, who informed him, "You are clearing up all Kharma [*sic*] and are also doing a momentous task, a task which evil powers seek to hinder" (p. 110). After nine weeks in the hospital he got a job as a dishwasher before being hired as a radio announcer in Schenectady, New York. He then took a job driving cars cross-country for a delivery service. In Quebec he sailed for England but upon his arrival was sent back to New York by a corrupt customs officer. Back in New York he was arrested but escaped by jumping off the police launch and was taken in by a family of African-Americans. Recuperating under their care, he was summoned once again to meet astrally with Lama Mingyar Dondup, who told him that there had been further discussions with the man who wanted to abandon his body. "At our behest he changed his name to one more suitable to you" (p. 134). For Rampa, the immediate task was "to get [his] body back to Tibet that it may be preserved" (p. 134). Before his departure he taught the African-Americans how to pray and about the Great Self and the ancient Egyptian art of creating thought forms. A benefactor bought him a ticket for the sea passage to India. In Kalimpong he met a delegation of disguised lamas who accompanied him to an isolated lamasery overlooking Lhasa. There he prepared himself to take over a new body, like the Dalai Lama "taking over the body of a new-born baby" (p. 147).

In the company of an elder lama he made an astral journey to the Akashic

Record to investigate the past of the man whose body he was to inhabit. The man was married and made surgical fittings for a living. During the war he had served as an air raid warden, having been unfit for active duty because of a medical condition. After being contacted by a lama in a dream, he changed his name "because that which he had previously had the wrong vibrations as indicated by our Science of Numbers" (p. 162). Rampa decided to meet with him in the astral plane. He learned that the man hated life in England because of the favoritism of the class system, but that he had always had an interest in Tibet and the Far East. He recounted how one day he had been approached by a lama after being knocked unconscious by a fall from a tree in which he had been trying to photograph an owl. The lama said

> I was drawn to you because your own particular life vibrations are a fundamental harmonic of one for whom I act. So I have come, I have come because I want your body for one who has to continue life in the Western world, for he has a task to do which brooks no interference. . . . Would you like the satisfaction of knowing that your Kharma had been wiped away, that you had materially contributed towards a job of utmost benefit to mankind? . . . Have you no thought for humanity? Are you not willing to do something to redeem your own mistakes, to put some purpose to your own mediocre life? You will be the gainer. The one for whom I act will take over this hard life of yours. (Pp. 167–169)

He agreed. Rampa told him that he would return in a month to take over his body, providing that the man had grown a beard to hide the damage done to Rampa's face by the Japanese.

One month later, accompanied by three lamas, he traveled astrally to London, where he would take over the man's body. The man was instructed to fall out of a tree again, at which point an operation was performed to sever the man from his silver cord and attach Rampa's cord to the man's body. He entered into the Western body with great difficulty, rose to his feet, and was helped inside by the man's wife. He immediately had to seek employment, and found a job developing photographs. He later had various freelance jobs and did "psychological work" to support his wife and himself. When he inquired about a job as a ghostwriter, the literary agent Cyrus Brooks of A. M. Heather & Company encouraged him to write his own book. He was reluctant. "*Me* write a book? Crazy! All I wanted was a job providing enough money to keep us alive and a little over so that I could do auric research, and all the offers I had was [*sic*] to write a silly book about myself" (p. 194). But at the insistence of the agent he undertook the arduous and unpleasant task of writing *The Third Eye*. After completing the book he suffered a heart attack and moved for health reasons to Ireland, "an island which was once part of the lost continent of Atlantis" (p. 198). There he wrote *Doctor from Lhasa*.

He was summoned once more by Lama Mingyar Dondup, who said that he must go to the "Land of the Red Indians," where he had one final task to accomplish. The lama added: "be not upset by those who would criticize you, for they know not whereof they speak, being blinded by the self-imposed ignorance of the West. When Death shall close their eyes, and they become born to the Great Life, then indeed will they regret the sorrows and troubles they have so needlessly caused" (p. 204). Rampa, his wife, and their two cats flew to New York and then to Windsor, Canada, but the climate did not suit him, and he decided to move as soon as he finished *The Rampa Story*, which ends with the prediction of a Chinese nuclear attack launched from Lhasa.

I HAVE RECOUNTED Rampa's story as, perhaps, he would have wanted it to be told, in a seamless chronology. But that is not of course how it was written or how it was read. Especially in the last two books, the narrative does not proceed smoothly but is interrupted with discussions and instructions on various occult arts, most often on astral travel but also on crystal-ball gazing. There are instructions on breath control and accounts of the earth's prehistory, the golden age when extraterrestrial giants visited the earth in flying saucers. There are instructions on ancient Egyptian death practices and discourses on "Kharma" characterized as an evolutionary system in which existence is a school in which we must learn before passing on to the next level; people are impoverished or lose their limbs in order to learn a lesson. He explains that the religion of Tibet is a form of Buddhism, but that "there is no word which can be transliterated." The closest name for the religion of Tibet is, he says, Lamaism, which is different from Buddhism: "ours is a religion of hope and a belief in the future. Buddhism, to us, seems negative, a religion of despair" (p. 115). The prayer of Lamaism is "Om mani pad-me Hum!" which literally means "Hail to the Jewel in the Lotus!" although initiates know that its true meaning is "Hail to Man's Overself!" (p. 116). Rampa would go on to write more than a dozen other books on these and related topics.

I have omitted to this point any mention of the prefaces to the first and second editions of *The Third Eye,* any mention of the persistent claims that everything in the books is true and derives from his personal experience. I have also not made mention of the reception of the book, the criticisms to which Rampa responded with such vehemence.

In 1955 E. P. Dutton in New York sent the manuscript of *The Third Eye* to Hugh Richardson. Born in 1905, Richardson had served as officer-in-charge of the British mission in Lhasa for nine years, beginning in 1936.[8] He returned the manuscript with many corrections (Rampa's father could not have been a "monk minister" because monks are celibate; Tibetan officials wear one earring, not two) and offered his opinion that the book was "a fake built from published works and embellished by a fertile imagination."[9] Dutton rejected the manuscript on Richardson's recommendation. The manuscript was then sent to Secker & Warburg in London. Fredric Warburg met with the author, who read his palm and correctly told him his age and that he had recently been involved in a criminal case. He also informed Warburg that his firm was the karmically appropriate publisher for his book. Secker & Warburg obtained a copy of Richardson's review. Some of the mistakes were corrected and the manuscript was sent to almost twenty experts on Tibet, including the Tibetologist David Snellgrove and the mountaineers Heinrich Harrer and Marco Pallis. When confronted with their objections, the author was offered the option of publishing the book as a work of fiction, but he insisted that it was entirely factual. Secker & Warburg published the book in 1956, with the following preface:

> The autobiographical account of the experiences of a Tibetan lama is such an exceptional document that it is difficult to establish its authenticity. We tried to obtain confirmation of the author's claims by submitting his manuscript to twenty readers chosen for their intelligence and experience, among whom were some who possess in-depth knowledge of the subject. Their opinions were so contradictory that we could not obtain a positive result. It was not always the same passages whose accuracy was disputed, and what appeared doubtful to one expert was accepted without reservation by another. But then we asked ourselves, was there any expert in the world who had undergone the full training of a Tibetan lama? Was there anyone who had been brought up in a Tibetan family?

From the documents furnished by Lobsang Rampa it can be ascertained that he holds a diploma from the Medical University of Chungking [the diploma was in English rather than Chinese, badly typed and festooned with what appeared to be bottle caps] and that he holds the title of Lama of the Monastery of the Potala in Lhasa. In the course of numerous conversations we were able to determine the exceptional character of his faculties and his knowledge. On many points of his personal life he displayed a discretion that was sometimes disconcerting. But each person has the right to a private life and Lobsang Rampa assures us that because Tibet is occupied by the Communists, he is obliged to maintain a certain discretion in order not to compromise the security of his family. That is why some details, such as the real position occupied by his father in the Tibetan hierarchy, for example, are reported in a deliberately inexact way.

All of this explains why the Author must bear—and willingly takes—sole responsibility for the statements made in his book. We might sometimes think that he stretches the limits of Occidental credulity, although our understanding in this field cannot be held to be definitive. The publishers are nonetheless persuaded that *The Third Eye* essentially constitutes an authentic document on the education and formation of a young Tibetan in the bosom of his family and in a lamasery. It is for that, and for that alone, that we are publishing this book. We think that those who believe differently will at least agree that one can recognize in the Author a rare talent for storytelling and a capacity of felicitously evoking scenes and characters as exceptional as they are captivating.[10]

It was an immediate bestseller and was translated into German and French. The book sold some three hundred thousand copies during the first eighteen months and went through nine hardback printings in the United Kingdom in two years. The small community of European experts on Tibet, most of whom had reviewed the manuscript, was outraged. Snellgrove's review began, "This is a shameless book."[11] Pallis declared the book to be a wild fabrication and a libel on both Tibet and its religion. Harrer denounced the book in a scathing review, occasioning the threat of a libel suit from the German publisher. Richardson, Britain's leading expert on Tibet, offered to review the book for the *Times Literary Supplement*. But the *Times* had already found a reviewer, who concluded, "There is no doubt that this book was worth publishing, since, though it would be a matter of extraordinary difficulty to say whether it is a work of truth, it comes near to being a work of art. . . . [E]ven those who exclaim 'magic, moonshine, or worse' are likely to be moved by the nobility of the ethical system which produces such beliefs and such men as the author." [12] Richardson published his own brief review on the same day (November 30, 1956) in the *Daily Telegraph and Morning Post* in London. I cite it here in full:

Imaginary Tibet

BY HUGH RICHARDSON

A book which plays up to public eagerness to hear about "Mysterious Tibet" has the advantage that few people have the experience to refute it. But anyone who has lived in Tibet will feel after reading a few pages of "The Third Eye" (Secker & Warburg. 18s) that its author, "T. Lobsang Rampa," is certainly not a Tibetan.

Local colour has apparently been borrowed from standard works, but is applied as inappropriately as the decoration of a magpie's nest. There are innumerable wild inaccuracies about Tibetan life and manners which give the impression of Western suburbia playing charades.

The samples of the Tibetan language betray ignorance of both colloquial and literary forms; there is a series of wholly un-Tibetan obsessions with cruelty, fuss and bustle and, strangely, with cats. Moreover, the turn of phrase in the slick colloquial English is quite unconvincing when attributed to a Tibetan writer.

Given that this is the work of a non-Asian mind—and if I am mistaken, I should be happy to make amends to the author in person and in Tibetan—one can regard only as indifferent juvenile fiction the catchpenny accoutrements of magic and mystery: the surgical opening of "the third eye"; the man-lifting kites; the Abominable Snowman; the Shangri-la valley and eerie goings-on in caverns below the Potala. [13]

But most reviews were positive, with *Kirkus* finding that "the prevailing effect is credible and unassuming," [14] and *Library Journal* observing that "Very few books have been written by 'insiders,' born and educated there, hence every such publication is of great interest. Recommended for specialized libraries, though the taste of the public for books of this nature seems to be increasing." [15]

In January 1957, the author was interviewed by Scotland Yard, which asked to see a Tibetan passport or residence permit, which he was unable to produce. Shortly thereafter he moved to Ireland. On January 7, 1958, Marco

Pallis, acting on behalf of a group of European experts on Tibet, retained the services of Clifford Burgess, a leading Liverpool private detective, in an effort to discover the true identity of T. Lobsang Rampa. By the end of the month and three thousand miles of travel, Burgess had produced the following report:

CYRIL HENRY HOSKIN—BIOGRAPHICAL DETAILS

Born 8th April, 1910, at Plympton, St. Maurice, Devonshire, England.
Father—Joseph Henry Hoskin, Master Plumber (born 1878 in Plymouth).
Mother—Eva Hoskin (name before marriage—Martin).
Sister—Dorothy Winifred Hoskin, born 21st March, 1905, Plympton, St.
    Maurice, Devonshire.
This sister is now married to the Rev. Illingsworth-Butler, rector of Linby,
    Nottinghamshire.
Hoskin's father kept a plumber's shop in the Ridgeway, Plympton, Devon.
He attended Plympton village school. Left at the age of 15.

He was always a delicate child. He never did any work after leaving school, except to potter around his father's shop, supposed to be helping his father. He was a very odd child. People considered him a complete crank. He was always experimenting with electrical things and insects. As a child he never played with other children. He was considered by people who knew him to be a spoilt child. As a teenager he helped in his father's shop occasionally, but would lay in bed for days at a time and was considered lazy.

The mother sold the property in Plympton and took Cyril to live at the married daughter's house.

In 1940 the mother and Cyril left Annesley and went to live at 13, Warwick Avenue, London, W. 2. Hoskin was then employed by a Surgical Goods Manufacturing Company and described as a Works Manager.

Later in 1940, he obtained a job as a Correspondence Clerk for a London firm offering education by correspondence courses. As a result of bombing, this firm moved to Weybridge, Surrey, and Hoskin went there, living in a flat provided by the Company.

On 13th August, 1940, he married Sarah Anne Pattinson, a nurse at a Richmond hospital. She is a native of Cumberland.

During his time with the Correspondence firm at Weybridge, he became more and more peculiar in his manner, and among many strange things he did was:—(1) he used to take his cat out for walks on a lead (2) during this period he began to call himself KUAN-SUO and he had all the hair shaved off his head.

He left his firm in September, 1948. After which he lived in rooms near Weybridge for some months and then went to South London where he was subsequently seen carrying on business of sorts as a photographer. His activities between 1950 and 1954 are somewhat vague, but he was seen by one person who knew him and said that he was "A Criminal and Accident Photographer."

He next appears living in Bayswater in 1954 calling himself Dr. Kuan-Suo and is about to write "The Third Eye."

Until he went to live in Dublin there is no evidence of his ever having left the British Isles.[16]

The report presents the picture of a man who grew up in a rural village, the son of a master plumber and thus a member of the working gentry and financially comfortable, sufficiently so that his son was able to attend school until the age of fifteen. The son seems to have been something of a disappointment, especially compared with his sister, who married above her station. He did not join the family business, but held a variety of jobs, including that of making "surgical fittings" (corsets, trusses, and other unmentionables). He seems also not to have served in the war.

The detective reported elsewhere that after he changed his name, the former Hoskin wrote a rhyme to the managing director of the career-counseling firm where he worked: "You may wonder why I go on so / But will you please remember I am Kuan Suo." He was fired shortly thereafter and some time later approached a literary agent with two manuscripts, one on corsets and one on Tibet.[17]

On February 1, 1958, the *Scottish Daily Mail* ran the story "Third Eye Lama Exposed as Fake," and for the next week it was the main story in the British press; the February 3 *Daily Express* ran the headline "The FULL truth about the Bogus Lama." The same edition carried an article by Fredric J. Warburg of Secker & Warburg, who claimed to have had doubts all along; he recounts that to test Rampa he had a Tibetologist phoneticize the phrase "Did you have a nice journey, Mr. Rampa?" which he read to Rampa. When Rampa did not reply, Warburg informed him that it was Tibetan. Rampa then fell on the floor in apparent agony, rising to explain that when he was tortured by the Japanese, who sought secret information about Tibet, he had hypnotically blocked his knowledge of Tibetan (as well as Chinese and Japanese) and had never recovered his native tongue. Even hearing Tibetan caused him torment, and he warned Warburg that it would be unwise to press him further on the matter.[18] In Germany, the February 6 issue of *Die Zeit* ran the story "Der Pseudotibetaner." On February 17, 1958, *Time* magazine ran the article "Private v. Third Eye." In response to reporters' questions, the lama's wife explained that her husband had written the book for the real Dr. Ku'an, a Tibetan whose family was in hiding from the Chinese Communists. For his safety, Dr. Kuan's whereabouts could not be revealed. Hoskin, who could not meet with reporters because of his health, sent a message: "This story is true, but for very special reasons the identity of the Tibetan author cannot be revealed."[19] Shortly thereafter, however, he made a tape recording for a British television program in which he said, "Some time ago, I had the strangest premonition, the strangest urges, and even against my will I was compelled to change my name. . . . I had a slight concussion. And my body was actually taken over by the spirit of an Easterner."[20]

When *The Third Eye* was reprinted it contained "A Statement by the Author," which begins, "In the East it is commonly acknowledged that the stronger mind can take possession of another body" (p. 7). It goes on to recount that in late 1947 Cyril Hoskin felt a strange and irresistible compulsion to adopt Eastern ways of living. Some months later he legally changed his name to Carl Kuon Suo (later to Carl Ku'an, to make it easier to pronounce in England). He quit his job and left for a "fairly remote district," where he was beset by hallucinations. His memories of his own life began to fade as impressions of "an Eastern entity" increased. On June 13, 1949, he sustained a concussion in an accident in his garden, after which he had no memory of his earlier life but "the *full* memory of a Tibetan from babyhood onwards." His wife told him enough about his previous identity that he could still pretend to be an Englishman. Furthermore, he declares, "with my Eastern memory I knew where I had papers, and I sent for them to prove my identity. Now I have sent away those papers again because I am not prepared to have them sullied by such doubts as have been caused in this case" (p. 8). He says that the book was written hurriedly and that nothing was copied from another book. Further, "No two 'experts' have been able to agree on any particular fault. The 'experts,' in fact, have managed to contradict each other thoroughly, and that should prove the authenticity of the book because none of them has lived in Tibet as a lama—has entered a lamasery at the age of seven as I have done" (p. 8). Toward the end he notes that there is a great deal of Theosophical literature about possession and that his publishers have a letter from an Indian swami stating that possession is quite common in the

East. In closing he writes, "I state most definitely that my books, *The Third Eye* and *Medical Lama* [apparently the working title of *Doctor from Lhasa*] are true." Signed "T. Lobsang Rampa (C. Ku'an)."

This statement is followed by one from his wife, who supports her husband's account of the name change. She writes, "to my dismay, my husband had an uncontrollable desire to wear Eastern dress and to behave as an Easterner" (p. 9). She confirms the story of the concussion, after which he was no longer the same person: "when I discussed an event of the past he would have no recollection of it. Instead he spoke of life in a lamasery, or his experiences in the war, prison-camp life, or Japanese tortures" (p. 10). Since the summer of 1949 "his whole make-up and manner have been those of an Easterner, his general appearance and colouring have also shown a marked change" (p. 10). She goes on to say that he never wanted to write *The Third Eye* but did so because he could not find employment. She signs her name "S. Ku'an."

The book also contains a foreword to the second edition dated May 25, 1964, in which he accuses English and German newspapers of waging a campaign against him when he could not defend himself because of a heart condition. Later, they would give him no opportunity to respond to the charges against him. He states again that all of his claims are absolutely true and that he has never been proven guilty. He explains that "My specific reason for insisting that all this is true is that in the near future other people like me will appear, and I do not desire that they should have the suffering that I have had through spite and hatred" (p. 5).

This was not his only response to his critics. In *Doctor from Lhasa* he describes an unpleasant incident during the funeral ceremonies for the thirteenth Dalai Lama: "A foreigner was there who wanted all consideration for himself. He thought that we were just natives, and that he was lord of all he surveyed. He wanted to be in the front of everything, noticed by all, and because I would not further his selfish aim—he tried to bribe a friend and me with wrist watches!—he had regarded me as an enemy ever since, and has indeed gone out of his way—has gone to extreme lengths—to injure me and mine" (p. 107). This is perhaps a reference to Hugh Richardson, officer-in-charge of the British mission in Lhasa, although Richardson did not go to Tibet until 1936, three years after the thirteenth Dalai Lama's death.[21]

THERE ARE A HOST of questions raised by Rampa's books, questions raised both by their content and by their reception. At the most cynical level, they are the works of an unemployed surgical fitter, the son of a plumber, seeking to support himself as a ghostwriter. The first book, as Richardson suggests, could have been drawn from various English language sources, all easily available at the time (Edwin John Dingle's *My Life in Tibet* seems one possible source), supplemented with an admixture of garden variety spiritualism and Theosophy; the books contain discussions of auras, astral travel, prehistoric visits to earth by extraterrestrials, predictions of war, and a belief in the spiritual evolution of humanity. It is this blending that may account in part for the book's appeal, providing an exotic route through Tibet back to the familiar themes of Victorian and Edwardian spiritualism, in which Tibet often served as a placeholder.

With the unexpected success of the book, the ghostwriter could go on to concoct a story that would allow the ghost to become flesh. The second and third books, indeed, have little to do with life in Tibet, even as described by Rampa. Their raison d'être, beyond the obvious demand for a sequel placed upon the author of an unexpected bestseller, seems to be to account, picaresquely, for the period between around 1930, when Rampa left Lhasa at the end of *The Third Eye*, and 1956, when *The Third Eye* was published. In a sense, the other two books serve as an extended apologia for the first in that they attempt to account not only for the time but more importantly for the authorship, explaining how an eyewitness account of life in Tibet in which everything is true could have been written by Cyril Hoskin, who had never left England.

If we were to leave it at that, the works of Rampa would have little reason to detain the scholar, who has better things to do than concern himself with works that are clearly the products of an impostor. As the anthropologist Agehananda Bharati described Madame Blavatsky's *The Secret Doctrine*: "[it] is such a melee of horrendous hogwash and of fertile inventions of inane esoterica, that any Buddhist and Tibetan scholar is justified to avoid mentioning it in any context." [22] In seeking information from colleagues in the United States about Rampa, I found that, although everyone I spoke to had heard of *The Third Eye*, few admitted to actually having read it. But *The Third Eye* was a bestseller in twelve countries in the first year of its publication (earning its author twenty thousand pounds in royalties), and forty years later remains in print and widely available in several languages. How are we to account for this appeal? Its very popularity may be one reason why it has generally been ignored by professional scholars of Tibet.

I recently used *The Third Eye* in a seminar for first-year undergraduates at the University of Michigan, having them read it without telling them any-thing of its history. (The edition currently available in the United States for some reason omits the "Statement by the Author.") The students were unani-mous in their praise of the book, and despite six prior weeks of lectures and readings on Tibetan history and religion (including classics such as R. A. Stein's *Tibetan Civilization*), they found it entirely credible and compelling, judging it more realistic than anything they had previously read about Tibet, appreciating the detail about "what Tibet was really like," giving them "a true understanding about Tibet and Buddhism." Many of the things they had read about Tibet seemed strange until then; these things seemed more reason-able when placed within the context of a lama's life. It is not that the things Rampa described were not strange; it was that they were so strange that they could not possibly have been concocted. When I told them about the book's author, they were shocked, but immediately wanted to separate fact from fiction. How much of the book was true?

With the author unmasked they awoke from their mystified state, and with eyes opened turned away from Rampa and toward me for authority. Each of their questions began, "Did Tibetans really . . . ?" "Did Tibetans really perform amputations without anesthesia, with the patients using breath control and hypnotism instead?" "Did monks really eat communally and in silence while the Scriptures were read aloud?" "If a monk violated the eight-fold path, was he punished by having to lie motionless face down across the door of the temple for a full day, without food or drink?" "Are the priests in Tibet vegetarian?" "Did priests really only ride white horses?" "Were horses really only ridden every other day?" "Did acolytes really wear white robes?" "Did cats really guard the temple jewels?" [23] "At the New Year's festival, did monks really dress as giant buddhas and walk through the streets on stilts?" "Were there really man-bearing kites in Tibet?" And of course, "Did they really perform the operation of the third eye?"

The answer to each of these questions was no. But by what authority did I confidently make such a pronouncement? I had not lived in old Tibet and so could not contradict Rampa's claims with my own eyewitness testimony. It was, rather, that I had never seen any mention of such things in any of the books that I had read about Tibet—in English, French, or Tibetan. From reading other books, I had learned the standards of scholarly evidence, the need for corroboration by citing sources in footnotes. [24] And because I had read a sufficient number of such books, I was awarded a doctorate some years ago, and with the proper documents in my possession to prove my identity had been given the power to consecrate and condemn the products of others, and the power to initiate others into this knowledge. This power, the power to speak both with authority and as an authority, that is, the power to bestow value, had been passed on to me by my teachers, who had in turn received it from their teachers. It was this power that was embodied in my "no." But this power had come at a price. For by accepting this power I had had to forever disavow any interest in the possible commercial profits that might derive from my work. It was necessary that I renounce any self-interest in the economic value of my work, exchanging such capital for something higher and more noble because it was severed from crass material interests. This was symbolic capital, which would in its own way provide for my financial security by insuring that I would never have to offer my services to a publisher as a ghostwriter in order to support my wife and my cat, as Cyril Hoskin had done.[25] The work of scholarship, like the work of art, retains its aura only when it is not reproduced too widely. Were it to sell a million copies, its aura of authority would fade.

It is not that Rampa's claims can be dismissed because they are too strange. Had his research extended to include Evans-Wentz's *Tibetan Yoga and Secret Doctrines,* he would have learned about 'pho ba, or "transference of consciousness," one of the six teachings of the tenth-century Indian tantric master Nāropa (*Na ro chos drug*), whereby one can transfer one's own consciousness into that of another being (preferably a well-preserved corpse). The most famous case of consciousness transference in Tibetan literature is found in the biography of Marpa (Mar pa, 1012–1096), the teacher of Tibet's great yogin Milarepa. Marpa's son, Darmadoday (Dar ma mdo sde), after fracturing his skull in an equestrian accident, transferred his consciousness into the body of a recently deceased pigeon, since no human corpse could be found on short notice. The bird was then given directions by Marpa for flying across the Himalayas to India, where it discovered the fresh corpse of a thirteen-year-old brahman boy; the bird transferred its consciousness into the boy and then expired. The boy rose from the funeral pyre prior to his immolation and grew up to become the great yogin Tipupa (Ti phu pa).[26] Compared to this a Tibetan taking over the body of an unemployed Englishman seems rather mundane.

Or Rampa may have appealed to Tibetan theories of possession. René de Nebesky-Wojkowitz, in *Oracles and Demons of Tibet* (published in 1956, the same year as *The Third Eye*), describes in detail the manner in which a deity, a mundane protector of the dharma (*'jigs rten pa'i srung ma*), takes possession of the body of another, descending uninvited into an unsuspecting person who will become its medium, called in Tibetan the *sku brten* (physical foundation) of the deity. Nebesky-Wojkowitz details the tests that Tibetans use to determine whether the possessing entity is a deity or the roaming spirit of the dead.[27]

Or Rampa might have made an appeal to one of the oldest and most storied Buddhist techniques of legitimation, the discovery of the text. Since scholars have little concrete knowledge about what the Buddha actually taught, it is in some ways misleading to use the term *apocryphon* to refer to a Buddhist text. Over the millennia, however, competing Buddhist groups have disputed the legitimacy of a given text. In arguing for the authenticity of the Mahayana sutras as the word of the Buddha, despite their having appeared some four centuries after his death, the proponents of those sutras explained that the discourses had indeed been spoken by the Buddha but to a select audience (which sometimes was not physically present but heard his words through the power of clairaudience). Then, at the Buddha's behest, they were hidden—in the heavens, under the sea, in the earth—until a predetermined point in the future when the world would be more receptive to their revelation.[28] As discussed in the last chapter, this argument was deployed as well for the teachings of Padmasambhava, who during his brief visit to Tibet at the end of the eighth century is said to have hidden teachings, called *terma* (*gter ma*), "treasures," throughout the landscape. Hidden in rocks, at the bottoms of lakes, or inside statues and pillars, the texts were discovered over the centuries (and into the present century) at the appropriate historical moment by the future incarnations of the prophesied disciples of Padmasambhava. The prophecies themselves were generally contained in the rediscovered texts. (As Wilde writes of Wordsworth, "He found in stones the sermons he had already hidden there.")[29] Treasure texts could also be discovered not in the earth but in the mind of the discoverer. These were *dgongs gter*, "mind treasures," teachings of Padmasambhava that had remained pristine and uncorrupted, concealed in the discoverer's mind, to be revealed first to the discoverer and then to the world. The literature of the Nyingma and Bönpo sects contains entire canons of treasure texts, and there is a substantial literature on techniques for determining their authenticity.[30] False discoverers of *terma* are said to be incarnations of evil ministers from Tibet's ancient history, supported in their nefarious efforts by demons. As one text states:

There are many people in this dark age whose minds are not stable, who want to do hundreds of things; who behave hastily like monkeys and start to carry out whatever ideas cross their minds without examining them. They are possessed by Theu ring and other spirits who enjoy playing with various kinds of deceptive miracles. These spirits exhibit many deceptive illusions in various forms such as psychic vision teachings and dream teachings, and they mislead such people. They have the same negative effects as in the case of false discovered texts.[31]

Yet the authenticity of a *terma* is difficult to judge, and the behavior of the text discoverer is explicitly excluded from the criteria. False discoverers may be of good conduct and have harmonious relations with their community, and true discoverers may indulge in all forms of reprehensible behavior, thereby taking onto themselves obstructions that would ordinarily beset others, while demonstrating that all experience is ultimately of one taste (*ro gcig pa*).[32]

Why not then see *The Third Eye* as a mind treasure, a *dgong gter*, discovered unexpectedly in the mind of Cyril Hoskin at a crucial moment, in 1956, soon after the People's Liberation Army had occupied Lhasa and the Dalai Lama had met with Chairman Mao? Why not see the book as having brought the plight of Tibet to an otherwise indifferent audience of hundreds of thousands of Westerners, who would remain unconcerned were it not for the trappings of astral travel, spiritualism, and the hope of human evolution to a new age?

What is perhaps of greater interest, however, is the compulsion of the scholar to "correct" Rampa, to point out those elements of the authentic Tibetan tradition that are somehow analogous to his fabrications, to suggest how, if only he had been better informed, if only he knew what the scholar knows, he could have made his hoax more credible. It is just such correction that I have provided with my duly footnoted reports on consciousness transference, spirit possession, and treasure texts.

With Caucasian children in Europe and America now being identified as incarnations of Tibetan lamas (as in Bertolucci's *The Little Buddha*), what is it about *The Third Eye* that so enrages the expert, apart from the fact that Cyril Hoskin was of the wrong social class to qualify as an authentic English eccentric? It is a question of authority, and how it is established and maintained. The classic exposition of authority is that of Max Weber, who distinguishes between charismatic and traditional authority, which together eventually yielded, at least in the West, to legal authority. Weber defines charisma as "an extraordinary quality of a person, regardless of whether this quality is actual, alleged, or presumed," and defines charismatic authority as "a rule over men, whether predominantly external or internal, to which the governed submit because of their belief in the extraordinary quality of the specific *person*." [33] Traditional authority is domination that rests, instead, "on the belief in the everyday as an inviolable norm of conduct"; it is a "piety for what actually, allegedly, or presumably has always existed." [34] The distinction between charismatic authority and traditional authority is difficult to discern, much less maintain, in the case of Tibet, where so much authority of both forms has rested with religious clerics. Indeed, the entire system of incarnate lamas can be seen, in Weber's terms, as an attempt to transform charisma into tradition, as something to be passed down through generations in time. Whether or not Rampa possessed charisma is difficult to judge; those who met him invariably noted the remarkable depression in the middle of his forehead. And *The Third Eye* derives its authority from the extraordinary quality of the person alleged to be the author. But Weber is less helpful on how charisma is lost, and that is perhaps the more mystifying question in the case of Rampa.

Authority derives, at least terminologically, from the Latin *auctoritas*, four kinds of which are specified in Roman law: the authority of the senate, of the emperor, of a trustee, and of the seller (*auctoritas venditoris*). The last refers to the authority of the seller to own the goods he sells; as a kind of speech, it is a guarantee of title required for a sale to occur. [35] We can read the protracted tale of T. Lobsang Rampa's possession of Cyril Hoskin's body as the author's attempt to rescue and restore his claim to the person of Rampa once it had been challenged by Richardson and others. That he was successful in securing the ability to sell is evident in the fact that he wrote a dozen more books after *The Rampa Story*. Yet he remains an object of derision among the cognoscenti, that is, the authorities.

In a recent book, Pierre Bourdieu describes authoritative speech:

> In fact, the use of language, the manner as much as the substance of discourse, depends on the social position of the speaker, which governs the access he can have to the language of the institution, that is, to the official, orthodox and legitimate speech. It is the access to the legitimate instruments of expression, and therefore the participation in the authority of the institution, which makes all the difference—irreducible to discourse as such—

between the straightforward imposture of masqueraders . . . . and the authorized imposture of those who do the same thing with the authority and authorization of an institution.[36]

Rampa's authority is established by his identity as a Tibetan lama. Once Rampa is shown to be nothing more than Cyril Hoskin the audience can no longer accept his authority. *Doctor from Lhasa* and *The Rampa Story* thus try to reclaim that authority by showing why Hoskin is Rampa. It is significant that in his various prefaces and author's statements Rampa makes no attempt to argue for the accuracy of the contents of his books; he simply declares that they are true. By 1971 and *The Hermit*, his author's statement had been reduced to the following: "I, the author, state that this book is absolutely true. Some people who are bogged down in materialism may prefer to consider it as fiction. The choice is yours—believe or disbelieve according to your state of evolution. I am NOT prepared to discuss the matter or to answer questions about it. This book, and ALL my books, are TRUE!"[37] In an attempt to reclaim his authority he offers his readers the possibility of once more regarding him as if he were a Tibetan lama. This authority is essential to his identity, a point that eluded Agehananda Bharati in his diatribe against "Rampaism" when he wrote, "I never saw why Don Juan must be a Yaqui (which he is not) to teach something important, nor why a Hoskins [*sic*] must be a Tibetan (which he is not) if *he* has something important to teach."[38]

The problem for Rampa, however, is that in the Tibetan tradition charisma is inextricable from institution. The authority to speak is passed on through a lineage, a lineage that operates regardless of historical gaps and fissures. Hoskin cannot serve as the authorized representative of Lamaism because he does not partake of the authority of any institution certified by Tibetans or Tibetologists. In his review of *Doctor from Lhasa*, Richardson wrote "No one of my acquaintance who has lived in Tibet and knows the Tibetans—including a genuine Tibetan lama to whom I read the book—had any doubt that it was an impudent fake." Like the *skeptron*, the scepter, that was passed among the speakers in the Argives' assembly, its possession authorizing speech, the institutions of Tibet, whether the monastic academy, the descent of a deity, or the identification of a *tulku* (even with a Golden Urn), authorize speech. As Bourdieu notes "The spokesperson is an impostor endowed with the *skeptron*."[39] Cyril Hoskin, like Thersites in book 2 of the *Iliad*, attempted to speak without the scepter being passed to him. And as Odysseus rebuked Thersites and struck him with the scepter, leaving a wound on his back, so Hugh Richardson (and the authorities he spoke for) showed Rampa to be an impostor who had no right to speak of Tibet, leaving one to wonder whether the depression between Hoskin's eyes was not the sign of a more fatal wound, one that brought an end to his short life as an authority on Tibet, but also caused him to be reborn in another realm, for the condemnation by a scholar carries with it a kind of consecration. In wrathful tantric rites in Tibet, demons are dispelled with an act of *sgrol*, a verb that means both to liberate and to kill. We are left to wonder whether Hoskin would have assumed the identity of Rampa if he had not been exposed by the experts, for it is important to recall that the elaborate explanation of the transformation of Cyril Hoskin into Lobsang Rampa appears only after the public furor caused by the private detective's report.

And so Hoskin, or Ku'an, or Rampa, who wanted only to be a ghostwriter, became a ghost. As he says in *The Rampa Story,* "my lonely Tibetan body [lay] safely stored in a stone coffin, under the unceasing care of three monks" (p. 174). The unlaid ghost was left to wander from England to Ireland to Canada, where he died in Calgary in 1981. In the process he acquired the traditional authority of another institution, that of the vast literature of spiritualism, going on to write more than a dozen books on such authorized occult topics as interstellar travel, ouija boards, and the lost years of Jesus. Like a ghost he seemed to wander between two worlds, finding a home in neither. The representation of Tibetan Buddhism historically has been and continues to be situated in a domain where the scholarly and the popular commingle, a domain that is neither exclusively one or the other. The confluence of the scholarly and the popular is strikingly evident in *The Third Eye,* where Rampa draws on the accounts of travelers and amateur scholars (themselves sites of the admixture of the popular and scholarly) and combines them with standard occult elements (astral travel, rites from ancient Egypt, etc.) into a work that is neither wholly fact nor wholly fiction. It is evident that by the time Rampa wrote his "memoir" there was ample material available from scholars, travelers, and Theosophists to enable him to paint a portrait of Tibet in which his own contributions seemed entirely plausible. Furthermore, he was able to represent the Tibet of Western fantasies in such a way that he himself could be embodied within it. Tibet, a domain with the power to allow him to assume a new identity without leaving England: the son of a Devon plumber could become the scion of the Lhasa aristocracy; a man who made surgical fittings could become a surgeon; a criminal and accident photographer, confined to a world of mechanical reproduction, could see auras.

The author of *The Third Eye*, decried as a fraud, was not exactly a fraud, because, if we are to believe the testimony of those who knew him, he really did believe that he was T. Lobsang Rampa. He may have been delusional; he may not have been a huckster. He set out to be a ghostwriter, someone who writes for and in the name of another, receiving payment in exchange for the credit of authorship. But he was not a ghostwriter in this sense, because he came to assume the identity of the one in whose name he wrote. And the book that he produced also confounds the standard literary categories. It may have begun as a bestseller, a book that is marketed for its short-term profitability, but in its own way it has also become a classic, a work that sells well over time. The bestseller is authorized by the public and those who serve it: the publishing companies and the popular media. The current edition of *The Third Eye* (which according to the cover is to be shelved under "Inspirational") contains raves from the *Times Literary Supplement*—"It comes near to being a work of art"—and the *Miami Herald*: "What fascinates the reader is not only a strange land—and what could be stranger than Tibet?—but [Rampa's] skill in interpreting the philosophy of the East." The classic, on the other hand, is certified by the scholar, who insures its commercial durability by providing a reliable market for the book in the educational system, as I have done by assigning *The Third Eye* to my class.

It is not simply that the scholar needs the dilettante to define his identity. Lobsang Rampa is rather like the *lü* (*glud*) (translated by some as "scapegoat" but derived from the verb *glu,* meaning "to deceive" and "to seduce"), the ransom offered to the demons in a Tibetan exorcism ceremony in exchange for the spirit of the possessed. The officiating lama, the person authorized to perform the exorcism, makes a dough effigy of the person possessed. In order to empower the simulacrum, the possessed person both breathes on the effigy and mixes his saliva into the dough. The effigy is then dressed in a garment made from clothing belonging to the possessed. In addition, precious substances, such as pieces of turquoise, are pressed into the dough. The lama then summons the demons, offers them gifts, and effusively praises the effigy. In return for releasing the person they possess, the demons are offered something of greater value, the effigy.

This does not seem to be a case of tricking the demons into thinking that the effigy is the person, but rather of convincing them that the effigy is of greater value. In effect, the person possessed, in order to save himself, gives up something of himself by pressing precious substances into the body of his substitute. Once the exchange is complete, the effigy, now considered to be in the possession of the demons, is carried to a safe distance outside the community, where it is abandoned. In this strange version of mimesis, then, a double is created: endowed with the qualities of beauty and wealth that one has so long desired, it is then expelled to be consumed by demons. To escape the demons, wealth and power must be renounced. The effigy is not, therefore, precisely a scapegoat because what is expelled from the city is not what is most vile, instead, the seductive and the exalted—beauty, wealth, and power—are ostracized.[40]

And so Rampa, invested with the wealth of his royalties, which the scholar must renounce, is given to the public disguised as a Tibetan. In the bargain he derives his livelihood. Rampa wrote nineteen books that have sold over four million copies as well as a large quantity of incense, meditation robes, and crystal balls. His subsequent works include *Living with the Lama* (1964), dictated telepathically by his cat Mrs. Fifi Greywhiskers, and *My Visits to Venus* (1966, the royalties of which were to be donated to Save a Cat League of New York). In return, the scholar, by renouncing the public, gets his identity as a scholar back. He receives symbolic capital by disavowing that upon which he is ultimately dependent (and which is embodied by Lobsang Rampa): the continuing fascination with Tibet that sells Rampa's books also brings students to our classrooms, the public to our lectures, and readers to our monographs. The question that remains is that of the persistent confluence of the two institutions that Rampa floated between, Tibetology and spiritualism, one that cast him out and one that embraced him. He remains a figure of ambivalence. When I was discussing Rampa with Tibetologists and Buddhologists in Europe, many confessed that *The Third Eye* was the first book about Tibet that they had ever read; for some it was a fascination with the world Rampa described that had led them to become professional scholars of Tibet. Thus, some said, despite the fact that Rampa was a fraud, he had had "a good effect."

The parable of the burning house in the *Lotus Sutra* tells of a father distraught as his children blithely play, unaware that their house is ablaze. Knowing their respective predilections for playthings, he lures them from the inferno with the promise that he has a cart for each waiting outside, a deer-drawn cart for one, a goat-drawn cart for another, and so on. When they emerge from the conflagration, they find only one cart, a magnificent conveyance drawn by a great white ox, something that they had never even dreamed of. The burning house is samsara; the children are ignorant sentient beings, unaware of the dangers of their abode; the father is the Buddha, who lures them out of samsara with a variety of vehicles to liberation, knowing that there is in fact but one vehicle, the Buddha vehicle, whereby all beings will be conveyed to enlightenment. After telling the parable, the Buddha asks his disciple Śāriputra whether the father lied to his children. Śāriputra says no, the prevarication was necessary to save the children's lives. The parable suggests that it is permissible for a buddha to teach what is not in fact true if it serves a greater good. Perhaps not surprisingly, this is the only Buddhist text cited by Rampa in the trilogy.[41]

Unlike Śāriputra, the scholars coaxed into Tibetology by Rampa must declare that what they learned in their academic study of Tibet was that the person who called them to their careers, Tuesday Lobsang Rampa, was a liar. In order to become professional scholars, they had to renounce any interest in that which had served as the precondition for their eventual scholarly identity. It is, indeed, the very reading of Rampa that ultimately brings about the death of Rampa. Some might see this as a case of killing the father, but it might be more accurately described in the Freudian sense as a disavowal or denial (*Verleugnung*), a mode of defense in which the subject refuses to recognize the reality of a traumatic perception: in this case the scholar fondly remembers Rampa for his "good effect," refusing to acknowledge that he represents everything that the scholar most loathes, that it was this fraud that brought them to their profession.[42]

At Borders Bookstore in Ann Arbor, Michigan, books on Asian religions are back to back with books on astrology, the tarot, and the New Age. The books face away from each other, making it impossible to peruse both at the same time, yet they support each other; one would fall without the other behind it. The ghost of Rampa continues to haunt us, sometimes looming behind, sometimes shimmering at the periphery. For not all bookstores have such an extensive inventory, and we will always be startled, in an uncanny moment, to find his books next to ours on the shelf marked "Occult."

CHAPTER FOUR

The Spell

Om Mani padme hum, O, the Jewel in the Lotus: Amen. This prayer is an invocation of Pad-mapāni who is believed to have delivered it to the Tibetans; it is the most frequently repeated of all prayers, and has on this account excited the curiosity of the earliest visitors to Tibet. Its real meaning, however, was long involved in doubt, and it is only by the most recent researches that a positive determination has been finally arrived at. EMIL SCHLAGINTWEIT, 1863

In the short story "The Three Hermits," Tolstoy tells of a bishop traveling by ship across the White Sea. En route he notices a sailor pointing out a small island in the distance where three hermits are said to live. The bishop has the captain divert the ship to the island, where he finds three old men waiting on the shore, standing hand in hand. The bishop offers to instruct them, but first asks them how they pray. They tell him that their prayer is "Three are ye, three are we, have mercy upon us." The bishop explains to them that, although well intentioned, they are not praying properly. He explains the doctrine of the Trinity and then teaches them the Lord's Prayer, phrase by phrase. The hermits have great difficulty; one has no teeth, the beard of another has grown over his mouth. Eventually, however, they are able to recite the entire prayer without prompting and the bishop is rowed back to the ship, listening to them recite as he leaves the island. He returns to the ship grateful to God that he has had this opportunity to teach the hermits.[1]

Tolstoy's story raises certain questions: Who knows how to pray, the professional or the unlettered (though pure in heart)? And what of the words? Is it their form, repetition, enunciation, or meaning that is more important?

When the term "prayer" occurs in accounts of Tibetan religion, it is often followed by the word "wheel." No Tibetan artifact, not the skull cup or the thigh bone trumpet, has elicited more comment than the so-called prayer wheel, perhaps because during a time in Europe when science and materialism were increasingly seen as the opponents of religion and the spirit, the mechanism of the prayer wheel was construed as something that transgressed a boundary, an unholy union of religion and science, a machine for communing with the divine. Carlyle referred to it as a "Rotatory Calabash" and the Sinologist James Legge wrote, "Go to Tibet and Mongolia, and in the bigotry and apathy of the population, in their prayer wheels and cylinders you will find the achievement of the doctrine of the Buddha."[2] Travelers to Tibet and Mongolia during the eighteenth and nineteenth centuries were intrigued by the cylinders packed with scrolls of mantras and fitted with paddles so that they could be turned by the current of a stream, or those that were stationed above a fire and mounted with wings, to be propelled around and around by convection. In his 1862 *Narrative of the War with China in 1860*, Garnet Wolseley observed:

> [S]ome indolent but ingenious devotee invented long ago a machine which is now generally used in all Lhama temples. . . . Prayers with the lips only, and not proceeding from the mind, we are told, avail nothing; but what would all our pastors say to those done by machinery? In Europe we have instruments for all sorts of curious purposes, from sewing trowsers up to calculating decimal fractions; but no one there has ever yet dreamt of carrying the substitution of machinery for mental or bodily labour to such an extent as to take out a patent for a prayer machine. Let me recommend the idea to my Roman Catholic friends as a good one to get through any number of penitential "Aves" at a brisk pace, and with comparative ease to themselves.[3]

Sir Monier-Williams put it more succinctly: "It is to be hoped that when European inventions find their way across the Himālayas, steam-power may not be pressed into the service of these gross superstitions."[4]

The most common prayer wheels were handheld. The Jesuit missionary Ippolito Desideri saw them in Lhasa in 1728: "A portable Manì is a small cylinder pierced by an iron rod, one end of which is fixed into a wooden handle so that the Manì can be carried, as they often are; when the carrier moves his hand the cylinder turns round and he utters the words: Om, manì, pemè, hum."[5] It is this prayer that is most commonly printed on the seemingly endless scrolls of paper and placed inside prayer wheels large and small throughout the vast expanse of Tibetan Buddhist influence. And it is this prayer of only six syllables that has elicited more comment and speculation by Western writers than any other Buddhist formula.

In his 1859 *Die Lamaische Hierarchie und Kirche,* Carl Friedrich Köppen described the role of the six syllables of the mantra in Tibetan life:

> [T]hey are the only thing the ordinary Tibetan and Mongol knows; they are the first words which the child learns to stammer, they are the last sigh of the dying one. The wanderer mutters them on his way, the herdsman at his flocks, the woman at her housework, the monk at all his studies of intuition, i.e., of doing nothing: they are the cry both of war and of triumph. They are to be read everywhere where the Lamaistic church has penetrated, on flags, rocks, trees, walls, stone monuments, implements, paper slips, human skulls and skeletons, etc. They are, according to the opinion of the believers, the essence of all religion, all wisdom and revelation, the path to salvation and the gate of bliss.[6]

Even in Desideri's day, more than a century before, this most famous of mantras was known to Europeans and its meaning was debated. Indeed, it has been an object of fascination since the thirteenth century, when William of Rubruck observed in 1254, "Wherever they go they have in their hands a string of one or two hundred beads, like our rosaries, and they always repeat these words, *on mani baccam,* which is 'God, thou knowest,' as one of them interpreted it to me, and they expect as many rewards from God as they remember God in saying this."[7] In 1626 the Portuguese Jesuit Andrade reported on his recent mission to western Tibet:

> Another time I asked a lama in the presence of the King what means of salvation a sinner could use to be restored to the grace of God, and he

replied that it was sufficient to utter the words *Om ma'ny patmeonry,* which is equivalent to saying: however much I have sinned, I shall still get to heaven. If that is true, I retorted, take a dagger and stab a man in the heart, rob the King of the pearls he wears, insult us with the most extravagant abuse, and then say simply *Om ma'ny patmeonry,* and you are at once absolved and purified from all sins. Do you think that is reasonable?[8]

It seems that Andrade could not find a lama who could tell him the meaning of the mantra, so he provided his own, telling a monk, "As you patter these words like parrots which do not understand what they say, know that *Om ma'ny patmeonry* signifies 'Lord, forgive me my sins.' And from that hour all the monks assigned this meaning to the mysterious words."[9]

Shortly thereafter, Europeans learned that the prayer was directed to a particular deity. In his *China Illustrata* of 1667, the German Jesuit Athanasius Kircher describes the religion of the Tanguts in the city of Lhasa (in the English translation of 1669):

> [I]t hath a King of its own, and is altogether intangled with the foul Errours of Heathenism, it worshippeth Idols with the difference of Deities; amongst which, that which they call *Menipe,* hath the preheminence, and with its ninefold difference of Heads, riseth or terminateth in a Cone of monstrous height. . . . Before this Demon or false God this foolish people performeth their Sacred Rites with many unwonted Gesticulations and Dances, often repeating of these words: *O Manipe Mi Hum, O Manipe Mi Hum,* that is, *O Manipe, save us*; and these sottish people are wont to set many sorts of viands and meats before the idol for the propitiating or appeasing of the Deity, and perform such abominations of idolatry.[10]

But Desideri, who unlike Father Kircher actually went to Tibet and learned the Tibetan language, disputed the rendering of the mantra as "O god Manipe, save us." He provided the mantra's first European translation:

> The interpretation given by the Thibettans of the real words is as follows: the word Om is not a definitive term, but an ornamental one. The second word, Manì, means a jewel, such as a pearl, diamond or any other precious stone. The third word Pemè is the name of a flower which grows in a pond or a lake, and in Hindustani is called Camel pul. The letter E, like our O, is a vocative particle. The last word Hum is not a definite term, but is also purely ornamental, and is used by magicians. To understand the meaning of these words, which have no syntactic construction, I must refer you

to what I have already said about a Thibettan idol called Cen-ree-zij, represented as a youth holding a jewel in his right hand and seated on a flower called Pêmà in Thibettan. These words are, therefore, only an invocation to Cen-ree-zij, the idol and principal advocate of the Thibettans. It runs thus: "O thou who holdest a jewel in Thy right hand, and art seated on the flower Pêmà." They believe that these words were taught to their ancestors by Cen-ree-zij himself as a prayer pleasing to him, and which would deliver them from the long and grievous travail of transmigration.[11]

Desideri's rendering remained unknown until the manuscript of his *Relazione* was discovered in Italy in 1875 and published in 1904. Thus Thomas Astley clearly relied on Kircher when, in his 1747 *New General Collection of Voyages and Travels,* he described the god Menippe: "This is the chief of all the Images, before which the People perform their sacred Rites, with many odd Gesticulations and Dances, often repeating, *O Manipe Mi-hum, O Manipe Mi-hum!,* that is, *O Manipe, save us!*"[12] The German naturalist Peter Simon Pallas, reporting on the religion of the Kalmyks in 1769, wrote:

> Great and holy Lamas, who have been zealous in their office and obtained a victory over all their passions, pass, when they die, by the aid of their prayers only, (of which the words, om ma wie pad, me chum have the greatest influence), immediately into heaven, to the abode of the burchans [buddhas], where they enjoy perfect rest with godly souls, and exercise themselves to divine service, till the time of their regeneration comes.[13]

From this point on, it seemed that no traveler to Tibet or Ladakh could let the mantra pass without comment. In a letter of August 25, 1830, written at "the frontier between Ladakh and Chinese Tartary," the French explorer Victor Jacquemont reported, "How strange it all seemed to me in Tibet, where they also sing a great deal (for there are one or two inhabitants to the square league) but never any song but one, having three words: *Oum mani padmei;* which means, in the learned language, which none of the villagers or their lamas understand: 'O, diamond lotus!'—and takes the singers straight into the paradise of Buddha."[14] In an 1836 article in the *Journal of the Bengal Asiatic Society,* Brian H. Hodgson, British resident at the Court of Nepal, explains in a footnote: "[*Padma-páni*] is figured as a graceful youth, erect, and bearing in either hand a *lotos* and a jewel. The last circumstance explains the meaning of the celebrated *Shadaksharí Mantra,* or six-lettered invocation of him, *viz., Om! Mani padme hom!* of which so many corrupt versions and more corrupt interpretations have appeared from Chinese, Tibetan, Japanese, Mongolian, and other sources."[15]

With the rise of the science of philology in the nineteenth century, the responsibility for the meaning of the mantra was transferred from missionaries, travelers, and colonial officers to professional scholars of Sanskrit, who put forth another interpretation. In an 1831 article entitled "Explication et origine de la formule Bouddhique OM MAṆI PADMÈ HOÛM," Heinrich Julius von Klaproth explains that *padmè* is the locative of *padma* (lotus), such that the mantra means "Oh! The jewel is in the lotus, Amen" (Oh! Le joyau (est) dans le lotus, Amen). He goes on to observe that "Despite this indubitable meaning, the Buddhists of Tibet and of Mongolia are seeking a mystical meaning in each of the six syllables that compose this phrase. There are entire books filled with fanciful explanations."[16] Later in the same article he explains that the meaning of the mantra derives from a legend in which Avalokiteśvara is born from a lotus; all other explanations are futile because "they are nothing but mystical and are in no way based on the meaning of the Sanskrit words that compose the mantra." He notes that if the mantra were to be found in India, it would be among the followers of Śiva, where it would mean "Oh! The lingam is in the yoni, Amen."[17] W. Schott in his 1844 "Über den Buddhaismus in Hochasien und in China" concurs that the mantra means "O the jewel in the lotus" (O Edelstein in der Padma-Blume).[18] He notes that in the Roman Catholic tome *Alphabetum Tibetanum* (to be discussed below) the statement that *padma* is in the vocative rather than the locative was apparently made by someone who was ignorant of Sanskrit.[19] Köppen concludes in his 1859 *Die Lamaische Hierarchie und Kirche* that "Properly and literally, the four words, the single utterance of which is supposed to bring incalculable blessings, mean no more than 'O! The gem in the lotus! Amen!'"[20] Scholarly opinion seemed unanimous by 1863, when, in his *Buddhism in Tibet Illustrated by Literary Documents and Objects of Religious Worship with an Account of the Buddhist Systems Preceding It in India*, Emil Schlagintweit wrote of the mantra, "Its real meaning, however, was long involved in doubt, and it is only by the most recent researches that a positive determination has been finally arrived at." That meaning is "O, the Jewel in the Lotus: Amen."[21]

From this point on, fixed by the authority of academic science, the jewel remained firmly in the lotus, and the scholar's rendering began to appear in more popular works. In their account *Travels in Tartary, Thibet and China: 1844–1846*, the Vincentian missionaries Huc and Gabet report that the mantra means "O the gem in the lotus, Amen," which they say can be paraphrased as "Oh, may I obtain perfection, and be absorbed in Buddha, Amen." [22] There were occasional voices of dissent, however. The Reverend Joseph Wolff, "missionary to the Jews and Muhammadans in Persia, Bokhara, Cashmeer, etc.," explains that "Mani" and "Peme" are the names of the prophets of the Buddhists of Tibet, seeing in the mantra evidence of Manichaeism. [23] In his 1863 *Diary of a Pedestrian in Cashmere and Tibet*, Captain William Henry Knight of the 48th Regiment was repeatedly frustrated in his attempts to determine what the mantra meant, going so far as to surreptitiously empty a prayer wheel of its contents while visiting the monastery at Hemis in Ladakh. His frustration drove him to devote an entire appendix to the meaning and, especially, the correct pronunciation of the mantra, neither of which the Tibetans seemed to know. (He had been told by a fat lama that it meant the "Supreme Being.")

> The Lamas themselves, no doubt, believe that the doctrine contained in these marvellous words is immense, and the higher dignitaries of the Church may know their derivation; but, to the great majority, even the mystic meaning and dim legendary history which the true pronunciation and rightful origin of the words would bring to their minds, are unknown, and they are thus deprived of that large amount of comfort and consolation which they would otherwise derive from the glowing and all-powerful sentence—"Oh, the jewel in the lotus, Amen!" [24]

In 1877 Madame Blavatsky wrote in *Isis Unveiled*, "*Aum* (mystic Sanskrit term of the Trinity), *mani* (holy jewel), *padme* (in the lotus, *padma* being the name for lotus), *hum* (be it so). The six syllables in the sentence correspond to the six chief powers of nature emanating from Buddha (the abstract deity, not Gautama), who is the *seventh*, the Alpha and Omega of being." [25] After the death of Tennyson, Edwin Arnold, the author of the 1879 poetic rendering of the life of the Buddha *The Light of Asia*, was nominated by Queen Victoria to be the next poet laureate. The nomination was opposed by then prime minister Gladstone in favor of Alfred Austin, and Arnold was knighted instead. Sir Edwin's poem, which contains no mention of Tibet, actually ends with the mantra:

> The Dew is on the Lotus!—Rise, Great Sun!
> And lift my leaf and mix me with the wave.
> Om mani padme hum, the Sunrise comes!
> The Dewdrop slips into the shining Sea! [26]

The Moravian missionary to Tibet H. A. Jäschke provided an extended discussion of the mantra in his 1882 *A Tibetan-English Dictionary,* as part of the entry for *oṃ.* He glossed the mantra as "O thou jewel in the lotus, *hūm!*" and referred the reader to Köppen before explaining:

> The Tibetans themselves are ignorant of the proper sense of these six syllables, if sense at all there be in them, and it is not unlikely that some shrewd priest invented this form of prayer, in order to furnish the common people with a formula or symbol, easily to be retained by the memory, and the frequent recital of which might satisfy their religious wants. And though there may be no obvious meaning in such exclamations or prayers, yet their efficacy is sure to be firmly believed in by a people, whose practical religion chiefly consists in the performances of certain rites and ceremonies, in a devout veneration of their Lamas, combined with frequent oblations to them. . . . The numerous attempts that have been made to explain Ommanipadmehūm satisfactorily, and to discover a deeper sense or even a hidden wisdom in it, have proved more or less unsuccessful. The most simple and popular, but also the flattest of these explanations is derived from the purely extrinsic circumstance, that the Sanskrit words of the prayer consist of six syllables, and accordingly it is suggested, that each of the syllables, when pronounced by a pious Buddhist, conveys a blessing upon one of the "six classes of beings." [27]

He concluded by observing that Köppen's conjecture (which, perhaps due to his Christian sensibility, he does not specify) that the mantra derives from Śaivism and has a sexual meaning ("Blessed be the lingaṃ in the yoni! Amen!") "is nothing but a smart thought of that learned author."

By the late nineteenth century the mantra and its meaning began to take on a life of its own; it was alluded to by writers who not only had never traveled to Tibet, but (unlike Madame Blavatsky) never even claimed to have done so. Thus in 1883 Mary Agnes Tincker published the novel *The Jewel in the Lotos.* Set in Italy, it contains no reference to Buddhism or Tibet. At the end the hero has a vision of the renewal of Christianity, freed from the shackles of Rome: "The mystic lotos-flower that symbolizes time afloat upon eternity had stirred before him, and he had caught a glimpse of golden peace hidden within the folded centuries." [28]

In his 1887 *Swedenborg the Buddhist: The Higher Swedenborgianism, Its Secrets and Thibetan Origin,* Philangi Dasa glossed the mantra as "Mystic Trinity! Holy Jewel in the Lotus! Amen!" going on to explain that the "six breath-sounds answer to the Six powers of Nature outflowing from the Seventh. The whole may be paraphrased, The One Life is in the pith of the heart." [29]

At the same time, the presence of the jewel in the lotus was being reconfirmed by scholars of India and of Tibet. In his 1888 Duff Lectures, "Buddhism, Its Connexion with Brāhmanism and Its Contrast with Christianity," Sir Monier-Williams, Boden Professor of Sanskrit at Oxford, translated the mantra as "Om! the Jewel in the Lotus! Hūm!" He wrote that "In all probability an occult meaning underlies the 'Jewel-lotus' formula and my own belief is that the majority of those who repeat it are ignorantly doing homage to the self-generative power supposed to inhere in the universe," explaining in a note that "the name Mani is applied to the male organ, and the female is compared to a Lotus-blossom in the Kāma-Śāstras. I fully believe the formula to have a phallic meaning, because Tibetan Buddhism is undoubtedly connected with Śaivism." [30] Citing this passage in his 1896 *The Buddhist Praying-Wheel*, William Simpson observed, "Some notion may now be formed why this celebrated six-syllabled sentence is so mystical, and is, at the same time, believed to be so potent." [31]

In his 1895 *The Buddhism of Tibet, or Lamaism*, Waddell wrote, "Thus, the commonest mystic formula in Lāmaism, the 'Om-ma-ṇi-pad-me Hūṃ,'—which literally means, *'Om! The Jewel in the Lotus! Hūm!'*—is addressed to the Bodhisat Padmapāṇi who is represented like Buddha as seated or standing within a lotus-flower." [32] In his later account of the Younghusband expedition, he rendered the mantra as "Hail! The Jewel [Grand Lama] in the lotus-flower!" and as "Hail! Jewel [Lord of Mercy] in the Lotus-Flower!" [33] Apparently unaware of Waddell, the Australian missionary J. Huston Edgar, who served in the China Inland Mission on the border of Tibet beginning in 1901, explained that the mantra is "without meaning in Tibetan" and is "addressed to no known man, demon, beast, or god." [34] William Carey's 1901 *Adventures in Tibet*, published by the United Society of Christian Endeavor, dissented mildly:

If you ask what it means, no one can tell you, but every one has a most astonishing faith in the efficacy of writing, reading, rotating, and repeating it on every possible occasion and an endless number of times. A literal translation is, *O Jewel in the Lotus! O!* But to whom the invocation is addressed and why the mere words should be invested with such extraordinary sanctity and merit-producing power, must remain a mystery. If they think upon the subject at all, probably the Tibetans of to-day consider that they are addressing Avalokita, who is always represented as sitting on a lotus, and his incarnation, the Dalai Lama, whose Tibetan name is Gyal-wa Rin-po-ch'e, "Great Gem of Majesty."[35]

In S. E. Brady's 1905 short story, "The Jewel in the Lotus," a lama who craved extinction but could not eradicate his love of living learned this lesson: "Turning the prayer-wheel quickly, his starved heart whispered, 'I understand O Perfect One! The jewel in the Lotus! It is love—I understand.'"[36]

After decades of variations on "the jewel in the lotus" in travel literature and fiction, scholars weighed in on the matter again after the turn of the century, but this time with little effect. In 1906, in a note in the *Journal of the Royal Asiatic Society*, F. W. Thomas wrote, "I see no reason whatever for departing from the view of Hodgson . . . that *Manipadme* is one word. . . . [W]ould it not be more probable that *manipadme* is a vocative referring to a feminine counterpart of that Bodhisattva, i.e. Tārā?"[37] In 1915 the Moravian missionary A. H. Francke published an article in which he explained that *manipadme* should be read as a compound, "jewel-lotus," in the vocative (O Jewel-Lotus) rather than the locative (jewel in the lotus) case:

> It has mostly been explained as meaning "Oh, thou jewel in the lotus!";
> and, to arrive at this explanation, it was considered necessary to look at the
> word *padme* as the locative case of a noun *padma,* "lotus." Dr. F. W. Tho-
> mas, of the India Office, was the first to recognize that the termination *e* is
> not that of the locative case of the masculine declension of nouns ending in
> *a*, but the vocative case of a feminine noun ending in *ā*. The connexion of
> this formula with the two other ones shows us that *manipadme* is the voca-
> tive case of the name of the female deity Manipadmā, the "deity of the
> jewel-lotus," apparently the *śakti* of Manipadma, who must be identical
> with Padmapāni or Avalokiteśvara.[38]

But by this time, the jewel was inextricable from the lotus, so much so that those who had spent long periods in Tibet (including a Tibetan) glossed the mantra as such. Thus a Tibetan Christian, Paul Sherap, explains in G. A. Combe's 1926 *A Tibetan on Tibet* that the mantra means "Oh, the Jewel in the Lotus."[39] David Macdonald, who spent fifteen years in Tibet as a British trade agent, explained that the mantra means "Hail! The Jewel in the Lotus!" in his 1929 memoir *The Land of the Lama: A Description of a Country of Contrasts & of Its Cheerful, Happy-Go-Lucky People of Hardy Nature & Cu-*

rious Customs: Their Religion, Ways of Living, Trade & Social Life.[40] Sir Basil
Gould, who served in the British foreign service in Sikkim, Bhutan, and
Tibet from 1935 to 1945 entitled his memoir *The Jewel in the Lotus*, explaining, "The title is a translation of the two central words in the mystic Buddhist
formula *Om Mani Padme Hum*. I have chosen it because wherever I served,
within or beyond the borders of India and of Pakistan, religion was a large
part of the way of life of the peoples with whom I had to deal, and nowhere
did I feel more at home than amongst those whose constant thought was of
the Jewel in the Lotus."[41]

The French explorer André Guibaut, who traveled in eastern Tibet in
1940, speculated that the meaning of the mantra "has been lost in the mist of
ages," and that it is perhaps best understood as a remnant of an atavistic
world: "It is doubtless an evocation to the unseen world, the territory of the
unknown, uncanny faces. Where, better than here, on these high tablelands
towering to the skies, can one recapture the terrors of the early ages of mankind."[42] But the mountaineer Marco Pallis in his 1949 *Peaks and Lamas* was
inspired to philosophize on the mantra:

> *Mani* means "jewel"; therefore a precious thing, the Doctrine. *Padme*
> means "in the lotus"; it may refer to the world which enshrines the doctrine
> of the Buddha (the jewel), or to the spirit in whose depths he who knows
> how to take soundings will discover Knowledge, Reality, and Liberation,
> these three being really one and the same thing under different names. Or
> possibly the lotus, the usual throne of divinities and saints, is simply at-
> tached as a divine attribute to the gem of the doctrine.[43]

The British missionary Geoffrey T. Bull, who was captured in Tibet by Chinese troops in 1950, described *mani* stones in his memoir, *When Iron Gates
Yield:* "These are stones on which are carved the mystic Buddhist formula
'Om mani padme Om.' To us it is meaningless, but it is revered above all
other speech by the Tibetans. The traditional interpretation is 'O the jewel is
in the heart of the lotus,' but one lama told me that there are some exponents
of Lama-istic teaching, who can discourse for three months on the supposed
content of the saying alone."[44] In his popular work of 1951, *Buddhism*, Christmas Humphreys explains that the outer meaning of the mantra is "merely
'Hail to the Jewel in the Lotus,' and its inward meaning is the meaning of the
Universe."[45] As we saw in chapter three, T. Lobsang Rampa explained in his
1956 *The Third Eye* that "The prayer of Lamaism is 'Om mani pad-me Hum!'

which literally means 'Hail to the Jewel in the Lotus!' although initiates know that its true meaning is 'Hail to Man's Overself!'" In 1959 Allen Edwardes published "a historical survey of the sexual practices of the East" called *The Jewel in the Lotus*. Devoted largely to the practices and perversions of Hindus and Muslims, it carries on the first page *"Ome! munnee pudmeh hum. O hail! the Jewel in the Lotus."* It contains a brief description of a secret rite of the devotees of Kali:

> In Benares, in May of 1857 the secret rites of the *Shukteh-Poojah*, propitiating the *lingam-yoni* and supplicating strength to destroy the East India Company incited the people to hysterical fervor. The ancient observance of *nurmeydha* (human sacrifice) was revived. . . .
>
> Vibrant, doleful chanting; and then, the tide ebbs. A lone wail echoes: *"Ome! munnee pudmeh hum—Ome! munnee pudmeh hum—Ome! munnee pudmeh hum—!"*[46]

Lama Govinda himself devoted an entire work to the meaning of the mantra, his 1960 *Foundations of Tibetan Mysticism according to the Esoteric Teachings of the Great Mantra Oṁ Maṇi Padme Hūṁ*, which despite its title is based on no Tibetan text. His chief sources are the Upanishads, Swami Vivekananda, Arthur Avalon, Alexandra David-Neel, and, especially, the tetralogy of Evans-Wentz. For Govinda, the mantra was too profound to be merely translated; he devoted entire chapters to *om, maṇi, padme,* and *hūṁ,* aligning them with the first four "Dhyāni Buddhas" (a term coined by Brian Hodgson that does not appear in Buddhist texts). But there are five such buddhas, and hence Govinda aligned the fifth, Amoghasiddhi, with what the mantra means when the four words come together:

> [I]f OṀ represents the Way of Universality, MAṆI the way of Unity and Equality of all beings, PADMA the Way of Unfolding Vision, and HŪṀ the Way of Integration—then it must be said, that behind all of them stands the act of realization, the mysterious spiritual power (Skt., *siddhi*), which not only encourages us to proceed on the chosen way, but which transforms us while proceeding, until we ourselves have become the aim of our striving.[47]

Lama Govinda's extravagant commentary may have inspired others to flights of exegesis, for in the 1960s and 1970s we find more and more elaborate discussions of the mantra. In the May 1963 article "Mountaintop War in Re-

mote Ladakh," W. E. Garrett, in the generally staid *National Geographic,*
provides the following gloss: "OM—I invoke the path and experience of
universality so that MANI—the jeweline luminosity of my immortal mind
PADME—be unfolded within the depths of the lotus-center of awakened consciousness HUM—and I be wafted by the ecstasy of breaking through all
bonds and horizons." [48] The missionary and anthropologist Robert Ekvall,
who spent many years prior to the Second World War in the Amdo region of
Tibet, made the mantra both vocative and locative, explaining that "It may
safely be said that there is no Tibetan—excluding the completely witless and
speechless—who does not personally participate in this enunciation and not
one who is completely certain just what the phrase means. The traditional
explanation is that it is a vocative . . . hailing the jewel in the lotus and thus
referring to the incarnation of the Buddhahood." [49] A long list of meanings of
the mantra is found in the 1965 account of the American Air Corps crew
whose plane crashed in Tibet on November 30, 1943. There the author ag-
nostically provides a dozen translations of the mantra, concluding, "The
meaning of *Om mani padme hum* is as different as the individual minds of
Tibet's millions." [50] Despite devoting all of *Foundations of Tibetan Mysticism*
to the mantra, Lama Govinda weighed in again in his 1966 *The Way of the
White Clouds,* where he offered a gloss that he seems to suggest was provided
by the Geluk lama, Tomo Geshe Rinpoche. He writes:

> The moment, however, we become conscious of him [the Buddha] as the
> light in our innermost being, the Mantra OṂ MAṆI PADME HŪṂ begins to
> reveal its meaning, because now the 'lotus' (*padma*) is our own heart, in
> which the 'jewel' (*maṇi*), namely the Buddha, is present. The OṂ and the
> HŪṂ, however, represent the universe in its highest and deepest aspects, in
> all its forms of appearance and experience, which we should embrace with
> unlimited love and compassion like the Buddha. [51]

In 1970 the noted student of Chinese religions John Blofeld provided this
lengthy neo-Vedantin commentary in his *The Tantric Mysticism of Tibet:*

> In common with all mantras, the Mani has *Om* as its first syllable. *Om*
> stands for the totality of sound and, indeed, for the totality of existence.
> Originally written *Aum,* it starts at the back of the throat and ends with the
> lips. It is chief among the sounds to which a mystical creative quality is
> attached. Translators who have rendered it as 'O,' 'Oh,' or 'Hail' have
> obviously misconceived its meaning and its function. The A stands for

consciousness of the external world; the U, for consciousness of what goes on inside our minds; and the M, for consciousness of the non-dual, unquali-fied emptiness of the void.

The next syllable is *Mani*, meaning the Jewel. It is equated with Vajra, the adamantine non-substance which is perfectly void and yet more imper-vious to harm or change than the hardest substance known to chemistry. *Mani* is the symbol of highest value within our mind, the pure void which is always to be found there when the intervening layers of murky con-sciousness are pierced.

Padma (of which *Padme* is the vocative form) literally means the Lo-tus. It is the symbol of spiritual unfoldment whereby the *Mani* is finally reached.

Hum, like *Om*, is untranslatable. *Om* is the infinite and *Hum* is the infinite within the finite and therefore stands for our potential Enlighten-ment, the perception of the void within the non-void, Mind in the form of mind, the unconditioned in the conditioned, the transcendental in the ephemeral, the subtle embodied in the dense. This above all other mantric syllables symbolizes the central truth of the Vajrayana—the truth of void-ness enclosed within the petals of the non-void.

Om and *Hum*, however, are much more than symbols. Properly used, they have the power to awake in the human consciousness an intuitive un-derstanding of truths impossible to clothe in words. *Mani Padme*, the Jewel and Lotus which form the body of the mantra, have, even at the surface level, a number of complementary meanings. For example, the Lotus stands for the Dharma and the Jewel for the liberating truth it enfolds; or the Lotus is the world of form and the Jewel, the formless world, the reality infusing form, and so on.[52]

In the 1970s, as in the late nineteenth century, the mantra again lost its moor-ings in Tibet and floated free to be seized upon by the devotees of other spiritual paths. Thus Grace Cooke, founder of the White Eagle Lodge, in her 1973 book on creative meditation called *The Jewel in the Lotus*, wrote, "This Christ Spirit is the shining jewel we see in the heart of the lily, the jewel within the lotus, the jewel within our own heart."[53] In 1974 the British The-osophist Douglas Baker published the first volume of his seven-volume *The Seven Pillars of Ancient Wisdom: The Synthesis of Yoga, Esoteric Science and Psychology*. Titled *The Jewel in the Lotus*, it was devoted to an exposition of the theory of hylozoism, the proposition that the organic and inorganic are filled with life. The work contained no mention of Tibet or of *oṃ maṇi padme hūṃ*, explaining instead that after the third initiation, "The three chakras in the head region now begin to merge at right angles to each other . . . to form a single gynaecium at the centre of which are to be found the Higher Triad of permanent atoms, the Jewel in the Lotus."[54] A 1983 volume entitled *The Jewel in the Lotus* consists of a collection of 648 quotations from various Hindu, Muslim, and Buddhist texts and from artists, writers, and philosophers such as Blavatsky, Balzac, Blake, Buber, Dante, Dickinson, Gibran, Mozart, Plotinus, Rilke, Spinoza, and Tagore. In the foreword, the editor explains:

> *The Jewel in the Lotus* is offered for regular use by ardent theophilanthropists, now and in the future. A key is suggested for such users. The entire collection of invocations, chants and intimations is dedicated to the unknown but undaunted pathfinders to the global civilization of tomorrow, the noble sowers of seeds in the numinous dawn of the Aquarian Age.[55]

In 1993, Donald Walters (Kriyananda), the founder and spiritual director of the Ananda World-Brotherhood Village, published *The Jewel in the Lotus*, a one-act play about his guru, Yogananda, in which neither Buddhism nor Tibet is mentioned. It contains the line "And we, while living in the shadow of this very peak, might never have known that on Lotus Mountain lives the jewel of our desires."[56] The Baha'i faith has produced a videotape about their religion called *The Jewel in the Lotus*.

The Tibetan diaspora of 1959 renewed interest among anthropologists in the Tibetan-speaking populations of Nepal and their religions. In 1981 the anthropologist Robert Paul, working among the Sherpas, claimed that although his subjects did not know that the mantra means that the jewel is in the lotus, they did know "from the inflection that the mani is in the pema." He noted that the sound *mm* is an attempt to reproduce the phonation produced while sucking, particularly at the mother's breast. Thus both *oṃ* and *hūṃ* (he seemed unaware that Tibetans pronounce the syllable as "hoong") gain their power because they evoke the experience of nursing. He also noted that the letter *m* (*maṇi*) is associated with the mother, and the letter *p* (*padma*) with the father. This would appear to present problems, since when the mantra is rendered as "the jewel in the lotus," the word that begins with *m* is associated with the male organ while the word that begins with *p* is associated with the female. His solution is to see in the mantra an evocation of the infant son at his mother's breast: the female *maṇi* is in the male *padma*. "The mother is still seen as the bisexual phallic mother of the Pre-Oedipal phase; and the thought expressed is not 'the phallus is in the vulva' but rather its earlier equivalent, 'the nipple is in the mouth.'"[57]

In Rodger Kamenetz's 1994 account of his encounter with Buddhism, *The Jew in the Lotus*, one finds the mantra in the glossary with the following explanation. "A Sanskrit mantra. According to the Dalai Lama, 'this is almost our national mantra.' The meaning is, 'The Jewel in the Lotus.' Jewel = thought of enlightenment, Lotus = mind." (Presumably, the latter part of the explanation was not provided by the Dalai Lama.) In the spectacular exhibition catalogue *Wisdom and Compassion*, co-authored with Marilyn Rhie, Robert Thurman wrote, "The Tibetan landscape is filled with *mani* stones, flat rocks with the mantra of compassion, OM MANI PADME HUM ('OM! the jewel in the lotus [itself a symbol of the union of compassion and wisdom, male and female, and so on] HUM')."[58] More recently, in his *Essential Tibetan Buddhism*, Thurman wrote of Tibet, "it was the land of his sacred mantra, OM MANI PADME HUM! 'Come! Jewel in the Lotus! In my heart!'"[59] And in 1996, Wolfgang von Effra explained in his *Uncompromising Tibet*, "Pious Tibetans daily move hundreds of thousands of prayer mills, murmuring this mantra. 'Oh jewel in the mystery of the lotus flower' is the popular translation. Another translation better reflects the true meaning: 'Blessed be your speech, body and soul by the jewel of the lotus flower.'"[60]

Today, a mail order catalog called *The Mystic Trader* (a division of Pacific Spirit Corporation in Oregon) offers crystals, pyramids, batik T-shirts, boomerangs, Balinese masks, bamboo blow guns, and Burmese gongs. One can also find advertised prayer wheels, *mani* stones, and even prayer wheel earrings, each inscribed with the mantra, which the catalog explains is a prayer for peace and good fortune that means "I bow down to the Jewel in the Lotus Blossom." Another catalog, *dZi: The Tibet Collection*, sells "Tibetan-made Clothing, Folk Arts, Good Karma and More!" and advertises *mani* stones. Here we are told that the mantra means "'hail to the jewel in the lotus,' generally considered a mantra or prayer for compassion and understanding in the world." On the World Wide Web, perhaps fulfilling Monier-Williams's worst fears about the use of technology for prayer, there is a site named "Click Here for Good Karma," which can convert the spinning hard drive of one's computer into a prayer wheel. By clicking on the appropriate icon, *om mani padme hūm* (which, we are told here, means "the jewel in the lotus of the heart") is copied onto one's hard drive.[61]

It is perhaps noteworthy that in all of these renderings of the mantra as some variation of "the jewel in the lotus," Tibetan texts are never cited in support, that once the early-nineteenth-century European Sanskrit scholars had translated it as "the jewel in the lotus," the rendering took on a life of its own. There are numerous Tibetan works on the mantra, but they are rarely concerned with the semantic meaning of the Sanskrit words, perhaps confirming André Padoux's assertion that "a mantra has a use rather than a meaning." [62] Instead, in a tradition that can be traced back to the *Kāraṇḍavyūha Sutra*, the Tibetan concern is generally with establishing a wide range of homologies between the six syllables of the mantra (in Tibetan the mantra is commonly referred to as *yi ge drug ma*, "the six syllables") and other sets of six in Buddhist doctrine. The most common of these homologies is that between the six syllables and the six realms of rebirth (gods, demigods, humans, animals, ghosts, hell beings), in which the recitation of each syllable is said to protect one from the sufferings of the corresponding realm. [63] (In his *Peaks and Lamas*, Marco Pallis notes, "One of the less profound interpretations current among the lamas is to establish a correlation between each of the six syllables and one of the six classes of beings in the Round.") [64] A typical Tibetan work on the mantra is *The Benefits of the Maṇi Wheel (Maṇi 'khor lo'i phan yon)*, which contains passages such as the following:

> The benefit of turning the [prayer] wheel once is equal to reading the translation of the [Indian] treatises (*bstan 'gyur*) once. Turning it twice is equal to reading the words of the Conqueror [the Buddha] once. Turning it three times purifies the obstructions of body, speech, and mind. Turning it ten times purifies sins equal to Mount Meru. Turning it one hundred times makes one equal to the king of dharma Yama [the Lord of Death]. Turning it one thousand times, one understands the meaning of the dharmakāya for one's own welfare. Turning it ten thousand times, one brings about the welfare of oneself and other sentient beings. Turning it one hundred thousand times, one is reborn in the retinue of Avalokiteśvara. Turning it ten million times, the sentient beings of the six realms attain the ocean of bliss. [65]

Nowhere in the work is the "meaning" of the mantra explained. In recent years, when its meaning has been explained by a Tibetan, it is often for the benefit of an Anglophone audience. The Dalai Lama has identified *maṇi* with compassion and *padme* with wisdom; *hūṃ* symbolizes the union of these two. "Thus the six syllables, *oṃ maṇi padme hūṃ*, mean that in dependence on a path which is an indivisible union of method and wisdom, you can transform your impure body, speech, and mind into the pure exalted body, speech, and mind of a Buddha." [66]

This is not to suggest that discussions of the meaning of the mantra are entirely absent in Tibetan literature, as several scholars have recently shown. In a 1987 article on the prayer wheel, Dan Martin refers to a seventeenth-century work by the prime minister of the fifth Dalai Lama, Desi Sangye Gyatso (Sde srid sangs rgyas rgya mtsho), in which translations of a number of Sanskrit mantras are provided. Here, *oṃ maṇi padme hūṃ* is rendered as "O, you who have the jewel [and] the lotus" (*Kye nor bu padma can*).[67] Pieter Verhagen has discovered an early Tibetan grammatical treatise, possibly from the ninth century, that offers the mantra as an example of the vocative case. The text reads, in part, "Because *oṃ* is the nature of the five wisdoms, it is stated first. It closes with *hūṃ*, 'take to mind.' Regarding the actual vocative in between, *maṇi* is jewel. *Padme* is the same [in Sanskrit and Tibetan] and is left [untranslated]. Then, 'jewel-lotus' is invoked in obeisance. The adding of *e* in *me* [of *padme*] means 'O'; as in 'O jewel lotus.'" [68]

Thus the correct interpretation of the mantra would seem to be that it is not two words, *maṇi padme*, with the latter in the locative, but rather, as Tibetans appear to have known for some time, a vocative, with *maṇipadmā* the name of a deity, the Jewel-Lotus One. As David Snellgrove wrote in 1957, "This seems to be the solution of the problem, and there is no justification for splitting the compound into such a phrase as 'jewel in the lotus,' for which a meaning can as always easily be found." [69]

But scholars remain unsure of the significance of the grammatical suggestion that the deity be female, despite the fact that in Tibet Avalokiteśvara is male, and they remain in doubt as to the relation between the jewel and the lotus. Verhagen offers as possible translations "(woman) who has the lotus of the jewel," "(woman) who has the lotus with the jewel," "(woman) who has the lotus in the jewel," and "(woman) who has the lotus that is a jewel." [70] Some decades earlier, in a 1925 article in the *Journal of the Bihar and Orissa Asiatic Society*, Sten Konow noted that the most important of the sutras associated with Avalokiteśvara, the *Kāraṇḍavyūha*, describes a mandala in which the six-syllable knowledge (*ṣaḍakṣarī vidyā*) appears as a goddess, white in color, with four arms, holding a red lotus in her left hand and a rosary in her right. Thus, he argues, the compound *maṇipadmā* is in the feminine because the mantra (or its "wisdom," *vidyā*) is embodied as a goddess, the *śakti* (he uses the Śaiva term that is not used in Buddhist tantra) of

Avalokiteśvara.[71] He convincingly shows (as Thomas had before him) that *maṇipadmā* is a *bahuvrīhi* compound in the vocative case, meaning "O Jewel-Lotus." What remained to be determined was the relation between the jewel and the lotus. It is perhaps inevitable that Konow concludes:

> It is evident that the meaning can only be "thou whose padma is a maṇi," or "thou in whose padma there is a maṇi." The former analysis does not seem to give any sense, the latter, on the other hand, is quite satisfactory and no doubt correct. The proper explanation of this designation has already been indicated by Koeppen, who drew attention to the fact that *maṇi* also means *liṅga* [penis] and *padma* the *yoni* [vagina]. Maṇipadmā is accordingly a female deity with a *liṅga* in her *yoni*.[72]

Thus, the jewel is once again back in the lotus.

One way of telling this tale would be, then, that early Catholic missionaries to Tibet, despite the fact that they did not know Sanskrit, correctly identified the mantra as an invocation of Avalokiteśvara, seeing *maṇipadme* not as two words, but as the name of a deity, whom they called Manipe. European philologists of the early nineteenth century dismissed this information as erroneous, derived, as it was, from Romish clerics who did not know Sanskrit grammar and thus did not recognize that *padme* was the locative of *padma* and that the mantra meant "the jewel in the lotus." Empowered by the authority of scholarship, this rendering of the mantra gained wide currency and took on a life of its own, floating free from Tibet and Tibetan Buddhism to be employed in a remarkable range of contexts. The occasional dissent has gone largely unheeded, even today, when Tibetan texts that specifically identify the mantra as a vocative have become available. Thus the missionaries, who lived among Tibetans, were right. The nineteenth-century philologists were wrong. Knowledge does not always march forward along the road of progress.

The penultimate irony is that a Tibetan text that describes it all quite clearly has been available to Europeans since 1762, and in the publication *Alphabetum Tibetanum*, a summary of the records of the Capuchin mission to Lhasa (1708–1745) by the Augustinian friar Antonio Agostino Giorgi. In this massive work one finds a Tibetan text that was included among the documents of Orazic della Penna. It is called *Brief Commentary on the Letters of the Six Syllable [Mantra]* (*Yi ge drug ma'i 'bru 'grel mdor sdus*) composed by one Ngawang (Ngag dbang) of Ra mo che monastery. It had been available to European scholars for two centuries, and thus did not need to be discovered among works previously unknown to the West. In this short text (which is followed by a Latin translation), many questions are answered. It explicitly states, for example, that *padma* is in the vocative.[73] It goes on to say, "O Jewel Lotus. For example, just as a young child fervently calls the name of its beloved mother, the practitioner fervently calls the deity Mahākāruṇika (Supreme Compassion), having a jewel and a lotus in his hands, calling, 'O Jewel Lotus.' Mahākāruṇika, remembering his prior promise, comes quickly."[74]

A modern Tibetan commentary on the mantra by the late tutor of the present Dalai Lama, Trijang Rinpoche (Khri byang rin po che, 1901–1981), contains a similar explanation but connects the jewel and the lotus to the four-armed form of Avalokiteśvara, who holds a crystal rosary in his right hand and a lotus in his left hand; his two other hands clasp a jewel at his heart:

> Regarding *maṇi padme*, "Jewel Lotus" or "Lotus Jewel" is one of the names of the noble Avalokiteśvara. The reason that he is called by that name is that, just as a lotus is not soiled by mud, so the noble Avalokiteśvara himself has, through his great wisdom, abandoned the root of saṃsāra, all the stains of the conception of true existence together with its latencies. Therefore, to symbolize that he does not abide in the extreme of mundane existence, he holds a white lotus in his hand. . . . He joins the palms of his two upper hands, making the gesture of holding a jewel to symbolize that, like a wish-granting jewel, he eliminates all the oppression of suffering for all sentient beings and bestows upon them all temporary and ultimate benefit and bliss.[75]

It would seem, in conclusion, that the early missionaries were correct that the mantra is a vocative invocation of Avalokiteśvara, who is depicted holding a jewel and a lotus, with the reason for the feminine form of the Sanskrit vocative remaining something of a mystery. In her recent *Traveller in Space,* June Campbell points out the unlikelihood of the term *maṇi* meaning phallus, *vajra* being the more common term. She suggests that, instead, *maṇi* means clitoris and that the mantra is thus an invocation of "the deity of the clitoris-vagina," a pre-Buddhist Tibetan deity whose gender was changed by "the zealous missionaries of Indian Buddhism."[76]

Be that as it may, based on the Tibetan sources and an analysis of the grammar, it appears that the mantra cannot mean "the jewel in the lotus" and that the endless variations on this misreading are merely fanciful. The ultimate irony, of course, would be to discover a Tibetan text that somehow supported this most famous but apparently erroneous rendering. And such a text exists. In the commentary mentioned above by the Dalai Lama's tutor, one of the most distinguished scholars of his generation, we find the following passage: "First, in terms of signification, *maṇi* indicates the vajra jewel of the father, *padme* the lotus of the *mudrā* [consort], and the letter *hūṃ* [indicates] that by joining these two together, at the time of the basis, a child is born and at the time of the path, the deities emanate."[77] Or, perhaps translated more loosely, "The jewel in the lotus. Amen."

In Tolstoy's story, the bishop gazes back at the island as the ship resumes its course. He is startled to see a white light in the distance moving toward the ship at high speed. Looking more closely, he sees that it is the three hermits, hand in hand, gliding across the surface without moving their feet, surrounded by gleaming light. As they reach the ship, they say in unison, "We have forgotten your teaching, servant of God. As long as we kept repeating it, we remembered, but when we stopped saying it for a while, a word dropped out, and now it's fallen to pieces. We can remember none of it. Teach us again."[78]

The Art

✾

What, then, is the characteristic feature, the basic element which makes such work typically Tibetan? It is, in the first place, that principle of placing borrowed features side by side. . . . Further, the typical colour scheme, the immense dynamic activity, demonic appearance, ferocity, savageness and rapacity. The unconditional service and submission to the religious cult, the piety, mysticism, and magic. And the great contrasts, in which two contradictions are clasped together and forced to live side by side in constant tension. LUMÍR JISL

Just as Victorian scholars could not see Tibetan Buddhism as anything other than the nadir in their history of Buddhism, so Tibetan art arrived too late to figure in any formation of a Western aesthetic of classical Asian art. The sculptures of buddhas and paintings of wrathful protectors could find no place among Ming vases, Sung landscape paintings, Edo prints, and Mughal miniatures. Sherman Lee's authoritative *History of Far Eastern Art* (1964) is credited with being the first book to successfully introduce Asian art to a wide audience in the United States. It opens with a two-page color map of Asia indicating the provenances of works of art: some three dozen in India, for example, five in Ceylon, four in Java. But although the name "Tibet" appears on the map, not a single site is marked, not Lhasa, not Gyantse. At the bottom of the map a disclaimer reads, "Only those sites mentioned in the book appear on the map." A perusal of the contents confirms the absence. Of the book's 656 paintings, sculptures, temples, shrines, ceramics, and lacquerware, none is described as Tibetan. It is not that Tibet is not mentioned (though almost always in the phrase "Nepal and Tibet"). It is rather that Tibetan art seems to be little more than a hopelessly complicated and desiccated elaboration of things already done better elsewhere. "With the developed use of the Buddha image, we begin to sense an impoverishment of imagination and subject. This is particularly true with the Mahayana material, where images are repeated for their own sake and ultimately reach their most elaborate forms in Nepal and Tibet, with frightfully complicated and seemingly endless systems of quantities and manifestations."[1] By 1994 and the publication of the fifth edition of *A History of Far Eastern Art*, the number of illustrations had increased to 801, including 66 in color. Two of the 735 black-and-white illustrations are of Tibetan works, a buddha and a wrathful deity. Lhasa has been marked on the map, but the name of the region (now enclosed by a line) is "Tibet (Xizang)." Xizang, China's name for its Tibetan colony, means "Western Treasury," a treasury that since 1959 has been rapidly emptied of its art. It was only then that these treasures would, for the first time, draw the sustained gaze of art historians who had neither been to Tibet nor read Tibetan, and a process of interpretation would begin in which, once again, Tibet and Tibetans were strangely absent.

This chapter will consider some of the assumptions and interpretative flights of fancy that were launched when Tibetan works came under the art historical gaze during the present century, flights of fancy that through the power of repetition came to acquire the status of knowledge.[2] The Tibetan works, sometimes seen as artifacts, sometimes as art, did not simply lose their contexts when they came under this gaze, transported, as they had been, from temples, monasteries, and private shrines in Tibet to museums, art dealers, and private collections in New York and London. Rather, because "objects are not only what they were made to be but what they become," these Tibetan works, materially stable yet somehow out of place, became a palette with which to paint a portrait of a Tibet unlocated in history.[3]

The dearth of Tibetan works in Lee's survey cannot be attributed to a lack of available scholarship on Tibetan art. In 1925 George Roerich published *Tibetan Paintings*, in which the major schools of Tibetan art were identified and Nepalese, Khotanese, and Chinese influences were noted. Nonetheless, art-historical scholarship on Tibet during the first half of the century was devoted largely to the vexing task of identifying deities; works from that period include Alice Getty's 1914 *The Gods of Northern Buddhism* (which speaks of "Lamaite painting"), Walter E. Clark's 1937 *Two Lamaistic Pantheons*, and Antoinette Gordon's 1939 *Iconography of Tibetan Lamaism*, which illustrates the process of identifying a deity: "Of what type are the ornaments and garments? (See Key to Sacred Images, p. 39.) Answer: Bodhisattva ornaments. To which group of Bodhisattvas does it belong—the non-Tantric or the Tantric forms? (See p. 39.) Answer: The Tantric group, since it has eleven heads and eight arms."[4] And in 1949 Giuseppe Tucci published his monumental, three-volume *Tibetan Painted Scrolls*, which begins prophetically, "Tibetan painting has not met so far with the same appreciation as that received by its Indian and Persian counterparts. In a way this is not surprising, as collections of Oriental art are rich of too many modern Tibetan paintings of little merit, in which the same subjects appear over and over again. For this reason it has been difficult to overcome the impression that Tibetan painters have little originality and are so subservient to the rules of iconography that they are hardly able to give individual forms to their own fancy."[5]

The Tibetan diaspora of 1959 made a great flood of Tibetan art available to dealers and collectors in the West, including both those works that Tibetans themselves carried out and often had to sell for their sustenance as well as works that the Chinese looted and sold through art dealers in Hong Kong and elsewhere.[6] These works attracted a special breed of connoisseur, one for whom the artistic commodity (whether a painting or sculpture or a skull cup or ritual dagger) was often further fetishized by the conceit that the work, through its acquisition and display, had been rescued from destruction so that a part of Tibet's unique and endangered cultural heritage could be preserved.

So by 1969, ten years after the Dalai Lama's flight from Lhasa, the Asia House Gallery in New York was able to mount a major show of Tibetan art, although the attitude toward it, expressed in an extended excerpt from the preface to the catalog by the gallery director, Gordon B. Washburn, remained largely the same as that expressed by Lee, but with certain elaborations:

> These remarkable relics of the culture of Tibet, together with other equally precious records of her inheritance that have come from museums and private collections in Europe and America, should give us a wholly new con-

ception of Tibetan art. We have been used to seeing the sterile repetitions produced by pious monks who often occupied their time in copying manuscripts or scroll paintings (*tankas*) as exercises in devotion. These hundreds, or even thousands, of dutiful artifacts cannot be counted among the great creations of the Tibetan genius. In a country where the number of monasteries has been reckoned in the thousands, and the number of monks had once comprised nearly a third of the population, it is not surprising to discover that so great a number of implements of worship of merely conventional value were produced across the centuries.

Tibetan art, whether in the form of scroll paintings, sculptures or "ritual implements," did not have the inciting of aesthetic delight as its primary function, if indeed this element could be included in its purpose at all. Both tankas and bronzes were regarded as instruments of invocation and meditation—tools, that is to say, to help the worshipper rid himself of the outer world of illusion and so find salvation within. This sacred art is not, therefore, the fruit of a free invention but is, rather, the product of strict theological and liturgical canons that have dictated the iconography, the proportions, and even the colors of the paintings and sculptures. Anonymity was always taken for granted, and it transpires that hardly a handful of artists' names are known to us from this Land of Snows. Effective paintings from famous shrines were endlessly repeated, and models of high excellence brought from foreign sources were deeply revered. . . .

In view of this ritual approach to the creation of art, it is quite natural that only a few images will exceed in quality the level of mere liturgical command. But Tibetans were not simply subservient copyists of Indian, Nepali, Mongol, or Chinese models, however much her artists may have been influenced by these works from earlier Buddhist cultures.[7]

Much is already familiar here. Tibetan artists are portrayed as anonymous (in fact, many names are known) and Tibetan art as the rote imitation of foreign forms, lacking in the freedom and individuality associated with creative genius. The eighteenth-century view of monastic life as the sterile copying of Latin manuscripts is here transferred to Tibet (where monks were not so occupied) and the number of Tibetan monks is exploded to encompass one-third of the population (the most recent research suggests that between 10 and 15 percent of males were monks). The anonymous artist is thus portrayed as concerned not with the aesthetic but with the instrumental, with mere ritual use, constrained by rigid liturgical requirements governing line and color. As the works are essentially ritual objects, the emphasis is on the repetition of borrowed models. Describing the placement of figures on a scroll painting,

Lumír Jisl explained, "This apparently mechanical arrangement and stiffness should, however, not be ascribed to a lack of invention on the part of the Tibetan artist. He cannot do otherwise. He is a monk. We have already spoken of his dependence on church orders which he cannot infringe without committing a sin."[8]

Among the uses to which the art is put, meditation is mentioned, characterized as a means of finding truth within a reality absent in the external world. As we will see below, meditation would come to be portrayed by some as the motivating aesthetic of Tibetan painting, rendering it somehow more sublime than other art forms. But here Tibetan art remains merely sacerdotal, mixing influences from elsewhere; as Pratapaditya Pal, the most prolific of the art historians on Tibet, writes in the Asia House catalog, "An account of this constant co-mingling is, in brief, the story of the art of Tibet."[9]

Apart from the notion of outside influence, an obligatory element in Western writing about Tibetan art has been a discussion of the Tibetan mentality, of precisely what it is that has moved Tibetans to produce such strange images. Here art historians honor a venerable tradition, one that includes some of the most famous travelers to Tibet. In his 1931 *The Religion of Tibet*, Sir Charles Bell describes the Tibetan mind: "The dry, cold, pure air stimulates the intellect, but isolation from the cities of men and from other nations deprives the Tibetan of subjects on which to feed his brain. So his mind turns inwards and spends itself on religious contemplation, helped still farther by the monotony of his life and the awe-inspiring scale on which Nature works around him. . . . There is all the difference in the world between the devout, religious outlook of Tibet and the philosophic materialism of agricultural China."[10] One wonders whether Bell was aware of the work of Ernest Renan, who some decades before argued that the character of Semitic religion (both its belief in one God and the minimalism of its language) derived from landscape: "The desert is monotheistic, sublime in its immense uniformity."[11]

Describing his visit to western Tibet in 1933 in *The Way of the White Clouds*, Lama Govinda offers a somewhat more mystical variation on the same theme: "Thus, a strange transformation takes place under the influence of this country, in which the valleys are as high as the highest peaks of Europe and where mountains soar into space beyond the reach of humans. It is as if a weight were lifted from the mind, or as if certain hindrances were removed. . . . Consciousness seems to be raised to a higher level, where the obstacles and disturbances of our ordinary life do not exist, except as a faint memory of things which have all lost their importance and attraction. At the same time one becomes more sensitive and open to new forms of reality; the intuitive qualities of our mind are awakened and stimulated—in short, there are all the conditions for attaining the higher stages of meditation or *dhyāna*." [12]

Repeated sufficiently, the role of landscape acquired an official explanatory power, finding its way over the decades into exhibition catalogs and reference works. Thus in 1975 we read, "Tibet is a country marked by extreme contrasts: an hallucinatory, geotectonic spectacle where light (because of the altitude) intensifies colour and the slightest detail; . . . An introspective awareness develops because of these unusual surroundings, one which eminently favoured the identification of the individual with the schemas imposed upon him by artistic canons which were entirely conditioned by mystical experience." [13] The 1970 *Oxford Companion to Art* explains that "Lamaism was not restricted to Tibet but became the ruling creed in those barren and desolate regions of Asia which alone could provide a solitude vast, calm, and inaccessible enough to nourish its intense spirituality and mysticism." [14]

Tibetans were thus portrayed as the observers of their environment, their minds, as if by reflex, turned inside by the overwhelming outside that surrounded them. With the impulse behind Tibetan Buddhism (and hence its art) detected, and the drudgery of identifying the bewildering pantheon largely completed, the art historian could turn next to consider the specific products of Tibetan art and their meaning. Three categories have proved to be of enduring fascination, the wrathful deity, the *yab yum* image, and the mandala, each regarded as a "symbol" of something else.

A characteristic view of wrathful deities is provided by Pratapaditya Pal in his introduction to the 1969 catalog *Lamaist Art: The Aesthetics of Harmony*. He repeats the by now familiar refrain that Lamaism is not simply Indian Buddhism transported to Tibet, but is "really an amalgam of early, native shamanist beliefs, Bon ideology, and imported Buddhist concepts." [15] When he turns to a discussion of "Lamaist imagery," we find wrathful deities (most of which were in fact derived from India) represented as manifestations of the Tibetan character. Pal discusses the "imagery of the terrifying deities" in Tibet's repressive society:

> Nothing is more characteristic of the Tibetan psyche than their love for the grotesque and the bizarre in their art. Terrifying gods and wrathful demons, malevolent spirits and grinning skeletons prance and dance about on the surface of tankas . . . in an orgiastic exhibition of their strength and power.

It is possible that these images are projected by the collective consciousness of the Tibetan and the Mongolian peoples as a release from their psychic and cultural tensions. To the average Tibetan or Mongolian, given to war and beset by the hardships imposed by an inhospitable terrain, concepts of "illusion" or "enlightenment" or "ultimate reality" must have meant very little. His own religion as well as the subjective quality of his mind was conditioned essentially by his environment, physical as well as social.

Living in tents amidst inhospitable, formidable mountains and exposed helplessly to the hostile elements, his fears took concrete shapes as he visualized the inexplicable terrors and occult forces as fearsome and wrathful spirits who must be constantly appeased if one were to survive. It seems as though afraid of nature, where violent, mysterious forces always lurk behind the next corner, he has extracted the very essence of nature, which, in a symbolic form, serves as a weapon against nature's evils.

Equally oppressive was the society he lived in, for the tyranny of the monks and the monasteries was absolute.[16]

Wrathful deities, although they are described in detail in Indian tantras, are thus somehow uniquely Tibetan, fulfilling what Giuseppe Tucci's photographer, Fosco Maraini, called the "need for horror." For Pal, they seem to be a kind of double projection. The credulous Tibetan peasant, unable to understand the profundities of Buddhist philosophy, oppressed by the power of the landscape and by the greed of the monks, reacts in horror to his environment, both physical and cultural. These external elements are processed in the Tibetan psyche and then projected back outside, to be embodied in the forms of wrathful deities who must be propitiated in order for the peasant to survive. As Pal writes elsewhere, "Hence, these fears and predispositions have resulted in the creation, out of his subconscious, of the terrifying and demoniacal divinities, who in turn enslaved the minds of their creators."[17] But as if this were not enough, there are other sinister forces at play, as devious monks concoct images to terrorize the laity. Describing the goddess Lha mo, Pal explains, "It seems clear that such forms and their explanations were invented by the theologians in order to impress upon the mind of the credulous man the fate that awaited him if he refused to join the church."[18]

In addition to the environmental and social theories of the wrathful, there were psychoanalytic explanations. In *Tibet's Terrifying Deities,* F. Sierksma calls Tibetan paintings of wrathful deities "the art of the diabolic," unsurpassed by any other culture in history. Other forms of Tibetan painting, those of buddhas and bodhisattvas, are mechanical and slavish; the serenity of the buddha is better expressed in art from beyond Tibet. It is only in the depiction of the wrathful deity, he argues, that the Tibetan artist finds the perfect freedom that results in true creativity, producing works that tell us more about ourselves than our own dreams. Sierksma finds historical reasons for the existence of the wrathful deities of Tibet. He concedes that Indian tantra had demonic gods and that Tibet had demonic gods prior to the introduction of Buddhism. But this cannot account for the "extremely aggressive character" of the protective deities of Tibet. For Sierksma, Indian Buddhism was a spiritual religion, quiescent and philosophical, while the religion of Tibet was a religion of the real world, a religion of the senses. For this reason, although Buddhism was able to triumph, its victory was never complete, and a gap remained between the old and the new. A kind of reaction-formation took place, fueled from two directions. Buddhism defeated the Tibetan gods and made them protectors of Buddhism, but the Tibetan gods were never fully subjugated, and thus were demonized. At the same time, the lusty, earthbound religion of ancient Tibet, although defeated, remained unrepentant, its resistance and resentment resulting in the terrifying forms of its former gods, and even in the wrathful depiction of such beatific figures as Tsong kha pa. These demonic forms are described by Sierksma as "symptoms of acculturative demonisation," standing for "a primary symptom of incomplete acculturation, of a warrior nation that for the sake of Buddhism has had to give up a part of itself, of a Buddhism that for that warrior nation has also had to abandon an integral part, while the two have not found ultimate reconciliation."[19]

At the same time that the wrathful deities of Tibet are explained as reflections of the darkest reaches of the Tibetan psyche, we find Tibetan art characterized as "an aesthetics of harmony." "Unity, order, and harmony—the sine qua non of mystical experience—are also present in every Lamaist image"; each work of Tibetan art is "a translation of a vision experienced by a mystic." For this reason, an analysis of the style and structure of a work, whether an icon or a temple, cannot contribute to an appreciation of the piece "without an acquaintance with the mystical vision that inspired it."[20] Tibetan painting therefore lacks "the subtle interplay of light and shade" because in Lamaism the true nature of the mind is the "Primal Clear Light." Tibetan painting lacks pictorial realism and the use of perspective not because these were unknown to the Lamaist artist but because he could not be bothered with them, committed as he was to "portraying the transcendental reality." It is not surprising, then, that Pal is struck by the fact that "the same artists who created with such consummate artistry the dreamlike, visionary landscape with its atmosphere of tranquility and harmony . . . could evoke the terrifying and fantastic forms with such convincing power of expression."[21]

Hence Tibetan art, devalued by some for its lack of creativity, is valued by others for an aesthetic that surpasses the merely creative: Tibetan art is portrayed as an evocation of (and hence a conduit to) a transcendent reality, inexpressible in words but not in art. And to avoid having to be overly concerned with a pantheon that is far too vast and with deities whose accoutrements are far too numerous, this transcendent reality is not depicted representationally but symbolically.

The symbol solves many problems, for it is famous as the site of the coincidence of opposites. Thus if Tibetan deities are merely symbols, the wrathful need not contradict the peaceful. Without the symbol, the wrathful deities seem unique to Tibet, the product of the interplay between the topography of Tibet and the psychology of the Tibetan. At the same time, however, the peaceful deities seem to represent a more timeless and transcendent reality. But if all the deities, wrathful and peaceful, are really symbols, the problem dissolves; both symbolize a universal and ancient truth, as Pal explains:

> It must be emphasized that although these terrifying deities of Buddhism may appear demonic, they are not "demons" in the Western sense. Nor are they personifications of evil or demonic forces. Rather, their fierce forms symbolize the violence that is a fundamental reality of the cosmos and the cosmic process in the universe in general, and of the human mind in particular. . . . Science now states that the cosmos was born in violence; perhaps the ancient visionaries realized this universal truth when they envisioned the divine principle in terms of a *mysterium tremendum*.[22]

This compulsion toward the symbolic, whether the symbols are peaceful or wrathful, reaches its apogee when Detlef Lauf declares, "These representations were not experienced as definite deities or real figures, but as symbols of a spiritual process which could be perfected and realized only in pure introspection."[23] Such symbols can only be depicted, furthermore, by an artist who is himself privy to their secret meaning, a meaning that the historian, not being an initiate, may be excused from understanding:

> He has learned the classical Indian Sâdhanas—those short meditative texts with Mantras (as invocations)—in which the deities were described

with all their attributes, Mudrâs and colours for the purpose of pictorial meditation. Meditating on such Sâdhanas himself, the artist, time and again, becomes the creator of these embedded images—images developed out of himself. The Tibetan artist, being initiated into the profound teachings of the themes represented by him, thus creates works which in turn can be, and are designed to be, understood only by the initiated. This is an important factor in the contemplation of Tibetan art, an art frequently so obscurely encoded that access to it often seems barred to a thinking mind.[24]

Even Tucci, who deemed it necessary to devote the first volume of his massive *Tibetan Painted Scrolls* to Tibetan history and religion in order to contextualize the works of art he was to describe, succumbed to the mystification of the artist who, he said "must be at one with the spiritual planes he wants to reproduce . . . drawing [infinite worlds] only out of himself, by virtue of the power of meditation and of ritual."[25]

Art historians have not only considered the Tibetan artist, but also the viewer, once again deriving their vocabulary from psychology, but offering two antithetical views. In one the viewer is passive, like the hypnotist's subject waiting to be shown the Queen of Diamonds, the painting precipitating progress on the path: "The icon-mirror functions by establishing within itself (and therefore in the field of physical perception), the inclinations of the celebrant which would otherwise remain unconscious, permitting him to recognize them with a view to progress along the path of deconditioning."[26] In the other, art reveals reality, but only to those who have eyes to see. As Pal explains, "In general, images of deities, whether painted or sculpted, are meant only for the initiated and adept. They are intended to help him or her to achieve that state of concentration in which external symbols can be dispensed with altogether."[27] Thus "the many varied icons represented in Tibetan art are not meant to depict separate objective or imaginary human-shaped beings, or even particular spirit-beings, but states of being which the human viewer is meant inwardly to adopt."[28] Here one sees a variation on a distinction that goes back to the eighteenth century, where Hindus were seen to hold two attitudes toward their gods: the elite knew that the images were symbols pointing to an unseen reality, while the unlettered masses were superstitious idolaters. Depending on their estimation of Tibetan society, art historians have tended to place all Tibetans in one or the other category. In his 1969 film *Requiem for a Faith* (Hartley Film Foundation), Huston Smith explains, "These gods that seem so solid, so objectively real, actually represent our own psychic forces."

Also subject to the symbol are the famous representations of male and female deities in sexual union, called *yab yum* (father mother) in Tibetan. Such images elicited the opprobrium of Europeans in China during the nineteenth century. Garnet Wolseley, in his *Narrative of the War with China in 1860* describes the Yonghe-gong (today known to tourists as the "Lama Temple") in Beijing:

> Lust and sensuality is represented in its hideous nakedness and under its most disgusting aspect. . . . The priests when exhibiting these beastly groups did so with the greatest apparent satisfaction, and seemed to gloat over the abominations before them, which to any but those of the most bestial dispositions must have been loathsome in the extreme. Surely it cannot be wondered at, that a people who thus deify lust, should be base and depraved, and incapable of any noble feelings or lofty aspirations after either the good or the great.[29]

But in the present century, the male and female pair are explained as symbols of the coincidence of any number of dualities. For Evans-Wentz the pair represents the unity of phenomena and noumena,[30] for Sierksma, it is the union of the self and the ego.[31] For Heinrich Zimmer, "Scarcely could the ultimate identity of Eternity and Time, Nirvāna and Samsāra, the two aspects of the revealed Absolute, be represented in a more majestically intimate way."[32] For Giuseppe Tucci's photographer, Fosco Maraini, it is "the Absolute, the Ultimate, the First, the Eternal, the Everlasting, and the All-pervading, in the form of a bejewelled prince voluptuously embracing his shakti. What fantastic imagination, what metaphysical daring, to represent the most abstract possible concept, a concept only definable by negatives, like mathematical infinity, by the most concrete, the most carnal picture that it is possible to imagine."[33] Yet, Lama Govinda explains, it is not really sexual, rather the union of male and female "is indissolubly associated with the highest spiritual reality in the process of enlightenment, so that associations with the realm of physical sexuality are completely ignored."[34]

After the terrifying deities and the *yab yum* pairs, the third category of Tibetan art that has most fascinated art historians is the mandala. A mandala is a representation of a buddha's palace, with a buddha (sometimes in union with a consort) in the center, surrounded by arrays of other buddhas, bodhisattvas, gods, and goddesses, with protectors standing guard in the doorways at the four cardinal directions. A mandala is sometimes depicted in three dimensions, but it is usually depicted schematically in two dimensions, in paint or in sand.[35] In tantric initiations, the mandala, kept hidden during the early phases, is eventually revealed to the initiate, who is then allowed to "enter." It is this perfected abode, inhabited by buddhas and their consorts, bodhisattvas, and protectors, that the initiate is then instructed to visualize, in minute detail, in the practice of "deity yoga" (*lha'i rnal 'byor*), in which one meditates upon oneself as the central buddha of the mandala.[36] The mandala is not, then, a diagram that one stares at to induce altered states. Chögyam Trungpa explains that "It should be understood that mandala representations are not used as objects of contemplation in an attempt to bring about certain states of mind."[37]

However, the ritual use of the mandala seems to have been lost on many, including initiates like Lama Govinda, who described it as "a concentric diagram or plastic model, used for the purposes of meditation."[38] John Blofeld glossed the term as "an intricate pattern of decorated squares and circles used as a support for instruction and meditation."[39] Sometimes the term was simply rendered as "magic circle." But like other elements of Tibetan art, the mandala became prey to psychologization. (The term was central to Jung.) Pal explained, "There can be no doubt that the mandala is one of the most complex symbols of Esoteric Buddhism. It has a precise esoteric character which, in its simplest terms, may be described as the visible projection of the scheme of the universe. It is the universe reduced, through abstract lines, from its phenomenal multiplicity to its quintessential unity, from chaos to order."[40]

Tibetologists were not immune from the psychologizing trend. Tucci explained that a mandala was "no longer a cosmogram but a psychocosmogram, the scheme of disintegration from the One to the many and of reintegration from the many to the One, to that Absolute Consciousness, entire and luminous, which Yoga causes to shine once more to the depths of our being."[41] Indeed, in his 1961 *The Theory and Practice of the Mandala: With Special Reference to the Modern Psychology of the Subconscious*, Tucci (who notes that he "is not unaware of the researches of Dr. Jung, whose work seems to me to be destined to leave lasting traces on human thought") seeks to

> reconstitute, in their essential outlines, the theory and practice of those psycho-cosmogratta which may lead the neophyte, by revealing to him the

secret play of the forces which operate in the universe and in us, on the way to the reintegration of consciousness. . . . You will find in this gnosis some striking analogies with comparable ideas expressed by currents of thought in other countries and in other ages; and often real anticipations of modern and more structural theories. Things could hardly be otherwise, since we are dealing with archetypes which are innate in the soul of Man and which, therefore, reappear in different lands and at different epochs but with a similar aspect, whenever Man seeks to reconstruct that unity which the predominance of one or other of the features of his character has broken or threatens to demolish.[42]

Thus, like the wrathful deity and the *yab yum* pair, the mandala is ultimately neither Tibetan nor even Buddhist, but a symbol of something ancient, universal, and timeless.

Many of the ways in which art historians have characterized Tibetan art and artists are echoed in the catalog that accompanied the most ambitious exhibition of Tibetan Buddhist art ever mounted, the "Wisdom and Compassion" show that opened in San Francisco in 1992, organized by Marilyn Rhie and Robert Thurman. The exhibition sought "to introduce Tibet's compelling and mysterious art *on its own terms*,"[43] an art that "seems to break the 'veil of illusion' and offer a complete, instantaneous vision of the radiant beauty and power of pure reality."[44] We find, for example, the observation, reminiscent of Tucci some four decades before, that "The erotic and terrific deities of Tibetan art and culture express the Tibetan mastery and further development of the sophisticated depth psychology inherited from Indian Buddhist civilization, anticipating discoveries in psychology made only recently in the West. And it is in this area, traditionally known as inner science (*adhyatma-vidya*), that Tibetan civilization has something else of its own, unique and of extreme value, to contribute to humanity."[45] Thurman and Rhie perhaps depart from their predecessors, however, in that they do not represent Tibetan art as an instantiation of psychological processes. Instead, in a more overtly theological tone, the images of Tibetan art are offered as a model for the world to emulate: "If we let ourselves observe and experience this [*yab yum*] image as Tibetans do, we can be inspired about the possibility of attaining enlightenment for ourselves."[46]

The "Wisdom and Compassion" exhibition was designed, according to the curators, like a mandala (which they rendered as a "sphere of spiritual nurture"). The first work the viewer encountered was a six-foot gilt brass statue of the wrathful bodhisattva Vajrapāṇi, serving as a protector, as he often does at the entrance of Tibetan temples. The viewer then entered the sacred space of the mandala itself, where the images were arranged in outer, middle, and inner halls. The outer hall, called "Tibet's Sacred History," was devoted to images of Śākyamuni Buddha, of arhats and bodhisattvas, and of various Indian *paṇḍitas* and *mahāsiddhas*, ending finally with three "Dharma Kings": the historical Tri Songdetsen (Khri srong lde btsan), during whose reign the first Buddhist monastery in Tibet was founded, as well as two mythological figures, Rudracakrin, who will lead the kingdom of Shambhala in its apocalyptic war against the barbarians, and Vaiśravana, god of the north. This final grouping of rather disparate figures under the rubric "Dharma Kings" suggests a blurring of any demarcation between the historical and mythological, a characteristic of the exhibition as a whole.

The middle hall was devoted to the four major sects of Tibetan Buddhism, described by Robert Thurman as "four great waves." This characterization implies that each earlier wave recedes as the next wave moves ashore, and supports a rather thinly veiled teleology that sees Tsong kha pa and the Geluk, the final wave, as the culmination of Tibetan Buddhist thought and practice. The important controversies that have occurred among the sects over the centuries were described as "very occasional conflicts" that always involved "political factions aligned with one or another 'regional' institution."[47] Each of the four sects was represented by images of important historical figures and examples of their preferred tutelary deities, or *yi dams*, with the same deity often appearing in the groupings of more than one sect.

The inner hall was devoted to pure lands, "Tibetan Perfected Worlds." Here one found images of "Cosmic Bodhisattvas" such as Avalokiteśvara and Tārā (who also appeared in the outer hall); "Cosmic Buddhas," including the "historical Buddha" Śākyamuni (also to be found in the outer hall); "Pure Lands" such as Padmasambhava's Copper Mountain and Samye monastery (the first Buddhist monastery in Tibet); figures of Milarepa and Tsong kha pa, who were also found in the middle hall in their respective orders; and a painting of the city of Lhasa. This mixing of mythical and historical figures, of heavenly pure lands and Tibetan cities, a mixing that some might see as merely incoherent, was perhaps intended by the curators to suggest that these lines should not be so sharply drawn, that if only we had the eyes to see we would also perceive Lhasa as a pure land as we approach the middle of the mandala. As they explain, "The Pure Land dimension of Tibet can be seen as the key to Tibet's mysterious fascination, as it revitalizes our dreams of the mandalic, sacred aspects of Earth itself and its ultimate potential as a paradise."[48] Or, more succinctly, "Through Tibet's seventeen-hundred-year association with the Buddha reality, the entire land of Tibet has become the closest place on earth to an actual Pure Land."[49] At the end of the exhibition, the viewer found in the middle of the mandala another mandala, one that monks from the Dalai Lama's monastery were in the process of constructing from colored grains of sand. Although the intent was to provide "the living context within which the ancient masterpieces come to life," one might also note that it is only here, in the inner sanctum of the symmetrical and static perfection of the pure land, at the center of the mandala and outside history, that Tibetan people, "real Tibetans" rather than idealized bodhisattvas and saints, were displayed, as in a *tableau vivant*.[50] (The monks were behind glass at the exhibition at the IBM Gallery in New York.)

FROM THE VARIOUS presentations surveyed in this chapter, one is confronted with a picture of Tibetan art as either a representation of the horrors that haunt the premodern mind or as a signpost to a sublime, hidden reality. The Tibetan artist is either an initiate of advanced mystical practice, translating his visions into line and color, or an automaton slavishly copying the iconographic conventions of a static and oppressive theology. The Tibetan viewer is either a credulous devotee who cowers before the frightful form or the knowing gnostic who looks through the numbing plethora of iconographic detail to an absolute beyond the veil of illusion. As Pal explained, "The tanka was not created for purely aesthetic enjoyment. Although some were hung as wall decorations, the tanka was primarily an image, an evocation. As the religion is essentially mystical, the tanka is intended to aid the devotee to look within himself."[51]

Perhaps much of such free association can be ascribed to the relatively late development (over the past two decades) of a scholarly knowledge about Tibetan art that may have deterred such representations, especially the kind of knowledge that could be derived from reading Tibetan texts and speaking to Tibetan artists.[52] Even when scholarly knowledge has been available, its belatedness and its limited circulation have kept it from displacing the popular, which gains authority through the power of repetition in exhibition catalogs and coffee-table books. Just as the insistence of Sanskritists that *oṃ maṇi padme hūṃ* does not mean "the jewel in the lotus" has gone largely unheeded, so Tibetological prefaces to Tibetan texts have done little thus far to dispel the notion of the Tibetan painter as an anonymous mystical monk. Nonetheless, research that involved actually speaking with contemporary Tibetan refugee artists about their work paints a rather different picture of the production and use of Tibetan art.

Paintings were commissioned from artists for reasons more quotidian than mystical. Commissioning a painting of a deity was a way of making merit, merit that could in turn be used to avert obstacles (*bar ched*). Paintings were requested, often on the advice of a lama, to dispel illness, to avert danger during an astrologically impropitious year, to help a recently deceased family member find a happy rebirth. Images of Amitāyus, the buddha of infinite life, were commissioned to promote longevity. Images of deities were above all objects of worship and propitiation to whom offerings were made and prayers were recited, and before whom prostrations were performed, thereby generating merit for the practitioner. Paintings also had didactic purposes, and itinerant teachers would often unroll a painting in public and tell miraculous tales of bodhisattvas. For those monks and lamas who engaged in meditation, visualization was an important part of their practice, but paintings were to be used as a template only in the preliminary stages of meditation until a sharp mental image could be produced. There were precise guidelines for the depiction of deities, although the storied use of iconometrics (the geometric grids specifying the proportions of a given deity) in Tibetan painting was as much a matter of interpretation and even controversy as it was of slavish repetition.[53]

Tibetan artists were generally ordinary artisans who learned their craft from their fathers. Although some accomplished masters of Buddhist doctrine and practice were also skilled artists, the majority of Tibetan artists were laymen with little specific Buddhist training. Buddhist texts require that before executing an image of a tantric deity, the artist must undergo the proper initiation and go on a meditational retreat, and then observe dietary restrictions while executing the work.[54] It seems, in fact, that such things were rarely done, apart from receiving an initiation that would permit them to depict the deities of a given tantric class. Although artists were generally well paid for their work, their fee was technically considered an offering since trafficking in sacred images was proscribed.[55] Thus the Tibetan artist may not have been as Thurman and Rhie describe him: "The artist has to be a person who is open enough to enlightenment to serve as a selfless vessel for its manifestations, who participates in the creation of a work of art out of dedication to the higher realm, and not primarily for fame and profit."[56]

To next consider the degree to which Tibetan art is "symbolic," one might begin by telling a Tibetan tale. As a young merchant is about to set off for India, his aging mother asks him to bring her back a relic of the Buddha. The son sets off on his journey, but forgets her request until he is almost back home. Coming upon the skull of a dog, he extracts a tooth, wraps it in silk, and presents it to his grateful mother, who worships it fervently, doing prostrations and making offerings daily. Soon the tooth begins to produce small pearls (*ring bsrel*) and emanate a rainbow light, as authentic relics do.[57] The story is thus told as an illustration of the power of faith. But a variation on the story (provided by Thurman and Rhie in *Wisdom and Compassion*) adds a fascinating twist. After presenting the dog's tooth to his delighted mother, the son begins to feel guilty and decides to confess his deception to her. The Buddha—more precisely, the Jowo (Jo bo) statue in Lhasa, the most sacred image of the Buddha in Tibet—appears and dissuades him, explaining that the relic is authentic, that the Jowo himself had magically placed the dog's skull in the son's path, so that the tooth was actually a manifestation of the Buddha, that is, of the Buddha's image in Lhasa, a relic created by an image. The son is convinced when he returns home and finds the tooth surrounded by a rainbow halo.[58]

This variation on the tale provides an important insight into Tibetan notions of symbolism and embodiment. A Tibetan image, whether painted or sculpted, is not considered finished until it has been animated in a consecration (*rab gnas*) ceremony. In the case of a sculpture, the interior must be filled with rolls of mantras wrapped around a wooden dowel, called the "life stick" (*srog shing*), which runs from the crown of the head to the base of the image. Often incense or the soil from a sacred place is added as well, before the bottom of the image is sealed shut and marked with the sign of a crossed *vajra*. Paintings are marked with mantras, often the letters *oṃ*, *āḥ*, *hūṃ* on the reverse of the scroll, aligned with the head, throat, and heart of the figure on the front. A consecration ceremony, sometimes brief, sometimes quite elaborate, is then performed, the purpose of which is to cause the deity represented in the image (most commonly, a buddha) to enter into and thus animate the image.[59] The ritual is said to cause the deity, which in the case of a buddha abides in what is called the "unlocated nirvana" (*rab tu mi gnas pa'i myang 'das, apratiṣṭhitanirvāṇa*), because he abides in neither samsara nor nirvana, to become located in the physical image. The image has to be transformed into a buddha in order to become a site of merit making. In the ceremony, the unconsecrated image is (in the visualization of the person performing the consecration) made to dissolve into emptiness (which is its true nature) and then reappear as the deity itself, often through the use of a mirror, which reflects the ultimate nature of the deity into the conventional form of the image.[60]

A standard component of the ceremony is the recitation of the verse "As all the buddhas from [their] abodes in Tuṣita heaven, entered the womb of Queen Māyā, likewise may you enter this reflected image."[61] The consecrated image of the deity thus is not a symbol of the deity but, effectively, is the deity, and there are numerous stories in Tibet of images speaking to their devotees. In the variation of the story above the dog's tooth did not glow because of the mother's faith, but because it was in fact a relic of the Buddha, created by the Buddha. In the "three body" (*trikāya*) theory of Mahayana Buddhism, the emanation body of the Buddha (*nirmāṇakāya*) includes not only the form of the Buddha that appears on earth, once in each age, in the guise of a monk, adorned with the thirty-two major marks and eighty minor marks of a superman (*mahāpuruṣa*); the Buddha can also appear in the guise of ordinary beings, as well as (apparently) inanimate objects (called "crafted emanation bodies," *bzo sprul sku*), such as paintings and sculptures. Thus, the dog's tooth is a relic, it is a tooth of the Buddha, because it is an emanation of the Buddha. The fact that it is a sculpture of the Buddha that appears to the son, speaks to him, and identifies the tooth as his own creation only emphasizes this identity. It is this identity, which in the case of the consecration of an image is effected through ritual, that may help to explain the general absence in Tibet of what might be termed "art-historical" literature.[62]

All of this would suggest that the Tibetan attitude toward the artistic representation of Buddhist deities might best be described with the term used by the early Catholic missionaries to Tibet: idolatry, defined as "the worship or paying of divine honors to a false god as represented by some image or idol in which he is believed to be present."[63] If the qualification "false" is removed and it is understood that Buddhist gods may be male or female, then the definition appears apt. The 1676 work *China and France, or Two Treatises* reports that the Catholic missionaries Grueber and d'Orville were not able to meet the Dalai Lama "because none is admitted that makes profession of the Christian Religion," but they saw his picture, "unto which, as much reverence is paid, when but represented in Pictures and Images, as if he were there in person, by these Idolaters."[64] One finds a similar view in the writings of the missionary and scholar Graham Sandberg, who wrote in 1906, "Whatever praises modern enthusiasts may lavish on Buddhism as a pure and philosophic form of belief, they cannot long observe its practice in any country where it actually prevails without discovering that it is largely idolatrous."[65]

One might prefer to call the Buddhist images icons, religious images that are believed to partake of the substance of what they represent, but the point remains the same.[66] The Tibetan attitude, from the point of view of an earlier anthropology of religion, would be seen as the product of a primitive mentality. E. B. Tylor explains that "the tendency to identify the symbol and the symbolized, a tendency so strong among children and the ignorant everywhere, led to the idol being treated as a living powerful being, and thence even to explicit doctrines as to the manner of its energy or animation."[67]

Thus, far from being the high symbolist art that is always pointing to something else, away from itself, always standing for something else, a Tibetan image is not, in an important sense, a representation of the deity at all, but is the deity itself. The inability of art historians to recognize this fact, observable not only in Tibet but throughout the Buddhist world, derives in large part from a lack of interest in the uses of works of art. And even when use is invoked, it is romantic: the mystic contemplation of the image, turning a blind eye to persons prostrating in its presence. Indeed, the reception of Tibetan Buddhist art in the West observes the law of the excluded middle (something "Eastern thinking" putatively lacks). When the art historian explains wrathful deities as the projection of the Tibetan unconscious onto the brutal landscape, what is missing is any mediation by a Tibetan consciousness, by a Tibetan agent between the unconscious and the landscape. The Tibetan is instead portrayed as the passive observer of his or her own projections; the only agency is ascribed to the sinister lama who manipulates the observer's fear for his own gain. When the art historian portrays the *yab yum* image as a symbol of the union of polarities, he ignores the fact that according to certain systems of Tibetan tantric theory (including the "conservative" Geluk), the attainment of buddhahood is impossible without at some point engaging in actual sexual union with an actual (rather than visualized) partner, and that the biographies and autobiographies of Tibetan lamas are replete with descriptions of their practice of sexual yoga.[68] When the art historian portrays the mandala as an abstract symbol of an archetypal universe, he ignores the fact that a mandala is a particular palace of a particular deity who occupies the central throne, a palace decorated in a particular way and inhabited by particular buddhas, bodhisattvas, gods, goddesses, and protectors, that there are many different mandalas, and that the initiate seeks to memorize the palace in all of its aspects in order to become that particular deity.

Just as Tibetan art is encountered not in Tibet but is located elsewhere, so its meaning is not specific but universalized away from Tibet, to an imagined state of enlightenment in the future or to a primitive state of human evolution in the past, but never in the present, never in Tibet. Thus, as with other portrayals of things marked with the adjective "Tibetan," Tibetan art is represented as a field of opposites, of Chinese influence or Indian influence, of peaceful deities or wrathful deities, of sexual degradation or high symbolism, of works that compel abject devotion or that point only beyond, works executed by evil magicians or enlightened sages, who inhabit a land that can inspire only terror or mystic visions of emptiness. Invisible in all of these portrayals are Tibetans, actors (both ritually and otherwise) in the middle of a universe constituted and populated in ways quite different from the universe of those who seek to explain Tibetan art to us and to them.

But is the perspective of the Tibetan, in the end, the determinative perspective? And, if so, which Tibetan, the artist in exile or the artist in Tibet? And which artist, the one producing *thangkas* for the Dalai Lama, the one producing *thangkas* for tourists, or the one producing modernist paintings? Perhaps it is ultimately a question of relevance (in the linguistic sense of having a contextual effect), as the popular and the scholarly once again converge. Travelers to Tibet have often remarked on the credulity of Tibetans who would trade an old buddha image for a new one, or who would repaint old *thangkas* that had lost their color. The age of the piece, unless it had once belonged to or was somehow associated with a past saint, was not as relevant as it would be to the Tibetologist or art collector. Yet it would be relevant to the Tibetan that the work be consecrated for use, that it be an animated icon. Some collectors, operating in a different system of relevance, have pried the bottom from a statue and emptied it of its contents, have, in effect, unknowingly deconsecrated it. Is it, then, blasphemous to display in a public gallery a mandala that would be revealed only to tantric initiates? Is it blasphemous to hang a *thangka* of the Buddha in one's bedroom, if one does not know that Tibetans consider it a sin to make love in the presence of the Buddha? What is relevant for the Tibetan may not be relevant for the Tibetologist. What is relevant for the Tibetologist may not be relevant for the collector (made all the more complicated when the collector is a Tibetan or the Tibetologist is a Buddhist).[69] Does the object, although remaining the same, also change as it moves from one incommensurable context to another, from the hands of one to another, like Belle's necklace in Cocteau's *La Belle et la bête?*

What, then, is a Tibetan Buddhist painting? For a Tibetan it may be a valued heirloom, but it is also, when properly consecrated, an object of devotion and a medium for making merit. For the scholar of Tibetan Buddhism, it is an artifact: the deity needs to be identified, the piece dated, its provenance established, its author named, its style analyzed. For the connoisseur, the painting is not an artifact but a work of art, not a datum but a commodity. The information provided by the scholar is important, but largely in order to establish the commercial value of the piece. Linked to the value is the question of enjoyment, and here the ritual use and the techniques of the artist may be irrelevant to the connoisseurship that has been inextricable from art history. With connoisseurship has come a certain compulsion to interpret as a way of increasing value, a compulsion that has resulted in some of the theories of Tibetan art recounted here, all of which, in one way or another, attempt to control Tibetan art by making it into what Anne Chayet has called "une forme exotique de l'art occidental."[70] But perhaps what we call "Tibetan art" or "Tibetan Buddhism" is already uncontrollable and perhaps it is in the renunciation of the compulsion to control that a certain liberation may lie.

The Field

In a 1977 survey of the available Western-language scholarship on Tibetan Buddhism, the noted Sinologist Michel Strickmann identified what he perceived as a dangerous trend: "a far more serious threat to the interests of the non-specialist, in my opinion, emanates from a mass of new writings that ostensibly deal with Tibetan Buddhism or Buddhist Tāntra. Though sometimes adorned with hitherto respectable names, many of these books appear in reality to be no more than tracts telling harassed Americans how to relax." [1] Strickmann refers to the commingling of the scholarly and the popular, a trend that, as we have seen, has a long history in the Western encounter with Tibet. It is a trend, also, that has only grown and diversified since Professor Strickmann bemoaned its existence two decades ago. This chapter will survey the development of Tibetan Buddhist Studies as an academic field in North America. Focusing especially on the changes that occurred in the wake of the Tibetan diaspora that began in 1959, it will attempt to demonstrate some of the ways in which the production of knowledge is always partial, always undertaken within the determining confines of time, place, and cultural climate.[2]

In the academic study of Tibetan Buddhism, perhaps differing only in degree from other academic fields, the popular is never wholly absent. But there is, indeed, a difference in degree, for a number of reasons. First is the fact that for most of its history, Tibet has been regarded as somehow peripheral by its neighbors. For India, it has been the place beyond the forbidding Himalayan range, a place of mythical kingdoms and divine abodes. For the various Chinese, Mongol, and Manchu dynasties, it has been a distant, somewhat unrefined yet magically potent neighbor, sometimes imagined as part of their empires, sometimes not. For the British and the Russians of the late nineteenth century, it was the land just beyond the borders of their empires, a place to be mapped by spies. Even the Tibetans have participated in this perception, portraying their land in both Buddhist and Bönpo histories as a wild and uncivilized place to which culture was introduced only from the outside, whether from Buddhist India or Bönpo Zhang Zhung.

The perception of Tibet as peripheral has persisted in large part because until the second half of this century Tibet was never colonized, not by the Chinese, Mongol, Manchu, British, or Russian empires. One of the many products of colonialism is knowledge, produced first by explorers and merchants, then by colonial officers and missionaries, later by specialists in archives and institutes in the metropole and colleges and universities in the colony. No such institutions emerged in Tibet until after the Chinese invasion and occupation that began in 1950. Hence, there was no factory for the production of official knowledge, leaving only unofficial knowledge, produced by travelers and enthusiasts, "gifted amateurs." Among trained Orientalists of the nineteenth and early-twentieth centuries, classical Tibetan was almost always a secondary language, learned by the Indologist to read translations of Sanskrit texts, learned by the Sinologist to read an edict on one of the four faces of a tetraglot stele or to read the non-Chinese manuscripts among the huge cache discovered in the caves and temples of Dunhuang in western China.[3]

Indeed, it was only after the Tibetan diaspora that began in 1959 that the study of Tibetan Buddhism "in its own right" began to be accepted as a legitimate academic field. This occurred as Tibetan lamas made their way, under various auspices, to North America and began to attract American and Canadian students. It was the more dedicated of such students who went on to form the greatest pool of graduate students for the newly founded programs in Bud-

dhist Studies, who were to receive the first doctorates, and who were to com-
pete for the increasing number of academic positions in Asian religion, having
to suffer the effects of the perception of Tibet and its Buddhism as peripheral,
somehow less central than the religions of India or China or Japan.

Buddhist Studies, as a recognized academic discipline, came into existence only in the present century. It began in Europe as an offshoot of Oriental philology, in which scholars of Sanskrit also read Buddhist texts. Many
of these works were first made available in Europe by Brian Houghton Hodgson, the British resident to the Court of Nepal, who in 1837 dispatched
bundles of Sanskrit manuscripts from his post in Kathmandu to the great
libraries of Europe. The first scholar to make extensive use of Hodgson's gift
was the French scholar Eugène Burnouf, who translated the *Lotus Sutra* into
French; it was published posthumously in 1852. It was this translation and his
1844 *Introduction à l'histoire du Buddhisme indien* that introduced Mahayana
Buddhism to European and American intellectuals, among them Wagner and
Thoreau. From that point on, a growing number of scholars concerned themselves with Buddhist literature, debating such questions as whether the original teachings of the Buddha were preserved in Sanskrit or in Pali, and later
considering such doctrinal questions as whether or not nirvana is a state of
utter annihilation.[4]

Beyond the work of Burnouf (and several others), the literature of Buddhism did not reach a significant Anglophone audience until the publication
in the last decades of the nineteenth century of The Sacred Books of the East
series, which was "translated by Various Oriental Scholars and edited by
F. Max Müller." Among the fifty volumes in the series, seven were devoted
to Buddhist works, for the most part works from Pali, but also a Chinese
translation of Aśvaghoṣa's life of the Buddha, another translation of the *Lotus
Sutra*, and a volume entitled *Buddhist Mahāyāna Texts*, which included the
same life of the Buddha, this time translated from the Sanskrit, the *Diamond
Sutra*, the *Heart Sutra*, and the shorter and longer Pure Land sutras. None of
the works in The Sacred Books of the East were of Tibetan authorship, nor
were they translated from the Tibetan.

This is not to suggest that Tibetan works were entirely neglected during
the nineteenth century. In 1837 Isaac Jacob Schmidt published a French translation of the *Diamond Sutra* from the Tibetan, followed in 1843 by a translation of the *Sutra on the Wise Man and the Fool*. In 1847 Philippe Édouard
Foucaux (1811–1894) published his French translation of a Tibetan transla-

tion of a Sanskrit life of the Buddha, the *Lalitavistara*.[5] The most significant work on Tibetan Buddhist literature to appear during this period, however, was that of Alexander Csoma de Kőrös, the Hungarian scholar who published a Tibetan-English dictionary and a survey of the Tibetan Buddhist canon.[6] Nonetheless, during the nineteenth century scholarly interest in Tibet was focused largely on those works that shed light on Indian Buddhism, that is, the various Tibetan canons of Sanskrit works translated into Tibetan, and Tibetan histories (*chos 'byung*) of Indian Buddhism.[7]

In the United States the diplomat William Woodville Rockhill, who had traveled extensively in China and Tibet, published in 1892 *Udanavarga: A Collection of Verses from the Buddhist Canon* and in 1907 *The Life of the Buddha and the Early History of His Order, Derived from Tibetan Works in the Bkah-hgyur and Bstan-hgyur*. In 1942 Ferdinand Lessing of the University of California at Berkeley published *Yung-ho-kung, An Iconography of the Lamaist Cathedral in Peking, with Notes on Lamaist Mythology and Cult;* he later collaborated with Alex Wayman on the translation of an important Geluk survey of tantra, *Mkhas grub rje's Fundamentals of the Buddhist Tantras*. Tibetan Buddhist Studies, however, did not become established in North America until the 1960s (after the diaspora). Its major figures were David Seyfort Ruegg, Herbert Guenther, and David Snellgrove.[8]

The study of Tibetan Buddhism received its first substantial philanthropic support in the United States when the Rockefeller Foundation provided funds to bring the distinguished Sakya scholar Deshung Rinpoche to the University of Washington in 1960. In 1961 the first graduate program in Buddhist Studies was established at the University of Wisconsin, under the direction of Richard Robinson, a Canadian who had received his doctorate from the School of Oriental and African Studies of the University of London, where he wrote a dissertation later published as *Early Mādhyamika in India and China*. The students that Robinson produced filled many of the positions in Buddhist Studies that opened at American colleges and universities during the late 1960s and early 1970s. The students included Lewis Lancaster, Stephan Beyer, Francis Cook, Jeffrey Hopkins, Roger Corless, Steven Young, Dennis Lishka, Charles Prebish, Douglas Daye, Stefan Anacker, and Harvey Aronson. Some remained in the field, some went on to other professions. Those who remained in the field of Buddhist Studies generally found positions not in departments of Sanskrit or Classics or Oriental Languages, as would have been the case in Europe, but in departments of Religion or Religious Studies, a shift that would significantly affect both the direction and the form that Buddhist Studies and, in particular, Tibetan Buddhist Studies would take in North America.[9]

The growth of Religious Studies as an academic discipline in the United States has been largely a postwar development, with especial growth during the 1960s. During the late nineteenth century, various anthropologists and students of "culture" (one thinks immediately of Frazer and Tylor) were examining certain practices of non-Western societies, practices that they identified as "religious." The work of such scholars, often identified as "history of religions," "comparative religion," or "world religions," paid much attention to the evolutionary development of religions from the animistic and fetishistic to the polytheistic and then to the monotheistic. Christianity was largely exempted from such studies, being regarded as the culmination of religious evolution when it was regarded as a "religion" at all. The study of Christianity was thus generally confined to theology faculties in Europe and to seminaries and divinity schools in the United States.

The expansion and liberalization of the humanities curriculum in the United States after the Second World War led to the study of Christianity being established in public universities and moved out of the divinity schools of private universities. There was a perceived need to wean the curriculum in Religious Studies from the seminary model, to mitigate Protestant dominance by including Catholic and Jewish Studies, and to take into account non-Christian religions.[10] However, in the formation of the curriculum of Religious Studies, much of the structure of the seminary faculty was retained. A typical seminary would offer training in Biblical Studies (Old Testament and New Testament, with their attendant languages), Church History, Theology, and Ethics, along with Pastoral Counseling and Homiletics. In the typical department of Religious Studies at a college, there would be positions in Old Testament, New Testament, Church History, Theology, and Ethics, although the names were sometimes changed. Old Testament could be subsumed under Jewish Studies, Church History sometimes became "Religion in America," and Theology would become "Religious Thought" or "Philosophy of Religion," the latter placing particular emphasis on Feuerbach and Kierkegaard. To this core was added "World Religions" or "Comparative Religion," designed to cover the non-Judeo-Christian world—that is, among the "world religions," Islam, Hinduism, Buddhism, Confucianism, Taoism, and sometimes Shinto. Larger or more prosperous institutions might also add positions in Psychology of Religion (where William James, the Freud of *The Future of* an *Illusion,* and Jung received particular attention) and Sociology of Religion (where Weber and Durkheim were regarded as the founders). Religious Studies in the United States (and perforce Buddhist Studies) therefore was concerned largely with questions of meaning, interpreting texts to discover beliefs and worldviews. In Europe, however, where Buddhist Studies remained firmly within the long tradition of Oriental studies and philology, meaning in this sense was far less important than the ostensibly more simple commitment to the further accumulation of knowledge.

With the rise of the colonial powers during the eighteenth and nineteenth centuries, the list of the great religions slowly lengthened. In order to qualify, each (if at all possible) should have a founder, an organized hierarchy of priests, a canon of sacred texts, and a set of defining "beliefs." The first to be admitted was Islam, which like Judaism and Christianity regarded Abraham as its progenitor; then Confucianism, for its ethics, and Hinduism, or at least "classical Hinduism," for its mystical philosophy; and "original" Buddhism, for its rationality and individualism. But the religion of Tibet, as discussed in the first chapter, remained largely unknown except from outside. Catholic missionaries accepted the Chinese view that the religion practiced at the Manchu court was not Confucianism, not Taoism, and not Buddhism, but rather *lama jiao,* the sect of the lamas, or "Lamaism." For European scholars of the Victorian period, the religion of the Tibetans was not authentically Buddhist. As Waddell wrote, "the Lamaist cults comprise much deep rooted devil worship, which I describe in some fullness. For Lamaism is only thinly and imperfectly varnished over with Buddhist symbolism, beneath which the sinister growth of poly-demonist superstition darkly appears." [11]

Tibetan Buddhism was thus largely excluded from the realm of "comparative religion" and "comparative philosophy"; when one surveys anthologies of "world philosophy" or various renditions of the perennial philosophy or peruses journals such as *Philosophy East and West* one rarely finds a Tibetan name, either the name of an ancient Tibetan philosopher or of a modern Tibetan arguing his case. [12] As mentioned above, this is largely because Tibet never became a European colony or fell under direct European influence. Thus, in Tibet, there was no attempt to "modernize" by establishing universities, importing European technologies, or sending elites to Europe for education. [13] The absence of Western colonial institutions in Tibet prevented Tibetan scholars from producing Western forms of knowledge. Since Tibet was not a European colony, institutes, libraries, archives, and museums were not created, either in Tibet or in a European metropole. In his account of the British invasion of Tibet in 1903 and 1904, L. Austine Waddell, chief medical officer during the invasion, made a prediction that never came true: "In the University, which must ere long be established under British direction at Lhasa, a chief place will surely be assigned to studies in the origin of the religion of the country." [14] This also impeded the teaching of European languages in Tibet and the teaching of the Tibetan language in Europe. At the same time, the Buddhism most valued in Europe was that which was controlled by Europe and long dead in Asia, Indian Buddhism. As described in the first chapter, it was this Buddhism, especially in its Pali form, that European scholars regarded as the "original" or "true" Buddhism, and in comparison to which Tibetan Buddhism was judged a late and corrupted form. All of these factors have contributed to the general exclusion of Tibetan Buddhism from the discourse of comparative religion and philosophy. [15]

With the growing commitment to adding non-Christian religions to the Religious Studies curriculum, graduates of Robinson's Buddhist Studies program at Wisconsin were well suited for the World Religions positions in the new and growing departments of Religious Studies. Because Buddhism was the one "pan-Asian" religion, scholars with training in Buddhist Studies had to know something of the traditions of the culture in which Buddhism had developed (India) and of those cultures to which it had migrated (China and Japan). (Other regions in which Buddhism held sway, such as Southeast Asia, Tibet, and Korea, received less attention prior to the 1980s.) Thus, when there was only one opening in World Religions in a given department, the Buddhologist was well positioned to fill it. Even when departments expanded to include an Islamicist or a specialist in Hinduism, there was often a position for someone in Buddhist Studies as well. Some of the larger departments subscribed to what was referred to as the "zoo theory," staffing a department with scholars of each of the major world religions, in some cases seeking scholars who were themselves adherents of those traditions. Positions in Jewish Studies were almost always filled by Jews. Positions in Islamic Studies have increasingly come to be held by Muslims (of Middle Eastern or South Asian ancestry). Positions in Buddhist Studies are often held by Buddhists, but, as will be discussed below, these Buddhists have generally been of the white variety.

Regardless of the number of "non-Western" positions, however, the majority of positions were still those inherited from the seminary model. As a result, the agenda of the scholarship was largely a reflection of its particular concerns, with research and teaching directed toward the exegesis of "sacred texts" and on "worldview" or "belief." In producing his scholarship, how-ever, the Buddhologist among the Christians was faced with a dilemma. The texts that he dealt with (the scholars of this generation were generally male) often presented daunting philological and historical problems, the solutions to which, when finally found, were generally of such a technical nature that they appeared hopelessly arcane to the Buddhologist's undergraduate students as well as to his colleagues in the Department of Religious Studies. It was therefore common, both in teaching and in scholarship (especially in the United States), to turn away from the details of doctrine and institution and instead to look back toward their putative source, the experience of medita-tion. Few scholars of this period would question the declaration by Edward Conze, an influential Buddhologist of the 1960s, that "each and every [Bud-dhist philosophical] proposition must be considered in reference to its spiri-tual intention and as a formulation of meditational experiences acquired in the course of the process of winning salvation."[16]

Of particular interest for the development of the field of Tibetan Bud-dhist Studies is the career of Jeffrey Hopkins, who came to Robinson's pro-gram in Wisconsin only after having received considerable training in Ti-betan Buddhism elsewhere. Hopkins had gone to Wisconsin on the advice of his teacher, Geshe Wangyal (1901–1983), whose influence on the current state of Tibetan Buddhist Studies in the United States is difficult to overstate. Geshe Wangyal was born in what is today Kalmykia, the region between the Black Sea and the Caspian Sea populated by the Kalmyks, a Mongol people who in the seventeenth century emigrated there after the Mongols retreated from their European conquests. The Kalmyks are Tibetan Buddhists. Geshe Wangyal was born there in 1901 and ordained as a Buddhist monk at the age of six. He excelled at his studies and was chosen by the prominent Buryat Mongol lama Agvan Dorzhiev to travel to Tibet to enroll at Drepung mon-astery. He arrived in Lhasa in 1922 and remained for nine years, completing the monastic curriculum. He intended to return to Kalmykia to teach, but en route learned of the Bolshevik persecutions of Buddhist institutions. He re-mained in Beijing for some years, serving as translator for Sir Charles Bell (1870–1945, British political officer for Sikkim, Bhutan, and Tibet) during his travels in China and Manchuria. He later traveled to India and met the British mountaineer Marco Pallis, with whom he spent four months in En-gland in 1937. During the Second World War, he divided his time between India and Tibet. With the first news of the Chinese invasion of Tibet, he left Tibet for good and moved to Kalimpong in Sikkim.[17]

By that time a community of Kalmyk immigrants had been established in Freewood Acres, New Jersey. During the Second World War, the Kalmyks, who had been brutally persecuted under the Soviets, sided with the Germans. One group followed the Germans in their retreat from the Soviet Union, finding themselves in Austria when the war ended. This group was allowed to emigrate to New Jersey rather than being repatriated to the Soviet Union to suffer Stalin's revenge. With their community established, they sought a monk to perform religious functions. In 1955 Geshe Wangyal arrived. Like so many Buddhist monks who first came to the United States to serve a refugee community, Geshe Wangyal soon attracted the attention of Americans interested in Buddhism. It became known to the Asian enthusiasts of Manhattan and Boston that there was a Tibetan lama living in New Jersey. Among the most enthusiastic were Robert Thurman and Jeffrey Hopkins, both of whom left Harvard to live at Geshe Wangyal's Lamaist Buddhist Monastery of America in 1963. Geshe Wangyal accompanied Thurman to India, where in 1965 he was the first American to be ordained as a Tibetan Buddhist monk. After Thurman returned to the United States, Geshe Wangyal encouraged him to return to Harvard, where he completed his B.A. and Ph.D. He is currently the Jey Tsong Khapa Professor of Buddhist Studies at Columbia University.

After ten years of study with Geshe Wangyal, Hopkins enrolled in the graduate program in Buddhist Studies at the University of Wisconsin, where he and Robinson established Tibet House, a place for students of Tibetan Buddhism to study with visiting refugee Tibetan lamas. After Robinson's death in 1971, Hopkins went to India to conduct his dissertation research. Living in Dharamsala, he soon attracted the attention of the Dalai Lama, who was impressed both by Hopkins's fluent Tibetan as well as his substantial knowledge of Madhyamaka philosophy. In 1972 Hopkins returned to the United States, where he completed his doctorate. In 1973 he was hired as a member of the Department of Religious Studies at the University of Virginia.

At that time the University of Virginia had one of the fastest growing departments of Religious Studies in North America, in the early years of the decade adding positions in Islam, Buddhist Studies, Hinduism, and Chinese Religions, along with Psychology of Religion and Philosophy of Religion. Hopkins had an immediate impact, teaching courses on Buddhist philosophy and meditation to huge classes, even attracting twenty students to his course in classical Tibetan, ten of whom survived the first semester. Hopkins's specialty was Madhyamaka philosophy; his massive dissertation, *Meditation on*

Emptiness, which was later published as a book, became the bible (in its University Microfilms International form) for a growing number of students. Some went so far as to have a rubber stamp made that read "Does Not Inherently Exist," which they stamped everywhere from their foreheads to the urinals in the Department of Religious Studies' men's room. During his second semester, he brought to campus a Tibetan lama, Khetsun Sangpo, from Dharamsala. In courses with titles like "Buddhist Meditation" and "Buddhist Yogis," the lama lectured to scores of students, speaking in Tibetan, pausing after each sentence for Hopkins to translate. This was to become the paradigm of the Virginia program. It was the learning of the lamas that was being passed on to the students, either in this mode of near-simultaneous translation or with Professor Hopkins reporting what he had heard or read in his prodigious studies with many of the leading Tibetan scholars of the refugee community. In this way the legendary oral tradition of Tibetan Buddhism, long locked in its Himalayan keep, appeared, as if magically, in a classroom in Charlottesville, Virginia. Tibetan lamas, long absent, were now present.

But refugee lamas were not the only sources of Tibetan learning to materialize in Charlottesville (and elsewhere). Thousands of Tibetan texts also appeared. Under Public Law 480, the government of India agreed that its huge debt to the United States for shipments of American wheat provided for famine relief would be repaid in the form of books. Specifically, beginning in 1961, a designated number of copies of every book published in India were to be provided to the Library of Congress, which would then distribute them to select regional depository libraries, including Alderman Library at the University of Virginia. To the eternal good fortune of Tibetan Studies, the head of the Library of Congress in New Delhi from 1968 to 1985 was E. Gene Smith, an eminent Tibetologist trained at the University of Washington. Through his efforts, thousands of heretofore unknown Tibetan texts, texts that had been brought out of Tibet in the diaspora, were published in India and sent to depository libraries across the United States. In this way, the long mysterious Tibetan archive became, as if magically, manifest in the stacks of American university libraries.

In 1976 the Department of Religious Studies added a track in "History of Religions" to its graduate program. The students enrolled in this track were almost exclusively Hopkins's students of Tibetan Buddhism. Early on, Hopkins discovered that these students had difficulty understanding and, especially, remembering the multiple relations between the myriad categories of Buddhist philosophy that were deemed essential in the Geluk monastic curriculum. In an effort to remedy this problem, he taught students to memorize the Tibetan definitions of some of the most basic terms used there. Thus a pot (the standard object about which qualities such as impermanence are posited) was "that which is bulbous, splayed-based and performs the function of holding water"—as difficult to say in Tibetan as it is in English. "Impermanent" was defined as "momentary." "Phenomenon" was defined as "that which bears its own entity."

With these simple definitions memorized, it was then possible to construct simple syllogisms, such as "The subject, a pot, is impermanent because of being momentary." Here pot was called the subject, impermanent was the predicate, and being momentary was the reason. In order for the syllogism to be true, the reason had to be a quality of the subject—that is, the pot had to be momentary—and there had to be "pervasion" between the category of the reason and the category of the predicate; that is, whatever was momentary had to be impermanent. Hopkins would test the students by saying in Tibetan, "It follows that whatever is momentary is necessarily impermanent," and the students would answer, "There is pervasion." Or he would say, "It follows that whatever is a phenomenon is necessarily impermanent," to which the students would answer, "There is no pervasion." He would say, "posit," meaning "posit something that is a phenomenon and is not impermanent," and the students would say, "the nonproduct space," because they knew that the definition of the nonproduct space is "the absence of obstructive contact." Because such an absence did not change moment by moment, it was not impermanent, but was rather permanent. In this way the students developed a rudimentary command of the categories of the elementary monastic curriculum, learning the kinds of things that novice monks learned in Tibet.

It may be useful to describe briefly the nature of the Geluk monastic curriculum in Tibet, upon which Hopkins modeled the Virginia program. Monasteries were often large and complex institutions serving many functions in traditional society, only one of which was the training of scholars; moreover, only certain monasteries offered such training. The majority of the monks in any given monastery were not actively engaged in philosophical training; even in the large teaching monasteries of the major sects, it has been estimated that only 10 percent of the monks undertook the study of the philosophical curriculum.

The monastic curriculum of the three major Geluk monasteries (Drepung, Sera, and Ganden) took from fifteen to twenty-five years to complete.

After learning to read and write (usually beginning between the ages of seven and twelve), a monk would study elementary logic, set forth in a series of three textbooks called the small, intermediate, and large "path of reasoning" (*rigs lam*). The first of these introduced students to the mechanics of the syllogism (technically closer to an enthymeme) through the topic of colors, traditionally beginning with the statement "It follows that whatever is a color is necessarily red," which would be followed by a statement designed to demonstrate the error of such a position: "It follows that the subject, the color of a white conch, is red because of being a color." The *Small Path of Reasoning* proceeded through chapters on color, "objects of knowledge" (*shes bya*), identification of the reverse (*ldog pa ngos 'dzin*), opposites, cause and effect, and so on, providing increasingly difficult exercises in logic while simultaneously adding to the student's store of definitions and categories of technical terms. After completing the study of the three paths of reasoning students would move on to study "types of awareness" (*blo rigs*), which introduced the basic categories of Buddhist epistemology, and "types of reasons" (*rtags rigs*), which provided further instruction in logic. The training in the "collected topics," "types of awareness," and "types of reasoning" took from one to five years.

These works constituted the preparation for the core of the Geluk curriculum, the study of five Indian treatises known simply as the "five texts." The first was the *Ornament of Realization* (*Abhisamayālaṃkāra*), attributed to Maitreya, which was studied for four to six years. The work purports to present the "hidden teaching" of the Perfection of Wisdom sutras, that is, the structure of the path to enlightenment. It is for the most part a list of terms known as the "seventy topics," each of which has multiple subcategories. There are, for example, twenty varieties of the aspiration to buddhahood (*bodhicitta*). The second text was the *Introduction to the Middle Way* (*Madhyamakāvatāra*) of Candrakīrti, a work organized around the ten perfections of the bodhisattva path, but the bulk of which is devoted to the sixth, the perfection of wisdom. This chapter forms the *locus classicus* of Madhyamaka philosophy for the Gelukpas. It was studied for two to four years. The third work was the *Commentary [to Dignāga's "Compendium on] Valid Knowledge"* (*Pramāṇavarttika*) of Dharmakīrti. Its logical categories are studied in a synthetic form in the "paths of reasoning" and "types of reasoning" textbooks. Monks of the three great monasteries would convene annually at Jang to debate about Dharmakīrti's text. This text contains arguments for the existence of rebirth, for liberation from rebirth, and for the omniscience of a buddha; discussions of the two valid sources of knowledge (direct perception and inference); classifications of proof-statements; and an analysis of the operations of thought. Written in a cryptic poetic style, it is considered one of the most difficult Indian *śāstras* and thus was a particular favorite of the most elite scholar-monks. The fourth text was the *Treasury of Knowledge* (*Abhidharmakośa*) of Vasubandhu, a compendium of Hinayana doctrine, providing the basis for Buddhist cosmology and karma theory, among other topics. It was studied for four years. The final work, also studied for four years, was the *Discourse on Vinaya* (*Vinayasūtra*) of Guṇaprabha, providing the rules of monastic discipline.

The successful completion of the entire curriculum took some twenty years of study. During this time the educational techniques were two: memorization and debate. It was customary for a monk over the course of his study to memorize the five Indian texts, his college's textbooks on the Indian texts, and Tsong kha pa's major philosophical writings; it was not uncommon for an accomplished scholar to have several thousand pages of Tibetan text committed to memory. This repository of doctrine was mined in the second educational technique of the monastic university, debate. Debate took place in a highly structured format in which one monk defended a position (often a memorized definition of a term or an interpretation of a passage of scripture) that was systematically attacked by his opponent. Skill in debate was essential to progress to the highest rank of academic scholarship, and was greatly admired. Particular fame was attained by those monks who were able to hold the position of one of the lower schools in the doxographical hierarchy against the higher. These debates were often quite spirited, and certain debates between highly skilled opponents are remembered with an affection not unlike that which some attach to important sporting events in the West. It was commonly the case that a monk, adept at the skills of memorization and debate, would achieve prominence as a scholar without ever publishing a single word.

At Virginia, Jeffrey Hopkins derived the graduate program in Buddhist Studies from this model. However, unlike in Tibet, where the entire day of study could be devoted to this curriculum, at Virginia there were other subjects that needed to be studied (Indian Buddhism, East Asian Buddhism, Sanskrit, History of Religions, a second religion, etc.), such that only the language classes in classical Tibetan could be consigned to the monastic curriculum. This severely truncated the amount of material that could be studied and absorbed. As the program eventually developed, students would begin with the *Small Path of Reasoning;* the first thing they would learn to say in Tibetan was "It follows that whatever is a color is necessarily red." They would move in the first year through a selection of topics from the *Small Path of Reasoning,* memorizing the definitions and divisions, as well as the debates. Unlike in Tibet, however, the students never really learned to improvise in their debating, but merely repeated what they had memorized, like a conversation drill in a Spanish textbook. Whereas in Tibet the passive and active sides of the intellect were exercised in memorization and debate, respectively, at Virginia even the debating was passive. The second year of classical Tibetan was devoted to the study of "types of awareness" and "types of reasoning," the third year to a "stages and paths" textbook, and the fourth year was left open, often devoted to a tantric text.

Whenever possible, a prominent Geluk scholar-monk, selected by the Dalai Lama, was invited to Charlottesville for a semester or a year to teach these and other classes, with Professor Hopkins, as always, providing sentence-by-sentence translation. On Friday afternoons and weekends, the Tibetan monk would teach meditation, first in a space provided by a local church and later at Hopkins's home. The graduate students of the program were regular participants in these sessions. Thus the notion of belonging to a tradition of scholarship that had been the model in Europe, a tradition that extended back to the great Orientalists of the nineteenth century, was replaced by a far more ancient model, in which the master was not *der Doktor-vater* but the lama, whose tradition, it is said, can be traced back to the Buddha himself.

The other topics of the monastic curriculum, that is to say, the formal study of the five texts, remained largely untouched; the four years of graduate study provided enough time to complete only the preliminary elements of the curriculum. Madhyamaka and Yogācāra philosophy, two of Professor Hopkins's areas of expertise, were studied in English-language seminars, and here some of the content of Candrakīrti's *Introduction to the Middle Way* was touched upon. But generally speaking, students would complete their graduate coursework with only a partial command of the material that would be required of a twelve-year-old monk enrolled in the scholastic curriculum of a Geluk monastery. Students completed the program with the ability to read one type of technical scholastic literature. One of the skills that was sacrificed in the process was a solid foundation in Sanskrit, long the lingua franca of Buddhist Studies, as it remains in Europe and Japan. It would be unthinkable there for a student to undertake the study of Tibetan without a strong knowledge of Sanskrit. In the United States, at least at Virginia, the requirements in Sanskrit were minimal, the focus being on the received tradition of Tibetan renditions of Buddhist doctrine.

This ability was put to use in the writing of the dissertation. In Tibetan Buddhist scholastic literature there is a genre called *grub mtha'*, often translated as "doxography." Its texts are compendia of the doctrines of the various schools of Indian philosophy. While works of this genre sometimes include summaries of the doctrines of non-Buddhist schools of classical Indian philosophy such as Jaina, Sāṃkhya, Nyāya, and Carvāka, the bulk of the exposition is concerned with the Buddhist schools, which are generally numbered as four: the two Hinayana schools of Vaibhāṣika and Sautrāntika, and the two Mahayana schools of Yogācāra (generally referred to as Cittamātra, "mind only"—*sems tsam*, in the doxographical literature) and Madhyamaka. The Tibetans brought their own approach to the study of Buddhist philosophy, cataloging the positions of the various Indian schools, ranking them, and comparing their assertions on a wide range of topics. Despite the fact that Vaibhāṣikas and Sautrāntikas never had adherents in Tibet and the Cittamātra view was only occasionally espoused, studies that move up through this hierarchy are considered, especially in the Geluk sect, to have a strong pedagogic and even soteriological value; the exposition begins with Vaibhāṣika and moves toward Prāsaṅgika-Mādhyamika. The tenets of the lower schools are seen as stepping stones to the higher, as a means of understanding increasingly subtle philosophical positions, providing an opportunity to discern a development and refinement of concepts and terminology that would be imperceptible if study were limited to what is judged by many to be the most profound, the Prāsaṅgika-Mādhyamika. The Tibetan doxographies are very much constructions of the Indian schools and to that extent artificial. They are largely ahistorical, juxtaposing and amalgamating positions that were often separated by centuries. They are also synthetic, erecting "schools" for which in India there is sometimes insufficient historical evidence.[18]

Professor Hopkins would assign a portion of one of these works to a doctoral student as his or her dissertation topic. For example, I was assigned the Svātantrika section of Jamyangshayba's ('Jam dbyang bzhad pa) *Great Exposition of Tenets* (*Grub mtha' chen mo*) and Anne Klein was assigned the Sautrāntika chapter. The task that Hopkins set for his students was "getting it straight," a multistage process that began first with coming up with a rough translation of the assigned text. We each would meet with Hopkins once a week to go over our translation with him and have it corrected (an extremely labor intensive task, requiring him to keep up with a number of different texts at once). We would discuss doctrinal points with him, sometimes in connection with an early-nineteenth-century work of annotations on Jamyang-shayba's text. We regarded the authors of the works we studied as great masters. Our goal was to understand their thought by partaking in a lineage of scholarship. In the case of my own dissertation, that lineage, moving from the present to the past, flowed to me from Professor Hopkins, from his own teachers, from the author of the nineteenth-century annotations, from Jamyangshayba in the eighteenth century, from Tsong kha pa in the fourteenth century, and then from Indian masters: from Kamalaśīla, from Candrakīrti, from Nāgārjuna, and from the Perfection of Wisdom sutras, traditionally regarded as the word of the Buddha himself. To seek to use the understanding gained from this lineage as a foundation for one's own evaluation and critique was considered presumptuous and somehow unseemly. It would be impossible for us to ever surpass their understanding; our task was to represent it accurately in English. This approach was in part borrowed from the tradition itself, in which a high premium is placed on a profound and detailed understanding of doctrine, especially of the Madhyamaka. It is the Geluk position, supported with copious quotations from Indian texts, that there is no higher philosophical position than that put forward by Nāgārjuna, and that in order to be liberated from rebirth it is necessary to have a full understanding of that position, eventually in meditation but initially in a discursive way. Thus, in the accurate translation and exposition of Buddhist philosophy we could also partake in a form of salvation by scholarship.

At the same time, we would be applying to the appropriate funding agencies (at that time, the American Association of Indian Studies and the U.S. Office of Education through the Fulbright-Hays Doctoral Dissertation Abroad program) for support for our doctoral research. Here, because of politics both international and scholarly, a degree of dissimulation was called for. The government of India did not permit research in Tibetan refugee communities because of political sensitivity over relations with China. At the same time, research on Tibetan Buddhism did not have the cachet of Sanskrit studies. For that reason, doctoral students from the Virginia program submitted proposals for projects that involved the translation of a Sanskrit text (that also existed in Tibetan translation), and asked to be based not in Dharamsala or in refugee monasteries in Karnataka State (which were barred to foreigners) but, for example, at Delhi University, which had the only Department of Buddhist Studies in India. With the grant successfully in hand, it was then possible to make extended visits to Tibetan communities to study at the feet of refugee Tibetan lamas. In our work with them we felt that in a sense we were doing what the Tibetans had done when, during the tenth century, they brought Buddhism to their land of snows. After their arduous trip across the mountains to India, they studied with the great Indian masters and then re-turned home to translate their works into Tibetan. In the same way we had crossed the ocean to India to study with Tibetan masters, now in exile there, and upon returning to America would translate texts based on their teachings. In that way we both preserved the wisdom of these masters and made the dharma available in English.[19] The precedent for this had been set earlier in the century by Evans-Wentz.[20]

Meanwhile, at the University of Wisconsin after the untimely death of Richard Robinson, one of the Tibetan scholars originally brought to America by Geshe Wangyal and invited to Wisconsin by Jeffrey Hopkins during his graduate studies there was hired as an assistant professor in the Department of South Asian Studies. This was Geshe Lhundup Sopa, a monk of Sera mon-astery. Now a professor emeritus, he is at this writing the only Tibetan *geshe* (the highest degree in the Geluk curriculum) ever hired as a tenured faculty member at a college or university in North America. Together, Jeffrey Hop-kins and Geshe Sopa published a volume that included translations of two works: a commentary on Tsong kha pa's poem on the three aspects of the path to enlightenment (renunciation, the aspiration to buddhahood, and the understanding of emptiness) and a brief doxography of the schools of Indian Buddhist philosophy. It was published under the apparently hyperbolic title of *Practice and Theory of Tibetan Buddhism* (later revised as *Cutting through Appearances*).

As a highly regarded product of the monastic curriculum described above, the many graduate students that Geshe Sopa trained tended in their dissertations to focus on works of Geluk scholastic philosophy. The other places in North America where one could study Tibetan Buddhism at the graduate level in the 1970s and 1980s, such as the University of Washington, the University of California at Berkeley, Indiana University, and the Uni-versity of Saskatchewan, produced far fewer graduates than Wisconsin and Virginia, which remained the primary centers of Tibetan Buddhist Studies during this period.[21] In these decades, then, it was perhaps not much of an overstatement to represent the *Practice and Theory of Tibetan Buddhism* with two works from just one Tibetan sect, the Geluk, because the bulk of the scholarship being produced at that time focused on the Geluk sect, an effect that can be traced back to Geshe Wangyal, a Geluk monk who was the forefather of the programs at Virginia and Wisconsin and the teacher of Robert Thurman. Indeed, one might say that during this century the most important figure in Tibetan Studies in Great Britain was David Snellgrove, that in France it was Marcelle Lalou or Rolf Stein, and that in North America it was Geshe Wangyal. This has had a profound effect on the history of Tibetan Studies.

Most of the graduates of the Virginia and Wisconsin programs eventually found academic positions; they often described their specialty with the neologism "Indo-Tibetan Buddhism," perhaps in an attempt to counter the old view of Tibet as a marginal civilization of Asia. In time, however, such precautions have seemed unnecessary, as Tibet has come more and more into the forefront of popular attention with the repeated visits of the Dalai Lama to the United States. The graduates of these programs have gone on to constitute a distinct class in the history of American Buddhism, an American version of what in Tibetan is called the "scholar-adept" (*mkhas grub*), that is, scholars who are also Buddhist practitioners. In Tibet, such persons were generally monks and almost always male. In America, they are almost always laypeople, and sometimes female. This peculiar feature of American Buddhism, at least when compared to the Buddhisms of Asia, derives largely from the fact that American Buddhism lacks a significant monastic component.

The histories of Buddhist nations traditionally tend to revolve around the founding of monasteries. In Tibet, for example, when King Tri Songdetsen wanted to establish Buddhism in his realm, he invited an abbot from India to found a monastery. It was his attempt that enraged the gods and demons of Tibet, requiring that Padmasambhava be called in to subdue them. Only then could the momentous act of founding a monastery succeed. Buddhist history and Buddhist texts agree that without monks there can be no Buddhism, a view supported by Buddhist myths of the endtime. In the last stages of the degeneration of the dharma, it is said that all Buddhist texts will disappear (the last to go will be those on monastic discipline), the saffron robes of the monks will turn white (the color of the robes of the laymen), and, in the end, all of the relics of the cremated Buddha—the teeth, the bones, the fingernails, the hair—will break free from their reliquaries, the stupas and pagodas, and magically travel to Bodhgaya, where they will reassemble beneath the tree where the Buddha achieved enlightenment. There they will be worshipped one last time by the gods before they burst into flames and vanish.

In Asia, the distinction between monk and layperson is generally sharply drawn, even in Japan, where, since the Meiji era, monks have married. The distinction is not so much about celibacy, although outside Japan the pretense of celibacy (and its attendant misogyny) remains important. The distinction is instead one of a division of labor. The role of the monk is to maintain a certain purity, largely through keeping an elaborate set of vows. Such purity renders the monk as a suitable "field of merit" to whom laypeople can make offerings, thereby accumulating the favorable karma that will result in a happy rebirth in the next life. By adopting a certain lifestyle, then, in which the transient pleasures of married life are renounced, monks provide the opportunity for the layperson to amass a certain karmic capital. In return, monks receive the fruits of the labor of the laity—labor that they themselves have eschewed—in the form of their physical support. More specifically, monks do what laypeople cannot do because they generally do not know how: recite texts, perform rituals, and sometimes meditate. Laypeople do those things that monks are forbidden to do: till the soil, engage in business, raise families. (In Tibet, where lay and state support for monks was less generous than in some Theravada countries, monks often engaged in commerce, either individually or on behalf of the monastery.)

In America, white Buddhists have not observed this distinction. Instead, American Buddhists, whether Zen, Theravadin, or Tibetan, have always wanted to do what monks do, but without becoming monks. Or perhaps it is more accurate to say that they have wanted to do some of the things monks do. They have been less interested in performing rituals, but have had a keen interest in reading and studying texts and in meditating. It is partly due to these interests and partly because of their wealth that American Buddhists have often been able to lure Asian monks away from the refugee communities they were brought to the United States to serve, founding instead "dharma centers" where the clientele is largely not of Asian descent.

But even now there are not always enough Asian masters to go around. Some Western men and women have become monks and nuns, but generally they have not attracted large groups of followers. American nuns in Tibetan traditions have led the movement to reestablish the order of fully ordained nuns, a movement motivated by a complicated feminism that seeks to restore the place of women in a patriarchal hierarchy in which a man who has been a monk for fifteen minutes is senior to a woman who has been a nun for fifteen years. But the impact in America of American monks and nuns has been relatively minor, in large part because there is no institution to support them. Life in America with shaved head and robes is a difficult one, with much time spent explaining to the uninformed that one is not a Hare Krishna; there is no established *sangha* in the United States (outside of a few communities) in which one can easily live as a monk or nun. Furthermore, many of those who have become monks and nuns in the Tibetan tradition have never learned to read Tibetan sufficiently to receive the requisite sanction from a Tibetan lama to teach or the requisite renown to attract American followers. Tibetan is difficult to learn outside of an academic setting. Those Western monks who spend long periods in Korea or India or Sri Lanka, who learn the language and the texts sufficiently to be qualified as teachers in Asia, rarely remain monks when they come back home, finding a more appropriate role in the academy, as scholars (witness, for example, Robert Thurman, Robert Buswell, José Cabezón, Georges Dreyfus). Many who remain monks and nuns in the United States derive their authority from their garb, but they would not have the credentials of a teacher in a traditional Buddhist society. And thus, in a strange way, the traditional role of the monk, as dispenser of Buddhist wisdom and interpreter of texts, has been arrogated to the academic, those students of Geshe Wangyal, Geshe Sopa, and other Tibetan lamas who have received the sanction to teach, not necessarily by virtue of the symbolic capital derived from traditional transmission (although this was often also there), but by virtue of symbolic capital derived from their possession of a doctorate in Buddhist Studies.

In order to continue in their positions, however, the new scholar-adepts also had to meet the demands of the institutions that paid their salaries. It was easy enough to attract large numbers of students to courses like "Introduction to Buddhism," where the dual role of scholar and adept only served to boost enrollments. (During my younger and more supple years, I would annually wow my students by demonstrating the lotus posture during a lecture on meditation.) But it was also necessary to publish. In the 1970s and 1980s, the established academic presses in Europe and America, and even the commercial presses, failed to recognize the growing market for Tibetan Buddhism. Oxford University Press had kept the old Evans-Wentz tetralogy in print, but little else had been added to its list over the decades. Four new presses were founded to meet the growing need, each connected with a particular refugee Tibetan lama.

The first was Shambhala Publications, founded in Berkeley in 1969 and named after the mythical Himalayan kingdom where the practice of tantric Buddhism is preserved in preparation for an apocalyptic war. In 1970 it published what would become its most successful title, *The Tassajara Bread Book* by Zen baker Edward Brown, and in 1975 it published what would become a New Age classic, Fritjof Capra's *The Tao of Physics*. Its most notable author in the early years, however, was Chögyam Trungpa, the Kagyu lama who settled first in Vermont and then in Boulder, Colorado. Works like *Cutting through Spiritual Materialism* (1973) brought Trungpa's urbane interpretation of Tibetan Buddhism to a large and enthusiastic audience; his followers eventually established a network of centers called "dharmadhātus," with a headquarters in Boulder. Trungpa's followers were highly organized, with local and national officers, appointed by Trungpa, including a Minister of External Affairs who was responsible for relations with those outside Trungpa's community.[22] Shambhala Publications also brought out translations of the works of a group of Trungpa's disciples, called the Nālandā Translation Committee. The press eventually added titles in Islamic mysticism and New Age psychology, with less emphasis on Tibetan Buddhism beyond the works of Trungpa. Few of Trungpa's disciples received doctorates in Buddhist Studies, and his influence on the academic study of Tibetan Buddhism largely has been limited to the small Buddhist Studies program at his Naropa Institute in Boulder.

The next press to be founded (in 1971) was Dharma Publishing, based in Berkeley, California. Its original and continuing purpose has been to publish the works produced by the Nyingma Institute under the direction of Tarthang Tulku. Dharma's publishing program has included works by Tarthang Tulku himself, such as *Time, Space, Knowledge* (1977), as well as the work of his largely anonymous group of disciples, who, under his direction, have brought out the multivolume traditional history of Buddhism called *Crystal Mirror*. In addition, the works of several European Buddhologists have been reprinted by Dharma (Christian Lindtner's *Nagarjuniana* was published as *Master of Wisdom*), as well as English translations of Tibetan works originally translated into French (such as Foucaux's 1847 translation of the *Lalitavistara*, published as *The Voice of the Buddha*). Several of Herbert Guenther's works, including his 3-volume *Kindly Bent to Ease Us*, were also published by Dharma. By far the most ambitious venture undertaken by Dharma was the publication of the Derge edition of the Tibetan canon, beautifully bound in 120 volumes and selling for $15,000. Unfortunately, although great expense was taken in the binding of the volumes, insufficient care was given to the reproduction of the contents, hurriedly photocopied from the blockprint edition housed in the University of California library. As a result, many folios are illegible, rendering the Nyingma edition an excellent canon to prostrate before (as Tibetan Buddhists often do) but a poor canon to read (as Tibetan Buddhists rarely do).

The next press was Wisdom Publications, founded in 1975 and now headquartered in Boston. It began as a publishing organ for the teachings of the Geluk *tulku* Thupten Yeshe (1935–1984, known as Lama Yeshe), who, along with Thupten Sopa, founded Kopan and Tushita, popular dharma centers outside of Kathmandu and Dharamsala, respectively, and later centers around the world. Thupten Yeshe attracted a large number of students with his engaging teaching delivered in an idiomatic English, commenting on a wide variety of Buddhist and non-Buddhist works, including the Christmas carol "Silent Night" in a work called *Silent Mind, Holy Mind*. The followers of Lama Yeshe and Lama Sopa were organized into a network of dharma centers around the world under the umbrella of the Foundation for the Preservation of the Mahayana Tradition (FPMT). Wisdom Publications published works by the Dalai Lama, as well as Jeffrey Hopkins's massive dissertation, *Meditation on Emptiness*. The press has also published a wide variety of titles on Buddhist practice, including translations from the Pali.

The last press to be established was Snow Lion Publications (originally Gabriel/Snow Lion) in 1980 in Ithaca, New York. The press was founded by Gabriel Aiello, Pat Aiello, and Sidney Piburn shortly after the Dalai Lama gave teachings there in 1979. The group took an early interest in the work of Jeffrey Hopkins and his students and conceived the idea of a press that would be devoted to the preservation of Tibetan Buddhism and Tibetan culture. Despite initial financial hardship, Snow Lion has gone on to become the largest press devoted to Tibetan Buddhism, having published almost 150 titles on Tibet and Tibetan Buddhism (printing over one million copies) and distributing over 500 titles published by other presses. In addition, Snow Lion distributes hundreds of video- and audiotapes of teachings by Tibetan lamas; *thangkas*; statues of buddhas; ritual items such as *vajras*, bells, and rosaries; software for Tibetan fonts; and T-shirts, posters, and postcards connected to Tibetan culture. The press has been particularly committed to publishing works by the Dalai Lama (edited transcripts of public teachings), such as *Kindness, Clarity, and Insight* (1984), which has sold over fifty thousand copies. Despite the relatively small market, Snow Lion has also been committed to publishing the dissertations of Jeffrey Hopkins's students, with such arcane titles as *A Study of Svātantrika*. Over the years, Snow Lion has sought to balance its initial Geluk emphasis by publishing translations from the other sects of Tibetan Buddhism. Most of the translators of these works are Westerners (often under the tutelage of a Tibetan lama) associated with dharma centers in Europe, America, or Nepal who do not hold academic positions. Its periodical newsletter, in which these products are marketed, is a major forum for advertisements for meditation retreats and appeals for aid by various Tibetan refugee religious groups. Recognizing the success of these presses, other more established houses, both academic (such as SUNY and the University of California Press) and commercial (such as HarperCollins, which in 1994 started a Library of Tibet) increased their titles in Tibetan Buddhism.

In another case of the confluence of the scholarly and the popular, it is these presses, founded to serve the growing popular interest in Buddhism in Europe and America, that have published much of the North American scholarship on Tibetan Buddhism produced during the last three decades. Furthermore, the preponderance of this scholarship has centered on works of the Geluk sect, for a number of reasons. First, Jeffrey Hopkins, who headed the Virginia program, studied with many prominent Geluk scholars, such that most of his own prolific scholarship and that of the first generation of his students focused on Geluk texts. Because Geshe Sopa was a Geluk monk, the same was true of his students at Wisconsin. However, this research also needed to be published. Here the graduates benefited from the fact that two of the new "dharma presses," Wisdom and Snow Lion, had strong ties to the Geluk, especially in their early years.

But this politics of knowledge becomes clearer when we compare the circumstances of the production of scholarship on Tibet at the end of the nineteenth century with the circumstances today. It was at the end of the nineteenth century that the two most widely used Tibetan-English dictionaries were produced. One was compiled by a Moravian missionary, H. A. Jäschke, in Ladakh, the other by a Bengali scholar, Sarat Chandra Das, who made several spying expeditions into Tibet on behalf of the British. This was a time when Tibet was coveted as a potential mission field and as a potential colony, both of which require knowledge of the Tibetan language. As we saw in chapter one, Tibet was often portrayed during this period as a corrupt and static society and its religion was largely denigrated in scholarly literature as a debased form of the original Buddhism of India, contaminated with magic, shamanism, and priestcraft to the extent that it should not properly be called Buddhism. Similar characterizations of Asian, African, and New World cultures often provided an ideological justification for colonialism.

This perspective began to change after the diaspora of 1959, with a more historically based variation on the Theosophical theme of Tibet as a domain in which ancient wisdom was held in safekeeping for the modern age. The view of Tibet as a closed society that had so fascinated and vexed European travelers in the colonial period now became a reason why Tibetan Buddhism was more authentic than any other. Tibet had never been colonized as had India and Southeast Asia, had never been "opened" to the West as had China and Japan, had never suffered a revolution as had occurred in China in 1911 and 1949, and had never attempted to adopt Western ways, as had Japan since the Meiji. Rather, Tibet was seen to have resisted all foreign influence, its monasteries having forced the thirteenth Dalai Lama to close down the English-language school in Lhasa, to abandon his plans to train a modern army, and to discourage the introduction of European sports by proclaiming that he who kicks a soccer ball kicks the head of the Buddha.

All of this meant that the Buddhism of Tibet was pure and this purity derived in large part from a connection with the origin, which Tibetans themselves often invoked. Like other Buddhist traditions, the Tibetan based claims to authority largely on lineage, and in its case claimed that the Buddhism taught in Tibet in 1959 could be traced in an unbroken line to the eleventh century, when the founders of the major Tibetan sects made the perilous journey to India to receive the dharma from the great masters of Bengal, Bihar, and Kashmir, who were themselves direct recipients of teachings that could be traced to the Buddha himself. Moreover, this lineage was represented as essentially oral, with instructions being passed down from master to disciple as unwritten commentary on sacred text. Now that lineage was in danger of extinction. For the oral tradition not to be lost, locked within the minds of aged and dying refugee lamas, it had to be passed on, and the scholar-adepts of North America dedicated themselves to the task.

It is the old legacy of religion and magic, India and Tibet, Buddhism and Lamaism that perhaps has caused the current generation of scholars of Tibetan Buddhism (especially in North America) generally to shy away from certain genres of Tibetan literature (propitiation of malevolent deities, exorcism texts, and works dealing in general with wrathful deities or mundane ends) and to gravitate to others (works on meditation, the bodhisattva path, and scholastic philosophy), texts that demonstrate unequivocally that the chief religion of Tibet is a direct and legitimate descendent of Indian Buddhism. The study of such works exalts the Tibetan Buddhist tradition in precisely those domains from which Tibetan Buddhism was so long excluded, the domains of the world religions, gaining for their scholarly experts academic positions that once would have gone to specialists in Indian or East Asian Buddhism. Simultaneously, Tibetan Buddhism, with its ethical systems, regimens of meditation, and profound philosophies, is demonstrated to have something to contribute to the discourse of Religious Studies, a discipline with deep roots in confessional Christianity and its emphasis on doctrine and belief. The Western scholar can thus promote a sympathetic portrayal of Tibetan Buddhism, write books that are bought by American Buddhists, and win tenure in the process; publication of one's dissertation by one of the once-scorned "dharma presses" has since proved sufficient for tenure in a number of cases.[23]

Something that was unthinkable in the late nineteenth century has become possible in the late twentieth: the curriculum of a Tibetan monastery has become the model for a doctoral program in the United States. The greatest Tibetologist of the twentieth century, Giuseppe Tucci, described the Tibetan monastery as a place where "Hardening of the arteries set in with the double threat of formulas replacing the mind's independent striving after truth, and a withered theology taking the place of the yearning for spiritual rebirth."[24] The products of those monasteries were now teaching in the classrooms of American universities and graduate students were memorizing the formulas of their theology. And now that Tibet was no longer the object of European or American imperial desire, another side of Tibetan religion has become subject to the scrutiny of scholars (often working in concert with exiled lamas), the side of logic, philosophy, hermeneutics, ethics, and meditation, all of which demonstrated the depth and value of Tibetan civilization precisely at the moment when it seemed most in jeopardy.

During the last decade these scholars have benefited greatly from a three-volume Tibetan–Tibetan-Chinese dictionary, published under Chinese colonial auspices in 1985. When an American scholar does not know the meaning of the words in the Tibetan definition, he or she can always open the Tibetan-English dictionaries compiled a century ago by the missionary and the spy.

CHAPTER SEVEN

The Prison

The first reference in English to Shambhala was made by Alexander Csoma de Kőrös in 1833:

> The peculiar religious system entitled the *Kála-Chakra* is stated, generally, to have been derived from *Shambhala*, as it is called in Sanscrit (in Tibetan "*b*dé-*h*byung," vulgó "dè-jung," signifying "origin or source of happiness") a fabulous country in the north, the capital of which was *Cálapa,* a very splendid city, the residence of many illustrious kings of Shambhala, situated between 45° and 50° north latitude, beyond the *Sita* or Jaxartes, where the increase of the days from the vernal equinox till the summer solstice amounted to 12 Indian hours, or 4 hours, 48 minutes, European reckoning.[1]

We can only appreciate the author's concern with providing its precise location on earth. In the century that followed, the site of Shambhala (the probable inspiration of Hilton's Shangri-La, the utopia from which one escapes at one's peril) and, indeed, the site of Tibet, which was often made to stand for Shangri-La, would become increasingly nebulous. This chapter will consider the confluence of various myths of Tibet, some Western and some Tibetan, myths that have come together to form a certain lingua franca of the fantastic, shaping a land of language surrounded by mountains difficult to scale.

In the texts associated with the *Kālacakra Tantra*, the kingdom of Shambhala is said to be located north of the Himalayan range. It is a land devoted to the practice of the *Kālacakra Tantra*, which the Buddha himself had entrusted to Shambhala's king. Shambhala is shaped like a giant lotus and is filled with sandalwood forests and lotus lakes, all encircled by a great range of snowy peaks. In the center of the kingdom is the capital of Kalāpa, where the luster of the palaces, made from gold, silver, and jewels, outshines the moon; the walls of the palaces are plated with mirrors that reflect a light so bright that night is like day. In the very center of the city is the mandala of the Buddha Kālacakra. The inhabitants of the 960 million villages of Shambhala are ruled by a beneficent ruler, called the Kalkin. The laypeople are all beautiful and wealthy, free of sickness and poverty; the monks maintain their vows without the slightest infraction. They are naturally intelligent and virtuous, devoted to the practice of the Vajrayāna, although all authentic forms of Indian Buddhism are preserved. The majority of those reborn there attain buddhahood during their lifetime in Shambhala.

But conflict looms in the future. In the year 2425, the barbarians (generally identified as Muslims) and demons who have destroyed Buddhism in India will set out to invade Shambhala. The twenty-fifth Kalkin, Raudracakrin, will lead his armies out of his kingdom and into India, where they will meet the forces of evil in an apocalyptic battle, from which the forces of Buddhism will emerge victorious. The victory will usher in a golden age in which the human lifespan will increase, crops will grow without being cultivated, and the population of the earth will devote itself to the practice of Buddhism.[2]

But even prior to the war, all has not been peaceful in Shambhala. At the time of the eighth king, Yaśas, there were 35 million brahmans living in Shambhala, devoted to the religion of the Vedas. The king foresaw that, because both the Vedas and the religion of the barbarians permit animal sacrifice, after eight hundred years the descendants of the brahmans would join the race of barbarians and, as a result of the ensuing miscegenation, the entire population of Shambhala would eventually become barbarians. The king thus asked the brahmans either to receive initiation into the Kālacakra mandala (and thus become Buddhists) or to leave Shambhala and emigrate to India.

The brahmans chose the latter course. During their journey south, the king realized that if the brahman sages were to leave, the people of the 960 million villages would lose faith in the practice of the Vajrayāna. In order to prevent this, the king assumed the form of a wrathful deity, appeared before the departing brahmans, and frightened them so much that they swooned into unconsciousness. When they awoke, they had been transported back to the capital, where they asked the king to allow them to convert to Buddhism and to receive initiation into the Kālacakra mandala.[3] They were constrained to become prisoners of this utopia.

IN HIS 1889 ESSAY "The Decay of Lying: An Observation," Oscar Wilde promotes the art of lying, of making fearless, irresponsible statements that show disdain for proof of any kind. Lying, he argues, is particularly important in Art, because, contrary to popular opinion, it is Life that imitates Art. He observes, for example, that the climate of London had changed a decade before with the advent of French Impressionism; prior to that, London had not been foggy. The sunsets admired by "absurdly pretty Philistines" are merely second-rate Turners, the pessimism analyzed by Schopenhauer was invented by Hamlet: "The world has become sad because a puppet was once melancholy."[4] Wilde writes, "Art takes life as part of her rough material, recreates it, and refashions it in fresh forms, is absolutely indifferent to fact, invents, imagines, dreams, and keeps between herself and reality the impenetrable barrier of beautiful style, of decorative or ideal treatment."[5] It is in this sense that we might regard Tibet as a work of art, fashioned through exaggeration and selection into an ideal with little foundation in history. We have observed in this study a variety of attempts by nature to imitate this art, as when Cyril Hoskin became Lobsang Rampa. As Wilde notes, "Art creates an incomparable and unique effect, and having done so, passes on to other things. Nature, upon the other hand, forgetting that imitation can be made the sincerest form of insult, keeps on repeating this effect until we all become absolutely wearied of it."[6] He is not speaking only of cityscapes and sunsets, but also of lands and peoples. The Japanese, he explains, are the creation of certain artists; the people who live in Japan are quite as commonplace and ordinary as the English. "In fact, the whole of Japan is a pure invention. There is no such country, there are no such people. . . . And so, if you desire to see a Japanese effect, you will not behave like a tourist and go to Tokio."[7]

If we extend Wilde's theory, it would seem that Western enthusiasts of Tibetan Buddhism are more authentic in their Buddhism than Tibetans precisely because they are more intimate with the simulacrum of Tibet that is the invention, that is the artifice. But what happens when the people of such an invented land leave it and come to the place of its invention? This chapter will consider certain of the consequences of the Tibetan diaspora. As with other refugees, the nation has followed the exile into diaspora. But in the case of Tibet, Tibetans fled Tibet to find a safe haven in India, Europe, and North America only to find themselves and their country already there. In previous chapters, we have seen how the "lie" about Tibet took shape. Here we will consider how Tibetans have both contributed to it and accommodated it, taking up more explicitly the question of the historical agency of Tibetans, an agency that must be acknowledged even when its products seem complicitous with those that we would judge as somehow less authentic. It will become clear, if it is not already, that agency, whether Tibetan or Western, is not a fixed point or an innate ability but rather a process of circulation and exchange, in which, for example, power is bestowed by enthusiasts upon Tibetan lamas, to whom they in turn offer their obeisance. But, as in any exchange, to receive this power the Tibetans must give up something in return. The emphasis here will be on the post-1959 period, in which Tibetan agency takes on a rather different form than it had prior to the diaspora. In 1959 the knowledge moves outside and the inside is, apparently, left with nothing.

The focus of these reflections will be the current Dalai Lama, so strongly identified with Tibet both by Tibetans and non-Tibetans. If national identity is commonly defined in terms of the head of state in cases of hereditary kingship, such identity is at once concentrated and magnified when the head of state has been, essentially, the same person since the assumption of temporal rule by the fifth Dalai Lama in 1642, or even since the mythological beginning, for the bodhisattva of compassion, of whom the Dalai Lama is the human incarnation, is also the progenitor of the Tibetan people. (Indeed, the institution of the incarnate lama in Tibet can be viewed as a form of ancestor worship in which the ancestor is always alive.) As the thirteenth Dalai Lama fled from the British in 1904 and from the Chinese in 1910 only to return, so the present Dalai Lama fled into exile in 1959 and has remained there since, facing situations unimagined by his predecessors. Still, for many Tibetans and non-Tibetans, where the Dalai Lama is, there is Tibet: the soul of Tibet need not stand on the soil of Tibet.

Heinz Bechert coined the term "Buddhist modernism" to describe tendencies that began in the late nineteenth century when monastic elites in Sri Lanka and Southeast Asia sought to counter the negative portrayal of Buddhism by colonial officials and Christian missionaries.[8] Although the characterizations of Buddhism put forward by figures such as Anagarika Dharmapala in Sri Lanka (with the initial help of Colonel Henry Olcott of the Theosophical Society), Tai xu in China, and Shaku Sōen in Japan are not sufficiently consistent to be labelled as a movement, they share a number of general characteristics. The first is the representation of Buddhism as a "world religion" fully the equal of Christianity in antiquity, geographical expanse, membership, and philosophical profundity, with its own founder, sacred scriptures, and fixed body of doctrine. Buddhists, however, have no compulsion to convert Christians, but instead wish to engage them in "dialogue." This Buddhism is above all a religion of reason dedicated to bringing an end to suffering. It is strongly ethical and is devoted to nonviolence, and as such is a vehicle for social reform. Because it is "atheistic" in the sense that it denies the existence of a creator deity and because it places a strong emphasis on rational analysis, it is, more than any other religion, compatible with modern science. Elements of traditional cosmology that do not accord with science may be dismissed as cultural accretions incidental to the Buddha's original teaching. Finally, the essential practice of Buddhism is meditation, with the rituals of consecration, purification, expiation, and exorcism so common throughout Asia largely dismissed as popular superstition.

This version of Buddhism was unknown in Tibet. In 1906, a vibrant time for Buddhist modernism elsewhere in Asia, the Christian missionary Graham Sandberg observes as much:

> In Tibet the exorcism of devils and mystic rites involving the invocation of deities of many orders are believed in and form part of the daily religion in the case of the learned and the upper classes. In Burmah and Ceylon, on the other hand, such ideas and ceremonials are now mainly confined to the general public. The lettered and philosophic among the Burmese and Sinhalese Buddhists, having been re-instructed in their Faith as interpreted by European theorists, have eradicated from their Buddhism even the mythology which from the earliest promulgation belonged to that religion. But their religion is no longer Primitive Buddhism, but Christianized Buddhism.[9]

However, since the diaspora of 1959, the leading proponent of Buddhist modernism has been a Tibetan, the Dalai Lama. A strong proponent of nonviolence, he invokes Gandhi and Martin Luther King as much as Buddhist figures, and explains that the essence of Buddhism is "Help others if you can;

if not, at least refrain from harming others" (although under such a formulation any physician who has taken the Hippocratic Oath would be a Buddhist).[10] The Dalai Lama has taken an active interest in modern physics and psychology, hosting a number of "Mind Science" conferences in Dharamsala in recent years. He has stated that when elements of Buddhist cosmology conflict with the findings of Western science, the Buddhist views can be dispensed with. Thus, for example, while other Tibetan scholar-monks still argue that the Buddhist universe with its central mountain rising from an ocean is visible to those with pure karma, the Dalai Lama has stated that such a cosmology is simply mistaken. He says in *The Way to Freedom*, "The purpose of the Buddha coming to this world was not to measure the circumference of the world and the distance between the earth and the moon, but rather to teach the Dharma, to liberate sentient beings, to relieve sentient beings of their sufferings."[11] He remains firmly committed to the doctrine of rebirth, however, drawing the distinction between those things that science has found to be false and those things that science simply has not yet found. The central practice of Buddhism, according to his view, is meditation, which is to be practiced by monks and laity alike, leading to salubrious psychological effects.

The Dalai Lama has been an active participant in the Buddhist-Christian dialogue. During the summer of 1996, his comments on selected passages from the New Testament were published as *The Good Heart: A Buddhist Perspective on the Teachings of Jesus*. In the introduction, he is described by Father Laurence Freeman, O.S.B., as "one of the most loved and accessible spiritual teachers in the world today. Tibet's agony, which he carries constantly with him, has elevated him to a global spiritual role in which the universal religious values of peace, justice, tolerance, and nonviolence find a joyful yet serious embodiment."[12] Throughout the book, the Dalai Lama finds points of comparison and confluence between Buddhism and Christianity, both in the lives of their founders and in their scriptures. He stresses throughout the centrality of meditation to the religious life. He argues, however, against conversion and is clear that the two religions have major differences on issues such as the existence of God and the nature of reality. "If we try to unify the faiths of the world into one religion, we will also lose many of the qualities and richnesses of each particular tradition."[13]

Here and elsewhere he alludes to the importance of having different religions to suit the dispositions and needs of different people. This is a version of the famous Buddhist hermeneutical device of "skillful methods" (*upāya*), which Buddhist scholastics have traditionally used to account for apparent contradictions in the Buddha's teachings. It is explained that the Buddha had, instead, taught different things to different people based on their capacities. The apparent inclusive nature of this device, however, is founded on the assumption of a knowledge of the Buddha's true intention and ultimate position, such that the doctrine of *upāya* has been used historically to hierarchize the positions of competing Buddhist schools beneath one's own. It can be put to similar use in the case of competing religions.[14] The Dalai Lama writes, "I feel there is tremendous convergence and a potential for mutual enrichment through dialogue between the Buddhist and Christian traditions, especially in the areas of ethics and spiritual practice, such as the practices of compassion, love, meditation, and the enhancement of tolerance. And I feel that this dialogue could go very far and reach a deep level of understanding. But when it comes to a philosophical or metaphysical dialogue I feel that we must part company."[15] As a proponent of the Prāsaṅgika-Mādhyamika school of Buddhist philosophy, the Dalai Lama takes the position that it is impossible to be liberated from rebirth without understanding the doctrine of emptiness as it is presented by that school; even other Buddhist philosophical schools (and hence all non-Buddhist traditions) are incapable of providing the insight required for liberation.[16] Thus, even in the context of dialogue, he, like other Buddhist modernists before him, maintains a certain Buddhist triumphalism.

In addition to being the spokesman, indeed the chief spokesman for Buddhist modernism, there are other roles, none of which he held in Tibet, that the Dalai Lama must play, roles that at times seem to come into conflict. As seen above, he is a world spiritual leader whose presence is sought by religious and academic groups around the world. Yet he is also the leader of the Tibetan independence movement. As such, he must constantly speak out against Chinese policies in Tibet, a realpolitik that is often beyond the immediate concerns of those who are more interested in his teachings of love and compassion. *The Good Heart,* devoted entirely to these teachings, contains a single page inserted at the back of the book entitled "Tibet Since the Chinese Occupation in 1950," which in addition to listing Chinese atrocities demonstrates how his political message is sometimes a mere appendage to the spiritual.

The Dalai Lama is at the same time the leader of the Tibetan Buddhist community, that is, the community of Buddhists who are Tibetans. He must represent all sects of Tibetan Buddhism rather than simply the traditional sect of the Dalai Lama, the Geluk. This is a role that is rarely seen in the West, conducted, as it is, in the Tibetan language. But in the summer of 1996, as *The Good Heart* was being published, the West had a brief glimpse of this other side in what has been called the "Shugden affair."

Shugden (Rdo rje shugs ldan, "Powerful Thunderbolt") is an important protective deity of the Geluk sect. He is a deity of relatively recent origin. According to his myth, he is the spirit of a learned and virtuous Geluk monk, Tulku Drakpa Gyaltsen (Sprul sku Grags pa rgyal mtshan, 1619–1655). Born into an aristocratic family, he was one of the candidates to become the fifth Dalai Lama. Another child was chosen, however, and Tulku Drakpa Gyaltsen was identified instead as the third incarnation of Panchen Sonam Drakpa (Pan chen Bsod nams grags pa, 1478–1554), an eminent scholar who had been the teacher of the third Dalai Lama. Tulku Drakpa Gyaltsen became a distinguished scholar and debater, and a favorite of the respected teacher Losang Chögyi Gyaltsen (Blo bzang chos kyi rgyal mtshan, 1570–1662), the first Panchen Lama. In the early years of their education, both the Dalai Lama (who had not yet been installed as temporal ruler of Tibet by the Mongols) and Tulku Drakpa Gyaltsen lived in Drepung monastery outside Lhasa. There seems to have been a rivalry between their followers.

As the story goes, one day after defeating the Dalai Lama in debate, Tulku Drakpa Gyaltsen was murdered. Other accounts say that having grown weary of foiling attempts on his life by jealous followers of the fifth Dalai Lama, he committed suicide by the traditional method of stuffing a ceremonial scarf down his throat and suffocating, but only after teaching his disciple how to identify certain signs that would prove that the rumors against him were false. The signs duly appeared, and his disciple prayed to his departed master to take revenge on his enemies. Shortly thereafter, central Tibet and the new government of the Dalai Lama suffered famines and earthquakes. A mysterious force even overturned the dishes when the Dalai Lama was served his noon meal. The source of the difficulty was eventually identified, and a series of lamas and magicians were called in to exorcise the wrathful spirit. After they had all failed, the government of the Dalai Lama and the hierarchy of the Geluk sect propitiated the spirit and requested that it desist from its harm and become a protector of the Geluk. The spirit agreed, and since that time Shugden has become one of the chief protectors of the Geluk sect, its monks, and its monasteries.

From this point on, rites invoking the aid of Shugden began to be composed, many of which contained detailed descriptions of his abode and his person:

> Inside the palace, corpses of men and carcasses of horses are spread out, and the blood of the men and horses stream together forming a lake. Human skins and hides of tigers are stretched into curtains. The smoke of the "great burnt offering" (i.e. human flesh) spreads into the ten quarters of the world. Outside, on top of the platform, revived corpses and *rākṣasas* [a class of demon] are jumping around, and the four classes of skeletons perform there a dance. On all sides are hung up as tapestries fresh skins of elephants and skins drawn from corpses. There are "banners of victory" and circular banners made from bodies of lions, tassels made from wet bowels, wreathes consisting of various kinds of heads, and ornaments made from the organs of the five senses, whisks of human hair, and other fearful things. . . .
>
> In the interior . . . [is] the frightful *rDo rje shugs ldan*, whose body is a dark-red colour, who becomes fierce like a savage *rākṣasa*, and whose mouth is bottomless like the sky. He bares his four teeth, sharp like the ice of a glacier, and between them he rolls his tongue with the speed of chain-lightning, causing the three worlds to quake. . . . His forehead is contorted in terrible anger. His three bloodshot eyes stare full of hatred at the inimical *vighnas* [obstructers]. The yellow-red flames, issuing from his eyebrows and from the hair of his face, burn completely the four kinds of *bdub* [demons]. The yellow-brown hair of his head stands on end and in the centre above it, with a sun-*maṇḍala*, resides the lord-protector and king of religion, the great *Tsong kha pa* bearing a placid expression.
>
> By moving his two ears vehemently, *rDo rje shugs ldan* produces a fierce, devil-destroying wind, with which he sweeps away completely all the dwellings of the evil-doers, oath-breakers, and inimical obstacle-creating demons. From his two nostrils come forth rain-clouds, and from these again issue raging thunder and lightning, striking with yellow flashes the land of the *vighnas*.[17]

Like certain other protective deities, Shugden will upon request take possession of a medium, through whom he can be asked questions about the future.[18] Although many of the oracular deities of Tibetan Buddhism—including the most famous, the Nechung oracle consulted by the Dalai Lamas—are worldly deities subject to rebirth, Shugden's devotees believe that

Shugden himself has already advanced to the supramundane rank, that he is, in other words, a buddha, unbound by samsara.

One of Shugden's particular functions has been to protect the Geluk sect from the influence of the Nyingma, cautioning Geluks even against touching a Nyingma text; he is said to punish those who attempt to practice a mixture of the two. Such eclecticism (often associated with the fifth Dalai Lama, whose dishes Shugden overturned) enjoyed a revival during the "unbounded" (*ris med*) movement that began in eastern Tibet during the late eighteenth century among Nyingma, Sakya, Kagyu, and some Bön scholars.[19] In the first decades of the twentieth century, the Dalai Lama made preliminary attempts at modernization (often without the support of the powerful Geluk monasteries) by improving the size, organization, and weaponry of the army, setting up a police force in Lhasa, sending a group of boys to England for education, and so on. Perhaps in response to these modernizing trends, in the early decades of the twentieth century the worship of Shugden enjoyed a "revival" led by the powerful Geluk monk Pha bong kha pa (1878–1943). Under his influence something of a charismatic movement occurred among Lhasa aristocrats and in the three major Geluk monasteries in the vicinity of Lhasa (just at the time when representatives of Buddhist modernism were active in Southeast Asia and Japan), with Vajrayoginī as the tutelary deity (*yi dam*), Shugden as the protector, and Pha bong kha pa as the lama. This practice, which appealed to monk and laity alike, seemed to instill a strong sense of communal identity at a time when that identity appeared under threat, both by a modernizing government and by external forces. Devotion to Shugden would revive again some fifty years later when similar threats were perceived.

Pha bong kha pa was the guru of many of the most important Geluk monks of this century (both in terms of their scholastic influence and political power), including Lama Govinda's teacher Tomo Geshe Rinpoche,[20] Song Rinpoche, and, most prominently, Trijang Rinpoche (Khri byang rin po che, 1901–1981) of Ganden monastery, the junior tutor of the current Dalai Lama and thus one (along with the senior tutor, Ling Rinpoche) of the two most important Geluk monks in the refugee community, especially influential among refugees from eastern Tibet (Khams).[21] He was a strong proponent of Shugden. The Dalai Lama himself for many years included prayers to Shugden in his nightly worship.

In 1976, the Dalai Lama, on the advice of the Nechung oracle, discouraged the propitiation of Shugden, saying that he personally disapproved of the practice and would prefer that those who were associated with him, either as his disciples or as members of his government, not publicly worship Shugden. Contrary to the view of many Geluk monks, the Dalai Lama saw Shugden not as a buddha and not as the incarnation of Drakpa Gyaltsen, but as a worldly god, even an evil spirit, whose worship was fomenting sectarianism in the refugee community and thus impeding the cause of Tibetan independence. It was not because the deity was especially grotesque (a wide variety of wrathful buddhas are described in similar terms);[22] the Dalai Lama regularly offers initiations into the worship of wrathful deities and does not make a major decision without consulting the ferocious warrior-deity who speaks through the Nechung oracle. It was, instead, that the situation of exile made the Dalai Lama less a Geluk hierarch and more the ecumenical head of Tibetan Buddhism. He told a gathering in Dharamsala in 1986:

> As the Dalai Lama, although I am not qualified, I am the only person to uphold the common cause of Tibet. Because this relates to our common cause I have no choice but to talk, even though it may seem like a slap in the face for some. Anyway, there have lately been some problems concerning the protector Gyalchen Shugden, those of you who live in India know well about this and I don't have to repeat it to you. But, if those of you from Tibet accept him merely on the basis of his reputation as a great protector of the Gelugpas, it will not do any good for Tibet, either religiously or politically.[23]

The Dalai Lama's renunciation of Shugden in 1976 caused great discord within the Geluk community, where devotion to the deity remained strong among the Geluk hierarchy and among large factions of the refugee lay community; spirited defenses of his worship were written and published. Some went so far as to claim that the Dalai Lama was not the true Dalai Lama, that the search party had selected the wrong child forty years before. This controversy, however, remained largely unknown outside the Tibetan refugee community. The Tibetan Buddhism practiced by Western adherents was generally of the Buddhist modernist variety, with an emphasis on meditation on emptiness and on compassion, and did not include ritual offerings of fire from a lamp made of human fat with a wick made of human hair. It was not that their Tibetan teachers did not worship Shugden; it was simply that they generally did not teach their students to do so.

The Dalai Lama's opposition to the worship of Shugden became more pronounced in 1996. He made strong public statements against the practice during teachings at the celebration of the Tibetan New Year. At a tantric initiation in a Tibetan refugee settlement in south India, he requested that those who did not disavow the deity leave the ceremony. Because of the powerful link that is established in such an initiation between the initiating lama and the initiate, he refused to give tantric empowerments to devotees of Shugden; to do so, he stated, would endanger his health and shorten his life. He said on March 4, "It is good that paying attention to my health you have passed a resolution regarding this matter. Danger to health does not exclusively mean an armed attack. This type is extremely rare in Tibetan society. If there is continued indifference to my injunctions, then there would not be any point in my continuing to live silently as a disappointed man. This would be a more apt interpretation." [24] That is, because the Dalai Lama is said to be able to decide when he shall die, he suggested that if his people do not heed his warnings, he might die soon. On July 15, 1996, the Tibetan government-in-exile issued a statement that read in part:

> The Tibetan Administration has instituted a nine-member Special Committee to look into allegations of religious persecution against the devotees of a particular spirit, known as Dholgyal (Dorje Shugden).
> The Tibetan Administration's basic policy on the issue of Dholgyal propitiation was spelled out in the unanimous resolution passed on 6 June 1996 by the Assembly of Tibetan People's Deputies. The resolution stated that the government departments and their subsidiaries, as well as monastic institutions functioning under the administrative control of the Central Tibetan Administration, should be strictly forbidden from propitiating this spirit. Individual Tibetans, it said, must be informed of the demerits of propitiating this spirit, but be given freedom "to decide as they like." The resolution, however, requested the propitiators of this spirit not to receive vajrayana teachings from His Holiness the Dalai Lama. [25]

Monks of the six major Geluk monasteries in the refugee community were asked to sign a statement supporting a ban on "dubious deities." The Tibetan government-in-exile requested that the abbot of Sera monastery, a traditional center of Shugden devotion, report the names of those monks who continued to worship Shugden. The Holder of the Throne of Ganden (dGa' ldan khri pa), the titular head of the Geluk sect, issued a remarkable statement denouncing the worship of Shugden, explaining that when he was worshipped in the past by great masters, they understood the union of the peaceful and the wrathful, something that the deluded worshippers of today cannot comprehend. He accused those monks who have criticized the Dalai Lama for his proscription of Shugden of "devoting time in framing detrimental plots and committing degrading acts, which seems no different from the act of attacking monasteries wielding swords and spears and drenching the holy robes of the Buddha with blood." [26]

One of the monks who denounced the Dalai Lama's decree was Geshe Kelsang Gyatso, a Sera monk who had established himself in England as the head of the New Kadampa Tradition. The Kadampa (*bka' gdams pa*, which is traditionally etymologized as "those who take all of the Buddha's words as instructions") was the first Tibetan Buddhist monastic sect, founded in the eleventh century by the followers of Atiśa. Tsong kha pa is said to have called his followers the "new Kadampa," implying a connection to this original sect, noted for its monastic purity. The name Geluk (*dge lugs*, "system of virtue") came into use only after Tsong kha pa's death. For Kelsang Gyatso to call his group the New Kadampa Tradition, therefore, is ideologically charged, implying as it does that he and his followers represent the tradition of the founder, Tsong kha pa, more authentically than the Geluk establishment and the Dalai Lama himself. Like so many other Geluk monks in the refugee community, Kelsang Gyatso is himself a devotee of Shugden, and his uncle has served as a medium for the deity in one of the Tibetan refugee communities in south India. Unlike some other Geluk teachers who may have themselves been devotees, however, Kelsang Gyatso instructed his English disciples to make the worship of the deity a central part of their practice. Thus, after the Dalai Lama increased his opposition to devotion to Shugden in 1996, the disciples of Kelsang Gyatso denounced the Dalai Lama for impinging on their religious freedom, actually picketing against him during his visit to Britain in the summer of 1996, accusing him of intolerance.

The following article by Madeline Bunting appeared in the *Guardian* of London on July 6, 1996, under the headline "Smear campaign sparks fears over Dalai Lama's UK visit."

Members of a British-based Buddhist sect are behind an aggressive international smear campaign to undermine the Dalai Lama—one of the world's most revered religious figures and political leader of Tibet—ahead of his visit to the UK this month.

The Dalai Lama is accused of being a "ruthless dictator" and an "oppressor of religious freedom" in direct contradiction to his message of religious tolerance, according to a spokesman for an organisation called the

Shugden Supporters Community, based in Pocklington, Yorkshire, which has been distributing press releases to 400 worldwide news outlets.

Members of the Shugden Supporters Community (SSC) belong to one of the fastest-growing and richest sects in the UK called the New Kadampa Tradition (NKT) whose headquarters are in Ulverston, Cumbria.

The sect has expanded dramatically since it was founded in 1991, and is now the biggest Buddhist organisation in the UK with more than 200 affiliated centres at home and more than 50 abroad. Membership is put at about 3,000. The founder of the NKT is a Tibetan monk, Geshe Kelsang, who has lived in Britain since the late seventies. NKT members believe they must obey, worship and pray to Kelsang because he is the Third Buddha.

Kelsang is in almost permanent semi-retreat in Cumbria and speaks little English, although he is the author of 16 books on Buddhism, two of which have reached the UK bestseller lists.

Former members maintain that the Department of Social Security has unknowingly played a critical part in funding the NKT's rapid expansion. NKT associates have acquired at least five large properties in the last year and a significant proportion of the 300-odd residents of their centres claim housing benefit of up to £360 a week.

The benefit is paid as rent and used to service the large mortgages on properties. Among the properties acquired recently is Ashe Hall in Derbyshire, a neo-Jacobean mansion in 38 acres.

Organisers are concerned for the safety of the Dalai Lama during his week-long visit to the UK, starting on July 15. There have been threats from the SSC of demonstrations in London and Manchester where he is scheduled to speak before large audiences. At a demonstration last month outside the Office of Tibet in London, hundreds chanted anti-Dalai Lama slogans and carried placards saying "Your smiles charm, your actions harm."

The SSC maintains that the Dalai Lama has banned a centuries old Buddhist practise and claims that Tibetans in India have been dismissed from their jobs, monks expelled from their monasteries, houses searched and statues destroyed. The Tibetan government-in-exile's London representatives at the Office of Tibet vigorously deny the allegations. Amnesty International says the SSC has yet to substantiate its allegations.

At dispute between Kelsang and the Dalai Lama—the latter has the backing of the majority of the Tibetan religious and political establishment—is the spiritual practice of worshipping a deity called Dorje Shugden.

To supporters of the Dalai Lama, this practice can become demonic. The Dalai Lama has warned his students against it and says this spiritual practice threatens his life and the future of the Tibetan people. The NKT and SSC maintain Dorje Shugden is a Buddha.

In the last few weeks, the SSC has launched a letter writing campaign to the Home Secretary asking for the Dalai Lama's visa to be stopped; draft letters have been distributed by NKT trained teachers to their students, claiming that his visit will "do nothing other than harm" and accusing him of "persecuting his own people."

The concern among British supporters of Tibet is that the SSC campaign will play directly into Chinese hands. As a Nobel Peace Prize winner, the Dalai Lama has had enormous success in raising the profile of the cause of Tibet—the country has been occupied by the Chinese since 1950. The Chinese see undermining of his reputation as a world religious leader as an effective way to weaken support for Tibet.

The UK's Tibet Society, one of the hosts for the Dalai Lama's visit along with 27 Buddhist organisations, accuses the SSC of being sectarian and of "going directly against the basic premise of Buddhism, which is compassion and benefit of others."

A special report in the same issue of the *Guardian* portrayed the NKT as a cult, documenting its financial improprieties and intimidation tactics while portraying its support of Shugden as a remnant of Tibet's shamanistic past. An article by Andrew Brown in the *Independent* of July 15, 1996, entitled "The Battle of the Buddhists" described a member of the NKT as having "the catechetical manner you find among Scientologists or Trotskyists" before concluding that, as if in testimony to the Dalai Lama's success in representing his religion as a variation on Buddhist modernism, "Some of the mud being flung at the Dalai Lama will probably stick. The reputation of Tibetan Buddhism as a uniquely clean and rational religion will certainly be damaged." [27] On August 22, 1996, the monks of Sera Je Monastery in India, the monastery of Kelsang Gyatso, issued a formal "Declaration of Expulsion," which stated, in part, "This demon with broken commitments, Kelsang Gyatso, burns with the flame of unbearable spite towards the unsurpassed omniscient 14th Dalai Lama, the only staff of life of religious people in Tibet, whose activities and kindness equal the sky." [28] On February 4, 1997, the highly respected scholar and principal of the Buddhist School of Dialectics in Dharamsala, Geshe Losang Gyatso (age 70), who had long supported the

Dalai Lama's position on Shugden, was stabbed to death along with two of his students, apparently by Tibetan supporters of Shugden.[29]

Unlike buddhas and bodhisattvas, who are of Indian origin, the class of deities such as Shugden, known as protectors (*chos skyong* or *srung ma*), are often of Tibetan origin. They are the regional deities of Tibet, some of whom date from pre-Buddhist times, said to have been defeated in magical battle by Indian masters such as Padmasambhava and then converted to Buddhism; rather than be killed by a Buddhist master they agreed to defend Buddhism. Thus these protectors, some of whom are quite ancient, are native Tibetan deities (not from India) and have traditionally enjoyed great devotion as ancestral guardians of a clan, a mountain range, or a region. Shugden, a kind of clan deity for the Geluk sect and for a region of Eastern Tibet, having been carried into exile, thus must himself be declared obsolete and be exiled by the Dalai Lama so that Tibetans in exile may develop a national, rather than clan, identity. This national identity is required only now, after they have fled the land that they regard as the site of the nation of Tibet. Tibetan culture becomes the same culture for all Tibetans only in retrospect.

This raises, of course, the contested question of Tibetan nationalism. Prior to the Chinese annexation of Tibet, there was a political entity referred to in the West as "Tibet" and imagined to be ruled by the Dalai Lama, a state with which the European powers sought trading privileges (exacted by force by the Younghusband expedition, for example) and to which delegations were sent (such as the 1942 mission of the OSS officers Tolstoy and Dolan, who were not granted permission to transport war material through Tibet during World War II).

In most senses of the term, it would seem that Tibet was a nation.[30] There are narratives of the nation of Tibet, although often contained within accounts of the arising of the dharma (*chos 'byung*), that is, histories of Buddhism. There is an emphasis on the origins, continuity, and timelessness of the Tibetan people, the lineages of kings that are traced to prehistoric times. What is noteworthy is that Tibetan traditions are usually depicted as originating outside Tibet: Tibetan identity is acquired through contrast with surrounding cultures, but those cultures are often depicted as the source of the constituents of Tibetan identity. Thus, Buddhism came from India, but it was preserved in its fullness only in Tibet. Tibet is often depicted as a benighted place populated by a (proudly) uncivilized people, into which culture is introduced. Thus, in Bön accounts, the priests responsible for instituting the royal funerary cult must be called in from outside (from Zhang Zhung); in Buddhist accounts, the first king (from the clan of the Buddha) arrives across the mountains from India; the most sacred image of the Buddha in Lhasa was brought to Tibet by Songtsen Gampo's Chinese bride; Padmasambhava came from India to tame the demons of Tibet and establish the first monastery.

Like those of other nations, the traditions of Tibet are invented, of more recent origin than they are represented as being. Many date from the fourteenth century and the reign of Jangchup Gyaltsen (Byang chub rgyal mtshan), others from the seventeenth century and the reign of the fifth Dalai Lama. Like other nations, Tibetans have a foundational myth about the origin of their race and their unique national character, born not from a divine pair but through miscegenation, the offspring of a monkey and a demoness (although the monkey was an incarnation of Avalokiteśvara).[31] Still, these are Buddhist myths, excluding the non-Buddhists who are also Tibetans, notably, the Bönpo, suggesting that Renan was correct when he remarked that "Forgetting . . . is a crucial factor in the creation of a nation."[32]

When asked what their fatherland (*pha yul*) is, Tibetans will usually respond with the name of a region. There was strong identification with local mountains and valleys and their deities, with local lamas, monasteries, and chieftains, with local (and mutually unintelligible) dialects. (There is a Tibetan saying: "Each valley a different language, each lama a different dharma system.") Tibetans from the regions of Kham and Amdo would often describe going to the central provinces or to Lhasa as "going to Tibet." The term translated as "Tibetan," *bod pa*, was used by nomads of the northern plains (located in the central provinces) to refer to inhabitants of the Lhasa Valley, not to themselves. (In the refugee community, the meaning of the term "Tibetan" has been extended to include the populations of Kham and Amdo under Chinese control, but not the Tibetan-speaking peoples of Ladakh, Sikkim, and Bhutan.)[33] During long periods of Tibetan history the rule of the government of the Dalai Lama extended only through the provinces of U and Tsang (where there were sometimes disputes with the Panchen Lama over jurisdiction and taxation);[34] the inhabitants of Kham and Amdo were often fiercely contemptuous of its rule.[35] For the monks who constituted as much as 15 percent of the male population, the monastery or college (*grva tshang*) was often the chief unit of allegiance and community of identity. And because Tibet was not a colony during the nineteenth century, it did not develop those institutions that some see as key to the development of a national consciousness, institutions such as print capitalism, the census, the map, and the museum.[36] Thus it would seem that Tibet was a nation in the sense of a *natio*, a community or condition of belonging, rather than a nation-state in the modern sense of the term, with its attendant secular state and polity, notions of citizenship, a global capitalist economy,[37] membership in an international system of states enjoying diplomatic relations, an advanced social division of labor, industrialism, and the dominance of secular cultural values.[38]

A traditional definition of what makes someone a Tibetan is based on ethnicity: someone who eats *tsampa*, a roasted barley flour generally found unpalatable by non-Tibetans (and who, therefore, are not Tibetans). This has largely been replaced in exile (where roasted barley flour is rarely eaten), especially in representations to non-Tibetans, by an exaggerated emphasis on the practice of Buddhism as that which is unique about Tibetan culture (although Buddhism and its role in rulership were key elements of Tibetan state identity prior to the Chinese invasion). The Dalai Lama has observed that young Tibetans in the refugee community have a renewed interest in Buddhism because "Europeans and Americans are showing genuine interest in Tibetan Buddhism."[39] But the Tibetan Buddhism of Europeans and Americans may differ from the Tibetan Buddhism of Tibetans. It is the Buddhism that interests Europeans and Americans that is represented as Tibet's unique cultural legacy; it is this Buddhism, it is argued, that must not be allowed to be lost. This universal inheritance is Tibet's gift to the world. Thus in an effort to maintain the link between the cause of Tibetan independence and the promotion of the universal good of Buddhist compassion, the Dalai Lama has described Tibet (to Western practitioners of Tibetan Buddhism) as certain Europeans described it in the nineteenth century, as a preserve of wisdom:

> As Buddhist practitioners, you should understand the necessity of preserving Tibetan Buddhism. For this the land, the physical country of Tibet, is crucial. We have tried our best to preserve the Tibetan traditions outside Tibet for almost thirty years, and we have been comparatively successful. But eventually, after our time, there is a real danger that they will change, that they will not survive away from the protective nurture of our homeland. So, for the sake of preserving Tibetan Buddhism, which can be seen as a complete form of the Buddha Dharma, the sacred land of Tibet is vitally important. It is very unlikely that it can survive as a cultural and spiritual entity if its physical reality is smothered under Chinese occupation. So we cannot avoid taking responsibility in trying to improve its po-

litical situation. Clearly, in this light, active support for the Tibetan cause is not just a matter of politics. It is the work of Dharma.[40]

But the Dalai Lama himself, especially in statements enunciated for Western consumption, sometimes blurs the distinction, moving away from a call for Tibetan independence to a call for the preservation of Tibetan culture. By culture he does not mean the material culture of cuisine and crafts, or the social culture of kinship and clan; he does not seem to be evoking the ethnographic view of culture, what E. B. Tylor defined in 1871 as "that complex whole which includes knowledge, belief, art, morals, law, custom, and other capabilities and habits acquired by man as a member of a society."[41] In this view religion is but one constituent of the complex whole that is culture, and, as such, is subject to change as a result of various social and historical conditions. The Dalai Lama, however, seems to have in mind something more universal and eternal, something closer to the view put forward by Matthew Arnold in 1869: culture as "a general humane spirit . . . the love of human perfection."[42] In an October 30, 1996, interview in *Le Monde* the Dalai Lama said, "A kind of cultural genocide is in progress in Tibet. And even if losing her independence is acceptable, then still the destruction of our spirituality, of Tibetan Buddhism, is unthinkable. Protecting the Tibetan heritage has become my primary occupation."

Having learned that they have something called a "culture," the leaders of the Tibetans in exile have selected one of the many elements that together are considered to constitute the changing composition of culture, namely, religion, and have universalized it into an eternal essence, compassion. And, since culture precedes nature, Tibetans in exile have subsequently also discovered that in Tibet they also had nature. Tibetan environmental awareness has appeared only recently; there are no references to it in exile publications prior to 1985, when the Dalai Lama sent a representative to the Global Forum of Spiritual and Parliamentary Leaders on Human Survival. Since then the depiction of Tibet as a society that was also environmentally enlightened has become a standard component of Tibetan independence literature, in which one finds statements such as, "For most of Asia, Tibet's environment has always been of crucial importance. And so for centuries Tibet's ecosystem was kept in balance and alive out of a common concern for all humanity."[43]

The Dalai Lama has said that what is most important about Tibetan culture is not the national cuisine or the mode of dress; these are superficial and transitory. What is enduring about Tibet is Buddhism. But there are myriad forms of Buddhist practice in Tibet, including, for example, the propitiation of Shugden. By Buddhism, however, the Dalai Lama means something else, foremost the practice of compassion, something not of Tibetan origin, but transmitted to Tibet by the great Indian masters of the Mahayana. It is this beatific Buddhism that he has offered to the West, hoping perhaps to get his country back as part of the exchange. It is unclear, however, why there must be a political entity called Tibet in order for this inheritance to be transferred. In universalizing his message in this way, has the Dalai Lama allowed Tibetan Buddhism, like Lamaism before it, to float free from its site in a process of spiritual globalization that knows no national boundaries? If Renan was correct that "A nation is a spiritual principle, the outcome of profound complications of history; it is a spiritual family not a group determined by the shape of the earth," then Tibet is everywhere, and nowhere.[44] In seeking the goal of Tibet as a modern nation-state, the Dalai Lama invokes the universal value of Tibet and Tibetan culture. The cause of Tibetan independence may thus be compromised by the traditional universalism of Buddhist discourse, with its appeal to all sentient beings of the ten directions in the three times (past, present, and future) projected onto the cultural market of global consumerism.[45]

It could be argued, then, that the national culture (and nature) of Tibet was unified in the discursive sense only once the Dalai Lama had gone into exile in 1959. Introduced by Western supporters to the notion of culture, Tibetan refugees could look back at what Tibet had been. But this gaze, at least as it would be represented to the West, saw the Land of Snows only as it was reflected in the elaborately framed mirror of Western fantasies about Tibet. It was only through this mirror, this process of doubling, that a Tibetan nation could be represented as unified, complete, and coherent. It was as if a double of Tibet had long haunted the West, and the Tibetans, coming out of Tibet, were now confronted with this double. In this sense the Tibetans stepped into a world in which they were already present, and since their belated arrival—often encouraged by the devotees of Tibet, missionaries of a different stripe—they have merged seamfully into a double that had long been standing. (In a recent visit to London the Dalai Lama was taken to Madame Tussaud's to inspect his wax image.) If to see one's double is to see one's fate, then what has occurred since 1959 has been a sometimes fitful accommodation of this double: as though mimicking a phantom, the Tibetans' self-presentation, as in a science fiction film, sometimes merges with its evil twin and sometimes stands alone, while the observer is rarely able to tell them apart. As in the mirror scene in *Duck Soup*, it is only when one of the pair has turned away for an instant that the viewer knows that in fact there is no mirror between them, that they are two and not one; one is in disguise. In this sense, at a time when many young lay Tibetans growing up in India have begun to criticize Tibetan monks for not living up to the image of Tibetan Buddhism they have read about in English, the Shugden affair might be read as an attempt by the devotees of the deity to return to some sense of the ancestral and the regional, the orthodox and the local, to something uniquely Tibetan, which Westerners, despite the efforts of the English disciples of Shugden, cannot share.

Still, the moments in which the images are separate seem increasingly rare and increasingly brief; the mirror movements are the norm. Just as the king of Shambhala would not allow the brahmans to leave utopia, just as the High Lama attempted to dissuade Conway from leaving Shangri-La, Wilde's "lie" seems difficult to escape, as the mimesis of Tibetan and Western discourse about Tibet persists into the present, as the following sequence of quotations may suggest.

In 1880 the master of the Great White Brotherhood, the Mahatma Koot Hoomi, described Tibet in a letter to A. P. Sinnett that materialized in Madame Blavatsky's cabinet. It read, in part, "For centuries we have had in Thibet a moral, pure hearted, simple people, unblest with civilization, hence —untainted by its vices. For ages has been Thibet the last corner of the globe not so entirely corrupted as to preclude the mingling together of the two atmospheres—the physical and spiritual." [46] From here we can trace a process by which Tibet becomes increasingly symbolic, ethereal, and epiphenomenal, a surrogate society, even a sacrificial victim. In the preface to *My Life in Tibet* (1939) by Edwin J. Dingle (founder of the Science of Mentalphysics), Louis M. Grafe, in keeping with Hilton's vision of Shangri-La described in *Lost Horizon* just a few years before, portrays Tibet as a preserve of ancient wisdom, a place where Orientals safeguard the wisdom of the white race: "Amid all these changes, was the great original wisdom saved? Yes—thanks to that land which was free of strife and war—Tibet, protected by Nature herself with barriers insurmountable to the greed and war lust of surrounding nations. Here, men of Mongolian extraction were to preserve for the Indo-European the original wisdom of his own white race, to be given back when he showed himself ready for it, or when, as now, the barriers of Nature seem no longer sufficient to protect the sanctuary." [47] Tibet is thus a service society for the white race, preserving a wisdom that originally belonged to it but in the meantime had been lost.

In 1966 the esoteric wisdom of Asia was once again in fashion. But by this time China had overrun Tibet, and the wisdom, held in safekeeping for so long, was in danger of being lost forever. Lama Govinda portrays Tibet as symbolic both of the ancient wisdom that all humanity laments and of the salvific knowledge it longs for in the future:

> Tibet, due to its natural isolation and its inaccessibility (which was rein-forced by the political conditions of the last centuries) has succeeded not only in keeping alive the traditions of the most distant past, the knowledge of the hidden forces of the human soul and highest achievements and eso-teric teachings of Indian saints and sages.
>
> But in the storm of world-transforming events, which no nation on earth can escape and which will drag even Tibet out of its isolation, these spiritual achievements will be lost forever, unless they become an integral part of a future higher civilization of humanity. . . .[48]
>
> Why is it that the fate of Tibet has found such a deep echo in the world? There can be only one answer: Tibet has become the symbol of all that present-day humanity is longing for, either because it has been lost or not yet been realised or because it is in danger of disappearing from human sight: the stability of a tradition, which has its roots not only in a historical or cultural past, but within the innermost being of man, in whose depth this past is enshrined as an ever-present source of inspiration.[49]

In 1991 these sentiments could be reiterated. By this time, however, the cause of Tibet had entered more fully into popular culture and the contrast between the old and the new Tibet could be more sharply drawn. To be preserved, Ti-bet's wisdom must now be integrated into the world's culture, for the inspira-tion it provides. Thus, perhaps the most famous of the Western adherents of Tibetan Buddhism, Richard Gere, echoing Madame Blavatsky, Evans-Wentz, and voices from a century ago, describes Tibet as everything that the materi-alist West wants. Here Tibet operates as a constituent of a romanticism in which the Orient is not debased but exalted as a surrogate self endowed with all that the West wants. It is Tibet that will regenerate the West by showing us, prophetically, what we can be by showing us what it had been. It is Tibet that can save the West, cynical and materialist, from itself. Tibet is seen as the cure for an ever-dissolving Western civilization, restoring its spirit. An internal absence is thus perceived as existing outside, and if it be outside, let it be found in the most remote, the most inaccessible, the most mysterious part of the world: "Prior to the Chinese invasion of Tibet in 1950, the Tibetans were unusually peaceful and happy. Isolated for centuries from a chaotic world they deeply mistrusted, they developed a wondrous, unique civilization based wholly on the practice of Buddhism's highest ideals. Theirs has been a revolutionary social experiment based on spiritual, psychological, and philosophical insights that provide us with models for achieving intimate and creative relationships with the vast and profound secrets of the human soul. Tibet's importance for our own time, and for the future survival of Earth itself, is more critical than ever. Being our most vibrant link to the ancient wisdom traditions, Tibet, and the sanity she represents, must not be allowed to disappear."[50]

From here it is a rather small step to the view of Tibet as a surrogate state and the Tibetan people as sacrificial victims. Such a view was expressed in a mimeographed document I received in 1993 from something called World Service Network; the document was titled "The New Tibet—The Pure Land." Here, in a bizarre amalgam of Christian, Theosophical, and New Age imagery, Tibet and the Tibetan people are portrayed as innocent sacrificial offerings immolated in the horror of the Chinese invasion and occupation so that Tibet might be purified and transformed into a New Age mission field, which, once converted, will serve as the headquarters of a global utopia. It reads, in part:

> The Spiritual (Tibet) has been defiled and temporarily overpowered by one of the heartless and self-centered elements (China) of the material world. The Spirit will only become Free and Liberated by transmuting the darkness, once and for all through a powerful alignment with and expression of the higher laws and principles.
>
> From an esoteric viewpoint, Tibet has passed through the burning ground of purification on a national level. What is the "burning ground?" When a developing entity, be it a person or a nation (the dynamic is the same), reaches a certain level of spiritual development, a time comes for the lower habits, old patterns, illusions and crystalized beliefs to be purified so as to better allow the spiritual energies of inner being to flow thru the instrument without distortion. The spiritualization of the entity has sufficiently strengthened it enough to endure this extremely stressful experience.
>
> After such a purification the entity is ready for the next level of expan-

sion in service. The Tibetans were spiritually strong enough to endure this burning ground so as to pave the way for its destined part in building the new world. . . .

It is time for the unveiling of Shangri-la—The Pure Land—the impending rebirth of the New Tibet. Where sister/brotherhood, compassion, respect for each other and all life forms, sharing and interdependence are the foundation stones of a Great New Society. . . .

When Tibet has regained its full independence and is designated the world's first Sacred Nation it will act as the Point of Synthesis, as the hub of the Wheel of Transformation for Universal Love, Wisdom and Goodwill. It is then that we will go there to initiate Tibet into becoming the integrating element which will start the process of serious and lasting global transformation to World Peace.[51]

On September 21, 1987, the Dalai Lama presented a five-point peace plan to the Congressional Human Rights Caucus. He called for (1) the transformation of Tibet into a "zone of peace," (2) a cessation of the Chinese policy of population transfer into Tibet, (3) respect for the human rights of the Tibetan people, (4) the restoration and protection of Tibet's natural environment, including the removal of nuclear weapons and waste from Tibet, and (5) commencement of serious negotiations with the Chinese on the future status of Tibet.[52] Receiving no positive response from the Chinese, he offered a new proposal before the European Parliament in Strasbourg on June 15, 1988, in which he moved away from his call for outright independence for Tibet, proposing instead that Tibet be "a self-governing democratic political entity . . . in association with the People's Republic of China," with China responsible for Tibet's foreign policy. Again, this proposal elicited only a negative response from the Chinese, as it did from certain members of the Tibetan refugee community, who saw it as an abandonment of the cause of independence.[53]

These two proposals can be read as the Dalai Lama's concession to the political reality of China's occupation and colonization of Tibet. Almost forty years after the Chinese invasion, there was no indication that China would renounce its claims on Tibet in the foreseeable future (the events in Tiananmen Square in 1989 provided a brief flicker of hope). By putting forward these two proposals, the Dalai Lama indicated his own flexibility to negotiate in order to improve the situation of the Tibetans in Tibet. It is difficult, however, for anyone, perhaps most of all the Dalai Lama, to speak about Tibet without a multitude of associations also coming into play. Thus his proposals of 1987 and 1988 can be seen as an abandonment of the goal of an autonomous Tibetan nation-state just as the idea of such a state had begun to take form in exile. At the same time, his turn away from the particularity of the nation-state to the ideal of a "zone of peace" is continuous with the Buddhist modernist universalism he espouses, with its strong emphasis on nonviolence as a fundamental component of Buddhism. He writes in *My Tibet*, "It is my dream that the entire Tibetan Plateau should be a free refuge where humanity and nature can live in peace and in harmonious balance. It would be a place where people from all over the world could come to seek the true meaning of peace within themselves, away from the tensions and pressures of much of the rest of the world. Tibet could indeed become a creative center for the promotion and development of peace. The Tibetan Plateau would be transformed into the world's largest natural park or biosphere."[54] What seems inevitable, however, is the way in which his proposals appear to blend so seamlessly with the pre- and post-diaspora fantasies of Tibet as a place unlike any other on the globe, a zone of peace, free of the weapons that harm humans and the environment, where the practice of compassion is preserved for the good of humanity and all sentient beings. The Dalai Lama presents his position succinctly in the foreword to Pierre-Antoine Donnet's *Tibet: Survival in Question:*

> Tibetan civilisation has a long and rich history. The pervasive influence of Buddhism and the rigours of life amid the wide open spaces of an unspoilt environment resulted in a society dedicated to peace and harmony. We enjoyed freedom and contentment. Since the Chinese invasion in 1950, however, the Tibetan people as a whole have endured untold suffering and abuse. Tibetan religion and culture has been attacked, its artefacts destroyed and its proponents condemned.
>
> Tibet's religious culture, its medical knowledge, peaceful outlook and respectful attitude to the environment contain a wealth of experience that can be of widespread benefit to others. It has lately become clear that no amount of technological development on its own leads to lasting happiness. What people need is that sense of inner peace and hope that many have remarked among Tibetans, even in the face of adversity. The source of this lies mostly in the Buddhist teachings of love, kindness, tolerance and especially the theory that all things are relative.
>
> Our cultural traditions form a precious part of the world's common heritage. Humanity would be poorer if they were to be lost.[55]

It would seem, then, that the Dalai Lama's teaching of universal compassion and of the relative unimportance of national distinction are ultimately antithetical to the case for an autonomous Tibetan state. They are compatible, instead, when Tibet is made a surrogate state, a fantasy for the spiritualist desires of non-Tibetans, desires that have remained remarkably consistent during the past century, as evidenced by the string of quotations from Master Koot Hoomi to Richard Gere.

From another perspective, however, the Dalai Lama's teachings have played a most traditional role. Since Tibet's submission to the Mongols in the twelfth century, Tibetans have often perceived the relationship between Tibet and China as that of "patron and priest" (*yon mchod*): the leading lama of Tibet (in subsequent centuries, generally the Dalai Lama or Panchen Lama) was seen as the religious advisor and chief priest to the emperor, who acted as the patron and protector of the lama and, by extension, of Tibet. It was a relationship of exchange. The lama provided rituals and instructions that would protect the emperor and his empire in this and future lives. In return, the emperor provided the lama and his state with material support and military protection.[56] Since the fall of the Qing dynasty in 1911, the patron-priest relation with China has effectively ceased, with the Chinese now arrogating the role of the selection of the priest (as in the case of the Panchen Lama controversy of 1995 and 1996) to themselves.

Tibetans in exile, led by the Dalai Lama, have thus been forced to turn to new patrons—in Europe, the Americas, Australia, Japan, and Taiwan—for whom they perform the role of the priest by giving religious instructions and initiations and from whom in return they receive financial contributions and political support for the cause of Tibetan independence. The measure of the success and of the sphere of patronage (and thus influence) of Tibetan lamas in this regard can be plotted historically by the increasingly larger geographical regions in which incarnate lamas are discovered. After the death of the third Dalai Lama, to whom the Mongol leader, the Altan Khan, had pledged his support, the Altan Khan's grandnephew was recognized as the fourth Dalai Lama. Today, incarnate lamas are discovered in Europe and America. (In a recent Wildean case of life imitating art, an American boy in Seattle was identified as the incarnation of a prominent lama, as in Bertolucci's *The Little Buddha*. More recently and too farcical for Wilde, action film star Steven Seagal was identified as the reincarnation of a Tibetan lama.) In this way Tibetans have quite literally incorporated foreigners into their patronage sphere through their own version of colonialism, what might be termed a spiritual colonialism. Rather than taking control of a nation, Tibetan Buddhists are building an empire of individuals who, inhabited from birth by the spirit of a Tibetan saint, become, in effect, Tibetans, regardless of their ethnicity. (Although, as seen in chapter three, Lobsang Rampa lacked the proper credentials, he was clearly something of a forerunner of this phenomenon.)

The Dalai Lama may have a long-term strategy, then, one that serves Buddhist universalism, the freedom of Tibet, and the utopian aspirations of Tibetophiles around the world. Since coming into exile, the Dalai Lama has given the Kālacakra initiation over twenty times. This initiation is unusual among tantric initiations in that it is given in public, often to large gatherings; recent attendance has exceeded 250,000 people. When the initiation is given in Europe or America (as in Madison Square Garden), it has often been called "Kalachakra for World Peace." As he writes in his autobiography, "I have given the Kalachakra initiation in more than one country outside India—my motive for doing so being not only to give some insight into the Tibetan way of life and thinking, but also to make an effort, on an inner level, in favour of world peace."[57] This peace may have a special meaning, however, for those who take the initiation are planting the seeds to be reborn in their next lifetime in Shambhala, the Buddhist pure land across the mountains dedicated to the preservation of Buddhism.[58] In the year 2425, the army of the king will sweep out of Shambhala and defeat the barbarians in a Buddhist Armageddon, restoring Buddhism to India and to the world and ushering in a reign of peace.

In Hilton's novel, the inhabitants of Shangri-La sometimes found it necessary to resort to kidnapping in order to populate their utopia, commandeering an airplane and bringing its occupants to the Valley of the Blue Moon. The Dalai Lama may have found a more efficient technique for populating Shambhala and recruiting troops for the army of the twenty-fifth king, an army that will defeat the enemies of Buddhism and bring the utopia of Shambhala, hidden for so long beyond the Himalayas, to the world. It is the Dalai Lama's prayer, he says, that he will someday give the Kālacakra initiation in Beijing.

Notes

INTRODUCTION

1. I am grateful to Stephen and Sean Hallisey of Cambridge, Massachusetts, for providing me with this reference. In the 1980 film *Caddyshack,* the caddy played by Bill Murray delivers the following monologue:

> So I jump ship in Hong Kong and I make my way over to Tibet. I set myself up as a looper over in the Himalayas, you know, a looper, a caddy, a jock. So I tell 'em I'm a pro jock and who do they give me? The Dalai Lama himself, twelfth son of the lama, the flowing robes, the grace, bald, striking. So I'm on the first tee and I give him the driver and he whacks one (big hitter the lama, long) right into a 10,000 foot crevasse at the base of a glacier. And so we finish eighteen, and he's gonna stiff me! So I says, "Hey Lama. How about a little something, ya know, for the effort, ya know." And he says, "Oh, there won't be any money, but when you die, on your deathbed, you will receive total consciousness." So I got that goin' for me, which is nice.

2. *Twin Peaks,* episode 2, written and directed by David Lynch, first broadcast April 19, 1990. In episode 9 (aired October 6, 1990), the following exchange occurs:

AGENT COOPER: Buddhist tradition first came to the Land of Snow in the fifth century A.D. The first Tibetan king to be touched by the Dharma was King Hop-thong-thor-bu-nam-bu-tsang. He and succeeding kings were collectively known as "the happy generations." Now some historians place them in a Water Snake year, 213 A.D. Others in a year of a Water Ox, 173 A.D. Amazing, isn't it? "The happy generations."

AGENT ROSENFELD: Agent Cooper, I am thrilled to pieces that the Dharma came to King Ho-ho-ho, I really am. But right now I am trying hard to focus on the more immediate problems of our century right here in Twin Peaks.

AGENT COOPER: Albert, you'd be surprised at the connections between the two.

3. Antonin Artaud, "Address to the Dalai Lama," in *Anthology* (San Francisco: City Lights Books, 1972), pp. 64–65.

4. Susie C. Rijnhart, *With the Tibetans in Tent and Temple* (New York: Fleming H. Revell, 1901), p. 125.

5. H. P. Blavatsky, "Tibetan Teachings," in *Collected Writings 1883–1884–1885* (Los Angeles: Blavatsky Writings Publication Fund, 1954), 6:105.

6. Christmas Humphreys, *Buddhism* (New York: Barnes and Noble, 1962), p. 189.

7. André Guibaut, *Tibetan Venture,* trans. Lord Sudley (London: John Murray, 1949), p. 43. Christmas Humphreys wrote, "Nowhere save in Tibet is there so much sorcery and 'black' magic, such degradation of the mind to selfish, evil ends." See Humphreys, p. 189.

8. In his classic 1957 work, *Oriental Despotism: A Comparative Study of Total Power,* Karl Wittfogel classed Tibet as a "marginal agrarian despotism." See Karl A. Wittfogel, *Oriental Despotism: A Comparative Study of Total Power* (New Haven: Yale University Press, 1957), p. 191.

9. Lama Anagarika Govinda, *The Way of the White Clouds: A Buddhist Pilgrim in Tibet* (London: Hutchinson, 1966), p. xi. The view of Tibet as mechanically backward but spiritually advanced, as lacking in "outer technology" but rich in "inner technology" is oft-repeated. See, for example, Walt Anderson, *Open Secrets: A Western Guide to Tibetan Buddhism* (New York: Penguin Books, 1980), pp. 5, 21. A particularly extreme version can be found in Robert A. F. Thurman, *The Tibetan Book of the Dead* (New York: Bantam Books, 1994), pp. 10–12.

10. Huston Smith, *Requiem for a Faith,* Hartley Film Foundation, 1968.

11. Marilyn M. Rhie and Robert A. F. Thurman, *Wisdom and Compassion: The Sacred Art of Tibet* (New York: Harry N. Abrams, 1991), p. 22. Such statements can be explained in part by the lack of detailed histories of pre-1900 Tibet, despite the wealth of available sources in Tibetan. The period of 1913–1951 is presented in detail

in Melvyn Goldstein, *A History of Modern Tibet, 1913–1951* (Berkeley: University of California Press, 1989). Although it does not rely on Tibetan or Chinese documents, a useful account of Tibet since 1959 is found in Warren W. Smith, Jr., *Tibetan Nation: A History of Tibetan Nationalism and Sino-Tibetan Relations* (Boulder, Colo.: Westview Press, 1996). The absence of reliable histories is another consequence of Tibet's not having come under the colonial domination of a European power. It is noteworthy that there has been a marked increase in the writing of history (in Tibetan and Chinese) since Tibet came under the colonial domination of China.

12. For an insightful critique of this view, see Toni Huber, "Traditional Environmental Protectionism in Tibet Reconsidered," *Tibet Journal* 16, no. 2 (autumn 1991): 63–77.

Tibetan women generally had greater freedom of movement, access to and control of financial resources, and sexual freedom than did women in India and China. There were no practices comparable to sati, female infanticide, or foot-binding in Tibet. It does not follow from this, however, that, as the historian Franz Michael claimed, "Tibetan Buddhism believed in the equality of all human beings in their temporary individuality and did not, in principle or practice, recognize any sexual discrimination." See Franz Michael, *Rule by Incarnation: Tibetan Buddhism and Its Role in Society and State* (Boulder, Colo.: Westview Press, 1982), p. 127. In fact, there were far fewer nuns than monks, for example. Being a nun carried little of the status held by a monk; there is a Tibetan proverb that if you want to be a servant, make your son a monk; if you want a servant, make your daughter a nun. Unmarried daughters often became nuns (sometimes remaining at home). Other women became nuns to escape a bad marriage, to avoid pregnancy, or after the death of a spouse. The educational opportunities and chances for social advancement open to monks were generally absent for nuns, whose chief activities involved the memorization and recitation of prayers and the performance of rituals. Among the some three thousand incarnate lamas in Tibet, only a few were women, and women did not hold government office in Tibet. A feminist critique of Tibetan religion and society, both in pre- and post-1959 Tibet (where anthropologists report domestic violence both in the exile community and in Tibet), is an urgent desideratum. For a feminist analysis of Tibetan Buddhism, see June Campbell, *Traveller in Space: In Search of Female Identity in Tibetan Buddhism* (New York: George Braziller, 1996).

13. Marco Pallis, *Peaks and Lamas*, 3d ed., rev. (London: Woburn Press, 1974), p. 358.

14. In Bataille's posthumously published work, *The Accursed Share*, he argues that every system and thus every society produces a surplus energy that must be expended. Some societies expend it on war, some on luxury. He argues that in Tibet this surplus was consumed by Lamaism. His only source for his study is Sir Charles Bell's 1946 *Portrait of the Dalai Lama*. Although Bataille's essay is thus limited and mistaken on many points, he nonetheless provides a fascinating materialist analysis

of the myth that, with the introduction of Buddhism, Tibet decided to transform itself from a bellicose to a pacifist state. See Georges Bataille, *The Accursed Share*, trans. Robert Hurley (New York: Zone Books, 1991), 1:93–110.

15. Ekai Kawaguchi, *Three Years in Tibet* (Adyar, Madras: Theosophical Publishing House, 1909), p. 422.

16. Robert Thurman, "The Nitty-Gritty of Nirvana," interview by Joshua Glenn, *Utne Reader*, January-February 1996, 97.

17. Philip Rawson, *Sacred Tibet* (London: Thames and Hudson, 1991), p. 5.

18. Cited in Peter Hansen, "The Dancing Lamas of Everest: Cinema, Orientalism, and Anglo-Tibetan Relations in the 1920s," *American Historical Review* 101, no. 2 (June 1996): 731.

19. On the stereotype, see Peter Hulme, *Colonial Encounters: Europe and the Native Caribbean, 1492–1797* (London: Methuen, 1986), pp. 49–50.

20. The fixation on "old Tibet" has resulted in a remarkable dearth of scholarship on Tibet and Tibetans under Chinese rule. As Tsering Shakya has noted, "[T]here was also a residual sense that there was nothing worthy of study in post-1950 Tibet; as if the apparent demise of traditional society rendered further studies valueless and uninteresting." An important reversal of this trend is the book in which this statement appears: Robert Barnett and Shirin Akiner, eds., *Resistance and Reform in Tibet* (Bloomington: Indiana University Press, 1994). Tsering Shakya's statement appears on page 9.

21. This view is also held among the Tibetan intelligentsia in exile. See, for example, Tsering Shakya, "Tibet and the Occident: The Myth of Shangri-La," *Lungta* 5 (special issue on Tibetan authors, 1991): 21–23.

22. The largest selling book about Tibet (translated into thirty-two languages, including Tibetan) may be Hergé's 1960 *Tintin in Tibet*, in which the boy reporter goes into Tibet in search of his friend Chang (whom he met in *The Blue Lotus*). Hergé also weaves a yeti (very much in the news during the 1950s and the object of numerous zoological expeditions) into the plot. Hubert Decleer (in an unpublished article entitled "The Tibetan World Translated into Western Comics") has discovered part of the reason why Tintin went to Tibet. Hergé's advisor on *The Blue Lotus* was a Chinese student at the Royal Academy of Fine Arts in Brussels named Chang Chong-jen (the inspiration for the character of Chang). They became close friends and corresponded after Chang returned to China in 1935, but lost touch after the Japanese invasion of China. Hergé was so concerned about his safety that he went to all the Chinese restaurants in Brussels asking whether anyone knew his friend. He eventually determined that he had interrogated people from every province in China. He never met anyone from Tibet, however, and concluded that Chang must be there. In the story Tintin receives a letter from Chang saying that he is enroute to London via Kathmandu. Captain Haddock reads in the newspaper of an air crash in the Himalayas, and a subsequent report confirms that Chang is among the missing. They

set off for Delhi and then Kathmandu, whence they undertake a trek into the Himalayas. They become lost in an avalanche but are rescued and taken to a Tibetan monastery, complete with levitating monks. They set out again and discover Chang, who had been rescued and protected by a yeti.

23. The popular fiction contains works such as Mark Winchester's *In the Hands of the Lamas*, Talbot Munday's *Om*, Douglas Duff's *On the World's Roof*, Mildred Cooke and Francesca French's *The Red Lama*, Lionel Davidson's *The Rose of Tibet*, Berkeley Gray's *The Lost World of Everest*, and two "sequels" to Hilton, Leslie Haliwell's *Return to Shangri-La: Raiders of the Lost Horizon* and Eleanor Cooney and Daniel Altieri's *Shangri-La: Return to the World of Lost Horizon*. (I am grateful to David Templeman for alerting me to the existence of many of these works.) The travel literature is even more substantial. Selected works are provided here to illustrate the range of titles. The works include Theos Bernard's (who styled himself the "White Lama") *Penthouse of the Gods*, William M. McGovern's *To Lhasa in Disguise*, W. N. Fergusson's *Adventure, Sport and Travel on the Tibetan Steppes*, Harrison Forman's *Through Forbidden Tibet*, M. L. A. Gompertz's *The Road to Lamaland*, Thomas Holdrich's *Tibet the Mysterious*, Edwin Schary's *In Search of the Mahatmas of Tibet*, Theodore Illion's *In Secret Tibet*, Frederick Bailey's *No Passport to Tibet*, P. Millington's *To Lhassa at Last*, and Lowell Thomas Jr.'s *Out of This World: Across the Himalayas to Forbidden Tibet*. On travelers to Tibet (especially of the British variety), see Peter Hopkirk, *Trespassers on the Roof of the World: The Secret Exploration of Tibet* (New York: Kodansha International, 1995); Peter Bishop, *The Myth of Shangri-La: Tibet, Travel Writing, and the Creation of Sacred Landscape* (Berlekey: University of California Press, 1989); and Laurie Hovell's 1993 Syracuse University dissertation, "Horizons Lost and Found: Travel, Writing, and Tibet in the Age of Imperialism." See also Graham Sandberg, *The Exploration of Tibet: Its History and Particulars from 1623 to 1904* (Calcutta: Thacker, Spink & Co., 1904). The writings of Protestant missionaries to Tibet in the late nineteenth and early twentieth centuries also remain largely unexplored. These include Geoffrey T. Bull's *When Iron Gates Yield*, J. H. Edgar's *Land of Mystery Tibet*, Isabella L. Bird Bishop's *Among the Tibetans*, Marion H. Duncan's *Customs and Superstitions of Tibetans*, Susie Rijnhart's *With the Tibetans in Tent and Temple*, Flora Shelton's *Sunshine and Shadow on the Tibetan Border*, Annie W. Marston's *A Plea for Tibet*, and the diary of Annie Taylor included in William Carey's *Adventures in Tibet*. For a useful survey of Western travelers to Tibet, see Barbara Lipton, "The Western Experience in Tibet, 1327–1950," *The Museum* (Newark), n.s. (spring/summer 1972): 1–9, 50–59.

Also worthy of research is the *New York Times* hoax of 1936–37 that culminated in the front page story of February 14, 1937, headlined "M. M. Mizzle Quits His Lamasery, Pursued by Sable Amazon on Yak: Famous Caraway Seed Expert also Tires of Tibetan Diet, So He Sets Out for Calcutta—Old Friend, Winglefoot, the Tea Taster, Gets News in Letter Written in Lion's Blood."

24. See Derek Waller, *The Pundits: British Exploration of Tibet and Central Asia* (Lexington: University of Kentucky Press, 1990); and Thomas Richards, *The Imperial Archive: Knowledge and the Fantasy of Empire* (London: Verso, 1993), pp. 11–44. On the Japanese, see Hisao Kimura, *Japanese Agent in Tibet* (London: Serindia Publications, 1990); and Scott Berry, *Monks, Spies and a Soldier of Fortune: The Japanese in Tibet* (New York: St. Martin's Press, 1995).

25. Some of the photographs taken by Tolstoy and Dolan in Tibet have been published in Rosemary Jones Tung, *A Portrait of Lost Tibet* (New York: Holt, Rinehart and Winston, 1980).

26. Their story is told in William Boyd Sinclair, *Jump to the Land of God: The Adventures of a United States Air Force Crew in Tibet* (Caldwell, Idaho: Caxton Printers, 1965). Sinclair reports that the crew was stoned by a mob of ten thousand Tibetans in Lhasa because they had flown over the Potala and thus looked down on the Dalai Lama. See pp. 122–124, 138–140.

CHAPTER ONE

A briefer version of this essay appeared under the title "'Lamaism' and the Disappearance of Tibet" in *Comparative Studies in Society and History*, 38 (January 1996).

1. Sherman E. Lee, "The Luohan Cūdapanthaka," (plate 309) in *Circa 1492: Art in the Age of Exploration*, ed. Jay A. Levenson (Washington, D.C.: National Gallery of Art; New Haven: Yale University Press, 1991), p. 459. At the National Gallery exhibition, one room among the four devoted to Ming China was labeled "Lamaist Art." In the coffee-table book produced for the exhibition, however, among the reproductions and descriptions of the more than eleven hundred works displayed, no painting, sculpture, or artifact was described as being of Tibetan origin.

2. Philip Zaleski, review of *The Tibetan Book of Living and Dying*, by Sogyal Rinpoche, *New York Times Book Review*, 27 December 1992, 21.

3. This always useful mnemonic appears in the poem "The Lama." It reads in its entirety: "A one -*l* lama, he's a priest / A two -*l* llama, he's a beast / And I will bet a silk pajama / There isn't any three -*l* lllama.* . . . *The author's attention has been called to a type of conflagration known as a three-alarmer." See Ogden Nash, *Many Long Years Ago* (Boston: Little, Brown, and Co., 1945).

4. For a discussion of this rite, see Ferdinand Lessing, "Calling the Soul: A Lamaist Ritual," *Semitic and Oriental Studies* 11 (1951): 263–84; and, more recently, Robert R. Desjarlais, *Body and Emotion: The Aesthetics of Illness and Healing in the Nepal Himalayas* (Philadelphia: University of Pennsylvania Press, 1992), pp. 198–222.

5. For a general discussion of *bla*, see Réne de Nebesky-Wojkowitz, *Oracles and Demons of Tibet* (The Hague: Mouton and Company, 1956), pp. 481–83; R. A. Stein,

Tibetan Civilization (Stanford: Stanford University Press, 1972), pp. 226–29; Giuseppe Tucci, *The Religions of Tibet* (Berkeley: University of California Press, 1980), pp. 190–93; Erik Haarh, *The Yar-luṅ Dynasty* (Copenhagen: G. E. C. Gad's Forlag, 1969), pp. 315, 378; and, especially, Samten G. Karmay, "L'âme et la turquoise: un rituel Tibétain," *L'Ethnographie* 83 (1987): 97–130. On the related notion of the *sku lha* during the dynastic period, see Ariane Macdonald, "Une lecture des P. T. 1286, 1287, 1038, 1047, et 1290: Essai sur la formation et l'emploi des mythes politiques dans la religion royale de Sroṅ-bcan sgam-po," in *Études Tibétaines dédiés à la mémoire de Marcelle Lalou* (Paris: Adrien Maisonneuve, 1971), pp. 297–309.

6. The early standardization of *bla ma* as the rendering for *guru* is attested by the presence of the term in the eighth-century compendium of Buddhist terminology, the *Mahāvyutpatti*. The term *bla* itself was not used in the Buddhist vocabularies as a translation for any notion of a soul, but to render the Sanskrit terms *pati* (lord) and *ūrdhvam* (elevated). For a citation of usages from the *Mahāvyutpatti*, see Lokesh Chandra, *Tibetan-Sanskrit Dictionary* (Kyoto: Rinsen Book Company, 1976), 2:1680.

7. Although such a pervasive practice might suggest to some that Tibetans place an inordinate emphasis on the lama, an emphasis unique in the Buddhist world, it is clear from the literature, notably the tantric literature of northern India, that such an emphasis was equally strong in the Indian practices from which the Tibetans derived their Buddhism. For instances available in English translation of the Indian Buddhist emphasis on devotion to the guru, see, for example, Atiśa, *A Lamp for the Path and Commentary*, trans. Richard Sherburne (London: George Allen and Unwin, 1983); Herbert V. Guenther, *The Life and Teachings of Nāropa* (London: Oxford University Press, 1963); Tsang Nyön Heruka, *The Life of Marpa the Translator*, trans. Nālandā Translation Committee (Boulder, Colo.: Prajñā Press, 1982); Aśvaghoṣa, *Fifty Stanzas of Guru-Devotion*, in *The Mahamudra Eliminating the Great Darkness*, trans. Alexander Berzin (Dharamsala, India: Library of Tibetan Works and Archives, 1978).

8. For some historical data and a rather incoherent argument on this event, see Turrell Wylie, "Reincarnation: A Political Innovation of Tibetan Buddhism," in *Proceedings of the Csoma de Kőrös Memorial Symposium*, ed. Louis Ligeti (Budapest: Akadémiai Kiadó, 1978), pp. 579–86.

9. It is therefore not the case, as Pratapaditya Pal and others claim, that "Every lama in Tibet is considered a reincarnation of a predecessor." See Pratapaditya Pal and Hsien-ch'i Tseng, *Lamaist Art: The Aesthetics of Harmony* (Boston: Museum of Fine Arts, 1969), p. 17.

10. Turrell V. Wylie, "Etymology of Tibetan: Bla ma," *Central Asiatic Journal* 21 (1977): 148. Wylie seems to derive this etymology from an unnamed informant of Sarat Chandra Das in the compilation of his dictionary. See Sarat Chandra Das, *A Tibetan-English Dictionary with Sanskrit Synonyms* (Calcutta: Bengal Secretariat

Book Depot, 1902), s.v. *bla ma*. That such a reading does not appear in traditional etymologies of the term could, alternately, suggest that the term *bla* was intentionally not rendered as "soul" by the early Buddhist translators so as to discourage the Tibetan belief in such a soul, something that Buddhism famously rejects. The modern Tibetan scholar Samten Karmay has recently argued that Buddhism was never able to suppress the concept of a soul in Tibet and that over the centuries the concept was gradually reintegrated into popular rites, despite being at odds with the Buddhist doctrine of no-self (see Karmay, p. 99). This would suggest that at some point in Tibetan history, the philosophical doctrine of no-self exercised a marked influence over popular religious practice, something that has yet to be demonstrated in any Buddhist culture.

It may be significant that the other standard Tibetan-English dictionary, that of Jäschke, also cites an "oral explanation" in offering "strength, power, vitality" as one of the definitions of *bla*. See H. Jäschke, *A Tibetan-English Dictionary* (1881; reprint, Delhi: Motilal Banarsidass, 1992), s.v. *bla*. The recently published three-volume Tibetan-Tibetan-Chinese dictionary defines *bla* as "that which is above" (*steng*) or "that which is fitting" (*rung*), but also mentions that *bla* is "the support of life explained in astrology" (*dkar rtsis las bshad pa'i srog rten*). See *Bod rgya tshig mdzod chen mo*, vol. 2 (Mi rigs dbe skrun khang, 1984), s.v. *bla*.

11. In this reading, *ma* would be taken as a substantive marker (as, for example, in *tshad ma* and *srung ma*).

12. Marco Polo, *The Book of Ser Marco Polo the Venetian concerning the Kingdoms and Marvels of the East*, trans. and ed. Sir Henry Yule, 3d ed., revised by Henri Cordier (1926; reprint, New York: AMS, 1986), 1:301–3. For a discussion of the term *bakshi*, see Yule's p. 314 n. 10, and, especially, Berthold Laufer's "Loan-Words in Tibetan," in his *Sino-Tibetan Studies*, comp. Hartmut Walravens, (New Delhi: Aditya Prakashan, 1987), 2:565–67, where Laufer identifies *bakshi* as being of Uighur origin and dismisses the connection, reported by Yule, between *bakshi* and the Sanskrit *bhikṣu* (monk).

13. See Elliot Sperling, "The 5th Karma-pa and Some Aspects of the Relationship between Tibet and the Early Ming," in *Tibetan Studies in Honour of Hugh Richardson*, ed. Michael Aris and Aung San Suu Kyi (Warminster, England: Aris and Phillips, 1980), p. 283.

14. In the *Records of the Qing (Qing shilu)* of June 24, 1775, one finds a command given by the Emperor Qianlong to generals during the Jinchuan War wherein appears the phrase, "Jinchuan and Chosijiabu have hitherto fully supported and spread your Lamaism [*lama jiao*]." See Gu Zucheng et al., *Qing shilu Zangzu shiliao* (Lhasa, 1982), p. 2586. I am indebted to Elliot Sperling for discovering this reference and for providing me with the other information contained in this paragraph.

15. See Ferdinand Diederich Lessing, *Yung-ho-kung: An Iconography of the La-*

maist Cathedral in Peking with Notes on Lamaist Mythology and Cult, vol. 1, Reports from the Scientific Expedition to the North-Western Provinces of China under the Leadership of Dr. Sven Hedin, Publication 18 (Stockholm, 1942), p. 59. This reading is drawn from Lessing's comments and his translation, based on the Chinese and the Manchu. The parenthetical remarks are added by Lessing. The Tibetan side of the stele provides a somewhat different reading. The Tibetan reads *zhva ser bstan pa mchog tu bzhung pa ni | sog po tsho'i 'dod pa dang bstun pa yin ste zhin tu mkho ba'i gnad che | de bas gtso che bar dgos | yvon gur gyi dus ltar bla ma rnams la kha bsags dang rgyab byas pa'i tshul gyis bkur ste bya ba min |* ("With regard to holding the teaching of the Yellow Hats to be superior, this accords with the wishes of the Mongol and is most essential. Therefore, it should be foremost. [I] do not honor the lamas by praising and protecting them, as in the Yuan dynasty.") For the Tibetan text, see Otto Franke and Berthold Laufer, *Epigraphische Denkmaler aus China I. Lamaistische Klosterinshriften aus Peking, Jehol, und Si-ngan* (Berlin, 1914). The passage appears in the third line of large script on the first Tibetan plate.

16. Lessing, *Yung-ho-kung,* p. 58. In the *Lama Shuo,* "lama" is rendered in phonetically equivalent Chinese characters, rather than translated, a convention that had been in use since the Ming dynasty. I have adapted Lessing's translation here. His last sentence reads, without justification, "Lama(ism) also stands for Yellow Religion." The Tibetan side of the stele reads *bla ma'i slab bya la zhva ser gyi bstan pa zhes yod* (The training of the lamas is called the teaching of the Yellow Hats). The first sentence also seems to differ. The Tibetan reads *bod kyi rab byung pa la bla mar 'bod nas brgyud pa yin* (It is traditional to call Tibetan renunciates lamas). For the Tibetan text, see Franke and Laufer. The passage appears in the second line of large script on the second Tibetan plate.

17. Bernard Picart, *The Ceremonies and Religious Customs of the Various Nations of the Known World* (in French) (London, 1741), p. 425. Ironically, a more detailed and accurate account of Tibetan religion had by this time already been written by the Jesuit missionary Ippolito Desideri, who lived in Tibet from 1716 to 1719. Unfortunately, his *Relazione,* completed in 1733, was not discovered until 1875.

18. Johann Gottfried von Herder, *Outlines of a Philosophy of the History of Man,* trans. T. Churchill (1800; reprint, New York: Bergman Publishers, 1966), pp. 302–3.

19. Jean-Jacques Rousseau, *The Social Contract and Discourses,* trans. G. D. H. Cole (London: J. M. Dent & Sons, 1973), p. 272. In his 1794 essay "The End of All Things," Kant made a disparaging reference to the pantheism "of Tibetans and other Eastern peoples." See Immanuel Kant, *Perpetual Peace and Other Essays on Politics, History, and Morals,* trans. Ted Humphrey (Indianapolis: Hackett Publishing Company, 1983), p. 100.

In Joseph Marie Amiot's 1777 *Mémoires concernant L'Histoire, Les Sciences, Les*

Moeurs, Les Usages, &c. des Chinois: Par les Missionaires de Pékin, vol. 2 (Paris, 1777), we find mention of "les trois sectes idolâtriques des *Tao-sée*, des Bonzes, des Lamas." See p. 395.

20. Pallas's reports were published in German in three volumes as *Reise durch verschiedene Provinzen des Russischen Reichs* (St. Petersburg, 1771–76). Trusler provided a much-abridged translation in the second volume of *The Habitable World Described* (London: Literary Press, 1788). The term "Lamaism" appears on pp. 255 and 260. On Pallas, see also Carol Urness, ed., *A Naturalist in Russia* (Minneapolis: The University of Minnesota Press, 1967).

A Mongolian term may provide (with the Chinese *lama jiao*) another source for the term "Lamaism." Buddhism is often referred to in Mongolian as *blam-a surğal*, "lama teaching." The term is attested as early as the second half of the thirteenth century in a text called *Čağan teüke*. See Klaus Sagaster, *Die Weisse Geschichte*, Asiatische Forschungen, vol. 41 (Wiesbaden: Otto Harrassowitz, 1976), where, on page 145, note 2, the following passage appears: *blam-a bağsi-yin surğal-dur ese orobasu mağu üilen oroyu* (If one does not embrace the teaching of the lama master[s], one will fall under the influence of evil deeds). I am grateful to Dr. Samuel Grupper for providing me with the text and the translation.

Possible evidence against the Mongolian derivation of Lamaism is the fact that Isaac Jacob Schmidt, who also studied among the Kalmyks, argued in 1836 that the term was a European fabrication. See I. J. Schmidt, "Ueber Lamaismus und die Bedeutungslosigkeit dieses Nahmens," *Bulletin Scientifique publié par L'Académie Impériale des Sciences de Saint-Pétersbourg* 1, no. 1 (1836): 11. His statement is translated below.

21. See Jean Pierre Abel Rémusat, *Mélanges Asiatiques ou Choix de Morceaux Critiques et de Mémoires* (Paris: Librairie Orientale de Dondey-Dupré Père et Fils, 1825), 1:134 n. 1. He says in this article (p. 139) that the word "lama" means "priest" (*prêtre*) in Tibetan. Sven Hedin interpolates the term "Lamaism" into Abel Rémusat's text. He translates "The first missionaries who came into contact with Lamaism," whereas Abel Rémusat's French text (p. 131) reads "Les premiers missionaries qui en ont eu connaissance," with the referent being simply "cette religion." See Sven Hedin, *Trans-Himalaya: Discoveries and Adventures in Tibet* (London: Macmillan, 1913), 3:325.

In 1795 C. D. Hüllmann published *Historisch-kritische Abhandlung über die Lamaische Religion* (Berlin, 1795).

Webster's Ninth New Collegiate Dictionary cites 1817 (without reference) as the year "Lamaism" first appeared in English. This is mistaken; as indicated in note 20, the term appears in 1788 in Trusler's *The Habitable World Described*. L. A. Waddell, then, is also mistaken when he writes in 1915 that the term appears to have first been used in Köppen's 1859 *Die Lamische Hierarchie und Kirche*. In the same article, Waddell, in contrast to his 1895 *The Buddhism of Tibet, or Lamaism* (discussed below), says that the term "Lamaism" is "in many ways misleading, inappropriate, and undesirable" and "is rightly dropping out of use." See L. A. Waddell, "Lāmaism," in *Encyclopedia of Religion and Ethics*, ed. James Hastings (New York: Charles Scribner's Sons, 1915), 7:784.

22. William Moorcroft and George Trebeck, *Travels in the Himalayan Provinces of Hindustan and the Panjab; in Ladakh and Kashmir; in Peshawar, Kabul, Kunduz, and Bokhara*, comp. and ed. Horace Hayman Wilson (London: John Murray, 1841), 1:346.

Moorcroft died of fever in Turkestan in 1825, his papers eventually becoming the property of the Asiatic Society of Calcutta. They were not published until 1841, after being compiled and edited by the Oxford Sanskritist Horace Hayman Wilson. There are indications that the term "Lamaism" may not have been used by Moorcroft but rather that it was introduced by Wilson. Of his task, Wilson writes, "I have, in fact, been obliged to re-write almost the whole, and must therefore be held responsible for the greater part of its composition" (Moorcraft and Trebeck, p. liii). Furthermore, Moorcroft reports that all of his information on the religion of Ladakh was received from Alexander Csoma de Kőrös (p. 339). In his extensive writings on Tibetan literature and religion, Csoma speaks only of Buddhism and does not use the term Lamaism.

Perhaps the first European to attempt to etymologize "lama" was the Jesuit Emanoel Freyre, who accompanied Ippolito Desideri on his arduous trip to Lhasa, arriving on March 18, 1716, only to return alone to India after one month; he could not bear the climate. In his report on the journey, he wrote, "Having spoken here and there of 'lamas,' before proceeding, I will say something about the etymology of their name, their clothing, the temples, their recitations, of prayers, and their Superiors. 'Lamo' in Botian [Tibetan] means 'way'; whence comes 'Lama'—'he who shows the way.'" Freyre here mistakenly attempts to derive lama from the Tibetan *lam*, meaning "path." See Filippo de Filippi, ed., *An Account of Tibet: The Travels of Ippolito Desideri of Pistoia, S. J., 1712–1727*, rev. ed. (London: George Routledge and Sons, 1937), p. 356.

23. G. W. F. Hegel, *The Philosophy of History*, trans. J. Sibree (New York: Dover, 1956), p. 170.

24. Victor Jacquemont, *Letters from India, 1829–1832*, trans. Catherine Alison Phillips (London: Macmillan, 1936), p. 324. For his opinion of Csoma and his work, see also pp. 112–13.

25. I. J. Schmidt, "Ueber Lamaismus und die Bedeutungslosigkeit dieses Nahmens," *Bulletin Scientifique publié par L'Académie Impériale des Sciences de Saint-Pétersbourg* 1, no. 1 (1836): 11. My thanks to Professor Constantin Fasolt for translating the passage.

26. Translation of the passage cited in Henri de Lubac, *La recontre du Bouddhisme et de l'Occident* (Paris: Aubier, 1952), p. 45. For an even earlier observation of

similarity, see the comments of the Flemish Franciscan friar William of Rubruck who visited the court of Möngke between 1253 and 1255:

> All the priests shave their heads, and are dressed in saffron colour, and they observe chastity from the time they shave their heads, and they live in congregations of one or two hundred. . . . Wherever they go they have in their hands a string of one or two hundred beads, like our rosaries, and they always repeat these words, *on mani baccam*, which is 'God, thou knowest,' as one of them interpreted it to me, and they expect as many rewards from God as they remember God in saying this.

See William W. Rockhill, *The Journey of Friar William of Rubruck to the Eastern Parts of the World, 1253–55, as Narrated by Himself* (London: Hakluyt Society, 1900), pp. 145–46. See also Willem van Ruysbroek, *The Mission of Friar William of Rubruck*, trans. Peter Jackson (London: Hakluyt Society, 1990), pp. 153–54. In addition to being the first Westerner to note the existence of the mantra *oṃ maṇi padme hūṃ*, William may also have been the first to encounter an incarnate lama: "there had been brought from Cathay a boy who, from the size of his body, was not more than twelve years old, but who was capable of all forms of reasoning, and who said that he had been incarnated three times; he knew how to read and write." See Rockhill, p. 232; see also van Ruysbroek, p. 232, where the boy is said to be three years old.

The missionary Odoric, who traveled among the Mongols from 1318 to 1330, wrote in reference to the capital of Tibet, "their Abassi, that is to say, their Pope, is resident, being the head and prince of all idolaters, upon whom he bestows and distributes gifts after his manner, even as our Pope of Rome accounts himself to be the head of all Christians." Cited in Christopher Dawson, *Mission to Asia* (Toronto: University of Toronto Press, 1990), p. 244. The description of the Dalai Lama as "pope" or "pontiff" continues to the present. Pratapaditya Pal refers to him as "the chief pontiff of the Lamaist Church," noting that the third Dalai Lama "founded the first Patriarchal See of Mongolia." See Pal and Tseng, p. 12.

27. See Sven Hedin, *Trans-Himalaya, Discoveries and Adventures in Tibet* (London: Macmillan, 1913), 3:308.

28. See Thomas Astley, *New Collection of Voyages and Travels* (1747; reprint, London: Frank Cass and Company, 1968), 4:459.

29. Evariste-Régis Huc and Joseph Gabet, *Travels in Tartary, Thibet, and China 1844–1846*, trans. William Hazlitt (2 vols. in 1, New York: Dover, 1987), 2:50.

30. Huc and Gabet, 2:52. Max Müller notes that "The late Abbé Huc pointed out the similarities between the Buddhist and Roman Catholic ceremonials with such *naïveté*, that, to his surprise, he found his delightful *Travels in Thibet* placed on the 'Index.'" See Müller's *Chips from a German Workshop: Volume I: Essays on the Science of Religion* (1869; reprint, Chico, California: Scholars Press, 1985), p. 187. Skepticism

about Christian influence, however, was expressed shortly after Huc published his theory. In his 1863 *Buddhism in Tibet Illustrated by Literary Documents and Objects of Religious Worship with an Account of the Buddhist Systems Preceding It in India,* Emil Schlagintweit temperately wrote, "We are not yet able to decide the question as to how far Buddhism may have borrowed from Christianity; but the rites of the Buddhists enumerated by the French missionary can for the most part be traced back to institutions peculiar to Buddhism, or they have sprung up in periods posterior to Tsonkhapa." See page 70 of the reprint of this work published in 1968 by Susil Gupta, London. In addition to a wealth of largely accurate information about Tibetan Buddhism, this work contains a remarkable analysis of the idealization of the human form in Tibetan iconography based on a comparison of the facial features of "Buddhas, Bodhisattvas," and "Dragsheds, Genii, Lamas" with those of actual "Brahmans" and "Bhots" (Tibetans). See pp. 216–26.

31. It is perhaps noteworthy that he of the prominent proboscis appears in none of the standard Tibetan biographies of Tsong kha pa, and also that Desideri, the first Catholic missionary to live for an extended time in Tibet, duly noted the resemblances in the ceremonies, institutions, ecclesiastical hierarchy, maxims, moral principles, and hagiographies but made no attempt to account for them, adding that in his reading of Tibetan history he found no "hint that our Holy Faith has at any time been known, or that any Apostle or evangelical preacher has ever lived here." See de Filippi, p. 302. See also C. J. Wessel's informative note on this passage.

In Huc and Gabet's explanation of the presence in Tibet of practices deserving their approbation, there is also another element at play here: the persistent European assumption that those whose whereabouts cannot be accounted for, whether Jesus himself during the "lost years," Prester John, or Sherlock Holmes, must have been in Tibet, and that otherwise inexplicable "parallels" may be explained by their presence. For a document purportedly discovered in Ladakh purporting to describe Jesus' travels in Tibet, see L. Huxley, *The Life and Letters of Sir Joseph Dalton Hooker* (London: John Murray, 1918), 2 : 334–35. See also Nicolas Notovitch, *The Unknown Life of Jesus Christ* (Chicago: Rand McNally, 1894), for the "translation" of a manuscript discovered by the author in Ladakh, "The Life of Saint Issa," which describes Jesus' activities in India and Nepal.

32. This opinion of Tooke is cited by Peter Pallas. See John Trusler, *The Habitable World Described* (London: Literary Press, 1788), 2 : 261.

33. See the appendix to Johannes Nieuhof, *An Embassy from the East India Company of the United Provinces to the Grand Tartar Cham Emperor of China,* trans. John Ogilby (1669; reprint, Menston, UK: Scolar Press, 1972), pp. 42–43. A similar passage appears in *China and France, or Two Treatises* (London, 1676), pp. 109–10, a work that also describes the Dalai Lama: "Their Arch-Priest or *Mufty* is called *Lamacongin,* whom they reverence as God; and believe to be related to their first King, but they name him the Brother of all the Kings of the World. They are per-

suaded that he riseth from the dead as often as he dies, and that this man hath already risen seven times." See pp. 4–5.

Kircher goes on to describe the process of discovering the Grand Lama after the death of his predecessor. He also explains that the Tanguts pay great bribes to the priests to receive meats that have been mixed with the urine of the Grand Lama ("Oh abominable nastiness!"). See also Hedin, *Trans-Himalaya*, p. 318, and Astley, pp. 462–63.

For numerous cases of the comparison of elements of Tibetan Buddhism to Roman Catholicism, see Hedin, *Trans-Himalaya*, pp. 310–29. A useful survey of the early missions to Tibet may be found in John MacGregor, *Tibet: A Chronicle of Exploration* (New York: Praeger Publishers, 1970), pp. 1–111. On the Jesuit missions, see Sir Edward MacLagan, *The Jesuits and the Great Mogul* (New York: Octagon Books, 1972), pp. 335–68. For a study of the evidence of possible Tibetan contacts with Nestorians and Manicheans, see Geza Uray, "Tibet's Connections with Nestorianism and Manicheism in the 8th–10th Centuries," in *Contributions on Tibetan Language, History, and Culture*, ed. Ernst Steinkellner and Helmut Tauscher (Vienna: Arbeitskreis für Tibetische und Buddhistische Studien Universität Wien, 1983), 1:399–430.

34. See, for example, Justin Martyr, *Apologies*, LIV.7–8; LXII.1–2; LXVI.1–4. I am grateful to Elizabeth Clark for providing these references. It is significant to note that not all the Catholic priests who encountered Buddhist monks believed that they looked exactly like themselves. The Flemish friar William of Rubruck thought they looked like the French: "When I went into the idol temple I was speaking of, I found the priests seated in the outer gate, and when I saw them with their shaved faces they seemed to me to be Franks, but they had barbarian mitres on their heads." See William W. Rockhill, *The Journey of Friar William of Rubruck to the Eastern Parts of the World, 1253–55, as Narrated by Himself* (London: Hakluyt Society, 1900), p. 146.

Also of interest is the following note in Friedrich von Schlegel's *The Philosophy of History* (London: Henry G. Bohn, 1984) by the translator James Burton Robertson:

So great was the [Chinese people's] expectation of the Messiah—"the Great Saint who, as Confucius says, was to appear in the West"—so fully sensible were they not only of the place of his birth, but of the time of his coming, that about sixty years after the birth of our Saviour they sent their envoys to hail the expected Redeemer. These envoys encountered on their way the Missionaries of Buddhism coming from India—the latter, announcing an incarnate God, were taken to be the disciples of the true Christ, and were presented as such to their countrymen by the deluded ambassadors. Thus was this religion introduced into China, and thus did the phantasmagoria of Hell intercept the light of the gospel. So, not in the internal spirit only, but in the outward history of Buddhism, a demonical intent is very visible.

See page 136. I am grateful to Richard Cohen for this reference.

35. Jacques Lacan, *Écrits: A Selection*, trans. Alan Sheridan (New York: W. W. Norton, 1977), p. 3.

36. Jane Gallop, *Reading Lacan* (Ithaca, N.Y.: Cornell University Press, 1985), p. 85. The language of the demonic has persisted in more recent descriptions of Tibetan religion. In the following passage, Helmut Hoffmann, a researcher at the Sven Hedin Institute in Nazi Germany and later professor of Tibetan Studies at Indiana University, describes the Bön appropriation of Buddhist practices: "Just as the medieval Satanist desecrated the Host, so the Bön-po turned their sacred objects not in a dextral but in a sinister fashion. For example, the points of their holy sign the swastika did not turn dextrally as that of Lamaism, but sinistrally, to left instead of right. The Bön religion had become ossified as a heresy, and its essence lay largely in contradiction and negation." See his *The Religions of Tibet*, trans. Edward Fitzgerald (New York: Macmillan, 1961), p. 98.

37. Cited in John Kesson, *The Cross and the Dragon or, The Fortunes of Christianity in China: With Notices of the Christian Missions and Missionaries, and Some Account of the Chinese Secret Societies* (London: Smith, Elder, and Co., 1854), p. 185.

38. Some mention should also be made of more recent Catholic pronouncements on Buddhism and Tibetan Buddhism. In his 1994 *Crossing the Threshold of Hope* (New York: Knopf), Pope John Paul II discusses the appeal of Buddhism and of the Dalai Lama in a chapter entitled "Buddha?" (his question mark). The chapter is followed by "Muhammad?" then by "Judaism?" moving apparently from an atheistic pagan religion to the monotheisms. At the beginning of "Buddha?" the interviewer asks the pontiff specifically to address Buddhism, which "seems increasingly to fascinate many Westerners as an 'alternative' to Christianity or as a sort of 'complement' to it" (p. 84).

The pope immediately mentions the world's most famous Buddhist, the Buddhist who has the most Western followers, the Dalai Lama. Acknowledging that he has met the Dalai Lama a few times, he describes him not as the leader of the cause of Tibetan independence or as an internationally honored proponent of human rights, but as a proselytizer: "He brings Buddhism to people of the Christian West, stirring up interest both in Buddhist spirituality and in its methods of praying" (p. 85). But Buddhism is "an almost exclusively *negative soteriology*" (his italics):

The "enlightenment" experienced by Buddha comes down to the conviction that the world is bad, that it is the source of evil and of suffering for man. To liberate oneself from this evil, one must free oneself from this world, necessitating a break with the ties that join us to external reality—

ties existing in our human nature, in our psyche, in our bodies. The more we are liberated from these ties, the more we become indifferent to what is in the world, and the more we are freed from suffering, from the evil that has its source in the world. (Pp. 85–86)

Detachment from the world, however, does not bring one into the presence of God, because Buddhism is an atheistic system. *"To save oneself* means, above all, to free oneself from evil by becoming *indifferent to the world, which is the source of evil"* (his italics).

There are many things that could be said about this characterization. One obvious response that students of Zen or of Tibetan Buddhism might make is that the pope seems wholly ignorant of the Mahayana, where the bodhisattva remains in samsara; hardly indifferent to the world, he finds reality immanent in it ("form is emptiness, emptiness is form"), working ceaselessly and in myriad compassionate ways to benefit others. The pope may be describing the arhat, but he is not describing the bodhisattva. But it is perhaps wise to resist such a response, because the degradation of the arhat, the Hinayana disciple of the Buddha, and the exaltation of the bodhisattva is itself part of a polemic, a polemic present from the earliest Mahayana sutras, designed to wrest authority from the older tradition. To answer the pope by invoking the Hinayana-Mahayana distinction is merely to answer one polemic with another.

Much of the pope's characterization of Buddhism derives directly from nineteenth-century missionary literature. With the rise of the science of philology, the notion was put forward that languages represented the "mentality" of a given culture. This idea of mentality was then incorporated, with devastating effect, into race theory. There was thus something called the "Oriental mind" that was passive, irrational, static, world-negating, and given to mysticism (a forerunner to Jung's view of Asians as "introspective"), all of which was reflected in the degenerate and corrupt societies of Asia in the nineteenth century. The European mind, on the other hand, was rational and dynamic, possessed both of superior technology and the superior religion that made that technology possible, Christianity. Such a view was used to justify both the colonial and missionary policies of Western nations. If Christianity is the true faith, then God's providence ordains the delivery of that faith to the non-Christian world.

[The Church] builds up civilization, particularly "Western civilization," which is marked by a *positive approach to the world*, and which developed thanks to the achievement of science and technology, two branches of knowledge rooted both in the ancient Greek philosophical tradition and in Judeo-Christian Revelation.

This passage, which could have been drawn from any number of nineteenth-century polemical treatises, Protestant or Catholic, is drawn instead from page 88 of *Crossing the Threshold of Hope*.

39. Astley, p. 220. Later, referring to the Dalai Lama, he writes, "In this Respect, the Church of *Tibet* has infinitely the Advantage of the *Romish*, inasmuch as the visible Head of it is considered to be God himself, not his Vicar, or Deputy; and the incarnate Deity, who is the Object of divine Worship, appears alive in human Shape, to receive the Peoples Adorations: Not in the Form of a senseless Bit of Bread, or playing at Bo-peep in a diminutive Wafer, which would be too gross a Cheat to impose on the Understandings of the *Tibetians*, however, ignorant and superstitious the Missioners, to their own Shame, represent them." See p. 461.

In his 1769 report, the German naturalist Peter Pallas describes "the principal points of the tedious religion of the Lamas, that, like other superstitions, they are the fabrick of priests, and illusions by which they contrive to awe the ignorant multitude." He goes on to compare it to Roman Catholicism: "Their head, or Delai Lama, may be considered as the Pope, except that his soul is continually wandering from one human body to another, and is deified." He reports the opinion of Tooke that the first Dalai Lama was Prester John. See John Trusler, *The Habitable World Described* (London: Literary Press, 1788), 2:259–61.

40. Astley, p. 212, n. f. Herder held a similar opinion, expressed more circumspectly, writing in 1784, "In short, the tibetian religion is a species of the papal, such as prevailed in Europe itself in the dark ages, and indeed without that morality and decorum, for which the mungals and tibetians are commended." See Johann Gottfried von Herder, *Outlines of a Philosophy of the History of Man*, trans. T. Churchill, (1800; reprint, New York: Bergman Publishers, 1966), p. 304.

For other British comparisons of Buddhism and Catholicism, see Philip C. Almond, *The British Discovery of Buddhism* (Cambridge: Cambridge University Press, 1988), pp. 123–28. There were also charges that Catholicism derived from Hinduism. See P. J. Marshall, ed., *The British Discovery of Hinduism in the 18th Century* (Cambridge: Cambridge University Press, 1970), p. 24.

Certain Jesuits also were not optimistic about converting Tibetans. In a 1703 report on the state of the Jesuit missions in China, Father Francis Noel wrote, "The conversion of these roving *Tartars* would be difficult, because of the high Regard they pay their *Lamas*, who, being their Teachers, are implicitly obeyed in all things." See John Lockman, *Travels of the Jesuits into Various Parts of the World* (London, 1743), 1:451.

41. Susie C. Rijnhart, *With the Tibetans in Tent and Temple* (New York: Fleming H. Revell, 1901), p. 106.

42. On this portrayal of India, see Ronald Inden, "Orientalist Constructions of India," in *Imagining India* (London: Basil Blackwell, 1990), especially pp. 85–130.

43. Elizabeth A. Reed, *Primitive Buddhism: Its Origin and Teachings* (Chicago: Scott, Foresman, 1896), p. 16.

44. Sir Monier Monier-Williams, *Buddhism, In Its Connexion with Brāhmanism and Hindūism, and In Its Contrast with Christianity* (1890; reprint, Varanasi: Cowkhamba Sanskrit Series Office, 1964), p. 253.

45. Max Müller, *Chips from a German Workshop, Volume 1: Essays on the Science of Religion* (Chico, Calif.: Scholars Press, 1985), p. 220.

46. James Freeman Clarke, *Ten Great Religions: An Essay in Comparative Theology* (Boston: Houghton, Mifflin and Co., 1871), pp. 142–44. For other instances of the comparison of Buddhism with Protestantism, and of the Buddha with Luther, as well as the cautions against such comparisons by scholars such as Rhys Davids and Oldenberg, notably when the Buddha began to be appropriated by socialists, see Almond, pp. 71–77.

The noble elements of Buddhism were regarded by many Western scholars and missionaries as things that contemporary Buddhists in Asia were largely unaware of, things that the West could reintroduce them to, with salubrious effect. As Sydney Cave writes in *Christianity and Some Living Religions of the East,* "The Living Religions of the East have changed much since the time of the beginnings of the modern missionary enterprise. In their transformation many influences have been at work. The translation by Western scholars of *The Sacred Books of the East* revealed to the East the rich heritage of the past, and brought to light treasures which had been forgotten. In consequence, many Orientals gained a new pride in their religion and learned to pass from its baser to its nobler elements." See Sydney Cave, *Christianity and Some Living Religions of the East* (London: Duckworth, 1929), p. 20.

The popularity of Buddhism among the French during roughly the same period is satirized by Flaubert in *Bouvard and Pécuchet,* in which Pécuchet declares the superiority of Buddhism to Christianity:

> "Very well, listen to this! Buddhism recognized the vanity of earthly things better and earlier than Christianity. Its practices are austere, its faithful are more numerous than all Christians put together, and as for the Incarnation, Vishnu did not have one but nine! So, judge from that!"
> "Travellers' lies," said Madame de Noaris.
> "Supported by Freemasons," added the curé.

See Gustave Flaubert, *Bouvard and Pécuchet,* trans. A. J. Krailsheimer (New York: Penguin Books, 1976), p. 251.

Monier-Williams went to some length to argue that there were not more Buddhists than Christians in the world. See his "Postscript on the Common Error in regard to the Comparative Prevalence of Buddhism in the World," in his *Buddhism,* pp. xiv–xviii.

47. On this period see Edward R. Norman, *Anti-Catholicism in Victorian En-*

gland (New York: George Allen and Unwin, 1968); Walter Ralls, "The Papal Aggression of 1850: A Study in Victorian Anti-Catholicism," *Church History* 43, no. 2 (June 1974): 242–56; and, especially, Walter L. Arnstein, *Protestant versus Catholic in Mid-Victorian England: Mr. Newdegate and the Nuns* (Columbia: University of Missouri Press, 1982). The mid-nineteenth century was also a time of strong anti-Catholic sentiment in the United States, led by groups such as the Order of the Star Spangled Banner. See Tyler Anbinder, *Nativism and Slavery: The Northern Know Nothings and the Politics of the 1850s* (New York: Oxford University Press, 1992).

48. Thomas W. Rhys Davids, *Buddhism: Being a Sketch of the Life and Teachings of Gautama, the Buddha*, rev. ed. (London: Society for Promoting Christian Knowledge, 1903), p. 199.

49. Sir Monier Monier-Williams, *Buddhism, In Its Connexion with Brāhmanism and Hindūism, and In Its Contrast with Christianity* (Varanasi: Cowkhamba Sanskrit Series Office, 1964), p. 261.

50. T. W. Rhys Davids, *Lectures on the Origin and Growth of Religion as Illustrated by Some Points in the History of Indian Buddhism*, Hibbert Lectures, 1881 (New York: G. P. Putnam's Sons, 1882), pp. 192–93.

51. Note, however, that Waddell in 1895 retains the possibility of influence, but unlike earlier Catholic authors (and as an affront to Catholics) suggests that the influence may have occurred in the other direction:

> But in Lāmaism the ritualistic cults are seen in their most developed form, and many of these certainly bear a close resemblance outwardly to those found within the church of Rome, in the pompous services with celibate and tonsured monks and nuns, candles, bells, censers, rosaries, mitres, copes, pastoral crooks, worship of relics, confession, intercession of "the Mother of God," litanies and chants, holy water, triad divinity, organized hierarchy, etc.
>
> It is still uncertain, however, how much of the Lāmaist symbolism may have been borrowed from Roman Catholicism, or *vice versâ*.

See his *Tibetan Buddhism*, pp. 421–22.

In 1861, the Reverend Joseph Wolff, a Jewish convert to Christianity and missionary to "the Jews and Muhammadans in Persia, Bokhara, Cashmeer, etc.," argued that the monotheism of Abraham had penetrated as far as Lhasa, where, he claimed, there is a statue dedicated to him. See Joseph Wolff, *Travels and Adventures of Rev. Joseph Wolff, D.D., LL.D.* (London: Saunders, Otley, and Co., 1861), p. 189.

52. Rhys Davids, *Lectures on the Origin and Growth of Religion*, p. 194.

53. Thomas W. Rhys Davids, *Buddhism: Its History and Literature*, American Lectures on the History of Religions, First Series (New York: G. P. Putnam's Sons, 1896), p. 6.

54. Cited from the 1972 Dover reprint issued under the new title, *Tibetan Bud-*

dhism: With Its Mystic Cults, Symbolism and Mythology (1895; reprint, New York: Dover Publications, 1972), p. 4. In later life Waddell would turn his research more explicitly to his Aryan ancestors, claiming an Aryan origin for the Sumerian and Egyptian civilizations in works such as his 1929 *The Makers of Civilization in Race and History.*

55. I. J. Schmidt, "Ueber Lamaismus und die Bedeutungslosigkeit dieses Nahmens," *Bulletin Scientifique publié par L'Académie Impériale des Sciences de Saint-Pétersbourg* 1, no. 1 (1836): 13–14. My thanks to Professor Constantin Fasolt for translating the passage.

Herder, writing some decades earlier, looked to a similar telos but offered a more sympathetic assessment. He writes, "Everything in nature, and consequently the philosophy of Budda, is good or bad, according to the use that is made of it. On the one hand it exhibits as fine and lofty sentiments, as on the other it is capable of exciting and fostering, as it abundantly has, indolence and deceit. In no two countries has it remained precisely the same: but wherever it exists, it has raised itself at least one step above gross heathenism, the first twilight of a purer morality, the first infantile dream of that truth, which comprehends the universe." See Johann Gottfried von Herder, *Outlines of a Philosophy of the History of Man,* trans. T. Churchill (1800; reprint, New York: Bergman Publishers, 1966), p. 305.

56. Waddell, *Tibetan Buddhism,* p. 10.

57. Ibid., p. 14. The charge of mixing has a long history in the case of Tibet. Centuries before Waddell, Tibetan authors had used the charge of mixing to condemn rival Buddhist sects; a work attributed (probably falsely) to Bu ston, the *Refutation of False Tantras (Sngags log sun 'byin),* contemptuously dismissed Rnying ma texts as an "admixture of gold and dog shit." The passage appears in Kunsang Topgyel and Mani Dorji, eds., *Chag Lo-tsa-bas Mdzad-pa'i Sngags-log Sun-'byin dang 'Gos Khug-pa Lhas-btsas-kyi Sngags-log Sun-'byin* (Thimpu, 1979), pp. 25.5–36.3. It appears in English in the source for this reference: Daniel Preston Martin, "The Emergence of Bon and the Tibetan Polemical Tradition" (Ph.D. diss., Indiana University, 1991), p. 159.

58. Waddell, *Tibetan Buddhism,* p. 19.

59. Ibid., p. 30. Köppen characterized Lamaism as a mixture of Buddhism and Śaivism in his 1860 *Die Lamaische Hierarchie und Kirche* (Berlin: Verlag von H. Barsdorf, 1906), p. 82.

60. Ibid., p. xi. It is noteworthy that Desideri, writing 150 years earlier, offers a very different assessment: "Though the Thibettans are pagans and idolaters, the doctrine they believe is very different from that of other pagans of Asia [meaning India]. Their Religion, it is true, came originally from the ancient country of Hindustan, now usually called Mogol, but there, in the lapse of time, the old religion fell into disuse and was ousted by new fables. On the other hand, the Thibettans, intel-

ligent, and endowed with a gift of speculation, abolished much that was unintelligible in the tenets, and only retained what appeared to comprise truth and goodness." See de Filippi, pp. 225–26.

61. Rudyard Kipling, *Kim* (New York: Bantam Books, 1983), p. 8. Kipling's views of Tibetan Buddhism were typical of those of most travelers to Tibet during the late Victorian and Edwardian periods. See Peter Bishop, *The Myth of Shangri-La: Tibet, Travel Writing and the Western Creation of Sacred Landscape* (Berkeley: University of California Press, 1989), pp. 136–90.

62. Sir Francis Younghusband, *India and Tibet* (1910; reprint, New Delhi: Low Price Publications, 1994), p. 310. This is a reprint of the 1910 edition published by John Murray of London.

63. H. P. Blavatsky, *The Secret Doctrine* (Los Angeles: Theosophy Company, 1947), p. xxi. This is a facsimile of the original 1888 edition.

64. H. P. Blavatsky, *Collected Writings 1877: Isis Unveiled* (Wheaton, Ill.: Theosophical Publishing House, 1972), 2:582.

65. Rhys Davids, *Buddhism: Its History and Literature*, p. 208.

66. See Clements R. Markham, ed., *Narratives of the Mission of George Bogle to Tibet and of the Journey of Thomas Manning to Lhasa* (London: Trübner and Company, 1879), p. 338. On the difficulties surrounding the term "tantra," see Donald S. Lopez, Jr., *Elaborations on Emptiness, Uses of the Heart Sūtra* (Princeton: Princeton University Press, 1996), pp. 78–104.

67. Monier-Williams, p. 147.

68. Ibid., p. 151. Others saw Lamaism more simply as the natural development of Indian Buddhism. In his address to the Ninth International Congress of Orientalists, James Legge declared:

> Buddhism has been in China but a disturbing influence, ministering to the element of superstition which plays so large a part in the world. I am far from saying the doctrine of the literati is perfect, nevertheless, it has kept the people of China together in a national union, passing through many revolutions, but still enduring, after at least four or five millenniums of its existence, and still not without measure of heart and hope. Europe and America can give it something better than India did, in sending it Buddhism in our first century, and I hope they will do so. You must not look to the civilization of China and Japan for the fruits of Buddhism. Go to Tibet and Mongolia, and in the bigotry and apathy of the population, in their prayer wheels and cylinders you will find the achievement of the doctrine of the Buddha.

Cited in Reed, *Primitive Buddhism*, p. 30.

69. See Waddell, *Tibetan Buddhism*, pp. 227, 229.

70. See Jonathan Z. Smith, *Drudgery Divine: On the Comparison of Early Christianities and the Religions of Later Antiquity,* Jordan Lectures in Comparative Religions, XIV (Chicago: University of Chicago Press, 1990).

71. Sax Rohmer (Arthur Ward), *The Hand of Fu Manchu* (New York: Robert M. McBride and Co., 1917), p. 7.

72. J. Strunk, *Zu Juda und Rom-Tibet: Ihr Ringen um die Weltherrschaft* (Munich: Lundendorffs Verlag, 1937).

73. Waddell, *Tibetan Buddhism,* p. 573.

74. Waddell, *Lhasa and Its Mysteries* (New York: Dover Publications, 1905), pp. 447–48.

75. Tenzin Gyatso, the Fourteenth Dalai Lama, *Opening the Eye of New Awareness,* trans. Donald S. Lopez, Jr. (London: Wisdom Publications, 1985), pp. 117–18. The use of the term "Lamaism" is also condemned in an article published in Tibetan in 1982 at the behest of the Chinese Peoples' Political Consultative Committee. It was published in an inadequate English translation in 1986. See Tseten Zhabdrung, "Research on the Nomenclature of the Buddhist Schools in Tibet," *Tibet Journal* 11, no. 3 (autumn, 1986): 43–44. Tsultrim Kelsang Khangkar, a Tibetan scholar living in Japan, has, however, approved the term. It is significant that his endorsement of the term is based on the opinion of Japanese, rather than Tibetan, scholars. He says in an interview, "I asked some Japanese scholars regarding the term 'Lamaism.' They have explained to me that Tibetans have great respect for teacher (Lama) which is why Tibetan Buddhism is called 'Lamaism.'" See "'Lamaism' Is an Appropriate Term" in *Tibetan Review* 13, no. 6 (June 1978): 18–19, 27.

76. Wangyal had come to the United States to serve a community of Kalmyk Mongolians, refugees from Stalin who had left their homeland in Russia between the Black Sea and the Caspian Sea. Although Wangyal, like other Kalmyk Buddhist monks, had been trained in Tibet, he was not a Tibetan nor was his community; they were ethnically Mongols and nationally Russians. He therefore had no interest in calling his monastery "Tibetan Buddhist." However, he wanted to evoke in the name of his institution the tradition of Buddhism to which he and his community adhered, a tradition that historically had spread as far west as the Black Sea, as far north as Siberia, as far east as Sichuan, and as far south as Nepal. The only alternative adjective, apparently, was "Lamaist."

77. On British representations of Tibet as an archive state in a variety of literatures of the late nineteenth and early twentieth centuries, see Thomas Richards, "Archive and Utopia," *Representations* 37 (1992): 104–33.

78. For an analysis of Tibetan Buddhist studies during this period, see my essay, "Foreigner at the Lama's Feet," in Donald S. Lopez, Jr., ed., *Curators of the Buddha: The Study of Buddhism under Colonialism* (Chicago: University of Chicago Press, 1995), pp. 251–95.

79. Antonin Artaud, "Address to the Dalai Lama," *Anthology* (San Francisco: City Lights Books, 1972), p. 65.

80. Pal and Tseng, p. 9.

81. Lee in Levenson, *Circa 1492*, "Virūpāksha" (plate 319), p. 472. Beyond this definition, Lee rather proudly excludes knowledge of the complicated theology of Lamaism from his narrative. In describing the final Lamaist piece in the National Gallery volume, "Portable Shrine in Triptych Form" (plate 320), he begins, "Identification of the twenty-one deities represented within the confines of this small folding shrine is beyond the competence of this writer." After identifying one of the figures as the Indian tantric master Padmasambhava, who visited Tibet in the late eighth century, Lee devotes the greater part of his entry to a description not of this portable shrine, but of another one (not included in the exhibition), a "perfectly preserved" Japanese Shingon shrine reportedly brought from China by Kūkai in 806. Lee notes that the iconographies of the two shrines are quite different: "The Kongōbu-ji shrine is a classic presentation of the historical Buddha Śākyamuni," whereas "the present Lamaist shrine is centered on a quasi-historical founder of a complex faith who, by the time this shrine was made, had acquired wholly legendary status and attributes." Ibid., p. 472. Again, Lamaism must suffer in comparison. The Japanese piece depicts a historical figure in a classical style; the Lamaist piece depicts a figure only "quasi-historical." Were this not enough, this figure was the founder, again, of a "complex" faith, complex presumably because it was somehow composite, in contrast to the imagined simple ethical teachings of the historical Buddha, who, Lee would seem to imply, did not acquire "wholly legendary status." This complexity of the Lamaist shrine marks its great distance, its differentiation from the plenum present at the origin.

82. Jay A. Levenson, *Circa 1492: Art in the Age of Exploration* (Washington, D.C.: National Gallery of Art, 1991), p. 13. In defense of the National Gallery, it must be said that as part of the Smithsonian Institution, the national museum funded by the federal government, the National Gallery must conform to State Department policy, which holds Tibet to be a part of China. This policy has been in place since the suspension of CIA support for Tibetan guerrillas in 1968 and the subsequent establishment of diplomatic relations with the People's Republic of China. The museum would therefore be instructed not to label any work as originating in Tibet.

83. Stuart and Roma Gelder's *The Timely Rain: Travels in New Tibet* (London: Hutchinson of London, 1964), p. 129. The characterizations of Tibetan Buddhism by British officers such as Landon and Waddell are quoted as authoritative by the Gelders as well as by another Chinese apologist who wrote for Western consumption, Han Suyin. See her *Lhasa: The Open City* (London: Jonathan Cape, 1977).

One can also note the section on Tibet in Hajime Nakamura's *Ways of Thinking of Eastern Peoples*, in which, drawing largely on Chinese sources, reports of colonial officers, and spurious linguistic analysis ("The linguistic fact that Tibetans used a single short word to denote 'committing suicide' suggests the hypothesis that it was a fairly frequent social phenomenon," p. 305), he characterizes Tibetans as a promiscuous, dirty, meat-eating, violent, ancestor-ignoring, corpse-abandoning, cruel race of nomads whose ways of thinking show both shamanistic and logical tendencies (although not as logical as the Japanese). Of Tibetan religion he writes:

> Tibetans did not accept the Buddhism of rigorous moralism wholeheartedly. Chinese Buddhists once tried to propagate their own brand of Buddhism in Tibet, but they were soon expelled by the natives. The strict morality of Chinese Buddhism could not take root in Tibet. What was accepted by Tibetans was the Buddhism of worldly enjoyment which sometimes leads people to engage in sexual enjoyment, the corrupted form of Indian Esotericism.

See Hajime Nakamura, *Ways of Thinking of Eastern Peoples: India-China-Tibet-Japan* (Honolulu: University of Hawaii Press, 1964), p. 316.

84. J. Huston Edgar, *The Land of Mystery, Tibet* (Melbourne: China Inland Mission, 1947), p. 11.

CHAPTER TWO

1. Jorge Luis Borges, "The Enigma of Edward FitzGerald," in *A Personal Anthology* (New York: Grove Press, 1967), pp. 93–96.

2. These works include Lati Rinpochay and Jeffrey Hopkins, *Death, Intermediate State, and Rebirth in Tibetan Buddhism* (Ithaca, N.Y.: Snow Lion Publications, 1985); Lama Lodö, *Bardo Teachings* (Ithaca, N.Y.: Snow Lion Publications, 1987); and Glenn H. Mullin, *Death and Dying: The Tibetan Tradition* (Ithaca, N.Y.: Snow Lion Publications, 1986). There is also a video dramatization of *The Tibetan Book of the Dead*, including film footage from Ladakh and an animated depiction of the *bardos*, narrated by Leonard Cohen. Entitled *The Tibetan Book of the Dead: The Great Liberation after Death*, it was coproduced in 1994 by NHK (Japan), Mistral Films (France), and the National Film Board of Canada.

3. The first of the three was Sardar Bahādur S. W. Laden La (1876–1936), a Sikkimese police officer from Darjeeling who served the British in the Younghusband expedition. He was later hired by the government of the thirteenth Dalai Lama to establish a police force in Lhasa. He attended the Simla conference in 1914, and in 1921 was the personal assistant to Sir Charles Bell on his mission to Lhasa. On Laden La, see Melvyn C. Goldstein's *A History of Modern Tibet, 1913–1951: The Demise of the Lamaist State* (Berkeley, Calif.: University of California Press, 1989), pp. 121–25, 159; and (for a rather more glowing portrayal), W. Y. Evans-Wentz, *The Tibetan Book of the Great Liberation* (London: Oxford University Press, 1971), pp. 86–89.

The other two translators were Geluk monks, Karma Sumdhon Paul and Lobzang Mingyur Dorje of Ghoom monastery in Sikkim. They were both disciples of the Mongolian monk Sherab Gyatso, the abbot of Ghoom. It was Sherab Gyatso who was the true author of Sarat Chandra Das's *Tibetan-English Dictionary*, a fact acknowledged only on the Tibetan title page of the work (my thanks to Dan Martin for pointing this out). On the lives of the two monks, see Evans-Wentz, pp. 89–92.

4. W. Y. Evans-Wentz, *The Tibetan Book of the Dead or the After-Death Experiences on the* Bardo *Plane, according to Lāma Kaᵶi Dawa-Samdup's English Rendering* (London: Oxford University Press, 1960), p. xix. All subsequent references are provided in the text by page numbers in parentheses following the citation.

5. See Jay M. Winter, *Sites of Memory, Sites of Mourning: The Great War in European Cultural History* (Cambridge: Cambridge University Press, 1995).

6. On the uses of this and related mortuary texts in the Nyingma sect, see David Germano, "Dying, Death, and Other Opportunities," in Donald S. Lopez, Jr., ed., *Religions of Tibet in Practice* (Princeton, N.J.: Princeton University Press, 1997), pp. 458–93. See also Henk Blezer, *Kar gliṅ Ẑi khro: A Tantric Buddhist Concept* (Leiden: Research School CNWS, 1997).

7. For a history of spiritualism in England during this period, see Janet Oppenheim, *The Other World: Spiritualism and Psychical Research in England, 1850–1914* (Cambridge: Cambridge University Press, 1985).

8. This notion persisted into the nineteenth and even the twentieth centuries. See Wilhelm Halbfass, *India and Europe: An Essay in Understanding* (Albany: State University of New York Press, 1988), pp. 58–59. Such speculation often centered on theories concerning where Jesus spent the "lost years."

9. For a document purportedly discovered in Ladakh purporting to describe Jesus' travels in Tibet, see L. Huxley, *The Life and Letters of Sir Joseph Dalton Hooker* (London: John Murray, 1918), 2:334–35. See also Nicolas Notovitch, *The Unknown Life of Jesus Christ* (Chicago: Rand McNally, 1894), for the "translation" of a manuscript discovered by the author in Ladakh, "The Life of Saint Issa," which describes Jesus' activities in India and Nepal. Some of the publications arguing for Jesus' presence in Tibet and Ladakh have been credulously collected in Elizabeth Clare Prophet, *The Lost Years of Jesus* (Livingston, Montana: Summit University Press, 1987).

10. Alfred Percy Sinnett, *Esoteric Buddhism* (London: Chapman and Hall, 1885), pp. 181–82. The conviction that there is a secret brotherhood in Tibet, its presence unknown to Tibetans (save, often, the Panchen Lama), has remained a constant in spiritualist literature. See, for example, something called *The Urga Manuscript*, which purports to be a 1921 letter from Do-ring, scribe of the Panchen Lama (rendered here as "Precious Green Sage"), to Wing On, "his friend concerning the inner life": "Here exists a conflict that is deep, yet understandable. The present religion of Tibet is not an ancient one as the history of Bod land goes. There

are those who are the servants of the present religion who do not support the work of the Inner Temple, who feel that the magic of the priests must not be the final word, yet we who have lived the life of the Inner Courts well know that in our courts there is more true light than has ever been shed in any age. Thus we of the courts have had much power and have been an influence for good in the High House which was not always welcomed." *The Urga Manuscript* (Gerrads Cross, England: Colin Smythe, 1976), p. 8.

11. H. P. Blavatsky, *The Secret Doctrine*, 6th ed. (Adyar, Madras: Theosophical Publishing House, 1971), 5:389. Proponents of Madame Blavatsky continue to argue that she did indeed study in Tibet and that the *Stanzas of Dzyan* and *The Voice of the Silence* derive from ancient tantras (*rgyud sde*, hence *Kiu-te*), thought by the uninitiated to have long since been lost. Hence, the devotees of HPB are undaunted by the fact that neither the Tibetan originals of the *Stanzas of Dzyan* nor *The Book of Golden Precepts* has been discovered in the tantras or tantric commentaries of the Tibetan canon. For defenses of the authenticity of these works, see Sylvia Cranston, *HPB: The Extraordinary Life and Influence of Helena Blavatsky, Founder of the Modern Theosophical Movement* (New York: G. P. Putnam's Sons, 1993), pp. 80–101; Gregory A. Barborka, *H. P. Blavatsky, Tibet and Tulku* (Adyar, Madras: Theosophical Publishing House, 1974); and David Reigle, *The Books of Kiu-te or the Tibetan Buddhist Tantras: A Preliminary Analysis*, Secret Doctrine Reference Series (San Diego: Wizards Bookshelf, 1983). For a sustained attempt at aligning Theosophical doctrine with Buddhism, see Alice Leighton Cleather, *Buddhism the Science of Life* (Beijing: China Booksellers, 1928).

12. The influence of Theosophy on the study of Buddhism in Europe and America remains a largely unexplored topic. On some of the esotericist and spiritualist precursors of the Theosophical Society in the eighteenth and nineteenth centuries, see James Webb, *The Occult Underground* (La Salle, Ill.: Library Press, 1974); Janet Oppenheim, *The Other World: Spiritualism and Psychical Research in England, 1850–1914* (Cambridge: Cambridge University Press, 1985); Antoine Favre, *Access to Western Esotericism* (Albany: State University of New York Press, 1994); and Joscelyn Godwin, *The Theosophical Enlightenment* (Albany: State University of New York Press, 1994). For a useful history of the Theosophical Society, see Bruce F. Campbell, *Ancient Wisdom Received* (Berkeley: University of California Press, 1980). For an entertaining account of the Theosophical Society and its legacies, see Peter Washington, *Madame Blavatsky's Baboon: A History of the Mystics, Mediums, and Misfits Who Brought Spiritualism to America* (New York: Schocken Books, 1995).

Links between Theosophists and Tibetan Buddhism also merit a book-length study. For defenses of Madame Blavatsky's claim that she studied in Tibet, see the works of Cranston and Barborka cited above. Although these claims are generally dismissed by scholars, other links between Tibetans and early members of the Theosophical Society warrant further research. An important key here is the Bhutia Boarding School in Darjeeling, Sikkim. The school opened in 1874. The first head-master was Sarat Chandra Das and the Tibetan teacher was Ugyen Gyatso, a "lama" of Tibetan-Sikkimese descent. The school had been opened on the orders of Sir George Campbell, the British lieutenant-governor of Bengal, in order to provide an education for Tibetan and Sikkimese boys. Its true purpose, as explained in Derek Waller's *The Pundits* (Lexington: University of Kentucky Press, 1990), p. 193, was to "train interpreters, geographers and explorers, who may be useful if at any future time Tibet is opened to the British." Thus, the boys were taught English, Tibetan, and surveying. Beginning in 1879, Das (sometimes disguised as a Tibetan lama or a Nepalese merchant) and Ugyen Gyatso made numerous trips into Tibet to make maps and gather intelligence as secret agents of the British Survey of India. On their first trip, they went to Tashilhunpo monastery, the seat of the Panchen Lama (gen-erally referred to by Europeans of the day as the "Tashi Lama," the "Teshu Lama," or "Teshoo Lama," the latter used by Kipling as the name of the lama in *Kim*; Das is said to have been the model for Huree Chunder Mookerjee). There they were welcomed by the "prime minister" of the Panchen Lama, one "Sengchen Tulku," the abbot of Dongtse monastery, whom Das instructed in Sanskrit, Hindi, and the use of the camera and the magic lantern. (He appears to have been the incarnation of Seng chen Blo bzang bstan 'dzin dpal 'byor, 1784–1843, whose collected works have been published.) Das describes his time with him in detail in his *Autobiography: Narrative of the Incidents of My Early Life* (Calcutta: Indian Studies: Past & Present, 1969), pp. 56–89, summarized by Waller, pp. 197–204. When it was later deter-mined that Das was a British agent, Sengchen was arrested, imprisoned, and publicly flogged in Lhasa, before being brutally drowned in the Tsangpo River in June 1887, described by Ekai Kawaguchi in his *Three Years in Tibet* (Benares and London: Theosophical Publishing Society, 1909), pp. 17–20. After his death, his line of incar-nation was proscribed.

Both Blavatsky and Olcott mention their acquaintance with Das, with the col-onel praising him in diary entries of June 1885 and July 1887, noting in the latter that he had read his *Narrative of a Journey to Lhasa in 1881–82*. See his *Old Diary Leaves* (Adyar, India: Theosophical Publishing House, 1974–75), 3:265–67, 4:4–6. In his *The Masters Revealed: Madame Blavatsky and the Myth of the Great White Lodge* (Albany: State University of New York Press, 1994), pp. 195–96, K. Paul Johnson speculates that one of the *chelas* of the Mahatmas, one Chandro Cusho, is a fiction-alization of Sarat Chandra Das, and that the Mahatma Ten-Dub Ughien is based on Ugyen Gyatso. Although it is also possible that Madame Blavatsky's obsession with Tashilhunpo and its secret archives and with the Tashi Lama may have come in part from a reading of Bogle, it may also have been derived from the connection of Das and Ugyen Gyatso to the monastery and to the Sengchen Lama, from whom they received Tibetan texts that they brought back to Darjeeling. (A preposterous connection between these texts and HPB's *Stanzas of Dzyan* and *The Book of Golden Precepts* is suggested by Johnson, pp. 203–4.) In her hagiography of HPB, Sylvia Cranston reproduces the Tibetan text (and provides a mistranslation) of a verse purportedly written by the sixth Panchen Lama and included in the 1927 Chinese edition of *The Voice of the Silence* (Beijing: Chinese Buddhist Research Society, 1927). See Cranston, p. 86.

Das had died by the time Evans-Wentz arrived in Sikkim, but another figure from Darjeeling provides a link between this remarkable cast of characters. He is the Mongolian monk Sherab Gyatso, the personal assistant to the Sengchen Lama who was able to escape the punishment that befell his master because he was in Sikkim, serving as abbot of Ghoom monastery in Darjeeling (where Lama Govinda met Tomo Geshe Rinpoche). Like Ugyen Gyatso, Sherab Gyatso had been involved in surveying activities for the British. See Lt. Col. G. Strahan, *Report of the Explorations of Lama Serap Gyatso, 1856–68* [and others] *in Sikkim, Bhutan, and Tibet*, published under the direction of Col. H. R. Thuillier, Surveyor General of India (Dehra Dun: Survey of India, 1889), pp. 3–7. See also Lt. Col. R. E. Holdich's "The Narrative Account of Lama Ugyen Gyatso's Third Season's Explorations in Tibet in 1883," in *Records of the Survey of India* 8, pt. 2 (Dehra Dun, 1915), pp. 339–57. Later, Sherab Gyatso taught Ekai Kawaguchi and was the chief author (as attested by the Tibetan title page) of Das's 1902 *Tibetan-English Dictionary*. Sherab Gyatso was also the teacher of two of the monks who provided translations for Evans-Wentz in *The Tibetan Book of the Great Liberation*.

13. See Sylvia Cranston, *HPB: The Extraordinary Life and Influence of Helena Blavatsky, Founder of the Modern Theosophical Movement* (New York: G. P. Putnam's Sons, 1993), p. 84.

14. See Mircea Eliade, *No Souvenirs: Journal 1957–1969*, trans. Fred Johnson, Jr. (New York: Harper and Row, 1977), p. 208.

15. On Tingley, see Peter Washington, *Madame Blavatsky's Baboon: A History of the Mediums, Mystics, and Misfits Who Brought Spiritualism to America* (New York: Schocken Books, 1993), esp. pp. 108–14.

16. See Daniel Caracostea, "Alexandra David-Neel's Early Acquaintances with Theosophy, Paris 1892," *Theosophical History* (July-October 1991): 209–13.

17. Alexandra David-Neel, *Magic and Mystery in Tibet* (New York: Dover Publications, 1971), pp. 15, 17, 19.

18. Ken Winkler, *Pilgrim of the Clear Light* (Berkeley, Calif.: Dawnfire Books, 1982), p. 44. The other biographical information on Evans-Wentz in this chapter is drawn from Winkler's book. A useful summary is provided by John Myrdhin Reynolds in *Self-Liberation through Seeing with Naked Awareness* (Barrytown, N.Y.: Station Hill Press, 1989), pp. 71–78.

19. This summary is drawn from Marion Meade's biography *Madame Blavatsky: The Woman behind the Myth* (New York: G. P. Putnam's Sons, 1980), pp. 413–17. For another useful summary, see Nicholas Goodrick-Clarke, *The Occult Roots of Nazism* (New York: New York University Press, 1992), pp. 18–22.

20. H. P. Blavatsky, *The Secret Doctrine* (Los Angeles: Theosophy Company, 1947), 2:743. This is a facsimile of the original 1888 edition.

21. Alfred Percy Sinnett, *Esoteric Buddhism* (London: Chapman and Hall, 1885), p. 68.

22. Blavatsky, *Secret Doctrine*, 2:445.

23. Ibid.

24. Ibid., 2:303.

25. Ibid., 2:196 n.

26. Ibid., 2:168.

27. On Jung's relation to spiritualism and Theosophy, see Richard Noll, *The Jung Cult* (Princeton, N.J.: Princeton University Press, 1994). Despite his apparent respect for Tibetan Buddhism, Jung refused to sign a letter protesting the Chinese invasion of Tibet in 1959. See Frank McLynn, *Carl Gustav Jung* (London: Bantam Press, 1996), p. 516.

28. See, for example, Luis O. Gómez, "Oriental Wisdom and the Cure of Souls: Jung and Indian East," in *Curators of the Buddha: The Study of Buddhism under Colonialism,* ed. Donald S. Lopez, Jr. (Chicago: University of Chicago Press, 1995), pp. 197–250.

29. The biographical details that follow are drawn from the rather reverential biography by Ken Winkler, *A Thousand Journeys: The Biography of Lama Anagarika Govinda* (Longmead, England: Element Books, 1990).

30. Lama Anagarika Govinda, *Foundations of Tibetan Mysticism* (New York: Samuel Weiser, 1969), p. 25.

31. Lama Anagarika Govinda, *The Inner Structure of the I Ching: The Book of Transformations* (New York: Weatherhill, 1981), p. xi.

32. Govinda, *Foundations of Tibetan Mysticism*, p. 13.

33. Ibid., p. 14.

34. In his introduction to *Tibet's Great Yogī Milarepa*, there is a less ambivalent statement: "As from mighty broadcasting stations, dynamically charged with thought-forces, the Great Ones broadcast over the Earth that Vital Spirituality which alone makes human evolution possible; as the Sun sustains the physical man, They sustain the psychic man, and make possible mankind's escape from Sangsāric Existence." See W. Y. Evans-Wentz, *Tibet's Great Yogī Milarepa* (London: Oxford University Press, 1969), p. 18.

35. Blavatsky, *Secret Doctrine*, 1:303.

36. H. P. Blavatsky, "Tibetan Teachings," in *Collected Writings 1883–1884–*

1885 (Los Angeles: Blavatsky Writings Publication Fund, 1954), 6:98. On the fascination of Madame Blavatsky and the Theosophists with Tashilhunpo monastery and the Panchen Lama, see note 12 above.

37. For the early Theosophists, "science" was often used as a synonym for "theosophy." See, for example, Henry Steele Olcott, *The Buddhist Catechism*, 44th ed. (Adyar, Madras: Theosophical Publishing House, 1947).

38. Evans-Wentz's deviation from Buddhist doctrine on the issue of rebirth as an animal was pointed out in 1968 by Francis Story (Anagārika Sugatānanda) in the essay "The Buddhist Doctrine of Rebirth in Subhuman Realms." The essay is reprinted in Francis Story, *Rebirth as Doctrine and Experience* (Kandy, Sri Lanka: Buddhist Publication Society, 1975), pp. 64–100. See also John Myrdhin Reynolds in *Self-Liberation through Seeing with Naked Awareness* (Barrytown, N.Y.: Station Hill Press, 1989), p. 137 n. 6.

39. W. Y. Evans-Wentz, *The Tibetan Book of the Great Liberation* (London: Oxford University Press, 1968), p. 116 n. 1.

40. In his introductory foreword, Lama Govinda argues that the book is "not merely a mass for the dead, to which the *Bardo Thödol* was reduced in later times" (p. lxi).

41. Evans-Wentz reminds the reader that as early as 1911, in *The Fairy-Faith in the Celtic Countries* (London: H. Frowde, 1911), he had argued that the ancient Druid theory of rebirth provided "a scientific extension and correction" of Darwin's theory of evolution. He was thus gratified to find support for the theory of human reincarnation among such eminent scientists as T. H. Huxley, E. B. Tylor, and William James (pp. x, 60–61).

42. Timothy Leary, Ralph Metzner, Richard Alpert, *The Psychedelic Experience: A Manual Based on the Tibetan Book of the Dead* (Secaucus, N.J.: Citadel Press, 1976), p. 12.

43. Ibid., pp. 11, 30, 31. That such sentiments remain exciting to some three decades later is evidenced by the fall 1996 special issue of *Tricycle: The Buddhist Review* (vol. 7, no. 1), which is devoted to "Buddhism and Psychedelics."

44. The life and teachings of Trungpa Rinpoche are discussed in chapters 13 and 14 of Rick Fields, *How the Swans Came to the Lake: A Narrative History of Buddhism in America* (Boston: Shambhala, 1986). See also his autobiography, *Born in Tibet* (Boulder, Colo.: Shambhala, 1977).

45. Francesca Fremantle and Chögyam Trungpa, *The Tibetan Book of the Dead* (Boulder, Colo.: Shambhala, 1975), p. xvi.

46. See "A Prayer for Deliverance from Rebirth," in *Religions of Tibet in Practice*, ed. Donald S. Lopez, Jr. (Princeton, N.J.: Princeton University Press, 1997), p. 451.

47. Fremantle and Trungpa, p. 4. Tibetan texts speak of passing through similitudes of the stages of death when passing in and out of dreams and view the space

between moments of thought as a kind of intermediate state. However, Trungpa Rinpoche appears to be referring to something else here.

48. Ibid., pp. 5, 6.

49. Ibid., p. 8.

50. Sogyal Rinpoche, *The Tibetan Book of Living and Dying* (San Francisco: HarperSanFrancisco, 1992), p. 14.

51. For example, a translation of a Geluk text on the stages of death, Lati Rinbochay and Jeffrey Hopkins's *Death, Intermediate State, and Rebirth in Tibetan Buddhism* (Ithaca, N.Y.: Snow Lion Publications, 1981), has sold some fourteen thousand copies.

52. He made the statement in a public lecture during a conference on Tibetan culture and religion at the University of California, Santa Barbara, on May 1, 1993.

53. He also makes the remarkable statement, "I think of Gandhi, Einstein, Abraham Lincoln, Mother Teresa, of Shakespeare, of St. Francis, of Beethoven, of Michelangelo. When Tibetans hear of such people, they immediately say they are bodhisattvas" (Sogyal Rinpoche, p. 101).

54. Robert A. F. Thurman, *The Tibetan Book of the Dead* (New York: Bantam Books, 1994), p. xx.

55. Blaise Pascal, *Pascal's Pensées*, trans. Martin Turnell (London: Harvill Press, 1962), pp. 200–205.

56. Michel de Certeau has described the contractual nature of belief. Under this contract, the believer, in a position of inferiority to the object of belief, gives something away in the hope of getting something back, not now, but in the future. In order for the contractual relation to be maintained, there must be the expectation of some return on the initial investment, a surety of some salvation, and this in turn depends on the presumption of the ability of the object of belief to guarantee the loan. For de Certeau, it is only when the believed object becomes severed from this contractual relation that it becomes a "belief," a mental occurrence, a representation in the mind of someone else, "known as 'beliefs' precisely because we do not believe them any longer." That is, the view of belief as an inner state, as an assent to a proposition, can occur only with a loss, when the believer has terminated the contract with the believed, leaving the object of belief as a lonely component of someone else's religion, either of another time or of another place. See Michel de Certeau, "What We Do When We Believe," in *On Signs*, ed. Marshall Blonsky (Baltimore: Johns Hopkins University Press, 1985), pp. 192–202. The discussion here is drawn from pp. 193–96, the quotation from p. 196.

57. Robert A. F. Thurman, *Essential Tibetan Buddhism* (San Francisco: HarperSanFrancisco, 1995), p. 35.

58. On the uses of this and related mortuary texts in the Nyingma sect, see David Germano, "Dying, Death, and Other Opportunities," in *Religions of Tibet in Practice*, ed. Donald S. Lopez, Jr. (Princeton, N.J.: Princeton University Press,

1997), pp. 458–93. Germano provides a useful bibliography of related works on pp. 479–80.

59. Paul de Man, *Blindness and Insight: Essays in the Rhetoric of Contemporary Criticism,* 2d ed., rev. (Minneapolis: University of Minnesota Press, 1983), p. 188.

CHAPTER THREE

1. T. Lobsang Rampa, *The Third Eye* (New York: Ballantine Books, 1964), pp. 24–25. Subsequent citations are noted by page number in the text.

2. Ibid., pp. 20–21. For a more accurate account of Tibetan law, see Rebecca Redwood French, *The Golden Yoke: The Legal Cosmology of Buddhist Tibet* (Ithaca, N.Y.: Cornell University Press, 1995).

3. After his return to England and his retirement from government service, Bell was apparently threatened with the loss of his pension when he refused to submit the manuscript of *The People of Tibet* (Oxford: Clarendon Press, 1928) for censorship. But because he had been out of government service for six years, he was no longer subject to the Official Secrets Act, and Bell was not required to submit the manuscript. I am grateful to Alex McKay for this information, which results from his research in the India Office Library. For further discussion of Bell's career, see Alex McKay, *Tibet and the British Raj: The Frontier Cadre 1904–1947* (Richmond, England: Curzon Press, 1997). The specific information here may be found in India Office Library and Records L/P + S/12/3982.

4. The theme of kites in *The Third Eye* appears to have inspired the short story "Kites" in Pierre Delattre's *Tales of a Dalai Lama* (Boston: Houghton Mifflin, 1971), pp. 20–25.

5. T. Lobsang Rampa, *Doctor from Lhasa* (New Brunswick, N.J.: Inner Light Publications, 1990), p. 37. Subsequent citations are noted by page number in the text.

6. T. Lobsang Rampa, *The Rampa Story* (New York: Bantam Books, 1968), p. 4. Subsequent citations are noted by page number in the text.

7. In his introduction to *The Tibetan Book of the Dead* Evans-Wentz reports that "So long as the body is the receptacle of the consciousness-principle, it is said to renew itself completely every seven years."

8. For a brief biography of Richardson, see the appreciation by David Snellgrove in Michael Aris and Aung San Suu Kyi, eds., *Tibetan Studies in Honour of Hugh Richardson* (Warminster, England: Aris & Phillips, 1980), pp. vii–xi.

9. Personal correspondence from Hugh Richardson, June 24, 1996.

10. The publisher's statement was included only in the first printing of the English edition, which I have been unable to locate. The statement provided here is translated from the French edition: T. Lobsang Rampa, *Le troisième oeil,* trans. François Legris (Paris: Club des éditeurs, 1957). My thanks to Professor William Ray for

assistance in translating the passage. The aura of authority is enhanced in the French edition by the addition of numerous black and white photographs of scenes of Tibetan monastic life, with captions containing quotations from *The Tibetan Book of the Dead*.

11. David Snellgrove, "The Third Eye: Autobiography of a Tibetan Lama," *Oriental Art* 3, no. 2 (summer 1957), p. 75.

12. Review of *The Third Eye*, by T. Lobsang Rampa, *Times Literary Supplement*, 30 November 1956, 715.

13. Richardson's dissent was shared by Guy Wint, who wrote in the *Manchester Guardian*, also on November 30, 1956 (p. 9), "It sounds all rather fishy. There is no Tibetan lama in the West, and almost certainly equally none inside Tibet, who is capable of writing in English such a book as Mr. Lobsang Rampa's . . . Mr. Lobsang Rampa's book is the more suspect because it is everything which the more simpleminded occultist could desire."

14. Review of *The Third Eye*, by T. Lobsang Rampa, *Kirkus* 25, no. 62 (January 15, 1957).

15. Review of *The Third Eye*, by T. Lobsang Rampa, *Library Journal* 82, no. 670 (March 1, 1957).

16. The report was kindly provided to the author by Hugh Richardson, June 24, 1996. For further biographical details, see Christopher Evans, *Cults of Unreason* (London: Harrap, 1973), pp. 245–46.

17. "Private v. Third Eye," *Time*, 17 February 1958, 33. An exposé of Rampa by the Tibetan scholar Chen Chi Chang was published in the spring 1958 issue of the journal *Tomorrow*, pp. 9–16.

18. *Daily Express* (London), 3 February 1958, 7. See also Christopher Evans, *Cults of Unreason* (London: Harrap, 1973), p. 243.

Richardson reports in his letter of June 14, 1996, that Rampa had been asked by "a very great lady" to inscribe a copy of the book to her. He replied, "Dear Lady. I do not have my Tibetan pen with me. Let me take the book home." Richardson describes the eventual inscription as "three lines of meaningless scribbles, some few resembling Tibetan letters."

19. *Scottish Daily Mail*, 1 February 1958, 2.

20. *Time*, 17 February 1958, 33.

21. Richardson apparently did not recognize this portrayal (or chose not to mention it) in his brief review of *Doctor from Lhasa* in the *Daily Telegraph and Morning Post* (London) of August 7, 1959 (p. 14), which reads in full, under the title "Still Rampa":

When "The Third Eye" was published I pointed out in THE DAILY TELE-GRAPH that there were so many mistakes of fact and of interpretation that it could not possibly be by a Tibetan. Later it was proved that "T. Lobsang

Rampa" was a Mr. Cyril Hoskins [*sic*] from Plympton who had never been outside the British Isles.

To wriggle out of this predicament Mr. Hoskins pretended that he had been possessed by the spirit of a Tibetan Lama. That is not likely to take in any but the most credulous and does not explain away the many mistakes in the book.

Now we have "Doctor from Lhasa" by the same writer. It is surprising that his present publishers should claim that experts were unable to disprove the "facts" of "The Third Eye." No one of my acquaintance who has lived in Tibet and knows the Tibetans—including a genuine Tibetan lama to whom I read the book—had any doubt that it was an impudent fake.

Most of "Doctor from Lhasa" is about alleged activities in China. So far as Tibet is concerned the most realistic part is the picture on the dust-jacket: and we see in the photograph of the author that he does not even know on which side the cross-over of a Tibetan robe should come. Everything points to it being another exercise in fiction based on information which could be collected from published works and garishly coloured by a lively Walter Mitty imagination.

22. Agehananda Bharati, "Fictitious Tibet: The Origin and Persistence of Rampaism," *Tibet Society Bulletin 7* (1974): 3.

23. Rampa's claims about the importance of cats in Tibet were accepted as ethnographic evidence of Tibetan feudalism by F. Sierksma in his *Tibet's Terrifying Deities* (The Hague: Mouton and Company, 1966), p. 107, in which he writes, citing *The Third Eye*, "In the Land of Snows a servant was required to address his master's cat as follows: 'Would honourable Puss Puss deign to come and drink this unworthy milk.'"

24. Couldn't resist.

25. See Pierre Bourdieu, "The Production of Belief: Contribution to an Economy of Symbolic Goods," in *The Field of Cultural Production* (New York: Columbia University Press, 1993), pp. 74–75.

26. For an account of this story in English, see Tsang Nyön Heruka, *The Life of Marpa the Translator* (Boulder, Colo.: Prajñā Press, 1982), pp. 156–81.

27. See René de Nebesky-Wojkowitz, *Oracles and Demons of Tibet: The Cult and Iconography of the Tibetan Protective Deities* (The Hague: Mouton and Company, 1956), pp. 409–66.

28. For an example, see Paul Harrison, *The Samādhi of Direct Encounter with the Buddhas of the Present: An Annotated English Translation of the Tibetan Version of the* Pratyutpanna-Buddha-Saṃmukhāvasthita-Samādhi-Sūtra (Tokyo: International Institute for Buddhist Studies, 1990), pp. 96–109.

29. Oscar Wilde, "The Decay of Lying," in *Complete Works of Oscar Wilde* (New York: Harper & Row, 1989), pp. 977–78.

30. For a traditional presentation of *gter ma*, see Tulku Thondup Rinpoche, *Hidden Teachings of Tibet: An Explanation of the Terma Tradition of the Nyingma School of Buddhism* (London: Wisdom Publications, 1986). For analyses of the tradition, see especially Janet B. Gyatso, "The Logic of Legitimation in the Tibetan Treasure Tradition," *History of Religions* 33, no. 1 (1993): 97–134; and Janet B. Gyatso, "Drawn from the Tibetan Treasury: The gter ma Literature," in *Tibetan Literature: Studies in Genre*, ed. Roger Jackson and José Cabezón (Ithaca, N.Y.: Snow Lion Publications, 1995), pp. 147–69. See also Michael Aris, *Hidden Treasures, Secret Lives* (London: Kegan Paul International, 1989), pp. 15–106.

31. Tulku Thondup, p. 156.

32. Ibid., p. 157. See also Janet B. Gyatso, "Guru Chos-dbang's gTer 'byung chen mo: An Early Survey of the Treasure Tradition and Its Strategies in Discussing Bon Literature," in *Tibetan Studies: Proceedings of the Sixth Seminar of the International Association of Tibetan Studies, Fagernes 1992*, ed. Per Kvaerne (Oslo: Institute for Comparative Research in Human Culture, 1994), pp. 275–86.

With the notable exception of Michael Aris in his *Hidden Treasures, Secret Lives*, Western scholars of Tibetan Buddhism have been reluctant to directly confront the question of the historical legitimacy of *gter ma*, to consider the rediscovered texts as, in fact, works composed by their discoverers and hidden only to be revealed. For a spirited defense of the authenticity of *gter*, see Lama Govinda's introductory foreword in Walter Y. Evans-Wentz, *The Tibetan Book of the Dead* (London: Oxford University Press, 1960), pp. liv–lvi. The fact that the pious fiction of authenticity has been tacitly maintained for so long by scholars of Tibet is itself a fascinating topic to be considered with the larger issue of mystification.

33. Max Weber, "The Sociology of the World Religions" in *From Max Weber: Essays in Sociology*, ed. and trans. H. H. Gerth and C. Wright Mills (New York: Oxford University Press, 1958), p. 295.

34. Ibid., p. 296.

35. See Bruce Lincoln, *Authority: Construction and Corrosion* (Chicago: University of Chicago Press, 1994), p. 3.

36. Pierre Bourdieu, *Language and Symbolic Power*, trans. Gino Raymond and Matthew Adamson (Cambridge: Harvard University Press, 1991), pp. 109, 111. Although Lincoln's and Bourdieu's analyses are directed at speech acts, they also pertain to certain cases of textual authority.

37. T. Lobsang Rampa, *The Hermit* (New Brunswick, N.J.: Inner Light Publications, 1971), facing p. 7.

38. Bharati, p. 11. Bruce Lincoln describes authoritative speech as "the effect of a posited, perceived, or institutionally ascribed asymmetry between speaker and au-

dience that permits certain speakers to command not just the attention but the confidence, respect, and trust of their audience, or—an important proviso—to make audiences act *as if* this were so." See Lincoln, p. 4.

39. Bourdieu, *Language and Symbolic Power,* p. 109. An earlier example of imposture, also from England, is that of George Psalmanazar (1679?–1763), a Frenchman who convinced his English hosts that he was a native of Formosa and lectured on Formosan culture, religion, and language, all of which he had invented. See Leslie Stephen and Sidney Lee, eds., *The Dictionary of National Biography: From Earliest Times to 1900* (London: Oxford University Press, 1973), 16:439–42.

40. For an analysis of a Tibetan exorcism rite, see Donald S. Lopez, Jr., *Elaborations on Emptiness, Uses of the Heart Sūtra* (Princeton, N.J.: Princeton University Press, 1996), pp. 216–38. The distinction between the scapegoat and the ostracized is drawn from J. P. Vernant, "Ambiguity and Reversal: On the Enigmatic Structure of Oedipus Rex," trans. Page du Bois, *New Literary History* 10, no. 3 (1978): 491–92.

41. For the full version of the parable, see Leon Hurvitz, trans., *The Scripture of the Lotus Blossom of the Fine Dharma* (New York: Columbia University Press, 1976), pp. 58–75. When Rampa is reluctant to write because so few will believe what he says (as has been the case with the first two books), he is telepathically reminded by the lamas that "the end justifies the means" (a view often associated with communism). It is unclear how this relates to his dilemma, but he is reminded by the lamas of the parable of the three chariots. In Rampa's version, when the children escape from the burning house, the father gives them each the kind of chariot he had promised them; he seems to have missed the key point of the parable. See Rampa, *The Rampa Story,* pp. 16–17.

42. On disavowal, see J. Laplanche and J.-B. Pontalis, *The Language of Psychoanalysis,* trans. Donald Nicholson-Smith (New York: W. W. Norton & Company, 1973), pp. 118–21.

CHAPTER FOUR

1. Michael R. Katz, ed., *Tolstoy's Short Fiction* (New York: W. W. Norton & Company, 1991), pp. 167–72.

2. Cited in Elizabeth Reed, *Primitive Buddhism: Its Origin and Teachings* (Chicago: Scott, Foresman, 1896), p. 30.

3. Garnet Wolseley, *Narrative of the War with China in 1860* (Wilmington, Del.: Scholarly Resources, 1972), pp. 221–22. Other theories were somewhat less suspicious. Emil Schlagintweit speculated in 1863 that the practice had originated when the study of scriptures was replaced by the "mere reading or copying of holy books" as a work of merit for delivery from metempsychosis. But because few knew how to

read and those who did were otherwise engaged, the lamas "taught that the mere turning of a rolled manuscript might be considered an efficacious substitute for reading it." See Emil Schlagintweit, *Buddhism in Tibet Illustrated by Literary Documents and Objects of Religious Worship with an Account of the Buddhist Systems Preceding It in India* (London: Susil Gupta, 1969), p. 230. For interesting speculations on the origin and influence of the prayer wheel, see Lynn White, Jr., "Tibet, India, and Malaya as Sources of Western Medieval Technology," *American Historical Review* 65 (1959–60): 515–26. Gregory Schopen has considered possible Indian antecedents in an unpublished paper, "A Note on the 'Technology of Prayer' and a Reference to a 'Revolving Book-Case' in an 11th Century Indian Inscription."

4. Sir M. Monier-Williams, *Buddhism: Its Connexion with Brāhmanism and Its Contrast with Christianity* (Varanasi, India: Chowkhamba Sanskrit Series Office, 1964), p. 378. In his 1926 *The Road to Lamaland*, M. L. A. Gompertz remarked, "Some day, when electricity is introduced into Thibet, salvation will become even cheaper than it is at present. An electro-motor prayer-wheel at 3,000 revolutions per minute would put heaven within the reach of all." See M. L. A. Gompertz, *The Road to Lamaland* (New York: George H. Doran Company, 1926), p. 186.

5. Filippo de Filippi, *An Account of Tibet: The Travels of Ippolito Desideri of Pistoia, S. J., 1712–1727*, rev. ed. (London: Routledge and Sons, 1937), p. 295.

6. Carl F. Köppen, *Die Lamaische Hierarchie und Kirche* (1859; reprint, Berlin: Verlag von H. Barsdorf, 1906), p. 59. The translation appears in Sten Konow, "Om Mani Padme Hum," *Journal of the Bihar and Orissa Research Society* 12 (1925): 1.

7. See William W. Rockhill, *The Journey of Friar William of Rubruck to the Eastern Parts of the World, 1253–55, as Narrated by Himself* (London: Hakluyt Society, 1900), pp. 145–46. See also Willem van Ruysbroek, *The Mission of Friar William of Rubruck*, trans. Peter Jackson (London: Hakluyt Society, 1990), pp. 153–54. Elsewhere, Rockhill cites the Latin text: "et dicunt semper hec verba, *on man baccam*, hoc est, *Deus tu nosti*." See William W. Rockhill, *The Land of the Lamas* (London: Longmans, Green, and Co., 1891), p. 326.

8. Cited in Sven Hedin, *Trans-Himalaya: Discoveries and Adventures in Tibet* (London: Macmillan, 1913), 3:307.

9. Ibid., p. 308.

10. See the appendix in Johannes Nieuhof, *An Embassy from the East India Company of the United Provinces to the Grand Tartar Cham Emperor of China*, trans. John Ogilby (1669; reprint, Menston, England: Scolar Press, 1972), pp. 40–41. For the French, see Athanasius Kircher, *La Chine Illustrée* (Geneva: Unicorn Verlag, 1980), pp. 95–96.

A similar description, in which Menipe has a head "that riseth up as a Sugar-loaf, in a monstrous manner," appears in *China and France, or Two Treatises* (London, 1676), p. 107.

11. de Filippi, pp. 295–96.

12. See Thomas Astley, *New Collection of Voyages and Travels* (1747; reprint, London: Frank Cass and Company, 1968), 4:461.

13. See John Trusler, *The Habitable World Described* (London: Literary Press, 1788), 2:257.

14. Victor Jacquemont, *Letters from India, 1829–1832*, trans. Catherine Alison Phillips (London: Macmillan, 1936), p. 124. A somewhat more colorful translation, in which the mantra is "Oum mani pani" and the translation is "Oh, diamond water-lily!" is in William Henry Knight, *Diary of a Pedestrian in Cashmere and Tibet* (London: Richard Bentley, 1863), p. 374.

15. He goes on to explain, "The mystic triform Deity is in him of the jewel and the lotos (Sangha). But the *præsens Divus*, whether he be Augustus or *Padma-páni*, is everything with the many. Hence the notoriety of *this mantra*, whilst the others are hardly ever heard of, and have thus remained unknown to our travellers." Hodgson's article is reprinted in Brian H. Hodgson, *Essays on the Languages, Literature and Religion of Nepal and Tibet* (New Delhi: Mañjuśrī Publishing House, 1972). The passage quoted appears in the footnote preceded by a † on page 88.

16. Julius von Klaproth, "Explication et origine de la formule bouddhique om maṇi padmè hoûm," *Nouveau Journal Asiatique ou Recueil de Mémoires, d'Extraits et de Notices Relatifs à l'Histoire, à la Philosophie aux Langues, et à la Littèrature des Peuples Orientaux* (Paris) 7 (March 1831), p. 188.

17. Ibid., pp. 205–6.

18. W. Schott, "Über den Buddhaismus in Hochasien und in China," *Philologische und historische Abhandlungen der Königlichen Akademie der Wissenschaften zu Berlin* (n.p., 1844), p. 187 n. 3.

19. Ibid., p. 221 n. 2.

20. Carl Friedrich Köppen, *Die Lamaische Hierarchie und Kirche* (1859; reprint, Berlin: Verlag von H. Barsdorf, 1906), pp. 59–60.

21. Emil Schlagintweit, *Buddhism in Tibet Illustrated by Literary Documents and Objects of Religious Worship with an Account of the Buddhist Systems Preceding It in India* (1863; reprint, London: Susil Gupta, 1969), p. 120.

22. Evariste-Régis Huc and Joseph Gabet, *Travels in Tartary, Thibet, and China 1844–1846*, trans. William Hazlitt (reprint, 2 vols. in 1, New York: Dover Publications, 1987), 2:245–46.

23. Joseph Wolff, *Travels and Adventures of Rev. Joseph Wolff, D.D., LL.D.* (London: Saunders, Otley, and Co., 1861), p. 194.

24. William Henry Knight, *Diary of a Pedestrian in Cashmere and Tibet* (London: Richard Bentley, 1863), p. 375. The encounter with the corpulent lama is described on pp. 158–61. The prayer-wheel incident is described on p. 200.

25. H. P. Blavatsky, *Collected Writings 1877: Isis Unveiled* (Wheaton, Ill.: Theosophical Publishing House, 1972), 2:616.

26. Sir Edwin Arnold, *The Light of Asia* (London: John Lane the Bodley Head Ltd, 1926), p. 177.

27. H. A. Jäschke, *A Tibetan-English Dictionary with Special Reference to the Prevailing Dialects* (London: Routledge & Kegan Paul, 1949), pp. 607–8. In the Tibetan orthography, *oṃ* is mistakenly written as *soṃ*. On the Moravian mission in Ladakh, see John Bray, "The Moravian Church in Ladakh: The First 40 Years 1885–1925" in *Recent Research on Ladakh,* ed. Detlef Kantowsky and Reinhard Sander (Munich: Weltforum Verlag, 1983).

28. Mary Agnes Tincker, *The Jewel in the Lotos: A Novel* (Philadelphia: J. B. Lippincott and Company, 1883), p. 330.

29. Philangi Dasa, *Swedenborg the Buddhist: The Higher Swedenborgianism, Its Secrets and Thibetan Origin* (Los Angeles: Buddhistic Swedenborgian Brotherhood, 1887), p. 33.

30. Sir M. Monier-Williams, *Buddhism, Its Connexion with Brāhmanism and Its Contrast with Christianity* (Varanasi, India: Chowkhamba Sanskrit Series Office, 1964), pp. 372, 373 n. 3.

31. William Simpson, *The Buddhist Praying-Wheel* (London, 1896), p. 39.

32. L. Austine Waddell, *Tibetan Buddhism* (New York: Dover, 1972), p. 148. Albert Grünwedel offered the same gloss in his *Mythologie des Buddhismus in Tibet und der Mongolia* (Leipzig: F. A. Brockhaus, 1900), p. 234.

33. L. Austine Waddell, *Lhasa and Its Mysteries* (New York: Dover, 1905), pp. 23, 29.

34. J. Huston Edgar, *The Land of Mystery, Tibet* (Melbourne: China Inland Mission, 1930), p. 55. For a long description of the use of the mantra by another missionary (without speculation as to its meaning), see Marion H. Duncan, *Customs and Superstitions of Tibetans* (London: Mitre Press, 1964), pp. 181–86.

35. William Carey, *Adventures in Tibet* (Boston and Chicago: United Society for Christian Endeavor, 1901), pp. 124–25.

36. S. E. Brady, *The Jewel in the Lotus and Other Stories* (Shanghai: Oriental Press, 1905), p. 42.

37. F. W. Thomas, "Om Maṇi Padme Hūṃ," *Journal of the Royal Asiatic Society* (1906): 464.

38. A. H. Francke, "The Meaning of the Om-mani-padme-hum Formula," *Journal of the Royal Asiatic Society of Great Britain and Ireland* (1915): 402–3. In *The Bodhisattva Doctrine in Buddhist Sanskrit Literature,* Har Dayal writes of the mantra, "This seems to be an invocation of a female deity, 'the deity of the jewel-lotus.' F. W. Thomas and A. H. Francke have shown that the popular interpretation is incorrect (Om, 'the Jewel in the Lotus')." See Har Dayal, *The Bodhisattva Doctrine in Buddhist Sanskrit Literature* (London: Kegan Paul, Trench, Trubner & Co., 1932), p. 49. See also Dan Martin, "On the Origin and Significance of the Prayer Wheel

according to Two Nineteenth-Century Tibetan Literary Sources," *Journal of the Tibet Society* 7 (1987): 13–29.

39. G. A. Combe, *A Tibetan on Tibet* (London: T. Fisher Unwin, 1926), p. 48.

40. David Macdonald, *The Land of the Lama* (London: Seeley, Service & Co., 1929), p. 78.

41. Basil J. Gould, *The Jewel in the Lotus* (London: Chatto & Windus, 1957), p. 1. In 1948 John Blofeld published an outline of contemporary Buddhism in China under the title *The Jewel in the Lotus.*

42. André Guibaut, *Tibetan Venture*, trans. Lord Sudley (London: John Murray, 1949), p. 43.

43. Marco Pallis, *Peaks and Lamas* (New York: Alfred A. Knopf, 1949), p. 162.

44. Geoffrey T. Bull, *When Iron Gates Yield* (London: Hodder & Stoughton, 1955), p. 79.

45. Christmas Humphreys, *Buddhism* (New York: Barnes and Noble, 1962), p. 203.

46. Allen Edwardes, *The Jewel in the Lotus: A Historical Survey of the Sexual Culture of the East* (New York: Julian Press, 1959), pp. 48–49.

47. Lama Anagarika Govinda, *Foundations of Tibetan Mysticism* (New York: Samuel Weiser, 1969), p. 261.

48. W. E. Garrett, "Mountaintop War in Remote Ladakh," *National Geographic* 123 (May 1963): 686.

49. Robert B. Ekvall, *Religious Observances in Tibet: Patterns and Function* (Chicago: University of Chicago Press, 1964), p. 116.

50. See William Boyd Sinclair, *Jump to the Land of God: The Adventures of a United States Air Force Crew in Tibet* (Caldwell, Idaho: Caxton Printers, 1965), p. 224 n. 2.

51. Lama Anagarika Govinda, *The Way of the White Clouds: A Buddhist Pilgrim in Tibet* (London: Hutchinson, 1966), p. 35.

52. John Blofeld, *The Tantric Mysticism of Tibet* (New York: E. P. Dutton, 1970), pp. 194–95. In 1979 Walt Anderson explained in *Open Secrets: A Western Guide to Tibetan Buddhism:*

> Perhaps the most famous mantra associated with Tibetan Buddhism is *om mani padme hum,* which is usually translated as "Hail to the jewel in the lotus." This isn't quite accurate, since *om* signifies the infinite cosmos and the principle of enlightenment, but the central words *mani* (jewel) and *padme* (lotus) do convey the essence of the mantra. They can be interpreted several ways; for example, the jewel can represent enlightenment and the lotus the human mind.

See Walt Anderson, *Open Secrets: A Western Guide to Tibetan Buddhism* (New York: Penguin Books, 1980), p. 77.

53. Grace Cooke, *The Jewel in the Lotus* (Liss, England: White Eagle Publishing Trust, 1973), p. 13.

54. Douglas Baker, *The Jewel in the Lotus* (Essendon, England: Little Elephant, 1974). The work has no page numbers. The quotation occurs six pages from the end of the book.

55. Raghavan Iyer, ed., *The Jewel in the Lotus* (London: Concord Grove Press, 1983), p. 7.

56. Donald Walters, *The Jewel in the Lotus* (Nevada City, Calif.: Crystal Clarity Publishers, 1993), p. 27.

57. Robert A. Paul, "A Mantra and Its Meaning," *The Psychoanalytic Study of Society* 9 (1981): 90.

58. See Marilyn M. Rhie and Robert A. F. Thurman, *Wisdom and Compassion: The Sacred Art of Tibet* (New York: Harry Abrams, 1991), p. 34. In 1994 Thurman rendered the mantra as "OM-the jewel in the lotus-HUM" in the glossary to his translation of *The Tibetan Book of the Dead*. See Robert A. F. Thurman, *The Tibetan Book of the Dead* (New York: Bantam Books, 1994), pp. 267–68. John Powers in his *Introduction to Tibetan Buddhism* provides the same translation. See John Powers, *Introduction to Tibetan Buddhism* (Ithaca, N.Y.: Snow Lion Publications, 1995), p. 230. Earlier in his book, Powers provides a long and fanciful explanation of the meaning of the mantra, describing a jewel inside a lotus blossom (without the sexual connotations), claiming (on page 15) that "All of these symbols are operating in the minds of the Tibetans who are making the circuit around the residence of the Dalai Lama."

59. Robert A. F. Thurman, *Essential Tibetan Buddhism* (San Francisco: HarperSanFrancisco, 1995), p. 38.

60. Wolfgang von Effra, *Uncompromising Tibet: Culture-Religion-Politics* (New Delhi: Paljor Publications, 1996), p. 28.

61. Here is the text from the site:

> This is where prayer wheels enter the cyber-age. Prayer wheels are used by Tibetan Buddhists to purify themselves and the entire world of its accumulated negative karma. Inside each prayer wheel is a paper or some other medium (such as microfilm) on which a mantra has been inscribed many times over. Typically the mantra is OM MANI PADME HUM, which Tibetans pronounce: Om Mani Pémé Hung.
>
> In English this means "the jewel in the lotus of the heart"; it is a reference to the hidden spark of divinity within each of us. The six syllables of the mantra are said to purify the six negative emotions: pride, jealousy, desire, ignorance, greed, and anger, while simultaneously engendering the six qualities of the enlightened heart: generosity, harmonious conduct, endurance, enthusiasm, concentration, and insight.

If the mantra is inscribed once and placed into a prayer wheel, each rotation of the prayer wheel accumulates the same merit as saying the mantra once. Similarly, a prayer wheel containing 100 million instances of the mantra yields the same purification power per rotation as saying the mantra 100 million times.

To set your very own prayer wheel in motion, all you have to do is download this mantra to your computer's hard disk. Once downloaded, your hard disk drive will spin the mantra for you. Nowadays hard disk drives spin their disks somewhere between 3600 and 7200 revolutions per minute, with a typical rate of 5400 rpm. Given those rotation speeds, you'll soon be purifying loads of negative karma.

If you occasionally post articles to netnews, you can exponentially increase the good karma that is generated by including the mantra in your .sig file. Shortly after posting an article, every news server in the world will be spinning your mantra round and round. If we assume that the news servers are Unix machines that operate continuously, a single news posting with this .sig will probably spin over 5 trillion times before the article expires. Sentient beings everywhere will be thanking you. However avoid spamming the net, as the negative karma produced by the spam tends to cancel out the good karma that might otherwise have been generated.

So if you're ready, click here for good karma. Remember you have to save the file locally to set the mantra in motion. If you prefer something a little fancier, click on the image below to save the mantra as it would be written by the Tibetans:

[The mantra appears in Tibetan script followed in brackets by] OM MANI PADME HUM

P.S. It wouldn't hurt to think of the mantra from time to time while it's spinning around on your disk drive.

This computerization of the sacred recalls Arthur C. Clarke's science fiction short story, "The Nine Billion Names of God." The monks of a Himalayan monastery believe that the world will end when the nine billion names of God are known, but calculate that even if they could recite one name a second, it would take almost 290 years to recite all the names. They have computers flown in to speed their work. At the airfield, the pilots who brought the computers prepare to leave and are discussing the monks' crazy beliefs when the stars start going out one by one.

62. André Padoux, "Mantras—What Are They?" in *Understanding Mantras,* ed. Harvey Alper (Albany, N.Y.: State University of New York Press, 1989), p. 302.

63. This correspondence was noted by European scholars of Mongolia such as P. S. Pallas in his *Sammlungen historischer Nachrichten über die Mongolischen Völkerschaften* (Saint Petersburg, 1801), 2:90; and Isaac Jacob Schmidt in *Forschungen im*

Gebiete der älteren religiösen, politischen und literärischen Bildungsgeschichte der Völker Mittel-Asiens, vorzüglich der Mongolen und Tibeter (Saint Petersburg and Leipzig, 1824), pp. 199–201. For some of the many Tibetan glosses of the mantra, see, for example, William W. Rockhill, *Land of the Lamas*, pp. 326–34; David Snellgrove, *Buddhist Himalaya*, p. 237; Khetsun Sangpo Rinbochay, *Tantric Practice in Nyingma* (London: Rider, 1982), pp. 25–26; and Matthew Kapstein, "The Royal Way of Supreme Compassion" in *Religions of Tibet in Practice*, ed. Donald S. Lopez, Jr. (Princeton, N.J.: Princeton University Press, 1997), pp. 73–76.

64. Pallis, p. 163.

65. *Maṇi 'khor lo'i phan yon*, Indo-Tibetan Buddhist Literature Series (Gangtok, Sikkim: Dzongsar Khyntse [*sic*] Labrang Palace Monastary [*sic*], 1985), 136: 8b2–9a2.

66. Tenzin Gyatso, Dalai Lama XIV, *Kindness, Clarity, and Insight*, trans. Jeffrey Hopkins (Ithaca, N.Y.: Snow Lion Publications, 1984), p. 117. The Dalai Lama's comments have recently been backtranslated into Tibetan in a Tibetan language version of *Kindness, Clarity, and Insight*. See *Nang pa'i lta spyod kun btus* (Dharamsala, India: Institute of Buddhist Dialectics, 1996), pp. 168–70.

67. See Dan Martin, "On the Origin of the Prayer Wheel according to Two Nineteenth-Century Literary Sources," *Journal of the Tibet Society* 7 (1987), p. 15. The passage appears at 574.4 in Sde srid Sangs rgyas rgya mtsho's *Blang dor gsal bar ston pa'i drang thig dwangs shel me long*. A similar gloss is provided by the fifteenth Karmapa in his commentary on Thang stong rgyal po's *'Gro don mkha' khyab ma*. For an English translation, see the Fifteenth Karmapa Kakhyab Dorje, *A Continuous Rain to Benefit Beings*, trans. Ken McLeod (Vancouver, B.C.: Kagyu Kunkhyab Chuling, n.d.), p. 24.

68. The Tibetan text appears in P. C. Verhagen, "The *Mantra 'Oṃ maṇi-padme hūṃ'* in an Early Tibetan Grammatical Treatise," *Journal of the International Association of Buddhist Studies* 13, no. 2 (1990): 134. My translation differs somewhat from Dr. Verhagen's more literal rendering. The Tibetan text is entitled *Sgra'i rnam par dbye ba bstan pa* (P 5838) and the passage occurs in *Mdo 'grel* section of the Peking *bstan 'gyur*, vol. ngo, 63b8–64a2. See also Pieter Verhagen, "Mantras and Grammar," in *Aspects of Buddhist Sanskrit*, ed. Kameshwar Nath Mishra (Sarnath, India: Central Institute of Higher Tibetan Studies, 1993), pp. 320–46. On versions of the mantra that appear in the Dunhuang manuscripts, see Yoshiro Imaeda, "Note préliminaire sur la formule *Oṃ maṇi-padme hūṃ* dans les manuscrits tibétains de Touen-houang," in *Contributions aux études sur Touen-houang*, ed. Michel Soymié, Hautes etudes orientales 10 (Geneva and Paris: Librairie Droz, 1979), pp. 71–76.

69. David Snellgrove, *Buddhist Himālaya: Travels and Studies in Quest of the Origins and Nature of Tibetan Religion*, 2d ed. (Kathmandu: Himalayan Book Sellers, 1995), p. 309 n. 26.

70. Verhagen, "*Mantra 'Oṃ maṇi-padme hūṃ*,'" p. 138 n. 19. For speculations

as to why the mantra of a male deity is in the feminine, see Agehananda Bharati, *The Tantric Tradition* (London: Rider and Company, 1965), p. 133; David Snellgrove, *Indo-Tibetan Buddhism* (Boston: Shambhala, 1987), 1:195 n. 134 (although he reads the mantra as "O thou with the jewelled lotus"); and Martin, p. 21 n. 4.

71. Sten Konow, "Om Mani Padme Hum," *Journal of the Bihar and Orissa Research Society* 12 (1925), p. 5. See also Edward J. Thomas, *The History of Buddhist Thought*, 2d ed. (London: Routledge and Kegan Paul, 1951), pp. 187–88. Thomas claims that there is no mention of a female deity Maṇipadmā in the sutra.

72. Konow, p. 11.

73. The text states (with orthographical errors corrected), *me ẓhes 'byung ba'i 'dreng bu ni kye ẓhes 'bod brda*. See Antonio Agostino Giorgi, *Alphabetum Tibetanum Missionum Apostolicarum Commodo Editum* (1762; facsimile, Cologne: Editiones Una Voce, 1987), p. 516. The passage is translated into Latin on page 521.

74. Ibid., pp. 516–17. The passage is translated into Latin, with editorial comment, on pp. 521–22.

75. Trijang Rinpoche, *Gẓungs sngags yi ge drug ma'i 'grel bshad*, in *The Collected Works of the Venerable Khri-byan rdo-rje-'chan blo-bẓan-ye-śes-bstan-'dẓin-rgya-mtsho, Junior Tutor of His Holiness the Fourteenth Dalai Lama*, vol. 3 (*ga*) (New Delhi: Mongolian Lama Gurudeva, 1978), p. 67a1–5. This is my translation. A translation of the text has been published as Kyabje Yonzin Trijang Dorje Chang Losang Yeshe Tenzin Gyatso Pal Zangpo, "The Significance of the Six Syllable Mantra Om Ma Ni Pad Me Hum," *Tibet Journal* 7, no. 4 (winter, 1982): 3–10.

76. See June Campbell, *Traveller in Space: In Search of Female Identity in Tibetan Buddhism* (New York: George Braziller, 1996), p. 64.

77. Trijang Ripoche, *Gẓungs sngags yi ge drug ma'i 'grel bshad*, p. 68b5–6. The Tibetan reads, *dang po mtshon byed rtags kyi dbang du byes na | maṇis yab kyi rdo rje nor bu dang | padmes phyag rgya'i padma dang | hūṃ yig gis de gnyis mnyam par sbyar ba la brten nas gẓhi dus su bu bskyed pa dang | lam dus su lha spro pa rnams bstan*. It does not appear that this interpretation of Trijang Rinpoche (who did not know any European languages) derives from "Western influence."

78. Katz, ed., *Tolstoy's Short Fiction*, p. 172.

CHAPTER FIVE

1. Sherman E. Lee, *A History of Far Eastern Art* (New York: Harry N. Abrams, 1964), p. 108. Lee was not the only art historian to commit this sin of omission. Dietrich Seckel's *The Art of Buddhism* (New York: Crown Publishers, 1964) contains no discussion of Tibetan art and no Tibetan works among its almost two hundred plates and figures.

2. This chapter focuses entirely on the twentieth century, especially on the years since the Tibetan diaspora. For an excellent historical survey of the European en-

counter with Tibetan art, see Anne Chayet's "Découverte de l'art Tibétain" in her *Art et archéologie du Tibet* (Paris: Picard, 1994), pp. 11–20.

3. Nicholas Thomas, *Entangled Objects: Exchange, Material Culture, and Colonialism in the Pacific* (Cambridge: Harvard University Press, 1991), p. 4.

4. Antoinette K. Gordon, *The Iconography of Tibetan Lamaism*, rev. ed. (Rutland, Vt.: Charles E. Tuttle Company, 1959), p. 45.

5. Giuseppe Tucci, *Tibetan Painted Scrolls* (Rome: La Libreria dello Stato, 1949), 1:ix. This masterpiece is so lavishly produced that it is usually seen only by initiates, that is, by those who have access to the rare-book rooms of select university libraries. In 1957 Tucci contributed a lengthy article on Tibetan art to the *Enciclopedia Universale Dell'Arte*. The work appeared in English as *Encyclopedia of World Art* (New York: McGraw-Hill, 1967). Tucci's article, "Tibetan Art," appears in vol. 14, on pp. 67–82. He observes on p. 76 that "Though Tibetan painting is derived from or influenced by Indian and Chinese painting, it cannot be favorably compared with either. It suffers from overproduction." Notable for its tempered appreciation of Tibetan art is the 1911 booklet by Jacques Bacot, *L'art Tibétain* (Chalon-sur-Saone: Émile Bertrand, 1911), which concludes, "Le seul but que je m'étais proposé en venant ici, et je crois l'avoir atteint par les seules projections, était de réhabiliter un peu les Tibétains, réclamer pour eux, non pas de l'admiration, mais de l'indulgence et montrer qu'en somme ils ne sont pas tout à fait des barbares" (p. 30). He does say earlier in the work, however, speaking of Tibetan religious and secular art, "Nous ne trouverons dans aucun des deux ce que nous demandons au grand art et ce que donnent les peintures japonaises et surtout chinoises, d'exprimer de la nature et de la vie, de synthétiser une idée, un mouvement par ce qu'ils ont d'essentiel et de plus propre à provoquer une émotion" (p. 4).

6. The history of the acquisition of Tibetan art in Europe and America remains to be written. For a brief account of the formation of one of the early collections in the United States, the Jacques Marchais Museum on Staten Island, see Barbara Lipton and Nima Dorjee Ragnubs, *Treasures of Tibetan Art: Collections of the Jacques Marchais Museum of Tibetan Art* (New York: Oxford University Press, 1996), pp. 3–18. Barbara Lipton also recounts the strange odyssey of "The Golden Pavilion of Jehol" on pp. 261–67.

7. Pratapaditya Pal, *The Art of Tibet* (New York: Asia Society, 1969), pp. 7–8.

8. Lumír Jisl, *Tibetan Art* (London: Spring Books, 1958?), p. 19.

9. Pal, *The Art of Tibet*, p. 14.

10. Charles Bell, *The Religion of Tibet* (Delhi: Motilal Banarsidass, 1992), pp. 5–6. Europeans were not the only ones to comment on the effects of the Tibetan landscape. A thirteenth-century Arabic text reports, "In the country of Tibet (balad at-Tubbat) are special properties in respect of their air and water, their mountains and plains. A man there laughs and rejoices continually. Sadness, danger, anxieties and grief do not affect him. . . . Smiling among them is general. It appears even

on the faces of their animals." See D. M. Dunlop, "Arab Relations with Tibet in the 8th and 9th Centuries A.D.," *Islam Tetkikleri Enstitüsü Dergisi* 5 (1973): 313–14.

A view similar to Bell's was put forward by an Australian missionary, who went to Tibet in 1901:

> The Tibetan, cut off from intercourse with surrounding states, and debarred from benefiting by the experience and knowledge of older civilisations, was fitted to specialise in the wrong things thoroughly, and he uninterruptedly continued to misunderstand the operations of the unkind natural forces with his whole heart. The result was a profound belief in a spirit world inhabited by beings bent on doling out misery to humanity. Such an error dogmatically held, if existence was to be endured, logically enough, demanded a class versed in the psychology and activities of the other world, and with means at hand to confound its machinations, and defeat its activities. The lama and his magical devices seemed to answer the requirements admirably, and to-day Lamaism is viewed locally as a grand redemptive scheme with ample machinery for safeguarding man's welfare here, and in the hereafter.
>
> So the religion of Tibet is first of all Animism, but with much Buddhism, some Manicheism, and perhaps Nestorian Christianity grafted on. The mysterious force, however, that has moulded them all into one system, and affixed its indelible stamp, is to be found in the geographical peculiarities of Tibet.

See J. Huston Edgar, *The Land of Mystery, Tibet* (Melbourne: China Inland Mission, 1947), p. 10.

11. See Maurice Olender, *The Languages of Paradise: Race, Religion, and Philology in the Nineteenth Century*, trans. Arthur Goldhammer (Cambridge: Harvard University Press, 1992), pp. 51–57. The quotation appears on page 55. Renan would go on to contrast the stark and sterile desert of Judea with the lush green land of Galilee, the place of Jesus. Renan thus saves Jesus from Judaism and makes him an Aryan. See Olender, pp. 68–74.

12. Lama Anagarika Govinda, *The Way of the White Clouds: A Buddhist Pilgrim in Tibet* (London: Hutchinson, 1966), pp. 62, 70. The present Dalai Lama offers a similar view when he writes: "A pilgrimage through wild, open lands provides visions that help shape the proper attitude and inner awareness for religious practice." See His Holiness the Fourteenth Dalai Lama, *My Tibet*, with photographs and an introduction by Galen Rowell (Berkeley: University of California Press, 1990), p. 140.

13. Armand Neven, *Lamaistic Art* (Brussels: Société Générale de Banque, 1975), p. 10. More recently, John Powers has explained that in Tibet "The grandeur of the land has inspired spiritual seekers for millennia. There is perhaps no better place on

earth to experience emptiness; space imposes itself on consciousness everywhere one looks, the land seems to stretch off into infinity, and the sweeping ranges of mountains naturally draw the gaze upward toward the open sky." See John Powers, *Introduction to Tibetan Buddhism* (Ithaca, N.Y.: Snow Lion Publications, 1995), p. 204.

14. Harold Osborne, ed., *The Oxford Companion to Art* (Oxford: Oxford University Press, 1970), p. 1135. As Philip Rawson stated more succinctly in 1991, "Tibetan art is inspired by the need both to collaborate with and reconcile the violent energies expressed in the country's landscape." See Philip Rawson, *Sacred Tibet* (London: Thames and Hudson, 1991), p. 6.

15. Pratapaditya Pal and Hsien-ch'i Tseng, *Lamaist Art: The Aesthetics of Harmony* (Boston: Museum of Fine Arts, 1969), p. 9. For a fascinating analysis of how Indian deities came to be seen as monsters by Europeans, see Partha Mitter, *Much Maligned Monsters: A History of European Reactions to Indian Art* (Oxford: Clarendon Press, 1977), pp. 7–31.

16. Pal and Tseng, p. 19.

17. Pratapaditya Pal, *The Art of Tibet* (New York: Asia Society, 1969), p. 13.

18. Pal and Tseng, p. 20.

19. F. Sierksma, *Tibet's Terrifying Deities: Sex and Aggression in Religious Acculturation* (The Hague: Mouton & Co., 1966), p. 168. Sierksma does not consult Tibetan sources, relying heavily on Evans-Wentz, Govinda, and David-Neel, along with Tucci, even citing T. Lobsang Rampa as an authority at one point.

Pal offers a simplified version of Sierksma's theory: "The aggressive nomads . . . could hardly have been content with the sort of life demanded by a pacifist religion and imposed by a body of monks. The creation of substitutes was thus essential, and these substitutes assumed the shapes and forms of the terrifying deities, who were constantly on the warpath, in the psychic as well as the physical world." See Pal and Tseng, p. 21.

The Oxford Companion to Art, however, maintains that there is a distinction between the wrathful deities of the "reformed" Yellow sect (the Geluk) and those of the "Red Cap" sect (a term that has no sectarian correlate in Tibetan but was sometimes used in the West to designate the Sakya and Kagyu): "The difference was primarily a psychological one. In the works of the Yellow sect the demonic forces were dominated by and subordinated to the ultimate serenity of spiritual contemplation while the Red Cap monks depicted them in their naked, undisciplined fury. The first aimed at inspiring awe, the second at paralysing dread and horror." See Osborne, ed., p. 1135.

20. Pal and Tseng, p. 24.

21. Ibid., p. 27.

22. Pratapaditya Pal, *Art of Tibet: A Catalogue of the Los Angeles County Museum of Art Collection*, exp. ed. (Los Angeles: Los Angeles County Museum of Art, 1990), p. 42. As Tucci explained, "Fearing nature, in which occult forces are hidden

in ambush, they have extracted its symbols in order to defend themselves from nature by operating on and through symbols." Cited in Pratapaditya Pal, *The Art of Tibet* (New York: Asia Society, 1969), p. 38.

23. Detlef Ingo Lauf, *Tibetan Sacred Art: The Heritage of Tantra* (Berkeley, Calif.: Shambhala, 1976), p. 47. To question the presence of the symbolic in Tibetan art as described by Lauf, Pal, and others (so reminiscent of German Romantic theories of the symbol) in no way denies that Tibetan Buddhists have developed elaborate systems of meaning to explain their iconography. As is often the case in Christian iconography, we see the connection of artistic forms with points of doctrine. For example, in the case of the famous Geluk wrathful buddha Yamāntaka, his two horns are said to represent the two truths of Mādhyamika philosophy: the ultimate truth and the conventional truth. His nine heads represent the nine categories of Buddhist scriptures. His thirty-four arms together with his body, speech, and mind signify the thirty-seven "harmonies of enlightenment," a list of meditative states that include the eight-fold path. His sixteen legs signify the sixteen emptinesses, which include the emptiness of the internal, the emptiness of the external, the emptiness of the ultimate, the emptiness of the beginningless, and, importantly, the emptiness of emptiness. The humans and animals that he tramples with his right foot represent the attainment of the eight accomplishments, magical abilities acquired through tantric practice, including the ability to fly, to become invisible, and to travel underground. The birds that he tramples with his left foot represent the attainment of the eight powers, another set of magical abilities, including the ability to travel anywhere in an instant and the power to create emanations. His erect phallus represents great bliss, his nakedness means that he is not covered up with obstacles, and his hair standing on end symbolizes his passage beyond all sorrow. For a discussion of the various symbols of Vajrayoginī, see the essay by Chögyam Trungpa Rinpoche in *The Silk Route and the Diamond Path: Esoteric Buddhist Art on the Trans-Himalayan Trade Route* (Los Angeles: UCLA Arts Council, 1982), pp. 234–35.

24. Lauf, p. 45.

25. Giuseppe Tucci, *Tibetan Painted Scrolls* (Rome: La Libreria dello Stato, 1949), 1:290.

26. Armand Neven, *Lamaistic Art* (Brussels: Société Générale de Banque, 1975), p. 9.

27. P. Pal, *Tibetan Paintings: A Study of Tibetan Thankas Eleventh to Nineteenth Centuries* (London: Ravi Kumar/Sotheby Publications, 1984), p. 19. In another catalog we learn that "To appreciate Tibetan art one must appreciate himself, the fact of his being, the quality of his awareness and all that is manifested therein. Tibetan art is a part of this miraculous process of manifestation, not a comment on it or an attempt at an entertaining alternative to it. If one fully understands this art, then he is aware of being a Buddha in a Buddhafield." See *Sacred Art of Tibet*, 2d ed.

(Berkeley, Calif.: Dharma Publishing, 1974), p. 6 of the text; the catalog does not have page numbers.

28. Philip Rawson, *Sacred Tibet* (London: Thames and Hudson, 1991), p. 13.

29. Garnet Wolseley, *Narrative of the War with China in 1860* (Wilmington, Del.: Scholarly Resources, 1972), p. 220.

30. W. Y. Evans-Wentz, *Tibetan Yoga and Secret Doctrines* (London: Oxford University Press, 1967), p. 147 n. 2.

31. Sierksma, p. 197.

32. Heinrich Zimmer, *Myths and Symbols of Indian Art and Civilization*, ed. Joseph Campbell, Bolligen Series 6 (New York: Pantheon Books, 1946), p. 146.

33. Fosco Maraini, *Secret Tibet* (Delhi: Book Faith India, 1993), p. 77.

34. Govinda, *Foundations of Tibetan Mysticism*, p. 101.

35. See Martin Brauen, *The Maṇḍala* (London: Serindia Publications, 1997).

36. For a detailed description of a tantric initiation, see Tenzin Gyatso, *The Kalachakra Tantra: Rite of Initiation,* trans. and ed. Jeffrey Hopkins (London: Wisdom Publications, 1985).

37. Chögyam Trungpa Rinpoche, *Visual Dharma: The Buddhist Art of Tibet* (Berkeley, Calif.: Shambhala, 1975), p. 23. Elsewhere, he states with equal clarity, "It is widely thought that thangka painting is a form of meditation. This is not true" (p. 18).

38. Govinda, *Foundations of Tibetan Mysticism*, p. 64 n. 1.

39. Blofeld, *Tantric Mysticism of Tibet*, p. 250.

40. Pal, *The Art of Tibet*, p. 39.

41. Giuseppe Tucci, *The Theory and Practice of the Maṇḍala: With Special Reference to the Modern Psychology of the Subconscious,* trans. Alan Houghton Brodick (New York: Samuel Weiser, 1970), p. 25.

42. Ibid., p. vii.

43. Marilyn M. Rhie and Robert A. F. Thurman, *Wisdom and Compassion: The Sacred Art of Tibet* (New York: Harry N. Abrams, 1991), p. 12. For other analyses of the exhibition and its catalog, see Meg McLagan, "Mystical Visions in Manhattan: Deploying Culture in the Year of Tibet," in *Tibetan Culture in Exile: Proceedings of the Seventh Seminar of the IATS, Graz, 1995,* ed. Frank Korom (Vienna, 1997); Malcolm David Eckel, "On the Road to Mandala," *B & R* (spring 1992): 1–8. For a historically informed critique of the misrepresentations of Tibetan history and society in the catalog, see David Jackson, "Apropos a Recent Tibetan Art Catalogue," *Wiener Zeitschrift für die Kunde Südasiens und Archiv für Indische Philosophie* 37 (1993): 109–30.

44. Rhie and Thurman, p. 39.

45. Ibid., p. 36.

46. Ibid., p. 18.

47. Ibid., p. 165.

48. Ibid., p. 13.

49. Ibid., p. 312. In his trenchant review of the catalog, David Jackson challenges this portrayal:

> To read Thurman's account, however, one gets the impression that Tibet was a sort of "zone of gentleness," and that its inhabitants also viewed it as some kind of blessed realm. But obviously such a picture is incomplete. Where in this portrayal do Tibet's nomads, for instance, fit in, a people who lived almost exclusively on animal products and on meat that they hunted, raided or slaughtered, and who out of a resultant sense of guilt were also great patrons of religious masters? And where are we to place the ruthless bandit chieftains who regularly terrorized Lama pilgrims and traders in desolated areas? And what would traditional life in the great monasteries have been like without the delinquent warrior monks (*ldob ldob*)? In Tibet as in many a country, in addition to genuine religious teachers there were also a host of dubious mendicants, madmen, and charlatans who plied their trade among the faithful, and life within the big monasteries witnessed the full range of human personalities, from saintly to coldly calculating.

See David Jackson, "Apropos a Recent Tibetan Art Catalogue," *Wiener Zeitschrift für die Kunde Südasiens und Archiv für Indische Philosophie* 37 (1993): 110. There are, however, numerous descriptions of certain sites in Tibet as being, in reality, mandalas, and of paradisical valleys hidden in the Tibetan landscape. On the landscape as mandala, see, for example, Toni Huber, "Guidebook to Lapchi," in *Religions of Tibet in Practice,* ed. Donald S. Lopez, Jr. (Princeton, N.J.: Princeton University Press, 1997), pp. 120–34. For a recent study of hidden valleys (*sbas yul*), see Franz-Karl Erhard, "A Hidden Land in the Tibetan-Nepalese Borderlands," in *Maṇḍala and Landscape,* ed. A. W. Macdonald (New Delhi: D. K. Printworld, 1996).

50. Rhie and Thurman, p. 14.

51. Pratapaditya Pal, *The Art of Tibet* (New York: Asia Society, 1969), p. 38. Jisl explains elsewhere that the purpose of Tibetan art is to "act, as it were, as aids and real tools, one might say instruments, for the monks, helping them to concentrate and turn their thoughts away from this world to the sphere of meditation and mystery." See Jisl, p. 10.

52. E. Gene Smith wrote in 1970, "As more of the considerable number of Tibetan literary sources become available and as discerning eyes have the opportunity of examining representative collections of significant pieces, there will be little room left for the obscurantism and dissimulation that currently fill museum catalogues as well as the popular works in the West." See E. Gene Smith, introduction to *Kongtrul's Encyclopedia of Indo-Tibetan Culture,* ed. Lokesh Chandra, pts. 1–3 (New Delhi: International Academy of Indian Culture, 1970), p. 52.

53. The best discussion of the theory and practice of iconometrics is found in David P. Jackson and Janice A. Jackson, *Tibetan Thangka Painting: Methods and Materials*, 2d rev. ed. (Ithaca, N.Y.: Snow Lion Publications, 1988), pp. 45–73, 144–48. See also Kathleen Peterson, "Sources of Variation in Tibetan Canons of Iconometry," in *Tibetan Studies in Honour of Hugh Richardson*, ed. Michael Aris and Aung San Suu Kyi (Warminster: Aris and Phillips, 1980); and Giuseppe Tucci, *Tibetan Painted Scrolls* (Rome: La Libreria dello Stato, 1949), 1:291–99.

David Jackson has recently published the best single study of Tibetan art since Tucci's *Tibetan Painted Scrolls*. See his *A History of Tibetan Painting: The Great Tibetan Painters and Their Traditions* (Vienna: Verlag der Österreichischen Akademie der Wissenschaften, 1996). It contains, for example, a very useful survey and assessment of Western scholarship on Tibetan painting styles (pp. 19–42). The emphasis of Jackson's study is the individual Tibetan artist. As he writes, "Excellent artists have always been prized, honored and patronized by the great lamas and donors in Tibet. Moreover, in the course of Tibetan history, a number of great artistic geniuses appeared who left the deep impress of their personal style on posterity, sometimes even founding schools of art named after them. The present study is precisely an attempt to find out more about these most exceptional artists and their traditions" (p. 15). If we judge Jackson's book as representing the state of the art in the study of Tibetan painting, it can be observed that over the decades of the twentieth century this study has moved from a concern with iconography to a concern with meaning (as seen in this chapter) to a concern with "style" and artistic schools to a concern with the individual artist. In the process the Tibetan painter has gone from being an anonymous monk slavishly repeating received forms to being a creative genius with a personal style. The study of Tibetan art is moving, then, in precisely the opposite direction of much other art history, away from the dispersed subject position and toward the great man.

54. See Loden Sherap Dagyab, *Tibetan Religious Art* (Wiesbaden: Otto Harrassowitz, 1977), 1:27–28.

55. The preceding description is drawn from Jackson and Jackson, pp. 9–13. For another useful discussion of traditional uses of Tibetan art (within a larger study of recent nontraditional uses), see Yael Bentor, "Tibetan Tourist Thangkas in the Kathmandu Valley," *Annals of Tourism Research* 20 (1993): 109–12. On the role of the artist, see also Anne Chayet, *Art et archéologie du Tibet* (Paris: Picard, 1994), p. 165 ff. It is important to note as well that art has continued to be produced by Tibetans, both in and out of Tibet, since 1959. See, for example, Clare Harris, "Desperately Seeking the Dalai Lama," in *Disrupted Borders: An Intervention of Definitions and Boundaries*, ed. Sunil Gupta (London: Rivers Oram Press, 1993), pp. 105–14; and Per Kvaerne, "The Ideological Import of Tibetan Art," in *Resistance and Reform in Tibet*, ed. Robert Barnett and Shirin Akiner (Bloomington: Indiana University Press, 1993), pp. 166–85. The most thorough study of contemporary Tibetan art is

Clare E. Harris, *Imagining Tibet: Painters of the Post-1959 Period* (London: Reaktion, forthcoming).

An earlier and somewhat neglected source on the uses of Tibetan art appears in Marco Pallis's *Peaks and Lamas*. Pallis provides an interesting discussion of Tibetan arts and crafts in situ in a detailed description of the interior of a Tibetan farmhouse in Ladakh, the home of a wealthy aristocrat, a monk's cell, and a temple. He is free of many of the interpretative excesses of later art historians. He describes how works of art were cared for and how artists spoke about their work with a general absence of aesthetic vocabulary. On the vexed question of originality, he writes, "As to originality and invention, most artists, but especially painters and sculptors, might even feel rather hurt at being suspected, as they would think, of irreverent self-assertion." See Marco Pallis, *Peaks and Lamas*, 3d rev. ed. (London: Woburn Press, 1974), p. 349. He does eventually succumb to metaphysics, however, writing that "The artist may therefore regard himself as an inventor of glosses upon the Doctrine, a mediator between its pure spirit and the intelligence of dwellers within the world of sense" (p. 352). He goes on to provide a lengthy hypothetical dialogue in which a Tibetan lama speaks of "symbolism" in the most unlikely terms (pp. 354–56).

56. Rhie and Thurman, p. 37.

57. The story appears, among other places, in Patrul Rimpoche, *Words of My Perfect Teacher*, trans. Padmakara Translation Group (San Francisco: HarperCollins, 1994), pp. 173–74.

58. Rhie and Thurman, p. 38. Unfortunately, the authors do not provide a Tibetan source for this variation.

59. For a translation of one of the shorter rituals, see Yael Bentor, "The Horseback Consecration Ritual," in *Religions of Tibet in Practice*, ed. Donald S. Lopez, Jr. (Princeton, N.J.: Princeton University Press, 1997), pp. 234–54. On the process of filling statues, see Yael Bentor, "Inside Tibetan Images," *Arts of Asia* 24, no. 3 (1994): 102–9, and "On the Indian Origins of the Tibetan Practice of Depositing Relics and Dhāraṇīs in Stūpas and Images," *Journal of the American Oriental Society* 115, no. 2 (1995) 248–61.

60. On this process, see Yael Bentor, "On the Symbolism of the Mirror in Indo-Tibetan Consecration Rituals," *Journal of Indian Philosophy* 23 (1995): 57–71; Yael Bentor, *Consecration of Images and Stūpas in Indo-Tibetan Tantric Buddhism* (Leiden: E. J. Brill, 1996); and Giuseppe Tucci, *Tibetan Painted Scrolls* (Rome: La Libreria dello Stato, 1949), 1:308–16.

61. Cited in Yael Bentor, "Literature on Consecration (*Rab-gnas*)," in *Tibetan Literature: Studies in Genre*, ed. Roger Jackson and José I. Cabezón (Ithaca, N.Y.: Snow Lion Publications, 1996), p. 294.

62. There are, however, a considerable number of Tibetan literary sources on art. For a discussion of one such work, see E. Gene Smith, introduction to *Kongtrul's Encyclopedia of Indo-Tibetan Culture*, ed. Lokesh Chandra, pts. 1–3 (New Delhi:

International Academy of Indian Culture, 1970), pp. 42–51. Recent studies that make extensive use of Tibetan sources include Anne Chayet, *Art et archéologie du Tibet* (Paris: Picard, 1994); Roberto Vitali, *Early Temples of Central Tibet* (London: Serindia Publications, 1990); Franco Ricca and Erberto Lo Bue, *The Great Stupa of Gyantse: A Complete Tibetan Pantheon of the Fifteenth Century* (London: Serindia, 1983); and David Jackson, *A History of Tibetan Painting: The Great Tibetan Painters and Their Traditions* (Vienna: Verlag der Österreichischen Akademie der Wissenschaften, 1996).

63. P. K. Meaghen, *New Catholic Encyclopedia* (New York: McGraw Hill, 1967), 7:348, s.v. "idolatry."

64. *China and France, or Two Treatises* (London, 1676), pp. 111–12.

65. Graham Sandberg, *Tibet and the Tibetans* (London: Society for Promoting Christian Knowledge, 1906), p. 195.

66. See Moshe Barasch, *Icon: Studies in the History of an Idea* (New York: New York University Press, 1992), pp. 6–8. For a fascinating study of images, icons, and iconoclasm in Western art, see David Freedburg, *The Power of Images: Studies in the History and Theory of Response* (Chicago: University of Chicago Press, 1989).

67. Edward Burnett Tylor, *Religion in Primitive Culture* (New York: Harper & Brothers, 1958), 2:255; originally published as *Primitive Culture.*

68. For a Geluk description of how Śākyamuni Buddha achieved enlightenment by this path, see Daniel Cozort, *Highest Yoga Tantra* (Ithaca, N.Y.: Snow Lion Publications, 1986), pp. 107–8.

69. As Anne Chayet writes, "On en arrive parfois à cette absurdité que deux spécialistes, tibétain et non tibétain, parlant d'une même peinture, par exemple, semblent traiter de deux sujets, voire de deux domaines différents." See Anne Chayet, *Art et archéologie du Tibet* (Paris: Picard, 1994), p. 20.

70. Ibid.

CHAPTER SIX

1. Michel Strickmann, "A Survey of Tibetan Buddhist Studies," *Eastern Buddhist* 10 (1977): 128.

2. This chapter will not consider the fascinating history of Tibetan Studies in Europe during this century. Such a history would recount, for example, the circumstances (such as the presence of Dunhuang manuscripts in Paris) that have led Tibetologists in Europe (especially in France) to focus largely on pre-Buddhist Tibet and the fall of the Tibetan monarchy, producing excellent studies in which Buddhism is sometimes portrayed (as it is in some Bönpo histories) as an alien influence that brought an end to authentic Tibetan culture. In his study, *The Yar-luṅ Dynasty*, Erik Haarh writes:

When, at last, Buddhism got a foothold in Tibet, its influence, however, became the very reason for the fall of the Dynasty and the disintegration of the Yar-luṅ Empire. This was not the result of a general mollification or pacification of the Tibetan mentality, but because Buddhism became a destructive agent to the spiritual life and tradition of the Tibetan people. To the Tibetan kings, adhering to Buddhism for the purpose of making their authority independent on the ancient national traditions, which at the same time meant its very basis and its restriction, Buddhism became disastrous, ruining the Dynasty in its own defeat against the last display of strength of the aboriginal traditions.

See Erik Haarh, *The Yar-luṅ Dynasty: A Study with Particular Regard to the Contribution by Myths and Legends to the History of Ancient Tibet and the Origin and Nature of Its Kings* (Copenhagen: Gad, 1969), p. 12.

The other emphasis in France has been on "popular" practice, such as ritual and pilgrimage, again generally eschewing Buddhist scholastic practice in Tibet, which, as will be considered below, has been the general focus in North America. A history of Tibetan Studies in Europe would also consider the circumstances that caused the study of Bön (today largely centered in Oslo under Per Kvaerne and in Paris under Samten Karmay) to be stronger in Europe than it has been in North America.

3. For an eloquent and learned argument for the importance of Tibetan for the study of Indian Buddhism, see David Seyfort Ruegg, *The Study of Indian and Tibetan Thought* (Leiden: E. J. Brill, 1967).

4. For an account of this controversy, see Guy Richard Welbon, *The Buddhist Nirvana and Its Western Interpreters* (Chicago: University of Chicago Press, 1968).

5. See J. W. de Jong, *A Brief History of Buddhist Studies in Europe and America*, 2d ed., Biblioteca Indo-Buddhica, no. 33 (Delhi: Sri Satguru, 1987), p. 21.

6. For a discussion of Csoma, with references to other studies of his life and work, see Donald S. Lopez, Jr., *Curators of the Buddha: The Study of Buddhism under Colonialism* (Chicago: University of Chicago Press, 1995), pp. 256–59.

7. See Narendra Nath Bhattacharya, *History of Researches on Indian Buddhism* (New Delhi: Munshiram Manoharlal, 1981), pp. 129–32.

8. For a useful survey of Western-language scholarship on Tibetan religions up to 1977, see the bibliographic essay by Michel Strickmann, "A Survey of Tibetan Buddhist Studies," *Eastern Buddhist* 10 (1977): 128–49.

9. For recent discussions and critiques of past and current paradigms in the field of Buddhist Studies, see Luis O. Gómez, "Unspoken Paradigms: Meanderings through the Metaphors of a Field," *Journal of the International Association of Buddhist Studies* 18, no. 2 (winter 1995): 183–230; and José Ignacio Cabezón, "Buddhist Studies as a Discipline and the Role of Theory," *Journal of the International Association of Buddhist Studies* 18, no. 2 (winter 1995); 231–68.

10. See Clyde A. Holbrook, "Why an Academy of Religion?" *Journal of Bible and Religion* 32 (1964): 97–105; reprinted in *Journal of the American Academy of Religion* 59, no. 2 (summer 1991): 373–87. See also John F. Wilson, "Developing the Study of Religion in American Colleges and Universities," *Journal of General Education* 20, no. 3 (October 1968): 190–208.

11. Waddell, *Tibetan Buddhism*, p. xi.

12. Tibetan Buddhism was placed in the tradition of perennial philosophy in 1968 by Huston Smith in his film *Requiem for a Faith* (Hartley Film Foundation). There amid a psychedelic kaleidoscope of sideways mantras and a Japanese painting of a buddha, Smith narrates: "Tibetans painted the truth." He explains that "Separate selfhood is a fiction. . . . Our real identity is with Being as a whole, the scheme of things entire. . . . We become compassionate not from altruism which denies the self for the sake of others but from insight that sees and feels that one is the other." In fact, the most famous argument for compassion in Tibet is that put forward by the eighth-century Indian scholar Śāntideva, who argues precisely that to practice compassion is to deny the self for the sake of the other. Smith continues in this neo-Vedantin tone by stating that "the deepest insights of Tibetan Buddhism are not foreign to any of them [the alternative religions of man]." In fact, it is the position of the Geluk sect that enlightenment is impossible unless one gains direct realization of emptiness as it is set forth by Candrakīrti (as understood by Tsong kha pa).

Smith's film is famous as the first recording of the chanting of overtones by Tibetan monks. The subsequent history of the representation of this skill (Smith explains that "overtones awaken numinous feelings") remains to be written.

13. There were limited and unsuccessful attempts by the thirteenth Dalai Lama. In 1913 he sent four boys from aristocratic families to England to study. In the early 1920s a telegraph line was established between Lhasa and Gyantse, the machinery for a hydroelectric plant was purchased from England, and weapons were purchased from the British with which to modernize the Tibetan army. In 1924 an English-language school was established in Gyantse. However, it closed in 1926 (and efforts to modernize the military ceased) under pressure from the powerful Geluk monasteries. Another English-language school, designed to train wireless and hydroelectric technicians, opened in 1944 but it was closed under similar pressures after six months. See Melvyn C. Goldstein, *A History of Modern Tibet, 1913–1951: The Demise of the Lamaist State* (Berkeley: University of California Press, 1989), pp. 120–38, 158–62, 421–26.

14. Waddell, *Lhasa and Its Mysteries* (New York: Dover Publications, 1905), pp. 447–48.

15. This situation, however, has recently begun to change in the decades following the Tibetan diaspora, as Tibetan Buddhism belatedly confronts modernity. The Dalai Lama, for example, has become an active participant in the Buddhist-Christian dialogue and the Buddhist-Jewish dialogue. In the domain of comparative philoso-

phy, we find works being published (by Wisdom Publications) such as Peter Fenner's 1995 *Reasoning into Reality: A System-Cybernetics Model and Therapeutic Interpretation of Buddhist Middle Path Analysis*. But as in other confrontations between Tibetan Buddhism and modernity, the way has once again been led by Robert Thurman. In his 1984 *Tsong Khapa's Speech of Gold in the* Essence of True Eloquence: *Reason and Enlightenment in the Central Philosophy of Tibet*, he writes of Wittgenstein, "Yet, the critical insight he achieved and cultivated on his own was already highly developed and systematically cultivated in a great tradition with many thousands of members in India, Tibet, Mongolia, China, and Japan. One aspect of our first 'western renaissance' was our discovery of the hidden treasures of Greek thought. Our second renaissance may now well come from our discovery of the even greater resources of Asian thought." See Robert A. F. Thurman, *Tsong Khapa's Speech of Gold in the* Essence of True Eloquence: *Reason and Enlightenment in the Central Philosophy of Tibet* (Princeton, N.J.: Princeton University Press, 1984), p. 111. See also his statement on page 79 that "Tsong Khapa precedes Wittgenstein by centuries in the exquisite and liberative understanding of the surface."

Here, in a standard strategy of the comparative philosopher, Thurman claims that Wittgenstein's insights had been in the possession of Asian masters for centuries. And like Schlegel two centuries before and Seal one century before, he also predicts another renaissance. Thurman thus attempts to legitimate Tsong kha pa and Tibetan philosophy by showing that it is just as profound as anything thought by Wittgenstein, the most sublime of modern philosophers. Furthermore, the West is trumped by the fact that Tibetans knew what Wittgenstein knew centuries before his birth. What is being posited, then, is a universal truth that the East (specifically Buddhists) has always possessed and that the West may soon gain access to. Buddhists thus appropriate both the origin and the telos.

Thurman next moves to subsume Western philosophical discourse within a Buddhist model: "Indeed, it may be that Berkeley and Hegel and Heidegger and so on will someday be claimed by Europe as representatives of the Maitreya lineage of magnificence, as Hume and Kant and Nietzsche and Wittgenstein and so on may be claimed to represent the Manjushri lineage of the profound. . . . They should be included in the refuge-field icon we are constructing under which to read this *Essence*" (p. 21). Western philosophy is thus subjugated by subsumption.

For a trenchant review of Thurman's book, see Paul Williams, "Tsong Khapa's Speech of Gold," *Bulletin of the School of Oriental and African Studies* 49 (1986): 299–303. On "comparative philosophy," see Donald S. Lopez, Jr., *Elaborations on Emptiness: Uses of the Heart Sūtra* (Princeton, N.J.: Princeton University Press, 1996), pp. 239–60.

16. Edward Conze, *Thirty Years of Buddhist Studies* (London: Bruno Cassirer, 1967), p. 213. For a powerful critique of the rhetoric of experience in Buddhist Stud-

ies, see Robert H. Sharf, "Buddhist Modernism and the Rhetoric of Meditative Experience," *Numen* 42 (1995): 228–83.

17. For a brief biography of Geshe Wangyal, see the preface to the new edition of his *The Door of Liberation,* rev. ed. (Boston: Wisdom Publications, 1995), pp. xxi–xxvii.

18. Perhaps the most striking instance of such a construction is the Svātantrika and Prāsaṅgika, terms that do not appear as the names of branches of Mādhyamika in any Indian text, but rather were coined in Tibet, probably in the late eleventh century. Later Tibetan scholars disagreed over what constituted the difference between the two subschools, which Indian figures belonged to which, and which of the two should be ranked above the other.

19. I have described my own experiences in this regard in an essay entitled "Foreigner at the Lama's Feet," in *Curators of the Buddha: The Study of Buddhism under Colonialism,* ed. Donald S. Lopez, Jr. (Chicago: University of Chicago Press, 1995), pp. 251–95.

20. It was an enterprise of which Lama Govinda apparently would have approved. He wrote in his 1955 foreword to *The Tibetan Book of the Dead:*

> In times of old . . . "no one would have undertaken to translate a text who had not studied it for long years at the feet of a traditional and authoritative exponent of its teaching, and much less would anyone have thought himself qualified to translate a book in the teachings of which he did not believe."
>
> Our modern attitude, unfortunately, is a complete reversal of this; a scholar is regarded as being all the more competent ("scholarly") the less he believes in the teachings which he has undertaken to interpret. The sorry results are only too apparent, especially in the realm of Tibetology, which such scholars have approached with an air of their own superiority, thus defeating the very purpose of their endeavours.
>
> Lāma Kazi Dawa-Samdup and Dr. Evans-Wentz were the first to reestablish the ancient method of Lotsavas (as the translators of sacred texts are called in Tibet). They approached their work in the spirit of true devotion and humility, as a sacred trust that had come into their hands through generations of initiates, a trust which had to be handled with the utmost respect for even the smallest detail.

See Lama Govinda, introductory foreword to Walter Y. Evans-Wentz, *The Tibetan Book of the Dead* (London: Oxford University Press, 1960), p. lxiii.

21. It is noteworthy that the graduates of the programs at Washington and Indiana, where the Tibetologists were European-trained scholars (David Seyfort Ruegg and Helmut Hoffmann, respectively), produced work that was closer to the European model than did the graduates of Virginia and Wisconsin. The graduates

of the program at Saskatchewan were influenced by the approach of their teacher, Herbert Guenther.

22. Trungpa Rinpoche was often a controversial figure. For one view, see Peter Marin, "Spiritual Obedience," *Harper's*, February 1979, 43–58.

23. Two recent cases of such sympathetic scholarship are Robert Thurman's *Essential Tibetan Buddhism* (San Francisco: HarperSanFrancisco, 1995); and John Powers's *Introduction to Tibetan Buddhism* (Ithaca, N.Y.: Snow Lion Publications, 1995). Like so much of the work produced by American students of Tibetan Buddhism, both books have a bias that is both scholastic and Geluk (suggested by the photograph on the cover of Powers's book of the five Geluk scholar-monks, complete with "yellow hats").

Thurman's book is part of HarperSanFrancisco's Essential Series, which includes volumes such as *Essential Zen, The Essential Tao, The Essential Koran, The Essential Kabbalah, The Essential Jesus,* and *The Essential Rumi*. The contents of Thurman's volume suggest that he believes that the essential Tibetan Buddhism is Geluk and scholastic. Of the thirty-two works in the volume, thirteen are Geluk (including six from Tsong kha pa), twelve are not Tibetan but Indian works (such as the *Heart Sutra* and selections from Śāntideva), and only seven are by non-Geluk Tibetan authors (of these, one consists of four lines from Gampopa, another, eight lines from Sachen Gunga Nyingpo). The Geluk bias is also evident in the length of the selections, with some 140 pages devoted to Geluk works (over half of these from Tsong kha pa), yet only roughly 30 pages are given to non-Geluk Tibetan authors. Indeed, there are twice as many pages from Indian texts (including a long extract from Nāgārjuna's *Pañcakrama*, particularly important in Geluk tantra) than there are from non-Geluk Tibetan authors.

In Powers's book, the scholastic perspective is evident in the 25 percent of the book that is devoted to Indian Buddhist doctrine, as well as in the summaries of the four "schools" of Tibetan Buddhism, in which the philosophical and contemplative discourse of the most elite monks and lamas remains the focus. Even the chapter "Festivals and Holy Days" is devoted largely to the monastically dominated (and Geluk) events of the Monlam festival held to celebrate the New Year in Lhasa and the festival of the butter sculpture at Kumbum. The ordinary practices of the majority of Tibetans, monks, nuns, and laity, are consigned to a three-page section in the chapter on Bön entitled "Animism in Tibetan Folk Religion" (pp. 432–34). Elsewhere, whether it is in the discussion of tantra or the stages of death, the Geluk position is that which is presented, with occasional quotations from texts and teachers from other sects provided as embellishments. In both books the discussion of Tibetan history is derived largely (and uncritically) from traditional Buddhist sources, failing to note, for example, that the existence of the Nepalese bride of Srong btsan sgam po and the persecutions of Glang dar ma have been called into question.

24. Giuseppe Tucci, *To Lhasa and Beyond: Diary of the Expedition to Tibet in the Year 1948* (Ithaca, N.Y.: Snow Lion Publications, 1987), pp. 32–33.

CHAPTER SEVEN

1. Alexander Csoma de Kőrös, "Note on the Origin of the Kála-Chakra and Adi-Buddha Systems," *Tibetan Studies* (Budapest: Akadémiai Kiadó, 1984), p. 21. The first European reference to Shambhala is generally believed to have been made by the Portuguese Jesuits João Cabral and Estevão Cacella, who refer to "Xembala" in their letters of 1627. See George N. Roerich, "Studies in the Kālacakra," *Journal of the Urusvati Himalayan Research Institute of the Roerich Museum* 2 (1931): 15–16. See also C. Wessels, *Early Jesuit Travellers in Central Asia 1603–1721* (1924; reprint, New Delhi: Asian Educational Services, 1992), pp. 147–48.

2. The preceding description of Shambhala is drawn from John R. Newman, "A Brief History of the Kalachakra," in *The Wheel of Time: Kalachakra in Context*, ed. Geshe Lhundub Sopa, Roger Jackson, and John Newman (Ithaca, N.Y.: Snow Lion Publications, 1991), pp. 51–80.

3. For a fuller version of this episode see Newman, pp. 59–63. Some version of this story may have been known to Madame Blavatsky. In *The Secret Doctrine*, she cites the commentary to the *Stanzas of Dzyan: "The last survivors of the fair child of the White Island* (the primitive Sveta-dwipa) *had perished ages before. Their* (Lemuria) *elect, had taken shelter on the sacred Island* (now, the 'fabled' Shamballah, in the Gobi Desert), *while some of the accursed races, separating from the main stock, now lived in the jungles and underground* ('cave men'), *when the golden yellow race* (the Fourth) *became in its turn 'black with sin.'"* That is, the elect who survived the demise of the Lemurian and Atlantean races took refuge in Shambhala, whence they became the teachers of the Aryan race. See Blavatsky, *Secret Doctrine*, 2:319. On Tibetan views of Shambhala, see also Edwin Bernbaum, *The Way to Shambhala* (Garden City, N.Y.: Anchor Press, 1980). A history of the idea of Shambhala in the West remains to be written. The term has circulated in spiritualist writings since at least the time of Madame Blavatsky. Its currency was boosted considerably by Nicholas Roerich with his 1928 essay "Shambhala, the Resplendent" and his promotion of the "Banner of Shambhala." See Nicholas Roerich, *Shambhala: In Search of the New Era* (Rochester, Vt.: Inner Traditions International, 1990). In his memoir of life in Kalimpong in the early 1950s, Sangharakshita (D. P. E. Lingwood) notes that Roerich's son, the esteemed Tibetologist George Roerich, seemed always to be in equestrian dress. Apparently his father had believed that those who wanted to prepare the way for the advent of Maitreya must always be ready to ride with the king of Shambhala and his army, who might appear over the Himalayas at any moment. See Sangharakshita, *Facing Mount Kanchenjunga* (Glasgow: Windhorse Publications, 1991),

p. 52. For a credulous compilation of theories about Shambhala, see Andrew Tomas, *Shambhala: Oasis of Light* (London: Sphere Books Limited, 1977). Shambhala has served as the name of a pop song by Three Dog Night and the names of a publishing house and a 1993 recording of duets by jazz drummer William Hooker and guitarists Thurston Moore and Elliot Sharp (called "Shamballa" on the Knitting Factory Works label). Hooker writes in the liner notes: "Shamballa [a variant of Madame Blavatsky's spelling] is dedicated to the leaders of Humanity, the Masters of Wisdom."

4. Oscar Wilde, *Complete Works of Oscar Wilde* (New York: Harper & Row, 1989), p. 983. At the end of the essay (p. 992) he writes, "At twilight nature becomes a wonderfully suggestive effect, and is not without loveliness, though perhaps its chief use is to illustrate quotations from poets."

5. Ibid., p. 978.

6. Ibid., p. 986.

7. Ibid., p. 988.

8. See Heinz Bechert and Richard Gombrich, eds., *The World of Buddhism* (London: Thames and Hudson, 1984), pp. 275–77. For a more detailed discussion, see Heinz Bechert, *Buddhismus, Staat und Gesellschaft in der Ländern des Theravāda-Buddhismus* (Frankfurt: Alfred Metzner Verlag, 1966), 1:37–108. Buddhist modernists included European devotees, such as Alexandra David-Neel, who may have coined the term. For her, a Buddhist modernist was a Buddhist reformer. See Alexandra David, *Le modernisme Bouddhiste et le Bouddhisme du Bouddha* (Paris: Librairie Félix Alcan, 1911), p. 6. I am grateful to Professor Steven Collins for bringing this title to my attention.

9. Graham Sandberg, *Tibet and Tibetans* (London: Society for Promoting Christian Knowledge, 1906), pp. 195–96. Sandberg oversimplifies the role of the European in the process. See, for example, Charles Hallisey, "Roads Taken and Not Taken in the Study of Theravāda Buddhism," in *Curators of the Buddha: The Study of Buddhism under Colonialism*, ed. Donald S. Lopez, Jr. (Chicago: University of Chicago Press, 1995), pp. 31–61; and Jonathan Spencer, "The Politics of Tolerance: Buddhists and Christians, Truth and Error in Sri Lanka," in *The Pursuit of Certainty: Religious and Cultural Formulations*, ed. Wendy James (London: Routledge, 1995), pp. 195–214.

10. His Holiness the Dalai Lama, *The Good Heart: A Buddhist Perspective on the Teachings of Jesus* (Boston: Wisdom Publications, 1996), p. 166.

11. His Holiness, the Dalai Lama of Tibet, *The Way to Freedom* (San Francisco: HarperSanFrancisco, 1994), p. 73.

12. Dalai Lama, *Good Heart*, p. 3. On his participation in the Buddhist-Jewish dialogue, see Rodger Kamenetz, *The Jew in the Lotus* (San Francisco: HarperSanFrancisco, 1994).

13. Dalai Lama, *Good Heart*, p. 41.

14. For a fuller discussion of *upāya,* see Donald S. Lopez, Jr., *Buddhism in Practice* (Princeton, N.J.: Princeton University Press, 1995), pp. 27–31.

15. Dalai Lama, *Good Heart,* pp. 81–82.

16. See Donald S. Lopez, Jr., "Do Śrāvakas Understand Emptiness?" *Journal of Indian Philosophy* 16 (1988): 65–105.

17. Cited from a sādhana to Shugden translated in Réne de Nebesky-Wojkowitz, *Oracles and Demons of Tibet: The Cult and Iconography of the Tibetan Protective Deities* (The Hague: Mouton & Co., 1956), pp. 137–38. See also Stan Royal Mumford, *Himalayan Dialogue: Tibetan Lamas and Gurung Shamans in Nepal* (Madison: University of Wisconsin Press, 1990), pp. 125–31, 261–64; and Geshe Kelsang Gyatso, *Heart Jewel* (London: Tharpa Publications, 1991), pp. 73–101, 137–69.

18. For an illustrated description of such a possession ceremony, see Nebesky-Wojkowitz, pp. 432–39.

19. On the *ris med* movement, see E. Gene Smith, introduction to *Kongtrul's Encyclopedia of Indo-Tibetan Culture,* ed. Lokesh Chandra, pts. 1–3 (New Delhi: International Academy of Indian Culture, 1970), pp. 1–52; and Geoffrey Samuel, *Civilized Shamans: Buddhism in Tibetan Societies* (Washington, D.C.: Smithsonian Institution Press, 1993), pp. 533–43.

20. See Samuel, p. 605 n. 8.

21. For some of the relevant Tibetan literature pro and con Shugden, see Matthew Kapstein, "The Purificatory Gem and Its Cleansing: A Late Tibetan Polemical Discussion of Apocryphal Texts," *History of Religions* 28, no. 2 (1989): 231 n. 40.

22.. See, for example, the description of Vajrabhairava, one of the three chief *yi dam* of the Geluk in Bulcsu Siklós, *The Vajrabhairava Tantras,* Buddhica Britannica, Series Continua 7 (Tring, England: Institute of Buddhist Studies, 1996), pp. 42–43.

23. The statement can be found on the World Wide Web at http://www.infra.de/eureka/buf/tibet_foerderkreis/dorje_shugden/dolgyal3.html.

24. The statement appears on the Web at http://www.infra.de/eureka/buf/tibet_foerderkreis/dorje_shugden/0008.txt.

25. Reported in the September 21, 1996, issue of *World Tibet News* on the Internet.

26. Reported in the September 21, 1996, issue of *World Tibet News* on the Internet.

27. In support of the view that the controversy would be exploited by the Chinese, the BBC news of July 16, 1996, reported that three Tibetan monks who had recently applied at the Chinese embassy in New Delhi for visas to visit Tibet were asked whether they worshipped Shugden. The two who said they did were granted visas; the third, who said he did not, was refused a visa.

In an article by Wei Se in the Chinese government magazine *China's Tibet* (vol. 7, no. 6), the Dalai Lama is called a "self-styled believer in 'religious freedom,'" and is ridiculed for his "staunch disavowal" of an "innocent guardian of

Tibetan Buddhist doctrine" and for having "declared a virtual war against a holy spirit of the Gelug Sect." Reported on the Internet on *World Tibet News Network*, February 6, 1997.

28. The declaration was printed in the newsletter and catalog of Snow Lion Publications, *Snow Lion* 11, no. 4 (fall 1996): 3.

29. The murders were covered in a lengthy story in *Newsweek*, April 28, 1997, 26–28. In the article the Dalai Lama (clearly speaking as a Buddhist modernist) is quoted as saying, "Nobody would pray to Buddha for better business, but they go to the Shugden for such favors—and this is where it has become like spirit worship."

30. There has been little scholarship in the wake of Benedict Anderson on the idea of Tibet as a nation, especially scholarship based on the extensive Tibetan historical literature. For preliminary considerations, see Georges Dreyfus, "Proto-Nationalism in Tibet," in *Tibetan Studies: Proceedings of the Sixth Seminar of the International Association of Tibetan Studies, Fagernes 1992*, ed. Per Kvaerne (Oslo: Institute for Comparative Research in Human Culture, 1994), pp. 205–18; Georges Dreyfus, "Law, State, and Political Ideology in Tibet," *Journal of the International Association of Buddhist Studies* 18, no. 1 (summer 1995): 117–38; Geoffrey Samuel, *Civilized Shamans* (Washington, D.C.: Smithsonian Institution Press, 1993), pp. 134–54; Warren W. Smith, Jr., *Tibetan Nation: A History of Tibetan Nationalism and Sino-Tibetan Relations* (New York: Westview Press, 1996), pp. 659–93; and the essays in Robert Barnett and Shirin Akiner, eds., *Resistance and Reform in Tibet* (Bloomington: Indiana University Press, 1994).

31. On the constituents of a narrative of national culture, see Stuart Hall, David Held, and Tony McGrew, eds., *Modernity and Its Futures* (Cambridge, England: Polity Press, 1992), pp. 293–95.

32. Ernest Renan, "What Is a Nation?" in *Nation and Narration*, ed. Homi Bhabha (London: Routledge, 1990), p. 11. Although the Bönpo tradition is largely absent from the discourse of the Tibetan government (both pre- and post-exilic), where Tibet is identified as a sanctuary for the practice of Buddhism (in Tibetan, "the religion of the insiders," *nang pa'i chos*), there has been an increased interest in Bön among scholars of Tibet in recent decades, beginning with David Snellgrove's *Nine Ways of Bon* (1967) and continuing with the work of the Tibetan scholar Samten Karmay and his colleagues in Paris. This work has led to the formation of a nativist discourse about Tibet, with an emphasis on local practice, such as the mountain cults, and the portrayal of Bön as the authentic Tibetan religion. Buddhism is seen as a late arrival and, with its universalism, a contributing factor to the demise of the Tibetan empire and the erosion of a sense of national identity. See Samten G. Karmay, "Mountain Cults and National Identity in Tibet," in *Resistance and Reform in Tibet*, ed. Robert Barnett and Shirin Akiner (Bloomington: Indiana University Press, 1994), pp. 112–20, which discusses the importance of the hardly nonviolent mountain gods and King Gesar of Ling in Tibetan national identity. Even prior to

the Chinese invasion, progressive thinkers such as the Buddhist scholar Gendun Chophel (dGe 'dun chos 'phel, 1903–1951) felt that Buddhism had destroyed Tibetan national identity. See Heather Stoddard, "Tibetan Publications and National Identity," in *Resistance and Reform in Tibet,* ed. Robert Barnett and Shirin Akiner (Bloomington: Indiana University Press, 1994), p. 129.

33. See Tsering Shakya, "Whither the Tsampa Eaters?" *Himal* (September-October 1993): 9. For a useful historical survey of the various meanings of "Tibet," see Melvyn Goldstein, "Change, Conflict and Continuity among a Community of Nomadic Pastoralists," in *Resistance and Reform in Tibet,* ed. Robert Barnett and Shirin Akiner (Bloomington: Indiana University Press, 1994), pp. 76–90. On the politics of culture in exile, see also Ashild Kolas, "Tibetan Nationalism: The Politics of Religion," *Journal of Peace Research* 33, no. 1 (1996): 51–66.

34. See, for example, Melvyn Goldstein, *A History of Modern Tibet, 1913–1951* (Berkeley: University of California Press, 1989), pp. 112–20. It is noteworthy here that even the most crass political disputes are expressed in terms of Buddhist doctrine and vocabulary.

35. Joseph Rock quotes a speech by a Golok from Amdo that illustrates this point (and also calls into question the putative "nonviolence" of the Tibetans):

> You cannot compare us Go-log with other people. You obey the laws of strangers, the laws of the Dalai Lama, of China, and of any of your petty chiefs. You are afraid of everyone; to escape punishment you obey everyone. And the result is that you are afraid of everything. And not only you, but your fathers and grandfathers were the same. We Go-log, on the other hand, have from time immemorial obeyed none but our own laws, none but our own convictions. A Go-log is born with the knowledge of his freedom, and with his mother's milk imbibes some acquaintance with his laws. They have never been altered. Almost in his mother's womb he learns to handle arms. His forebears were warriors—they were brave fearless men, even as we today are their worthy descendants. To the advice of a stranger we will not hearken, nor will we obey ought but the voice of our conscience with which each Go-log enters the world. This is why we have ever been free as now, and are the slaves of none—neither of Bogdokhan nor of the Dalai Lama. Our tribe is the most respected and mighty in Tibet, and we rightly look down with contempt on both Chinaman and Tibetan.

See Joseph Rock, *The Amnye Ma-chhen Range and Adjacent Regions: A Monographic Study,* Serie Orientale Roma 12 (Rome: Instituto Italiano per il Medio ed Estremo Oriente, 1956), p. 127.

36. See Benedict Anderson, *Imagined Communities,* rev. ed. (London: Verso, 1991), pp. 163–85.

37. Tibetans exported wool, furs, yak tails, and musk to India and China and

had extensive diplomatic and trade relations with Nepal. Tibet's first international trade mission was launched in 1947, with the representatives carrying passports to which Britain and the United States granted visas, subsequently claiming after Chinese protests that the visas had been granted in error. For an account of the trade mission, see Melvyn Goldstein, *A History of Modern Tibet, 1913–1951* (Berkeley: University of California Press, 1989), pp. 570–610.

38. Hall, Held, and McGrew, eds., pp. 2–3. Some have seen the alliance between the clergy and the aristocracy as the defining characteristic of the medieval period in Europe. The warrior class (the aristocracy) provided protection and endowment for the clergy and in return the clergy provided legitimation, at the same time adopting celibacy and thus renouncing claims to kingship via the primogenitor. The situation in Tibet, often characterized as a medieval society, is similar and different. The chief difference comes in the institution of the incarnate lama, whereby celibacy does not preclude sovereignty.

39. Cited in Rodger Kamenetz, *The Jew in the Lotus* (San Francisco: HarperSanFrancisco, 1994), p. 213.

40. H. H. the Dalai Lama, "The Practice of Buddhism," *Snow Lion Newsletter* (spring 1993).

41. Edward Burnett Tylor, *The Origins of Culture*, chaps. 1–10 (New York: Harper and Brothers, 1958), p. 1; originally published as *Primitive Culture*.

42. Matthew Arnold, *Culture and Anarchy*, ed. Samuel Lipman (New Haven: Yale University Press, 1994), p. 73. For studies of the evolution of the idea of culture, see Raymond Williams, *Culture and Society, 1780–1950* (London: Chatto & Windus, 1958), and, more recently, Tomoko Masuzawa, "Culture," in *Critical Terms for Religious Studies*, ed. Mark C. Taylor (Chicago: University of Chicago Press, 1998).

Tibetan terms rendered as "culture" or used to render the term "culture" include *rig gzhung* (literally, "knowledge-system"), *rig gnas* (literally, "knowledge-abode," also used for "science"), and *shes rig* (literally, "understanding-knowledge"). The term "cultural revolution" in Tibetan is *rig gnas gsar brje*, literally, "knowledge-abode-new-change." I am grateful to Professor Elliot Sperling for this information.

43. See T. P. Atisha, "The Tibetan Approach to Ecology," *Tibetan Review* 26, no. 2 (1991): 9. For an insightful critique of this phenomenon, see Toni Huber, "Traditional Environmental Protectionism in Tibet Reconsidered," *Tibet Journal* 16, no. 2 (autumn 1991): 63–77; and Toni Huber, "Green Tibetans: A Brief Social History," in *Tibetan Culture in Exile: Proceedings of the Seventh Seminar of the IATS, Graz, 1995*, ed. Frank Korom (Vienna, 1997), pp. 103–119.

Some of the Dalai Lama's statements on the environment can be found in His Holiness the Fourteenth Dalai Lama, *My Tibet*, with photographs and an introduction by Galen Rowell (Berkeley: University of California Press, 1990).

44. Renan, pp. 18–19.

45. The Dalai Lama's message of universal human rights and nonviolence has had a different effect in Tibet, to which it is also directed. Whereas in Tibet prior to 1959 Geluk monks were among the most conservative members of the society, thwarting, for example, the thirteenth Dalai Lama's preliminary attempts at modernization, since the Chinese occupation, monks and nuns, especially in the vicinity of Lhasa, have been the leaders of protests against the Chinese, calling for Tibetan independence in a Buddhist vocabulary. These demonstrations reached their peak in 1987 and 1988, at the time the Dalai Lama was making his proposals before the U.S. Congress and the European Parliament. Buddhism has become a focus of resistance, in part because its practice has been suppressed by the Chinese and because its embodiment, the Dalai Lama, has been forced from Tibet; his anticipated return has taken on messianic proportions in Tibet. This is not to suggest that all Tibetan resistance has been nonviolent. Occasional bombings continue to be reported by the Chinese. For a study of Tibetan resistance during the 1987–88 period, see Ronald D. Schwartz, *Circle of Protest: Political Ritual in the Tibetan Uprising* (New York: Columbia University Press, 1994). See also Elliot Sperling, "The Rhetoric of Dissent," in *Resistance and Reform in Tibet,* ed. Robert Barnett and Shirin Akiner (Bloomington: Indiana University Press, 1994), pp. 267–84. See also Jamyang Norbu, "The Tibetan Resistance Movement and the Role of the C.I.A.," in the same volume. Such scholarship suggests that the Tibetans in Tibet are not passive victims of Chinese rule. On the current state of Buddhism in Tibet, see Melvyn Goldstein and Matthew Kapstein, eds., *Buddhism in Contemporary Tibet: Religious Revival and Cultural Identity* (Berkeley: University of California Press, 1998).

For recent studies of Tibetan culture in exile, see Frank J. Korom, ed., *Tibetan Culture in the Diaspora* (Vienna: Austrian Academy of Sciences, 1997); and Frank J. Korom, ed., *Constructing Tibetan Culture: Contemporary Perspectives* (World Heritage Press, 1997).

46. A. T. Barker, *The Mahatma Letters to A. P. Sinnett from the Mahatmas M. & K. H.,* ed. Christmas Humphreys and Elsie Benjamin (New York: Rider and Company, 1948), p. 434.

47. Louis M. Grafe, "Prelude to the Pilgrimage," in *My Life in Tibet,* Edwin John Dingle (Los Angeles: Econith Press, 1939), p. 10.

48. Lama Anagarika Govinda, *Foundations of Tibetan Mysticism* (New York: Samuel Weiser, 1969), p. 13.

49. Lama Anagarika Govinda, *The Way of the White Clouds: A Buddhist Pilgrim in Tibet* (London: Hutchinson, 1966), p. xi.

50. Marilyn M. Rhie and Robert A. F. Thurman, *Wisdom and Compassion: The Sacred Art of Tibet* (New York: Harry N. Abrams, 1991), p. 8. In his 1968 film *Requiem for a Faith* (Hartley Film Foundation), Huston Smith narrates in a statement reminiscent of Madame Blavatsky, "The importance of the Tibetan tradition for our time and for the spiritual history of mankind lay in the fact that Tibet was the last

living link connecting us to the civilizations of the ancient past. The mystery cults of Egypt and Mesopotamia are gone and the traditional civilizations of ancient India and China have been eroded by waves of Westernization. But modernity passed Tibet by."

51. This tract was presented to me in a sealed envelope during a conference at the University of California, Santa Barbara, in 1993. The address provided at the bottom of the text is World Service Network, P.O. Box 725, Topanga, California 90290. Robert Thurman offers a rather similar view when he presents various "theories" of the Chinese conquest of Tibet:

> The most compelling, if somewhat dramatic, is that Vajrapani [the bodhisattva of power] emanated himself as Mao Tse-tung and took upon himself the heinous sin of destroying the Buddha Dharma's institutions, along with many beings, for three main reasons: to prevent other, ordinarily human, materialists from reaping the consequences of such terrible acts, to challenge the Tibetan Buddhists to let go of the trappings of their religion and philosophy and force themselves to achieve the ability to embody once again in this terrible era their teachings of detachment, compassion, and wisdom, and to scatter the Indo-Tibetan Buddhist teachers and disseminate their teachings throughout the planet among all the people, whether religious or secular, at this apocalyptic time when humanity must make a quantum leap from violence to peacefulness in order to preserve all life on earth.

See Robert A. F. Thurman, *Essential Tibetan Buddhism* (San Francisco: HarperSanFrancisco, 1995), pp. 7–8. The Dalai Lama does not seem to ascribe to this view:

> Perhaps the only good thing that has come from our tragedy is the spread of the teaching and practice of Tibetan Buddhism. Of course, it would have been much better for everyone if it could have happened without such an unspeakable toll of human suffering. Imagine, Tibetan lamas could have come out to teach in different countries, travelling with their visas stamped on Tibetan passports! Western Dharma students could have freely come into Tibet's peaceful mountains to enjoy her fresh air, study at her monastic universities, and meditate in her inspiring solitudes. I say this not just to complain about our ordeal but because I have noticed that people tend to adopt a sort of fatalism about the history and problem of Tibet: "Well, it had to happen that way—otherwise Tibetans would not have come out of isolation into the world." Thinking this way can make them slow to take action to try to improve the real Tibetan situation, to solve the Tibetan problem, the human problem of six million Tibetan human persons.

See H. H. the Dalai Lama, "The Practice of Buddhism," *Snow Lion Newsletter* (spring 1993).

52. See Warren W. Smith, Jr., *Tibetan Nation: A History of Tibetan Nationalism and Sino-Tibetan Relations* (New York: Westview Press, 1996), p. 601.

53. Ibid., p. 609, for the terms of the proposal; pp. 610–16 for a discussion of the Chinese and exiled-Tibetan responses.

54. His Holiness the Fourteenth Dalai Lama, *My Tibet*, with photographs and an introduction by Galen Rowell (Berkeley: University of California Press, 1990), p. 18.

55. Pierre-Antoine Donnet, foreword to *Tibet: Survival in Question*, trans. Tica Broch (New Delhi: Oxford University Press, 1994), p. viii. The statement is dated December 1, 1993.

56. See David Seyfort Ruegg, *Ordre spirituel et ordre temporel dans la pensée Bouddhique de l'Inde et du Tibet: Quatre conférences au Collège de France* (Paris: Collège de France, 1995).

57. Tenzin Gyatso, *Freedom in Exile: The Autobiography of the Dalai Lama* (New York: HarperCollins, 1990), p. 204.

58. In 1820, a Tibetan scholar located Shambhala in Europe. See Turrell V. Wylie, "Dating the Tibetan Geography *'Dʒam gling rgyas bshad* through Its Description of the Western Hemisphere," *Central Asiatic Journal* 4 (1958–59): 300–311; and Turrell V. Wylie, "Was Christopher Columbus from Shambhala?" *Bulletin of the Institute of China Border Area Studies* (Taipei) 1 (July 1970): 24–34. See also the insightful discussion by Dan Martin in his "Anthropology on the Boundary and the Boundary of Anthropology," *Human Studies* 13 (1990): 119–45, especially 127–30. The key passage in the Tibetan text reads, in Wylie's translation, "That great scholar known as Me-pa ra-dza, or also as Ka-lam-pa-tsha [Columbus], i.e., 'King of the Boot,' who was born in the city of Tsi-na-ba [Genoa] of the country of glorious Shambhala, on the occasion of going to the Northern Continent first arrived at that island named Sa-kam [San Salvador]."

Index